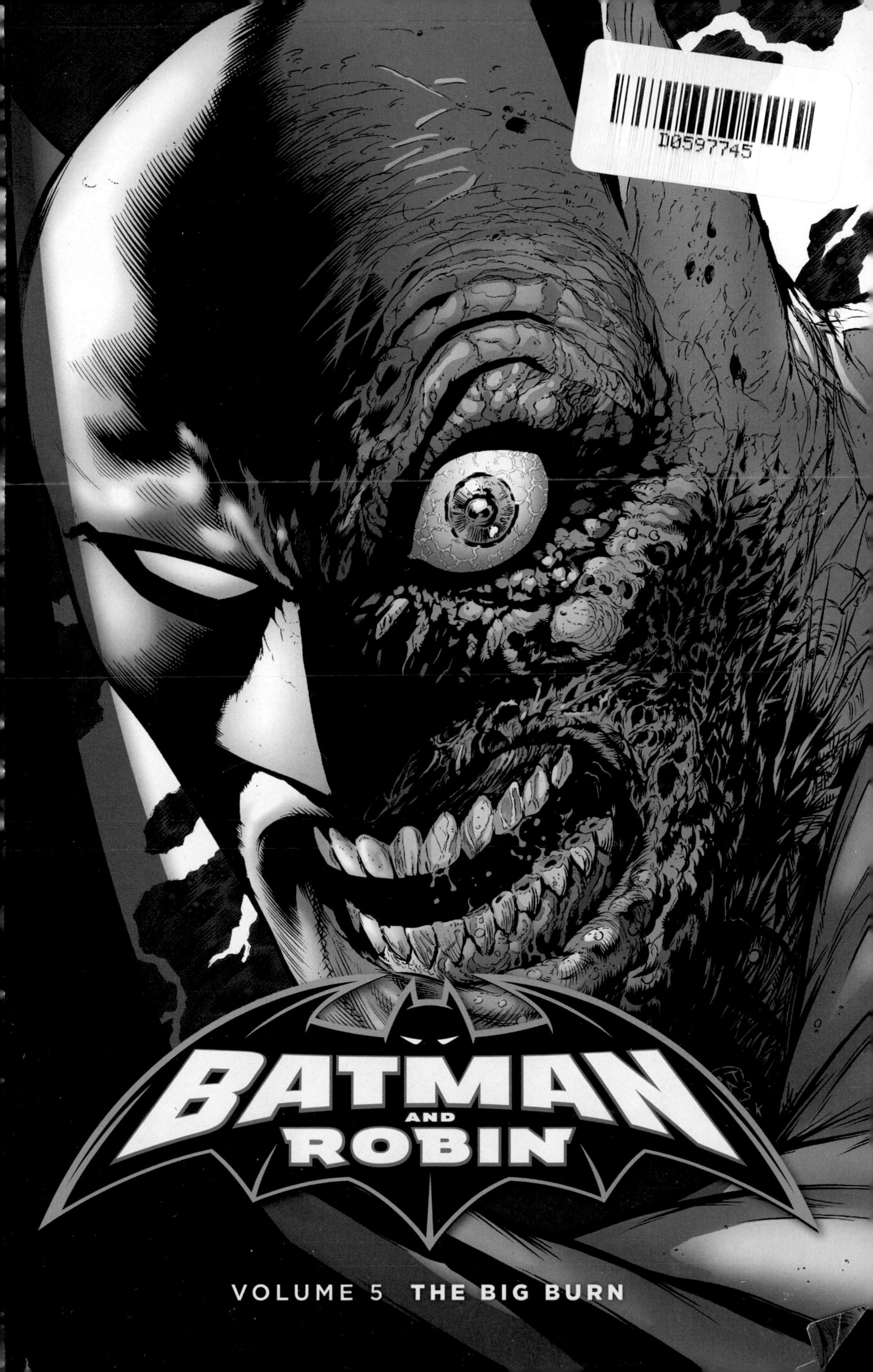

BATMAN AND ROBIN

VOLUME 5 THE BIG BURN

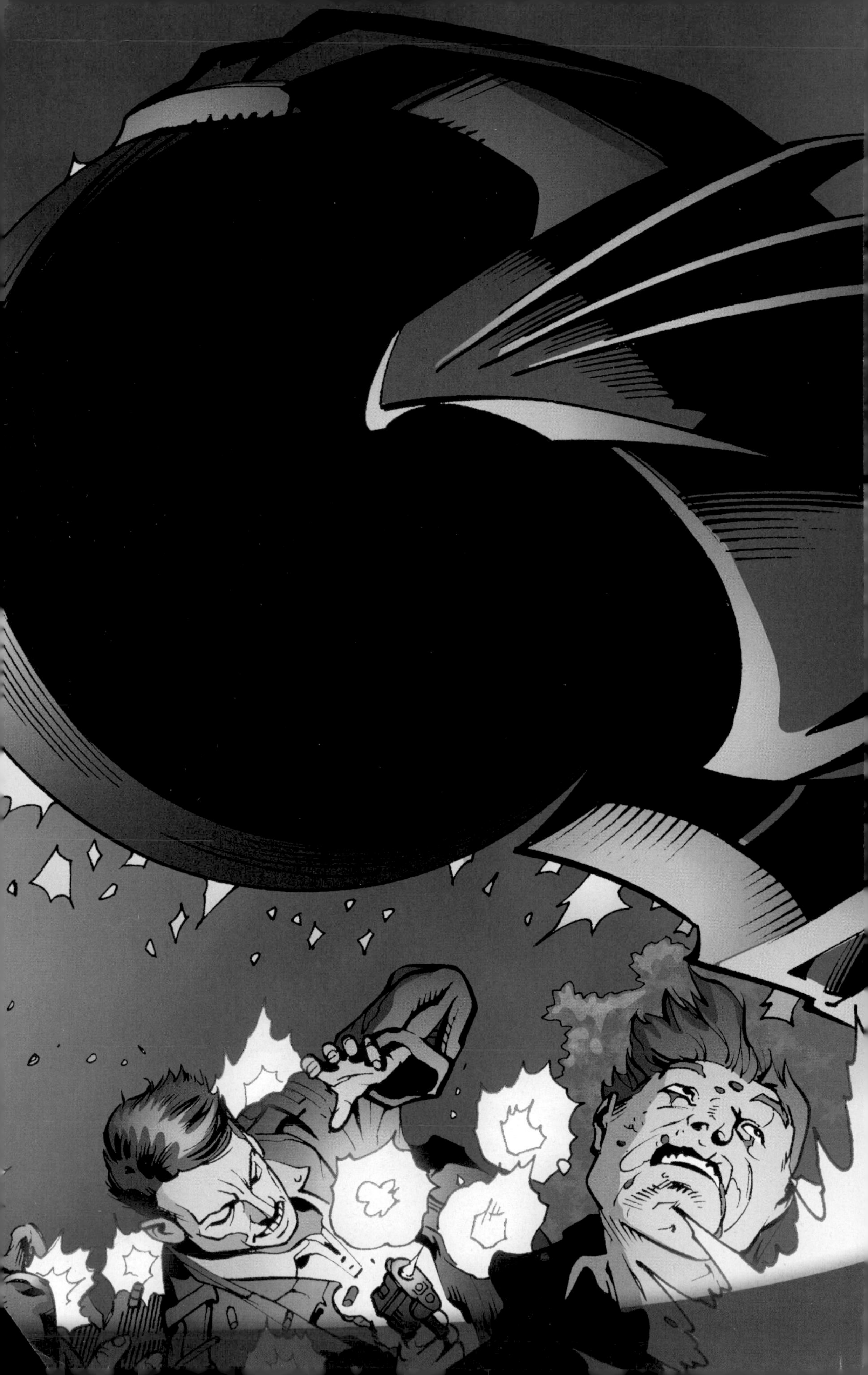

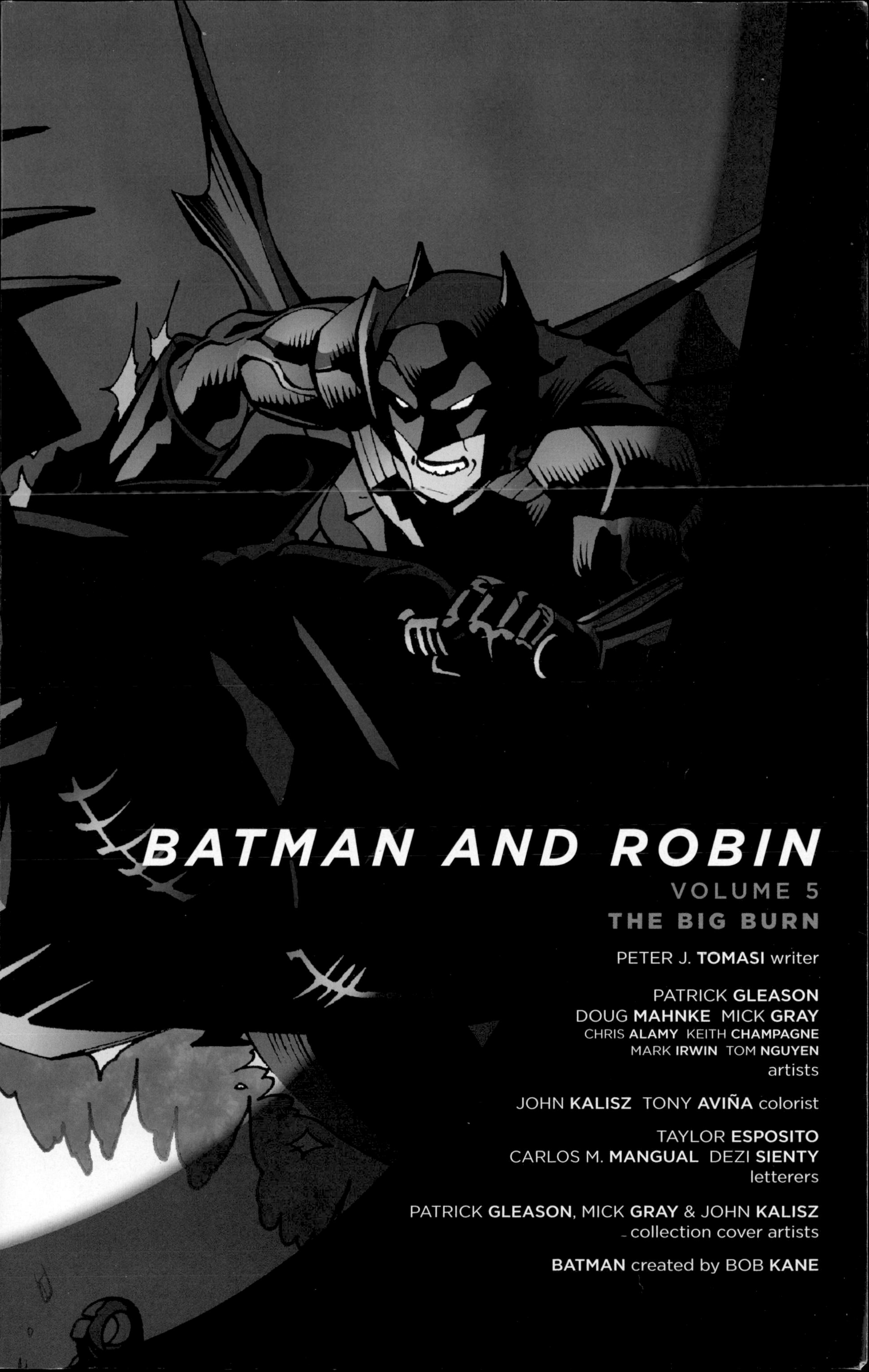

BATMAN AND ROBIN

VOLUME 5
THE BIG BURN

PETER J. **TOMASI** writer

PATRICK **GLEASON**
DOUG **MAHNKE** MICK **GRAY**
CHRIS **ALAMY** KEITH **CHAMPAGNE**
MARK **IRWIN** TOM **NGUYEN**
artists

JOHN **KALISZ** TONY **AVIÑA** colorist

TAYLOR **ESPOSITO**
CARLOS M. **MANGUAL** DEZI **SIENTY**
letterers

PATRICK **GLEASON**, MICK **GRAY** & JOHN **KALISZ**
collection cover artists

BATMAN created by BOB **KANE**

RACHEL GLUCKSTERN MIKE MARTS Editors – Original Series DARREN SHAN Assistant Editor – Original Series
RACHEL PINNELAS Editor ROBBIN BROSTERMAN Design Director – Books ROBBIE BIEDERMAN Publication Design

BOB HARRAS Senior VP – Editor-in-Chief, DC Comics

DIANE NELSON President DAN DIDIO and JIM LEE Co-Publishers GEOFF JOHNS Chief Creative Officer
AMIT DESAI Senior VP – Marketing and Franchise Management
AMY GENKINS Senior VP – Business and Legal Affairs NAIRI GARDINER Senior VP – Finance
JEFF BOISON VP – Publishing Planning MARK CHIARELLO VP – Art Direction and Design
JOHN CUNNINGHAM VP – Marketing TERRI CUNNINGHAM VP – Editorial Administration
LARRY GANEM VP – Talent Relations and Services ALISON GILL Senior VP – Manufacturing and Operations
HANK KANALZ Senior VP – Vertigo and Integrated Publishing JAY KOGAN VP – Business and Legal Affairs, Publishing
JACK MAHAN VP – Business Affairs, Talent NICK NAPOLITANO VP – Manufacturing Administration SUE POHJA VP – Book Sales
FRED RUIZ VP – Manufacturing Operations COURTNEY SIMMONS Senior VP – Publicity BOB WAYNE Senior VP – Sales

BATMAN AND ROBIN VOLUME 5: THE BIG BURN

Published by DC Comics. Compilation Copyright © 2015 DC Comics. All Rights Reserved.

Originally published in single magazine form in BATMAN AND ROBIN 24-28 and BATMAN AND ROBIN ANNUAL 2.
Copyright © 2013, 2014 DC Comics. All Rights Reserved. All characters, their distinctive likenesses and related elements featured
in this publication are trademarks of DC Comics. The stories, characters and incidents featured in this publication are entirely fictional.
DC Comics does not read or accept unsolicited ideas, stories or artwork.
SCRIBBLENAUTS and all related characters and elements are trademarks of and © Warner Bros. Entertainment Inc.

DC Comics, 4000 Warner Blvd., Burbank, CA 91522
A Warner Bros. Entertainment Company.
Printed by RR Donnelley, Owensville, MO, USA. 5/22/15. First Printing.
ISBN: 978-1-4012-5333-2

Library of Congress Cataloging-in-Publication Data

Tomasi, Peter, author.
Batman and Robin. Volume 5, The big burn / Peter Tomasi, writer ; Patrick Gleason, artist.
pages cm. — (The New 52!)
ISBN 978-1-4012-5333-2
1. Graphic novels. I. Gleason, Patrick, illustrator. II. Title. III. Title: Big burn.

PN6728.B36T647 2014
741.5'973—dc23

2014027355

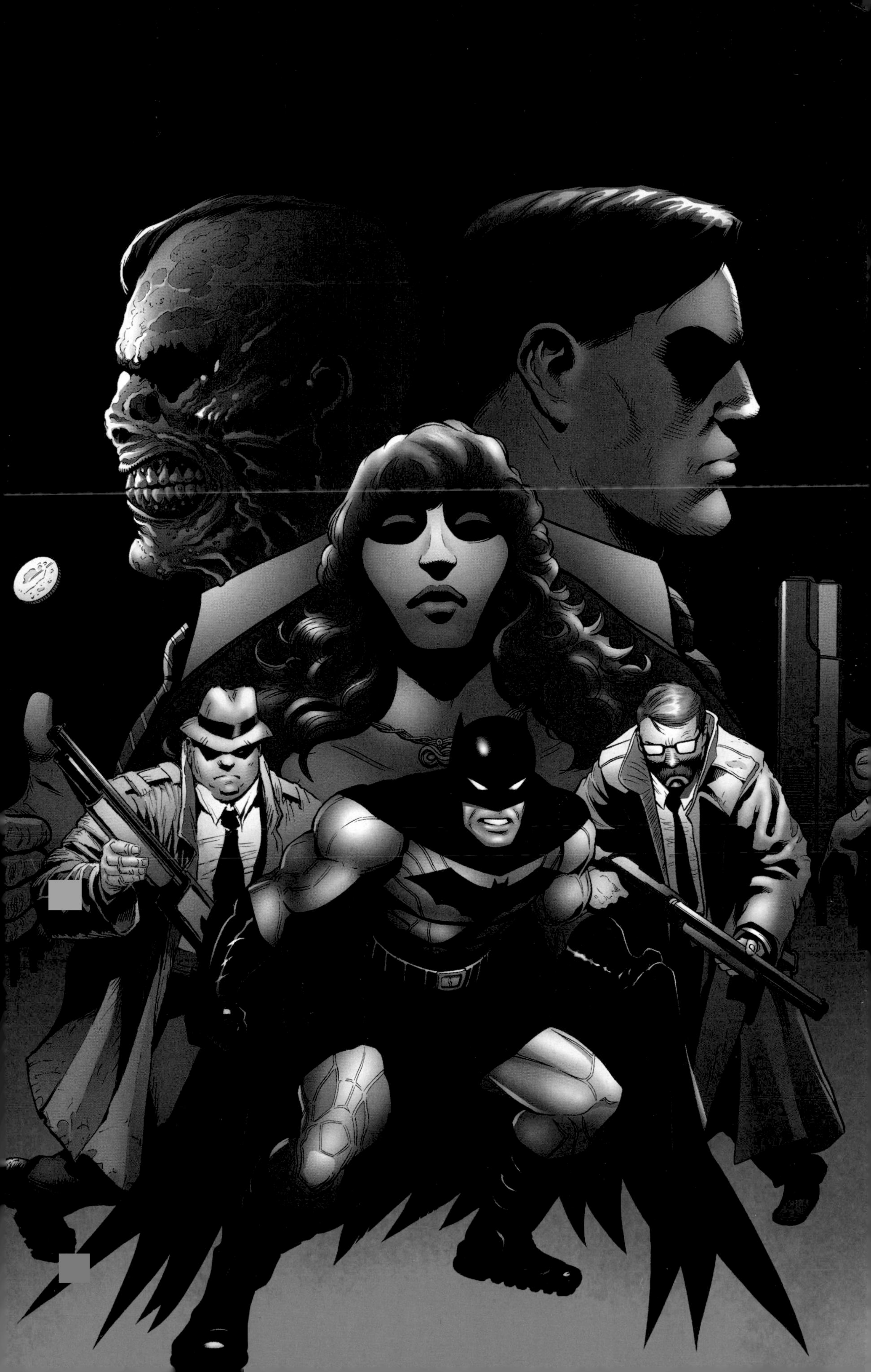

THE BIG BURN: FIRST STRIKE

PATRICK GLEASON penciller **MICK GRAY** inker **JOHN KALISZ** colorist cover art by **GLEASON, GRAY & KALISZ**

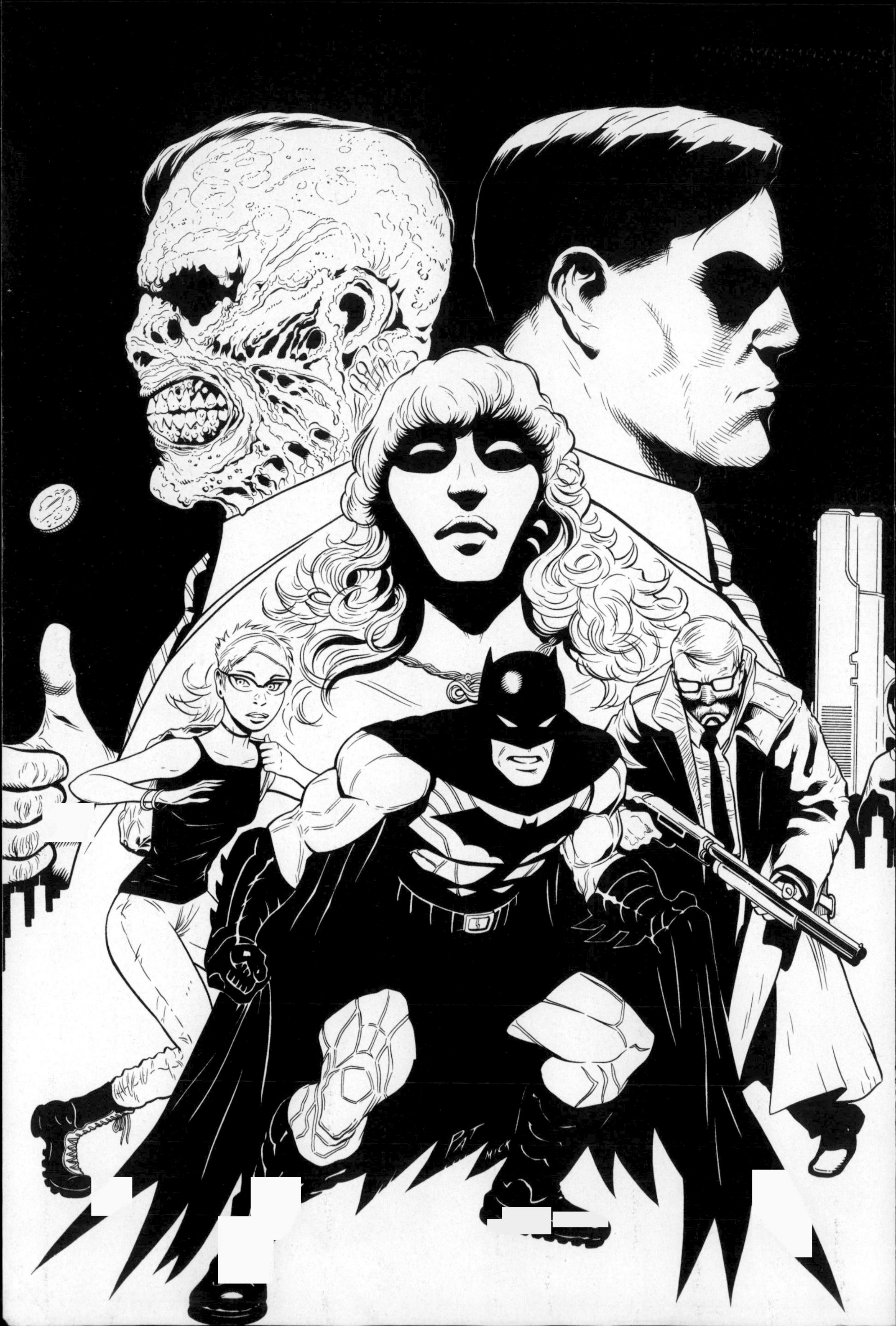

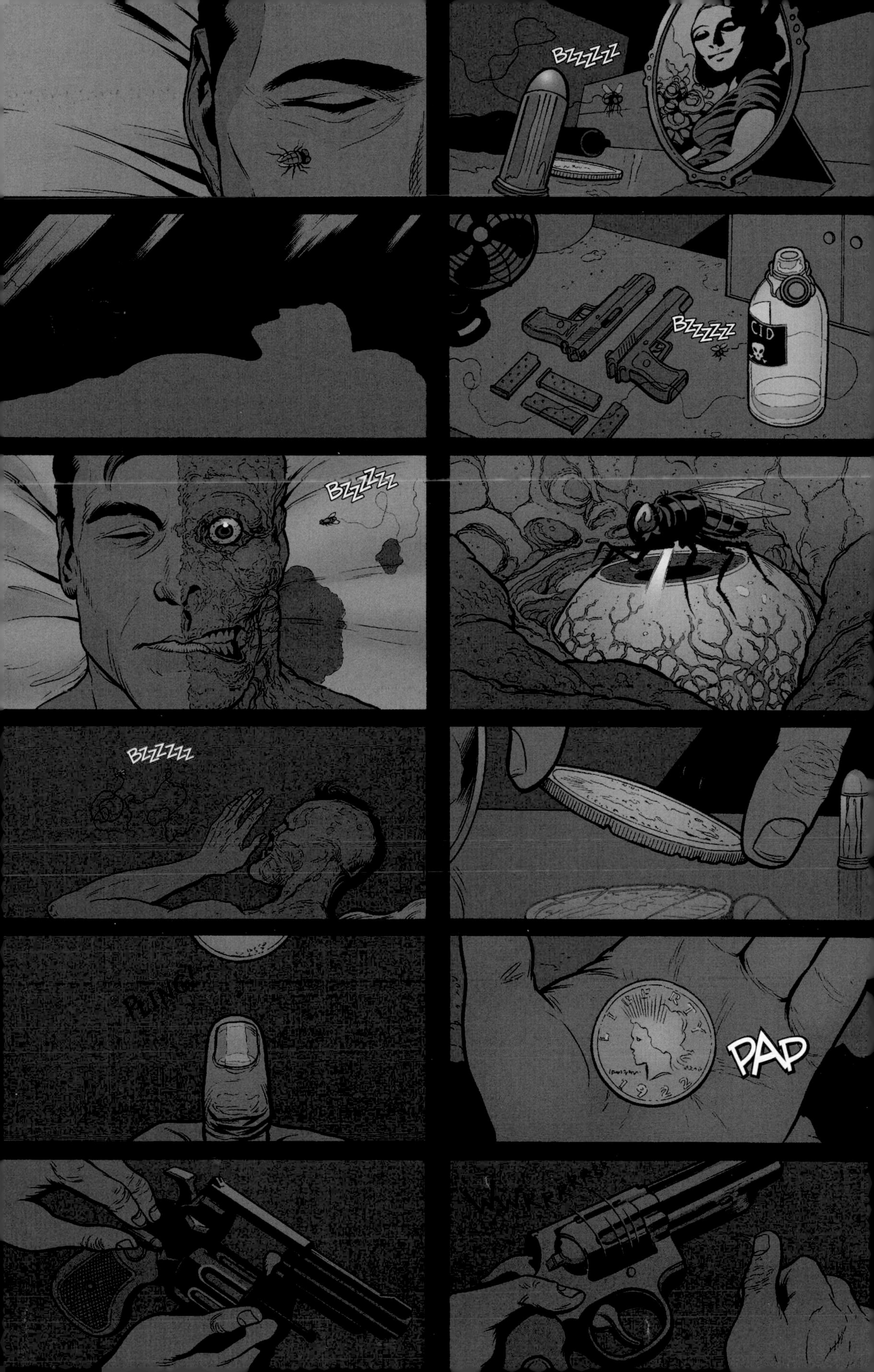
BZZZZZZ
BZZZZZZ
CID
BZZZZZZ
BZZZZZZ
PLING!
LIBERTY
1922
PAP

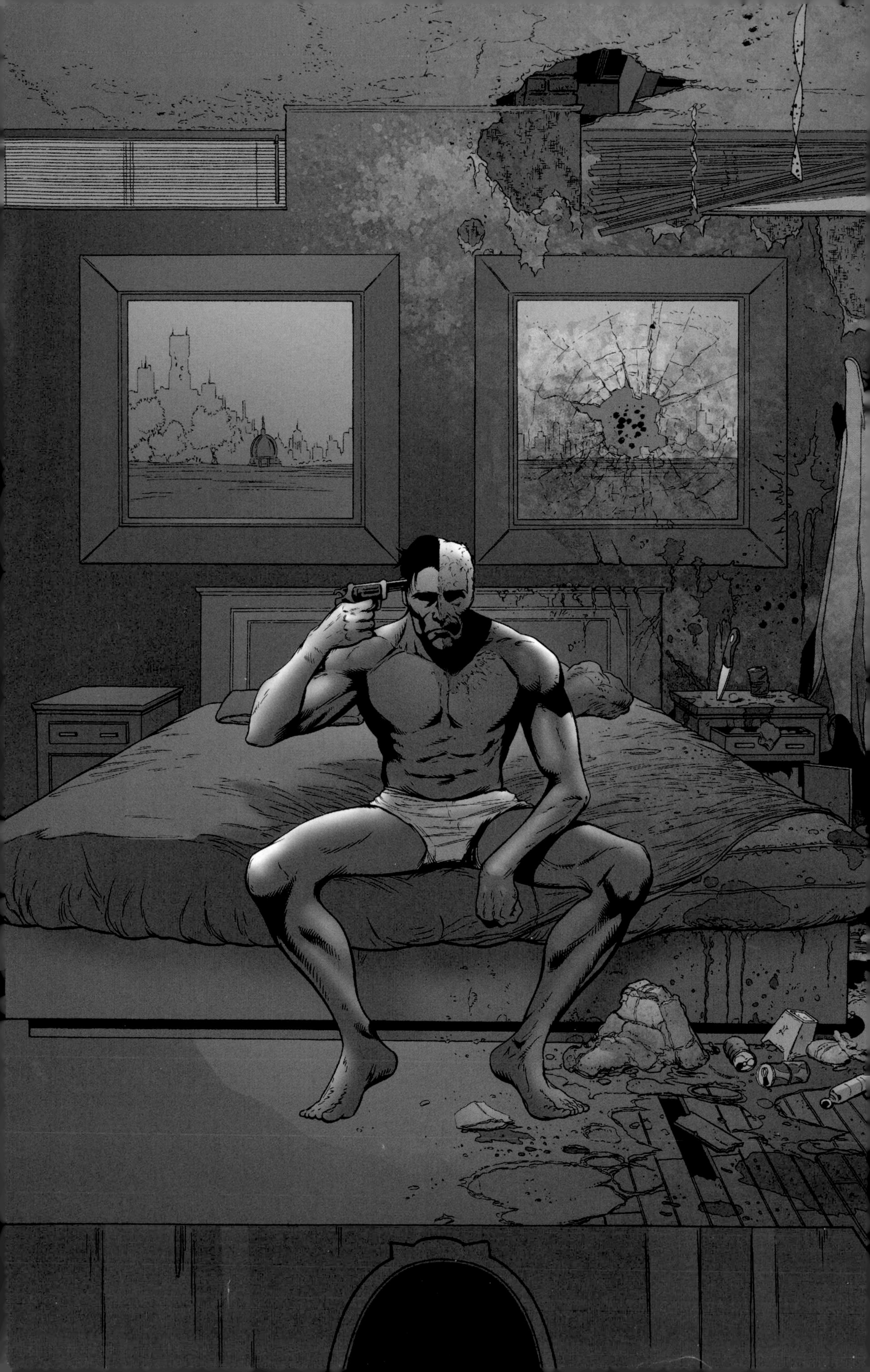

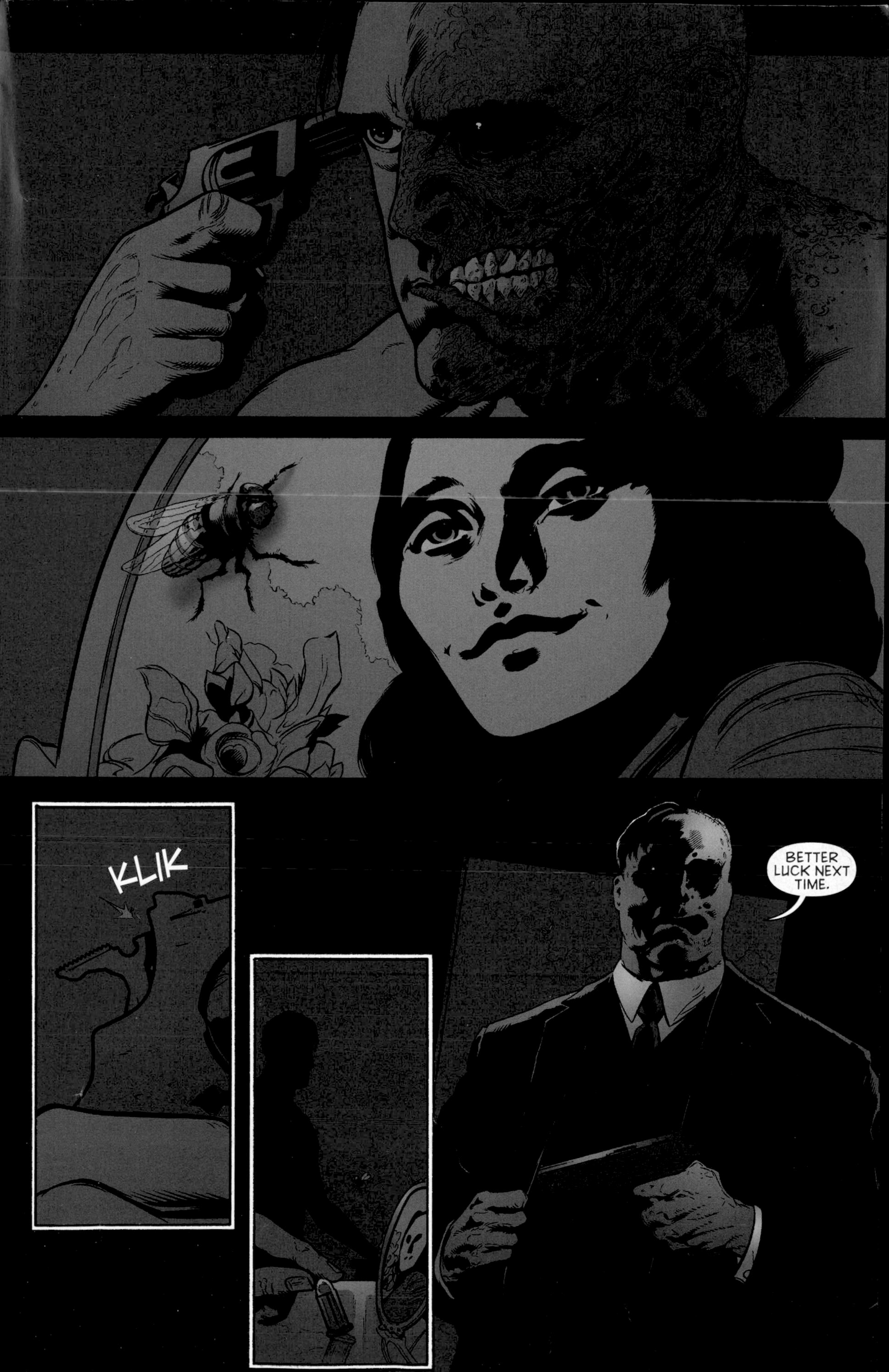
KLIK
BETTER LUCK NEXT TIME.

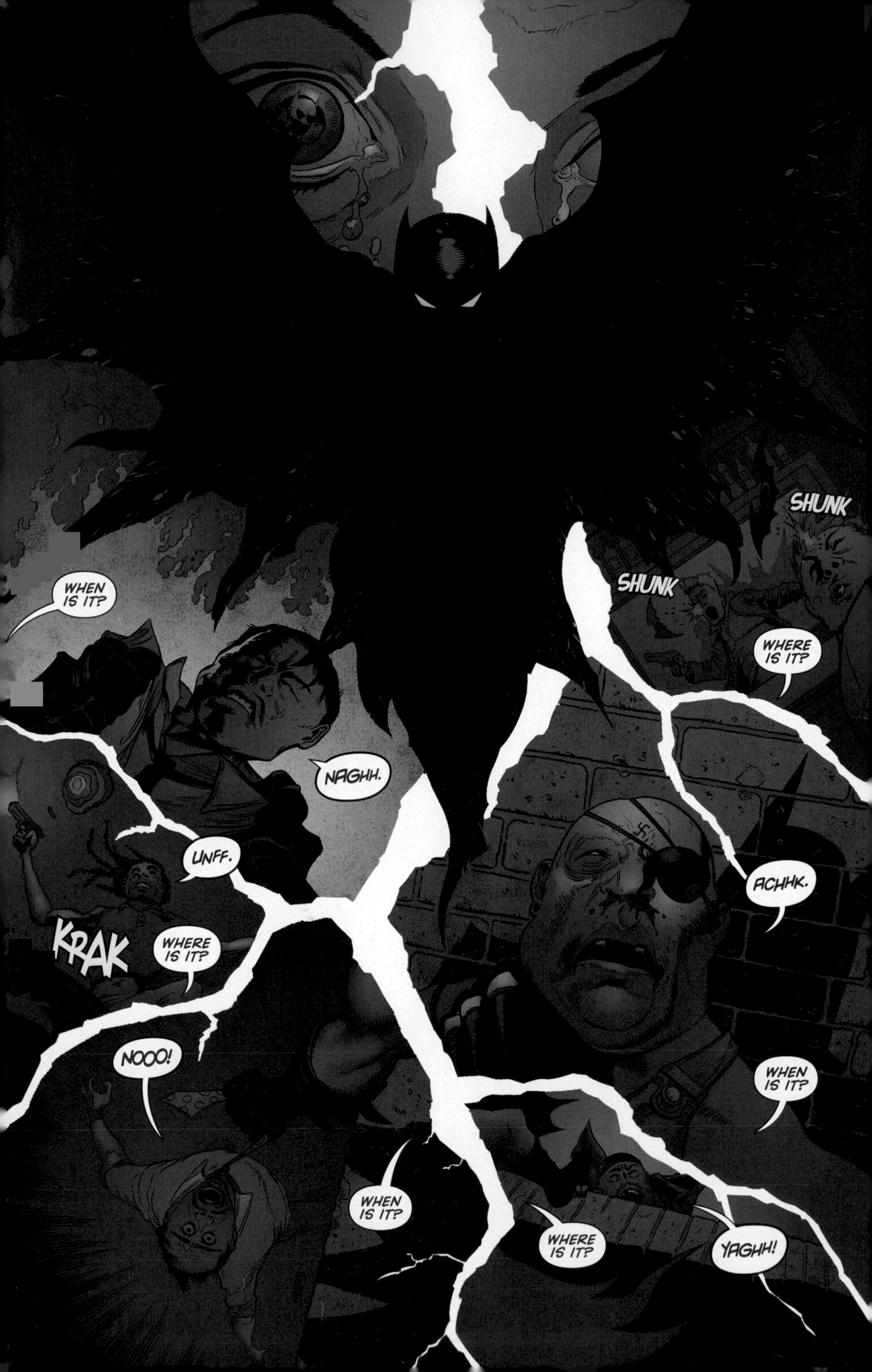
SHUNK
SHUNK
WHERE IS IT?
WHEN IS IT?
NAGHH.
UNFF.
KRAK
WHERE IS IT?
ACHHK.
NOOO!
WHEN IS IT?
WHEN IS IT?
WHERE IS IT?
YAGHH!

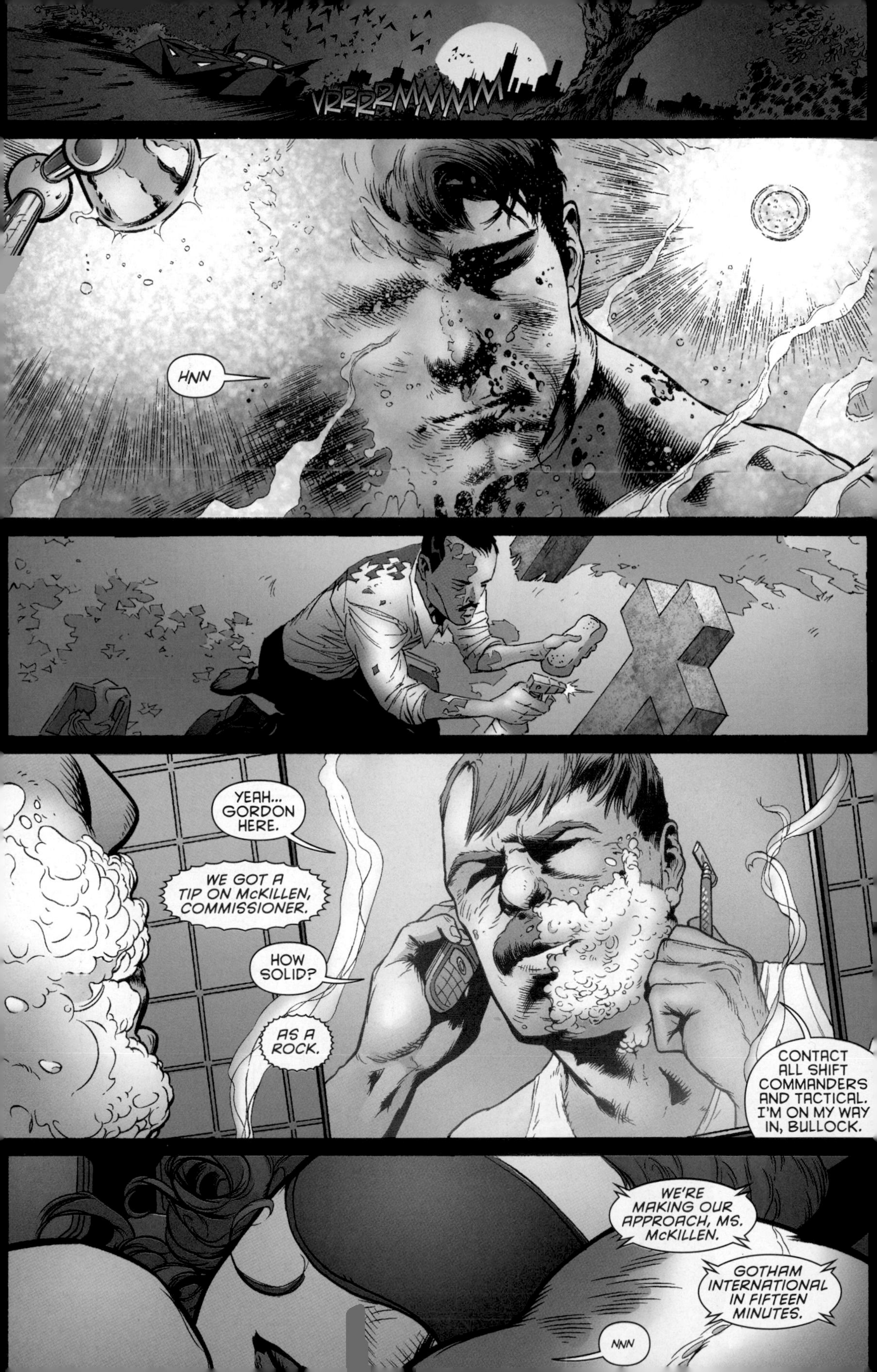
VRRRRZMMMMM
HNN
YEAH... GORDON HERE.
WE GOT A TIP ON McKILLEN, COMMISSIONER.
HOW SOLID?
AS A ROCK.
CONTACT ALL SHIFT COMMANDERS AND TACTICAL. I'M ON MY WAY IN, BULLOCK.
WE'RE MAKING OUR APPROACH, MS. McKILLEN.
GOTHAM INTERNATIONAL IN FIFTEEN MINUTES.
NNN

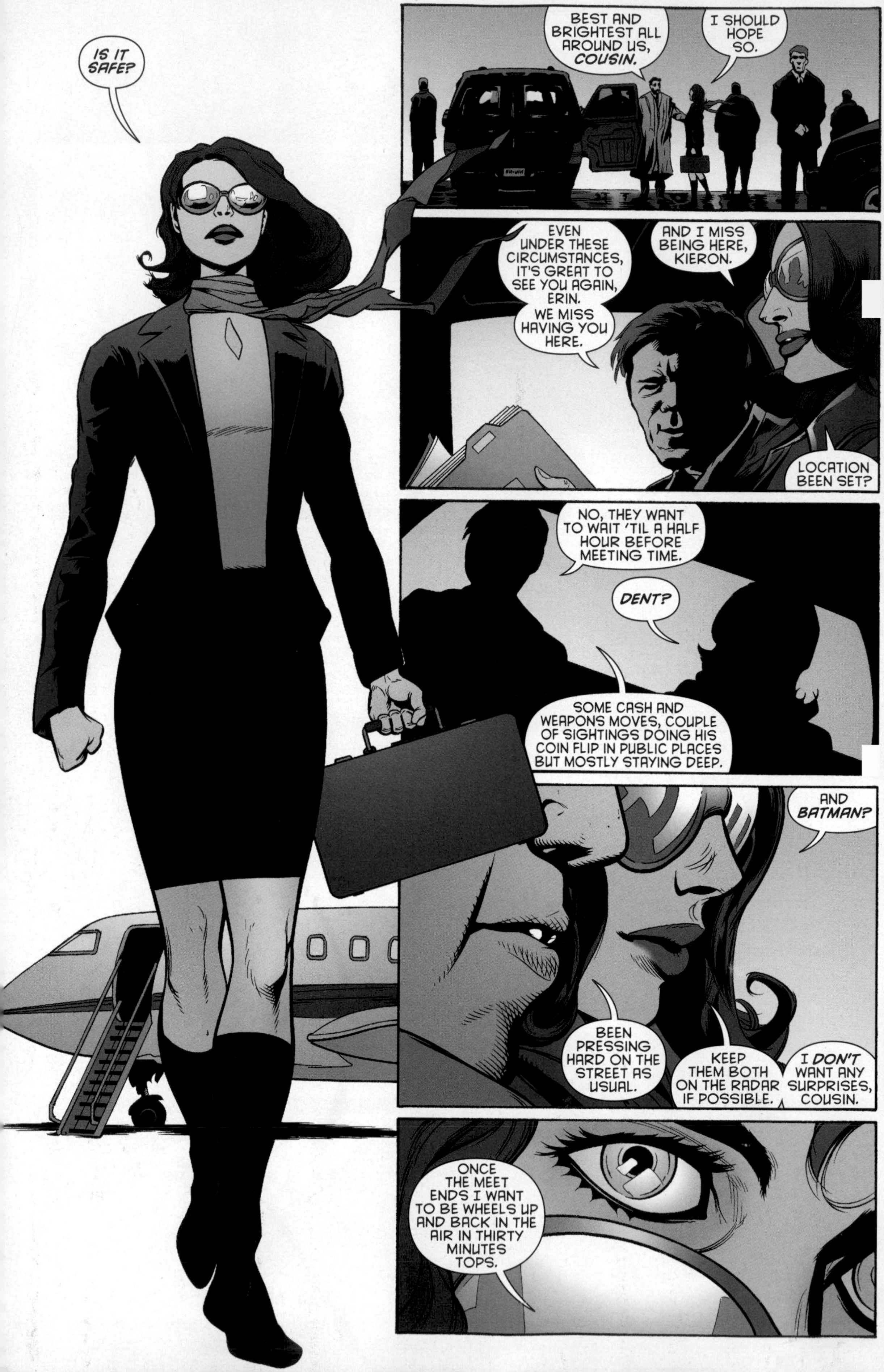
IS IT SAFE?
BEST AND BRIGHTEST ALL AROUND US, COUSIN.
I SHOULD HOPE SO.
EVEN UNDER THESE CIRCUMSTANCES, IT'S GREAT TO SEE YOU AGAIN, ERIN.
WE MISS HAVING YOU HERE.
AND I MISS BEING HERE, KIERON.
LOCATION BEEN SET?
NO, THEY WANT TO WAIT 'TIL A HALF HOUR BEFORE MEETING TIME.
DENT?
SOME CASH AND WEAPONS MOVES, COUPLE OF SIGHTINGS DOING HIS COIN FLIP IN PUBLIC PLACES BUT MOSTLY STAYING DEEP.
AND BATMAN?
BEEN PRESSING HARD ON THE STREET AS USUAL.
KEEP THEM BOTH ON THE RADAR IF POSSIBLE.
I DON'T WANT ANY SURPRISES, COUSIN.
ONCE THE MEET ENDS I WANT TO BE WHEELS UP AND BACK IN THE AIR IN THIRTY MINUTES TOPS.

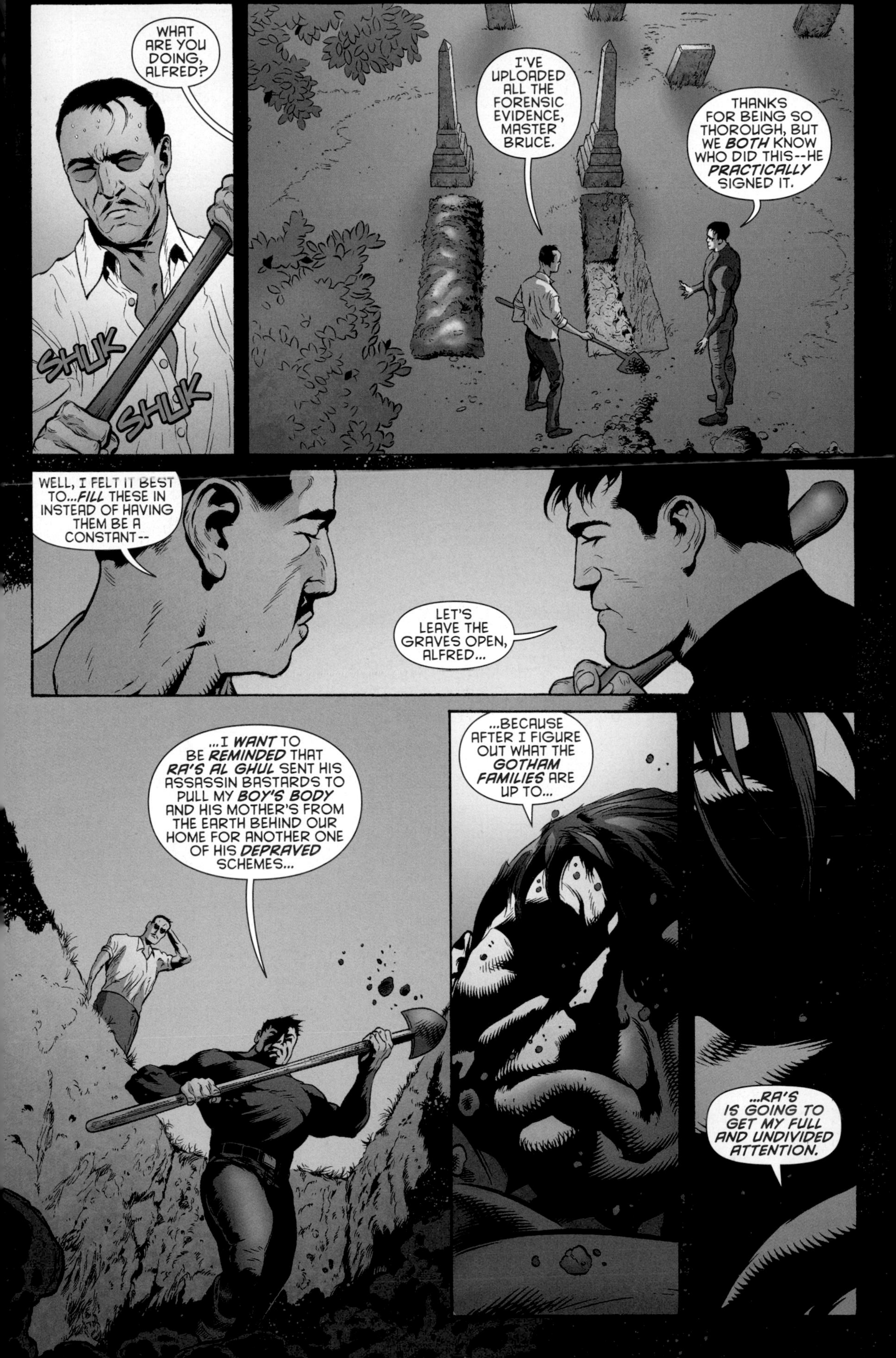

WHAT ARE YOU DOING, ALFRED?
SHUK
SHUK
I'VE UPLOADED ALL THE FORENSIC EVIDENCE, MASTER BRUCE.
THANKS FOR BEING SO THOROUGH, BUT WE BOTH KNOW WHO DID THIS--HE PRACTICALLY SIGNED IT.
WELL, I FELT IT BEST TO...FILL THESE IN INSTEAD OF HAVING THEM BE A CONSTANT--
LET'S LEAVE THE GRAVES OPEN, ALFRED...
...I WANT TO BE REMINDED THAT RA'S AL GHUL SENT HIS ASSASSIN BASTARDS TO PULL MY BOY'S BODY AND HIS MOTHER'S FROM THE EARTH BEHIND OUR HOME FOR ANOTHER ONE OF HIS DEPRAVED SCHEMES...
...BECAUSE AFTER I FIGURE OUT WHAT THE GOTHAM FAMILIES ARE UP TO...
...RA'S IS GOING TO GET MY FULL AND UNDIVIDED ATTENTION.

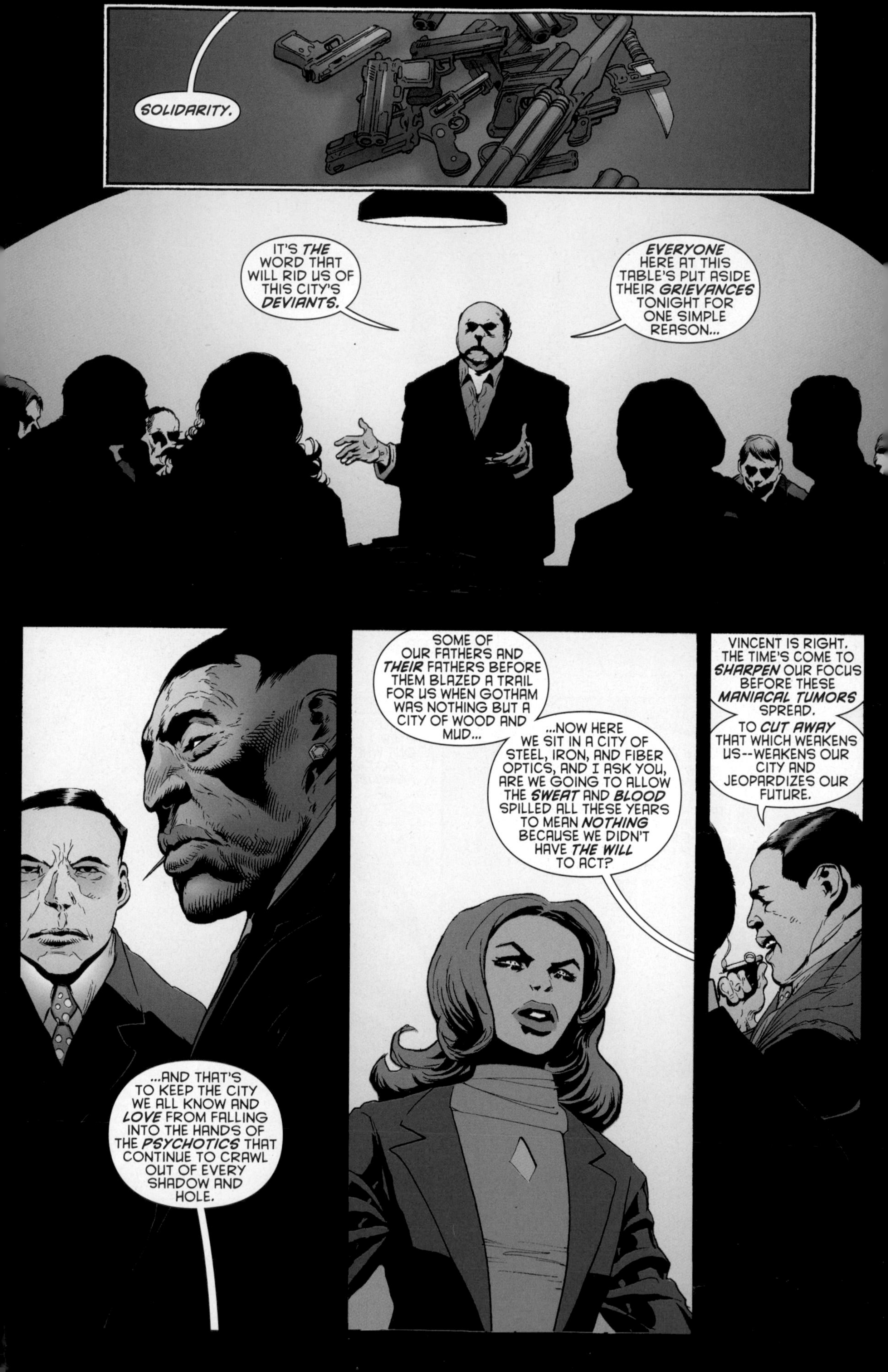
SOLIDARITY.
IT'S THE WORD THAT WILL RID US OF THIS CITY'S DEVIANTS.
EVERYONE HERE AT THIS TABLE'S PUT ASIDE THEIR GRIEVANCES TONIGHT FOR ONE SIMPLE REASON...
...AND THAT'S TO KEEP THE CITY WE ALL KNOW AND LOVE FROM FALLING INTO THE HANDS OF THE PSYCHOTICS THAT CONTINUE TO CRAWL OUT OF EVERY SHADOW AND HOLE.
SOME OF OUR FATHERS AND THEIR FATHERS BEFORE THEM BLAZED A TRAIL FOR US WHEN GOTHAM WAS NOTHING BUT A CITY OF WOOD AND MUD...
...NOW HERE WE SIT IN A CITY OF STEEL, IRON, AND FIBER OPTICS, AND I ASK YOU, ARE WE GOING TO ALLOW THE SWEAT AND BLOOD SPILLED ALL THESE YEARS TO MEAN NOTHING BECAUSE WE DIDN'T HAVE THE WILL TO ACT?
VINCENT IS RIGHT. THE TIME'S COME TO SHARPEN OUR FOCUS BEFORE THESE MANIACAL TUMORS SPREAD.
TO CUT AWAY THAT WHICH WEAKENS US--WEAKENS OUR CITY AND JEOPARDIZES OUR FUTURE.

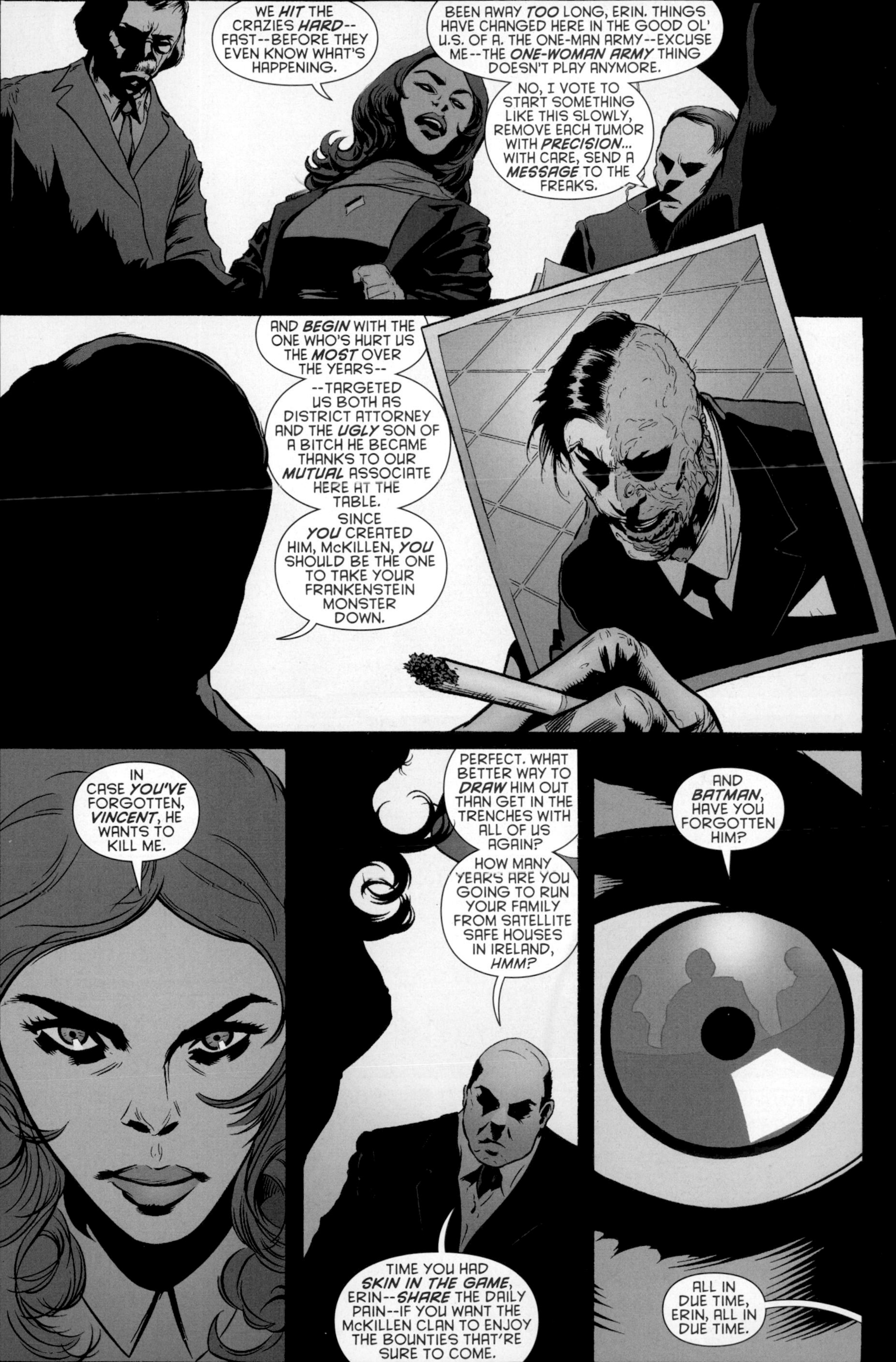
WE HIT THE CRAZIES HARD--FAST--BEFORE THEY EVEN KNOW WHAT'S HAPPENING.
BEEN AWAY TOO LONG, ERIN. THINGS HAVE CHANGED HERE IN THE GOOD OL' U.S. OF A. THE ONE-MAN ARMY--EXCUSE ME--THE ONE-WOMAN ARMY THING DOESN'T PLAY ANYMORE.
NO, I VOTE TO START SOMETHING LIKE THIS SLOWLY, REMOVE EACH TUMOR WITH PRECISION... WITH CARE, SEND A MESSAGE TO THE FREAKS.
AND BEGIN WITH THE ONE WHO'S HURT US THE MOST OVER THE YEARS--
--TARGETED US BOTH AS DISTRICT ATTORNEY AND THE UGLY SON OF A BITCH HE BECAME THANKS TO OUR MUTUAL ASSOCIATE HERE AT THE TABLE.
SINCE YOU CREATED HIM, McKILLEN, YOU SHOULD BE THE ONE TO TAKE YOUR FRANKENSTEIN MONSTER DOWN.
IN CASE YOU'VE FORGOTTEN, VINCENT, HE WANTS TO KILL ME.
PERFECT. WHAT BETTER WAY TO DRAW HIM OUT THAN GET IN THE TRENCHES WITH ALL OF US AGAIN?
HOW MANY YEARS ARE YOU GOING TO RUN YOUR FAMILY FROM SATELLITE SAFE HOUSES IN IRELAND, HMM?
TIME YOU HAD SKIN IN THE GAME, ERIN--SHARE THE DAILY PAIN--IF YOU WANT THE McKILLEN CLAN TO ENJOY THE BOUNTIES THAT'RE SURE TO COME.
AND BATMAN, HAVE YOU FORGOTTEN HIM?
ALL IN DUE TIME, ERIN, ALL IN DUE TIME.

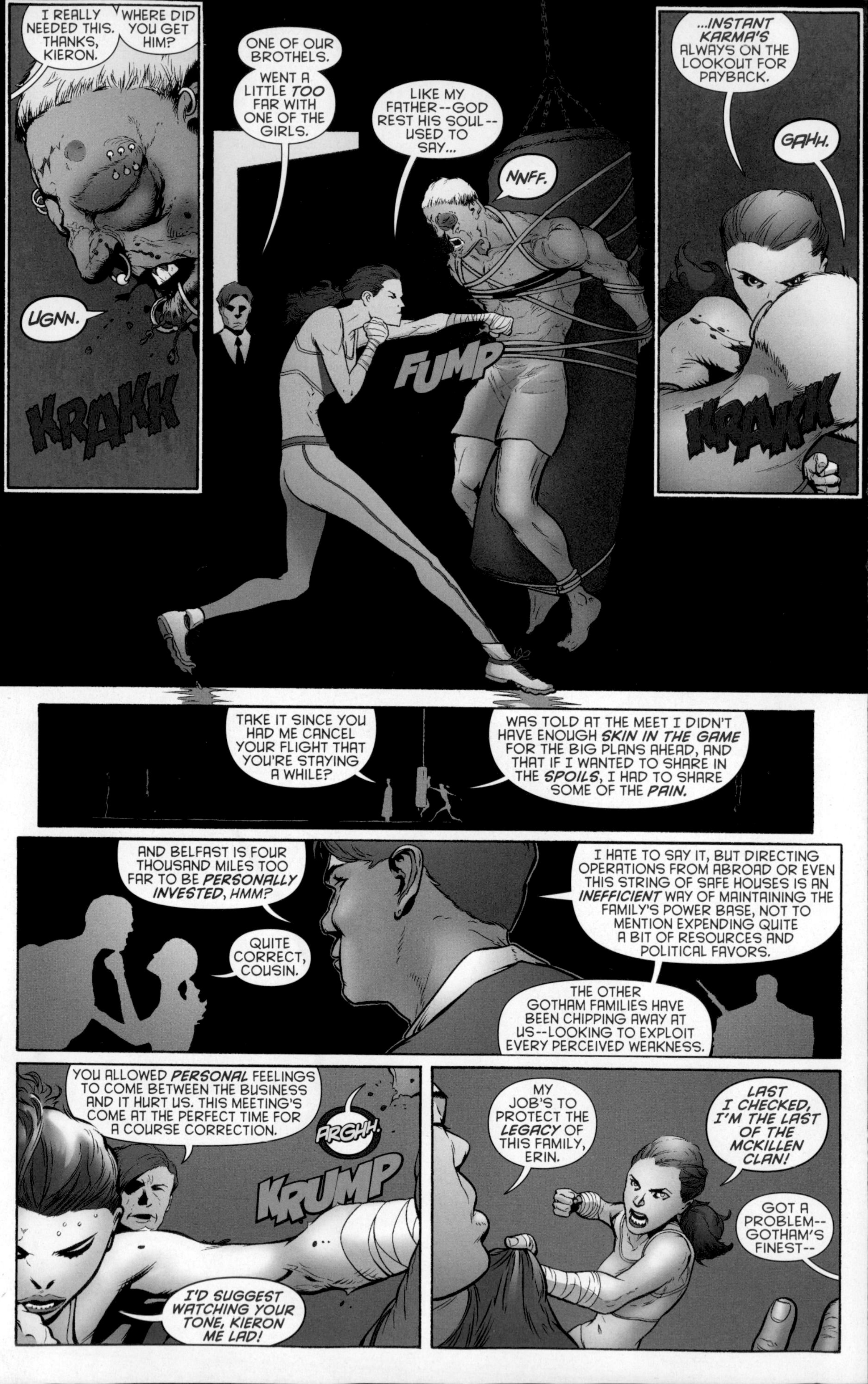

I REALLY NEEDED THIS. THANKS, KIERON.
WHERE DID YOU GET HIM?
UGNN.
KRAKK
ONE OF OUR BROTHELS.
WENT A LITTLE TOO FAR WITH ONE OF THE GIRLS.
LIKE MY FATHER--GOD REST HIS SOUL--USED TO SAY...
NNFF.
FUMP
...INSTANT KARMA'S ALWAYS ON THE LOOKOUT FOR PAYBACK.
GAHH.
KRAKK
TAKE IT SINCE YOU HAD ME CANCEL YOUR FLIGHT THAT YOU'RE STAYING A WHILE?
WAS TOLD AT THE MEET I DIDN'T HAVE ENOUGH SKIN IN THE GAME FOR THE BIG PLANS AHEAD, AND THAT IF I WANTED TO SHARE IN THE SPOILS, I HAD TO SHARE SOME OF THE PAIN.
AND BELFAST IS FOUR THOUSAND MILES TOO FAR TO BE PERSONALLY INVESTED, HMM?
QUITE CORRECT, COUSIN.
I HATE TO SAY IT, BUT DIRECTING OPERATIONS FROM ABROAD OR EVEN THIS STRING OF SAFE HOUSES IS AN INEFFICIENT WAY OF MAINTAINING THE FAMILY'S POWER BASE, NOT TO MENTION EXPENDING QUITE A BIT OF RESOURCES AND POLITICAL FAVORS.
THE OTHER GOTHAM FAMILIES HAVE BEEN CHIPPING AWAY AT US--LOOKING TO EXPLOIT EVERY PERCEIVED WEAKNESS.
YOU ALLOWED PERSONAL FEELINGS TO COME BETWEEN THE BUSINESS AND IT HURT US. THIS MEETING'S COME AT THE PERFECT TIME FOR A COURSE CORRECTION.
ARGHH.
KRUMP
I'D SUGGEST WATCHING YOUR TONE, KIERON ME LAD!
MY JOB'S TO PROTECT THE LEGACY OF THIS FAMILY, ERIN.
LAST I CHECKED, I'M THE LAST OF THE MCKILLEN CLAN!
GOT A PROBLEM-- GOTHAM'S FINEST--

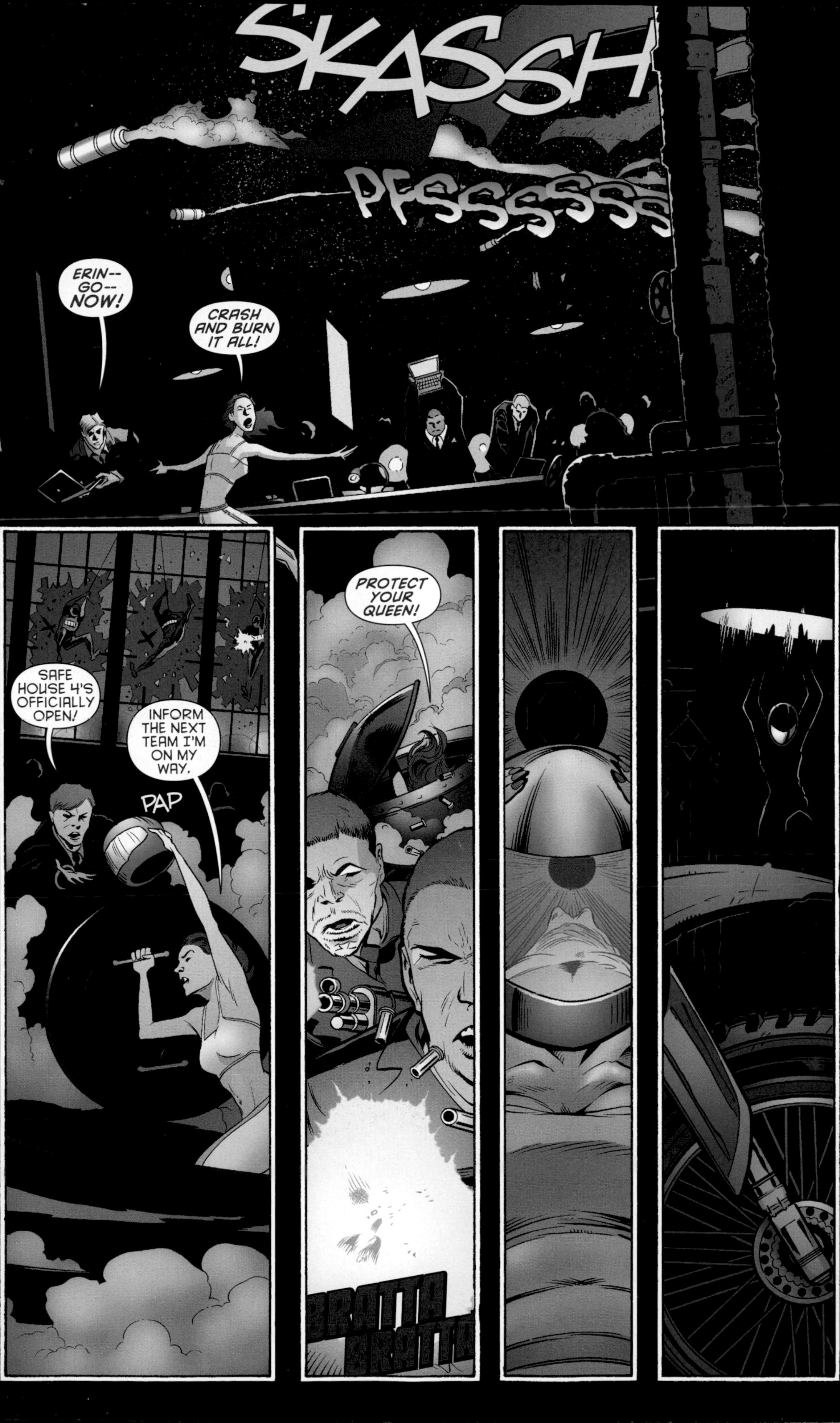
SKASSH
PFSSSSSSS
ERIN-- GO-- NOW!
CRASH AND BURN IT ALL!
SAFE HOUSE 4'S OFFICIALLY OPEN!
INFORM THE NEXT TEAM I'M ON MY WAY.
PAP
PROTECT YOUR QUEEN!

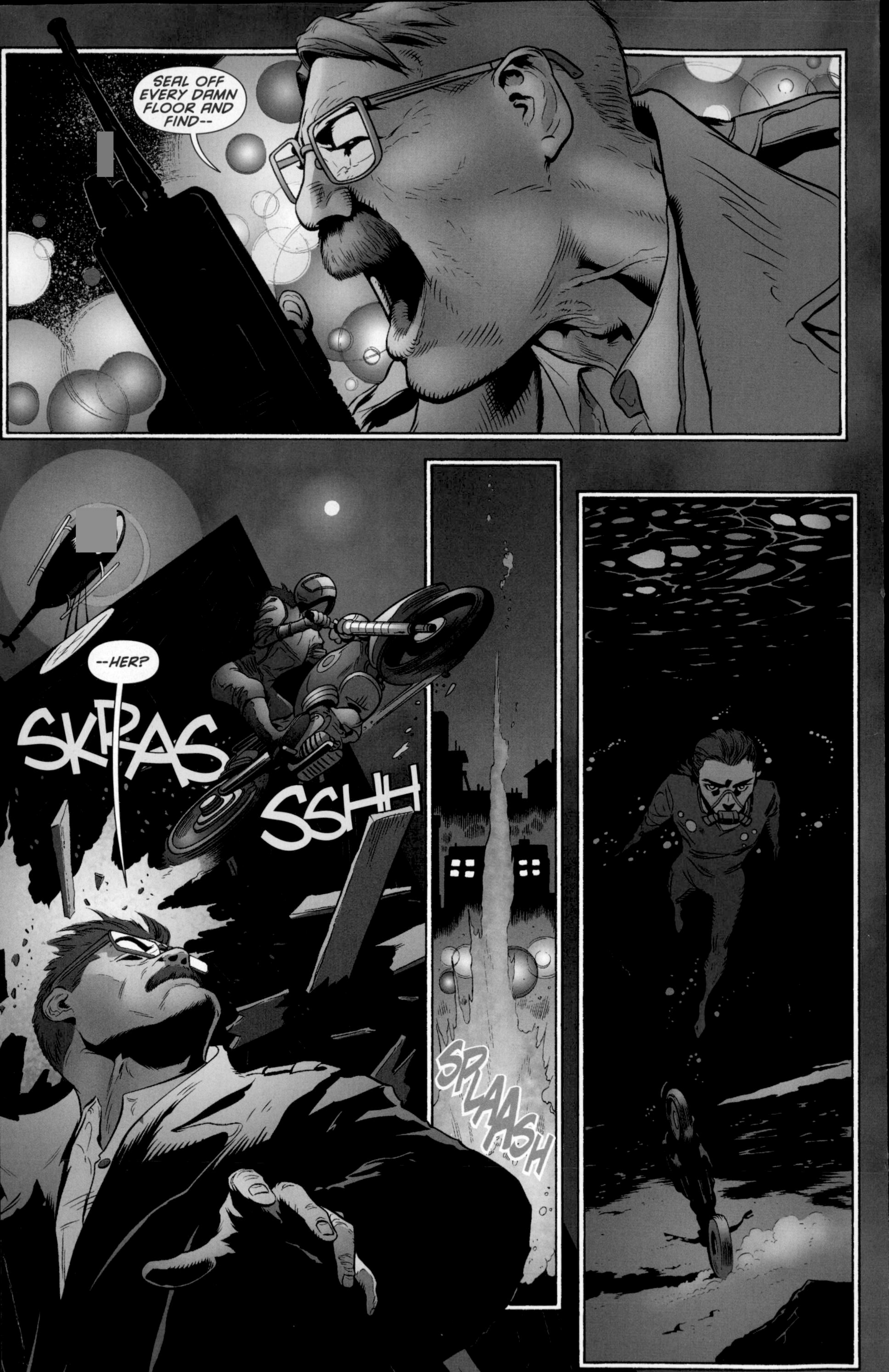
SEAL OFF EVERY DAMN FLOOR AND FIND--
--HER?
SKRAS
SSHH
SPLAAASH

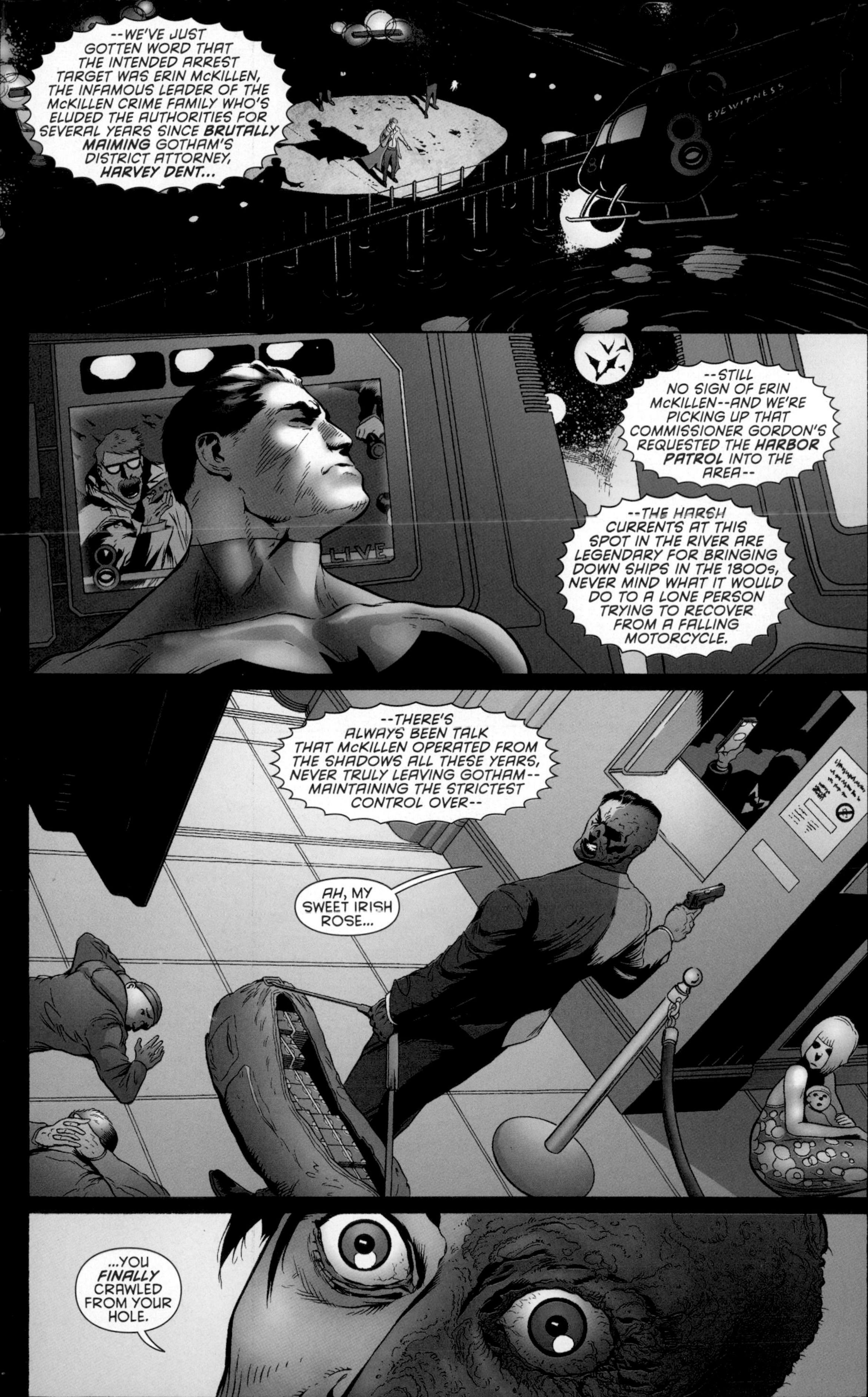
--WE'VE JUST GOTTEN WORD THAT THE INTENDED ARREST TARGET WAS ERIN McKILLEN, THE INFAMOUS LEADER OF THE McKILLEN CRIME FAMILY WHO'S ELUDED THE AUTHORITIES FOR SEVERAL YEARS SINCE BRUTALLY MAIMING GOTHAM'S DISTRICT ATTORNEY, HARVEY DENT...
EYEWITNESS
LIVE
--STILL NO SIGN OF ERIN McKILLEN--AND WE'RE PICKING UP THAT COMMISSIONER GORDON'S REQUESTED THE HARBOR PATROL INTO THE AREA--
--THE HARSH CURRENTS AT THIS SPOT IN THE RIVER ARE LEGENDARY FOR BRINGING DOWN SHIPS IN THE 1800s, NEVER MIND WHAT IT WOULD DO TO A LONE PERSON TRYING TO RECOVER FROM A FALLING MOTORCYCLE.
--THERE'S ALWAYS BEEN TALK THAT McKILLEN OPERATED FROM THE SHADOWS ALL THESE YEARS, NEVER TRULY LEAVING GOTHAM--MAINTAINING THE STRICTEST CONTROL OVER--
AH, MY SWEET IRISH ROSE...
...YOU FINALLY CRAWLED FROM YOUR HOLE.

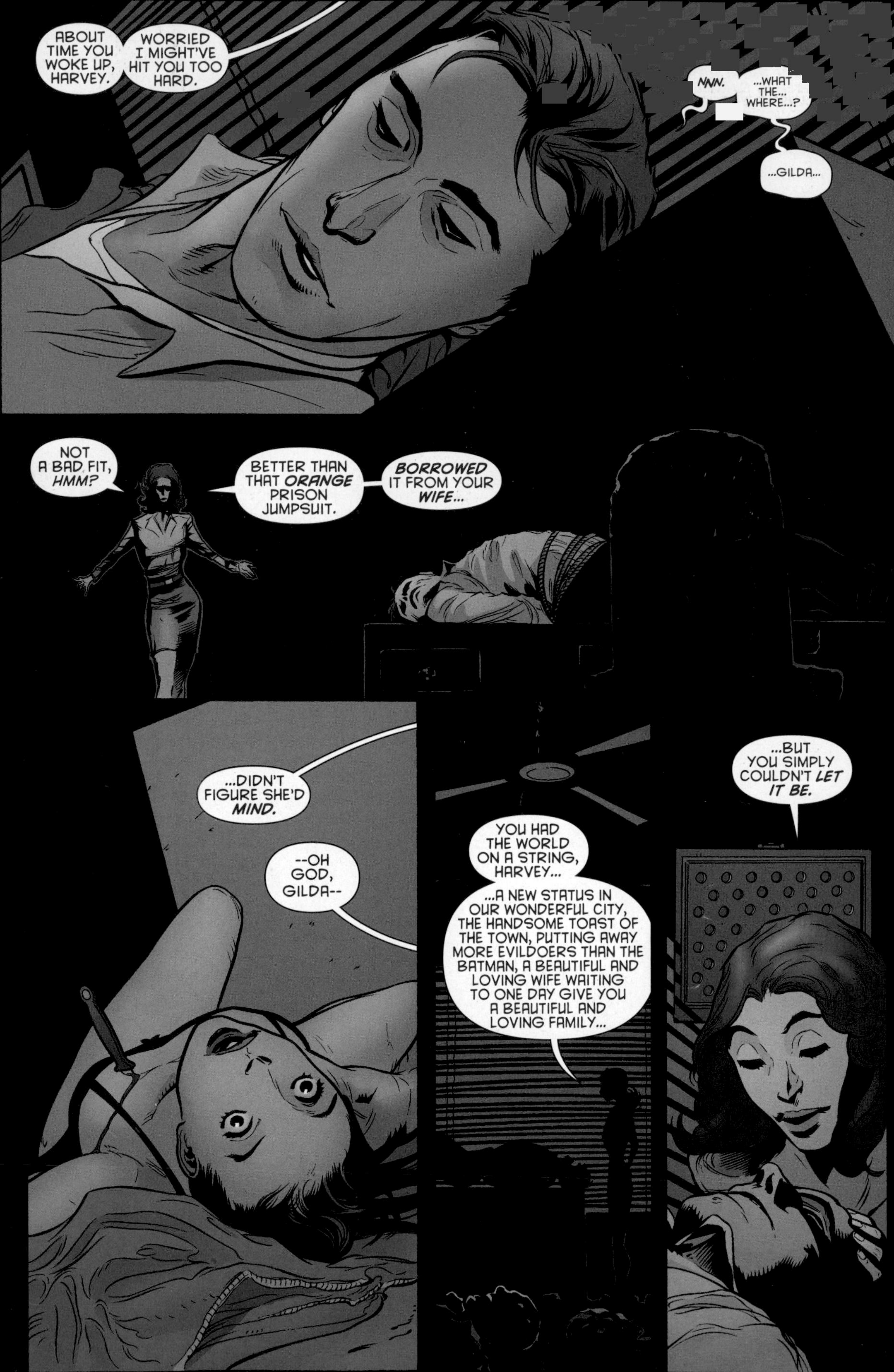
NNN.
...WHAT THE... WHERE...?
...GILDA...
ABOUT TIME YOU WOKE UP, HARVEY.
WORRIED I MIGHT'VE HIT YOU TOO HARD.
NOT A BAD FIT, HMM?
BETTER THAN THAT ORANGE PRISON JUMPSUIT.
BORROWED IT FROM YOUR WIFE...
...DIDN'T FIGURE SHE'D MIND.
--OH GOD, GILDA--
YOU HAD THE WORLD ON A STRING, HARVEY...
...A NEW STATUS IN OUR WONDERFUL CITY, THE HANDSOME TOAST OF THE TOWN, PUTTING AWAY MORE EVILDOERS THAN THE BATMAN, A BEAUTIFUL AND LOVING WIFE WAITING TO ONE DAY GIVE YOU A BEAUTIFUL AND LOVING FAMILY...
...BUT YOU SIMPLY COULDN'T LET IT BE.

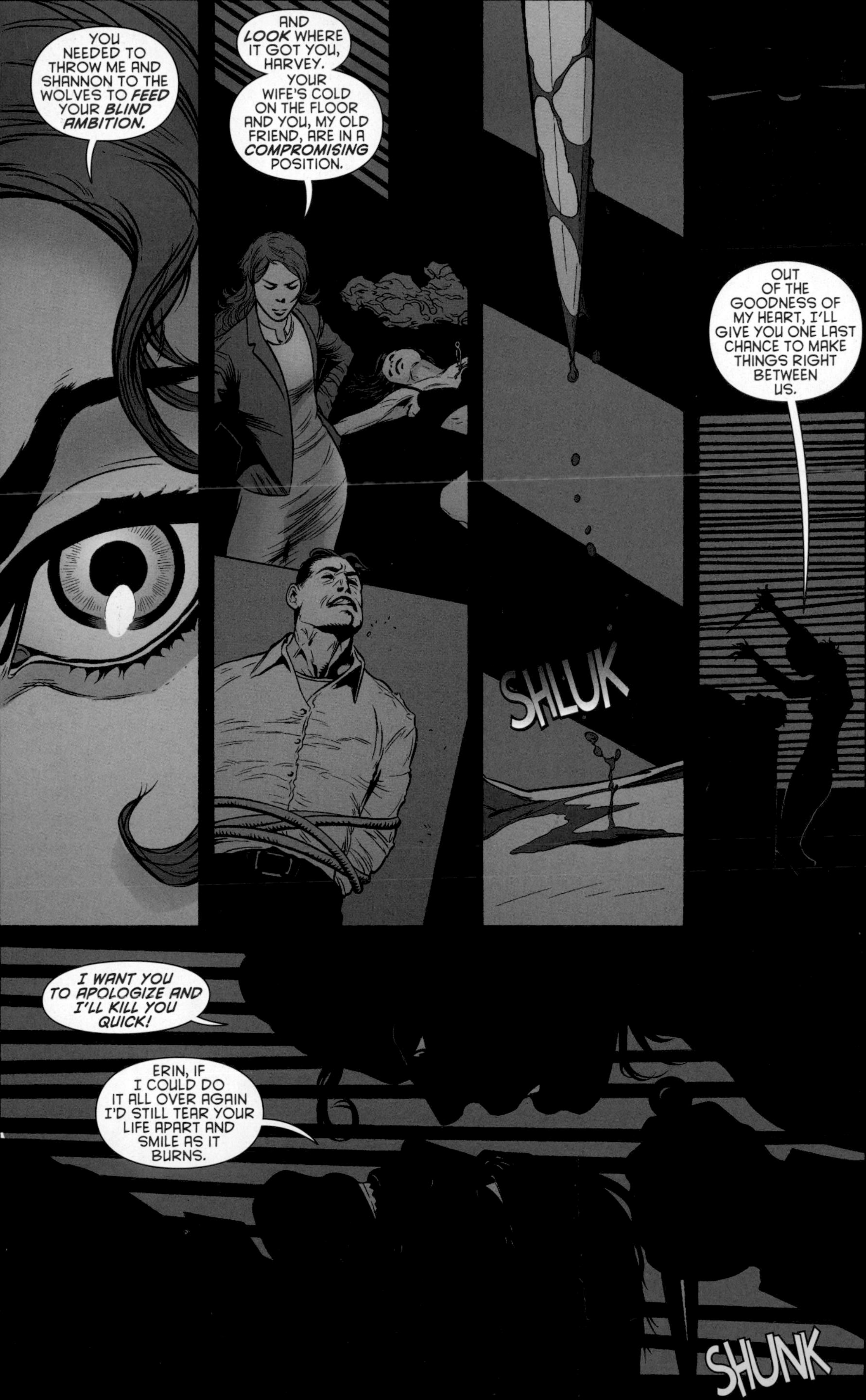

YOU NEEDED TO THROW ME AND SHANNON TO THE WOLVES TO FEED YOUR BLIND AMBITION.
AND LOOK WHERE IT GOT YOU, HARVEY.
YOUR WIFE'S COLD ON THE FLOOR AND YOU, MY OLD FRIEND, ARE IN A COMPROMISING POSITION.
SHLUK
OUT OF THE GOODNESS OF MY HEART, I'LL GIVE YOU ONE LAST CHANCE TO MAKE THINGS RIGHT BETWEEN US.
I WANT YOU TO APOLOGIZE AND I'LL KILL YOU QUICK!
ERIN, IF I COULD DO IT ALL OVER AGAIN I'D STILL TEAR YOUR LIFE APART AND SMILE AS IT BURNS.
SHUNK

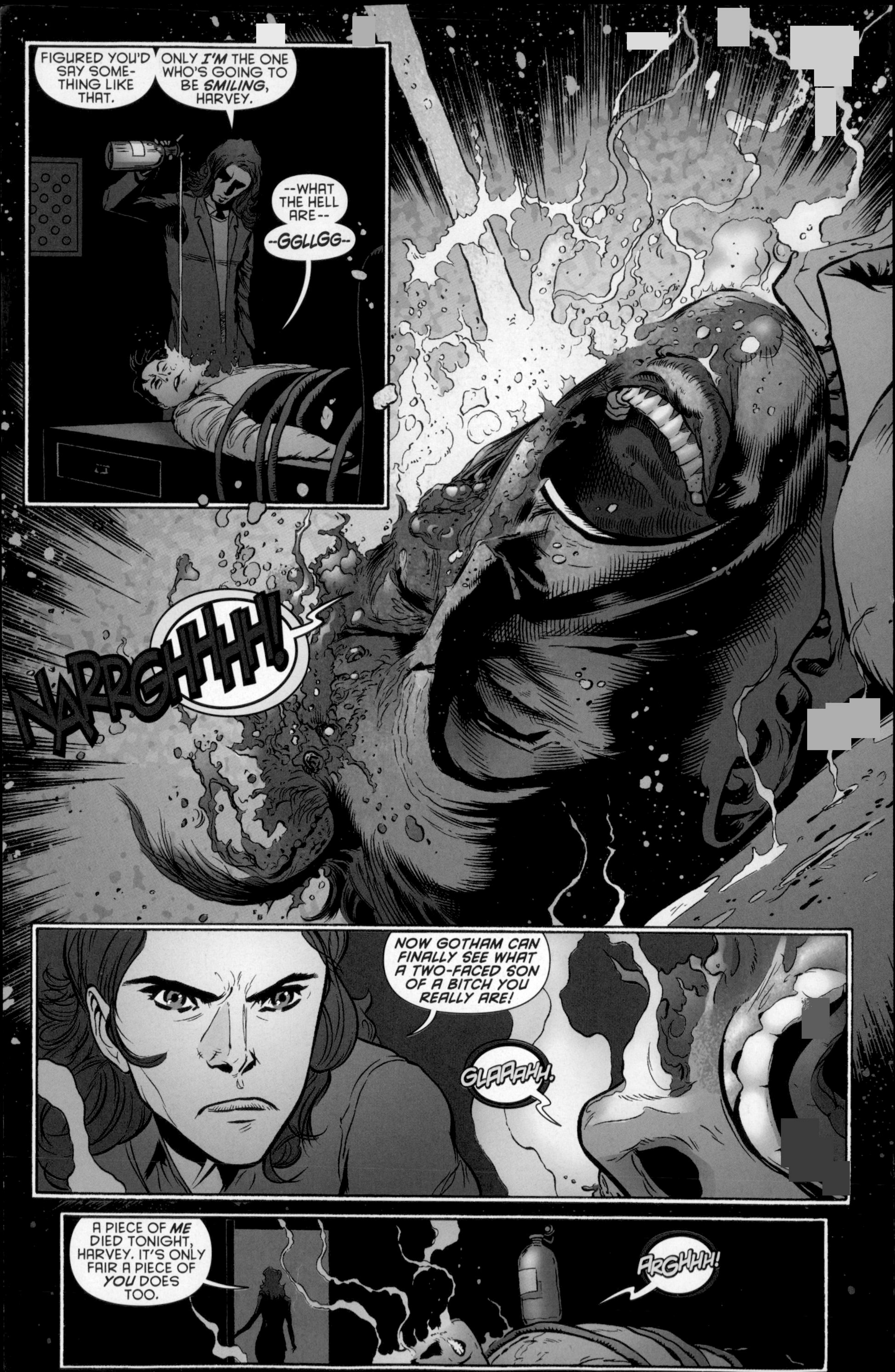

FIGURED YOU'D SAY SOME-THING LIKE THAT.
ONLY I'M THE ONE WHO'S GOING TO BE SMILING, HARVEY.
--WHAT THE HELL ARE--
--GGLLGG--
NARRGHHHH!
NOW GOTHAM CAN FINALLY SEE WHAT A TWO-FACED SON OF A BITCH YOU REALLY ARE!
GLAAAHH.
A PIECE OF ME DIED TONIGHT, HARVEY. IT'S ONLY FAIR A PIECE OF YOU DOES TOO.
ARGHHH!

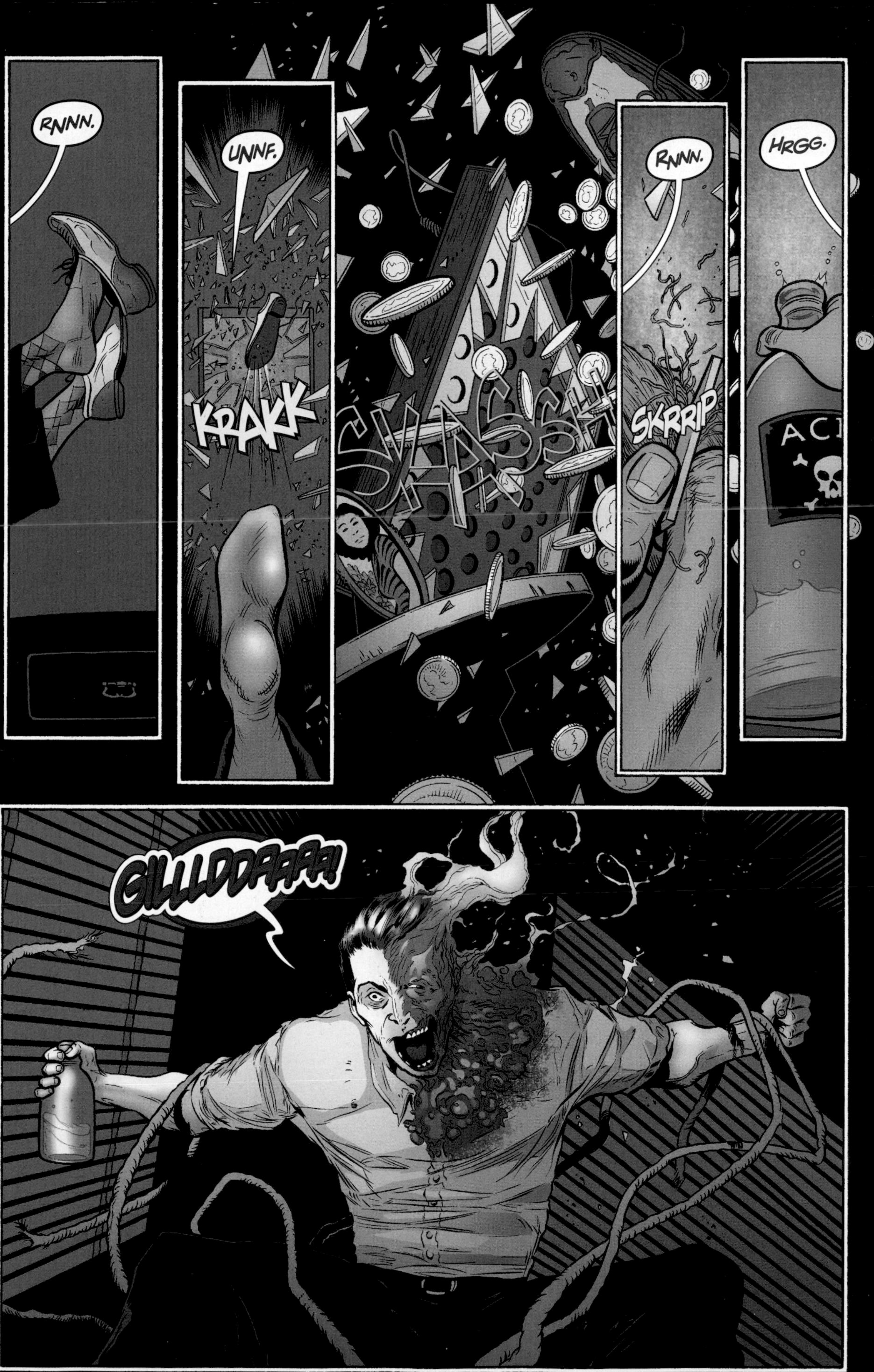
RNNN.
UNNF.
KRAKK
SMASSH
RNNN.
SKRRIP
HRGG.
ACI
GILLLDDAAAA!

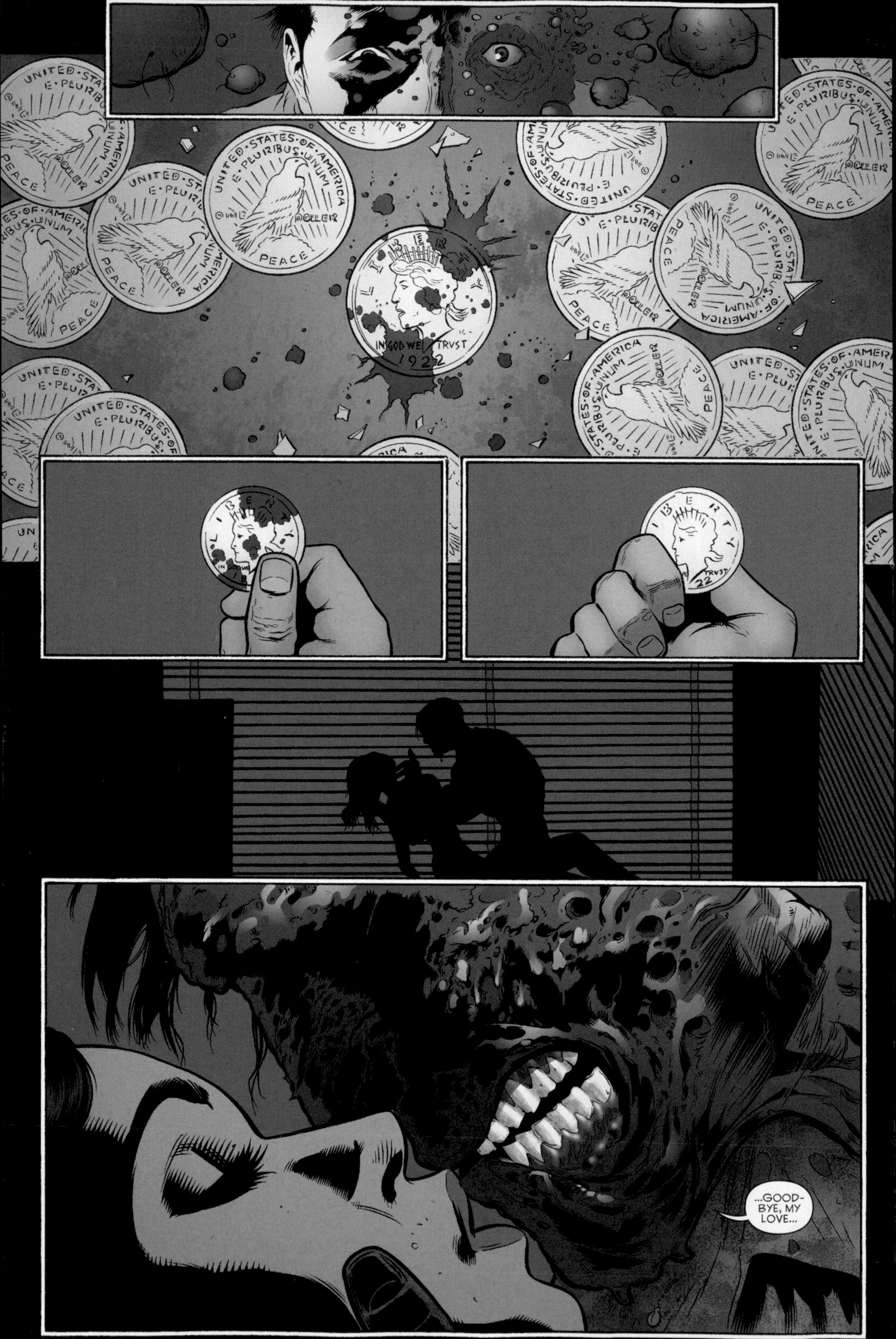
...GOOD-BYE, MY LOVE...

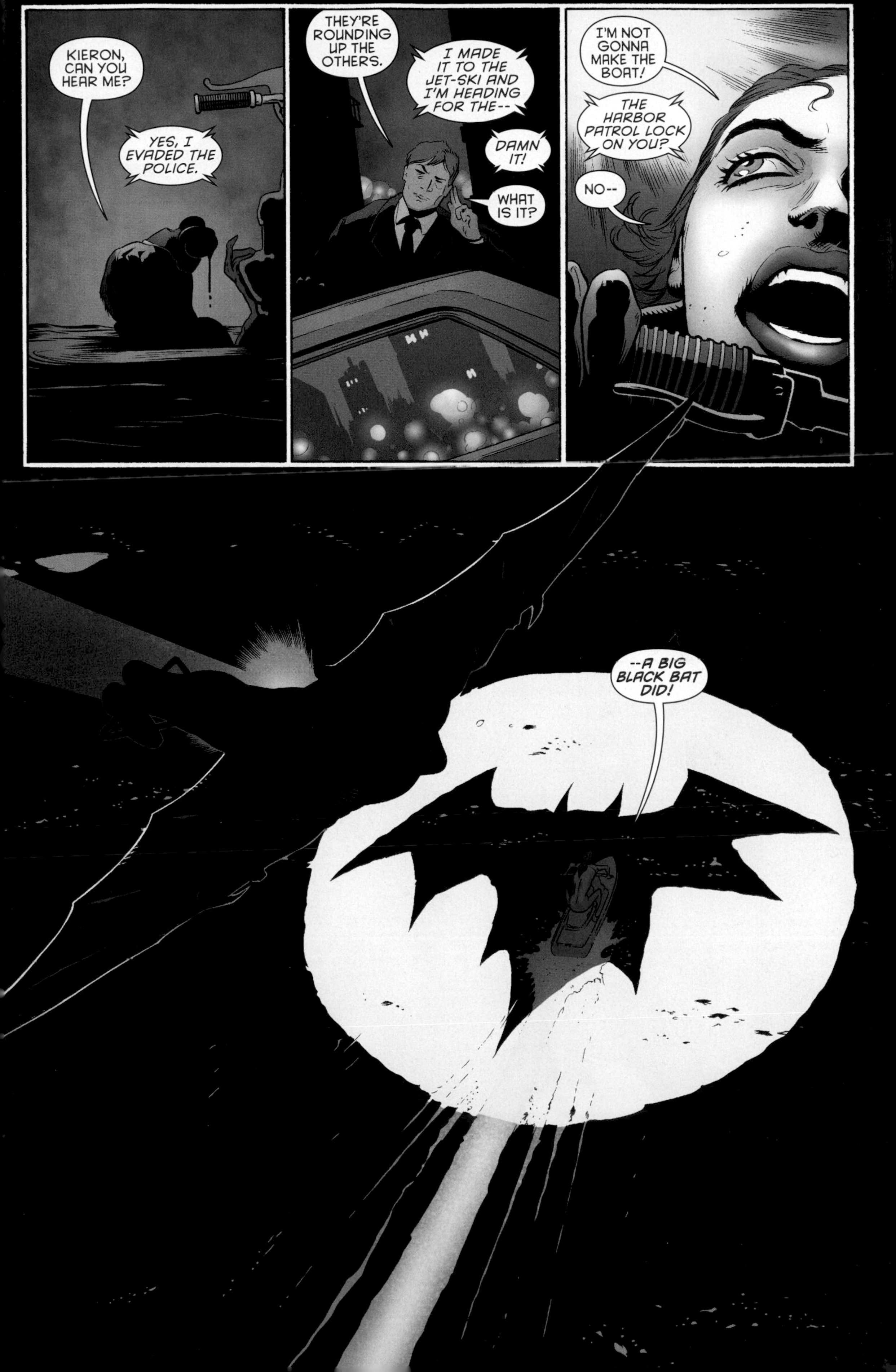
KIERON, CAN YOU HEAR ME?
YES, I EVADED THE POLICE.
THEY'RE ROUNDING UP THE OTHERS.
I MADE IT TO THE JET-SKI AND I'M HEADING FOR THE--
DAMN IT!
WHAT IS IT?
I'M NOT GONNA MAKE THE BOAT!
THE HARBOR PATROL LOCK ON YOU?
NO--
--A BIG BLACK BAT DID!

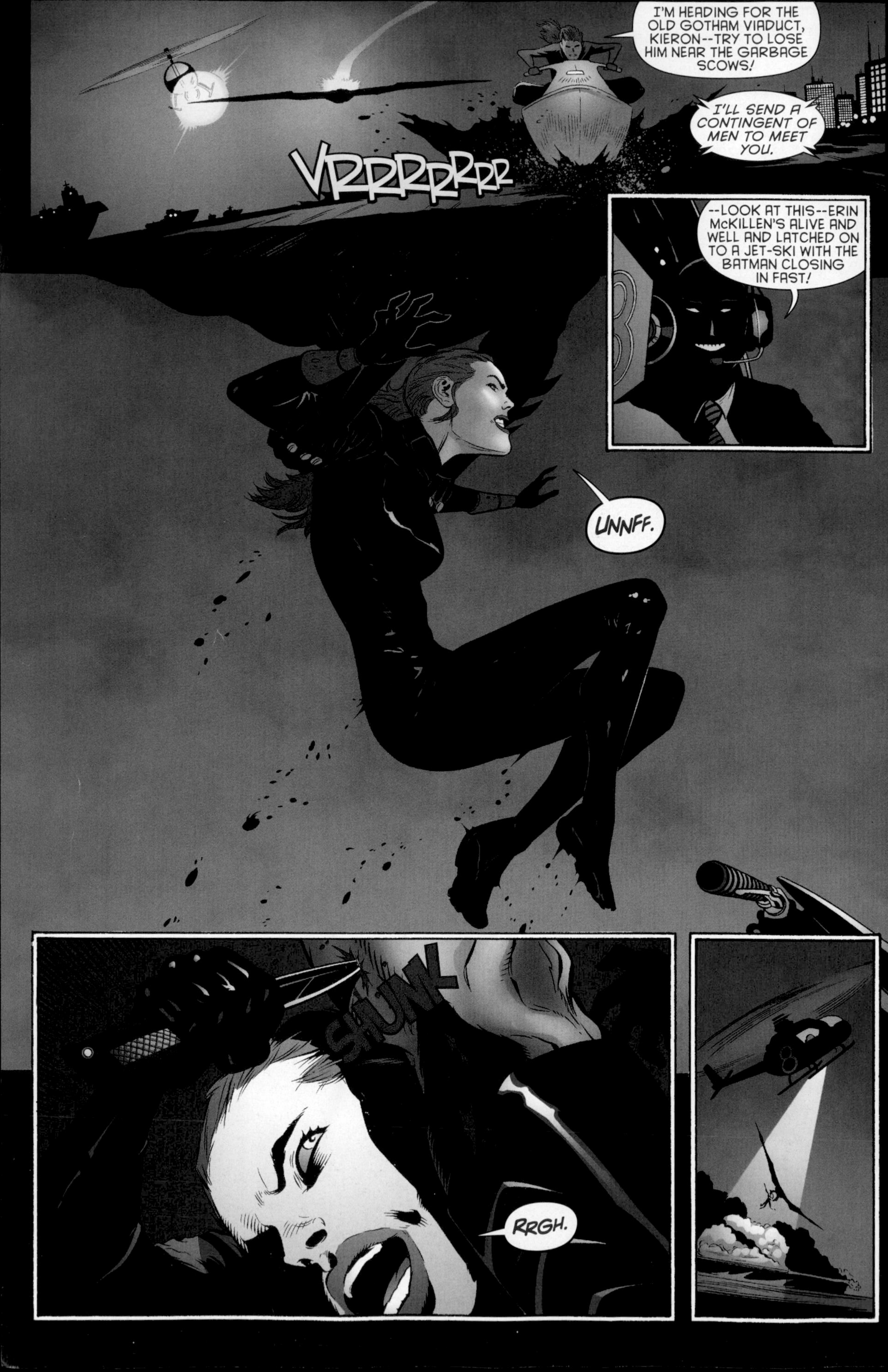
I'M HEADING FOR THE OLD GOTHAM VIADUCT, KIERON--TRY TO LOSE HIM NEAR THE GARBAGE SCOWS!
I'LL SEND A CONTINGENT OF MEN TO MEET YOU.
VRRRRRRRR
--LOOK AT THIS--ERIN McKILLEN'S ALIVE AND WELL AND LATCHED ON TO A JET-SKI WITH THE BATMAN CLOSING IN FAST!
UNNFF.
SHUNK
RRGH.

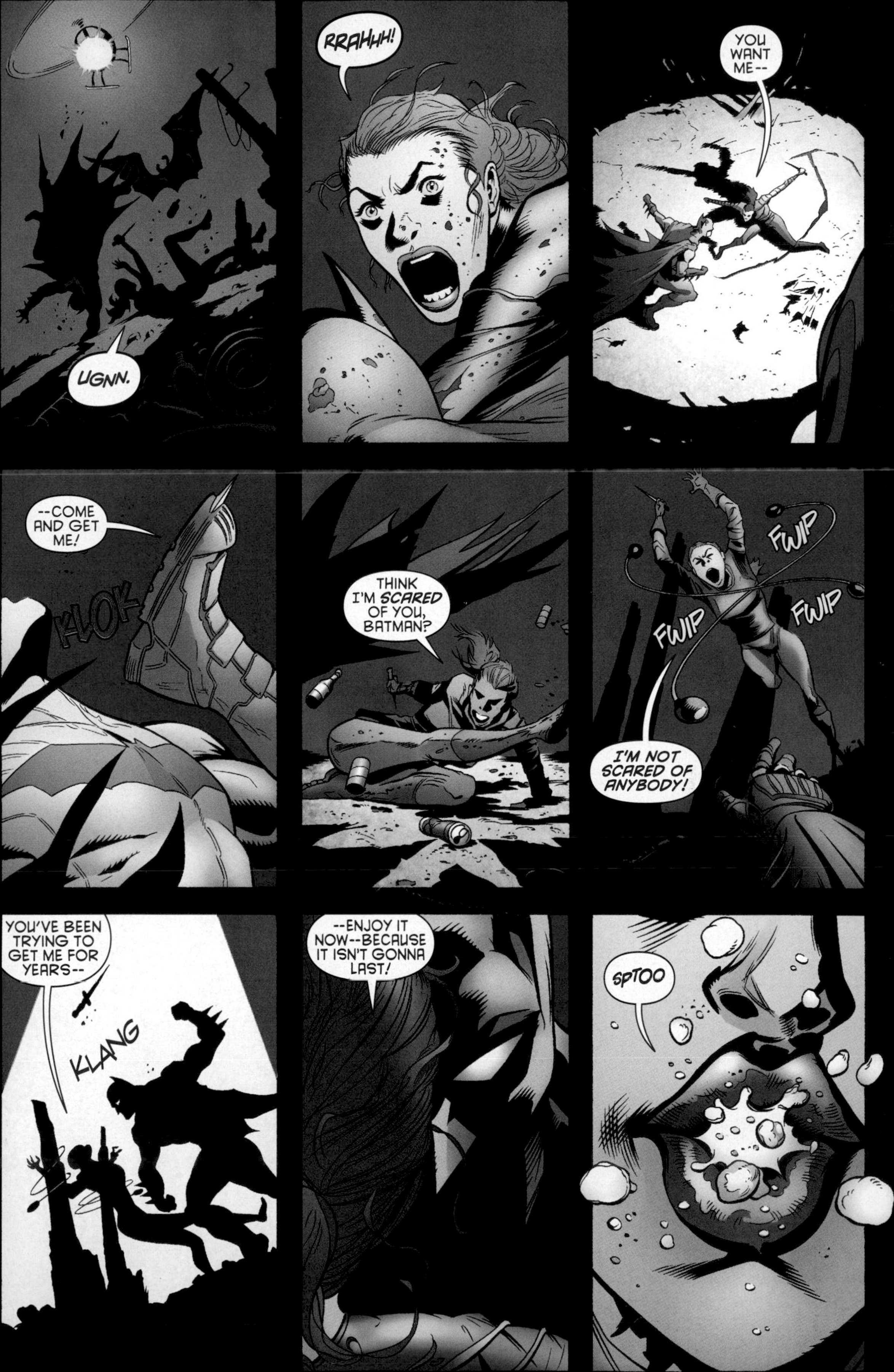

UGNN.
RRAHHH!
YOU WANT ME--
--COME AND GET ME!
KLOK
THINK I'M SCARED OF YOU, BATMAN?
FWIP
FWIP
FWIP
I'M NOT SCARED OF ANYBODY!
YOU'VE BEEN TRYING TO GET ME FOR YEARS--
KLANG
--ENJOY IT NOW--BECAUSE IT ISN'T GONNA LAST!
SPTOO

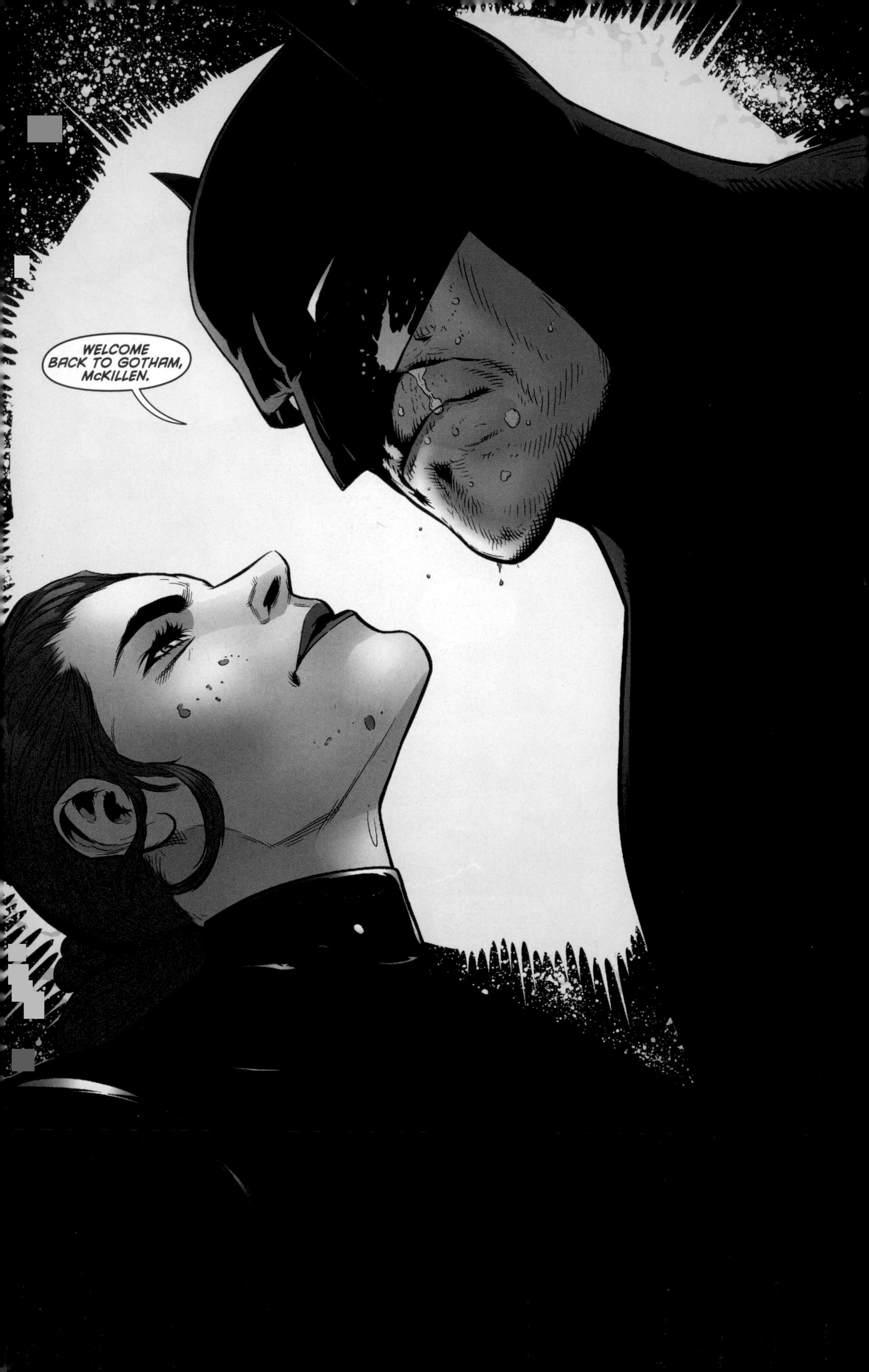
WELCOME BACK TO GOTHAM, McKILLEN.

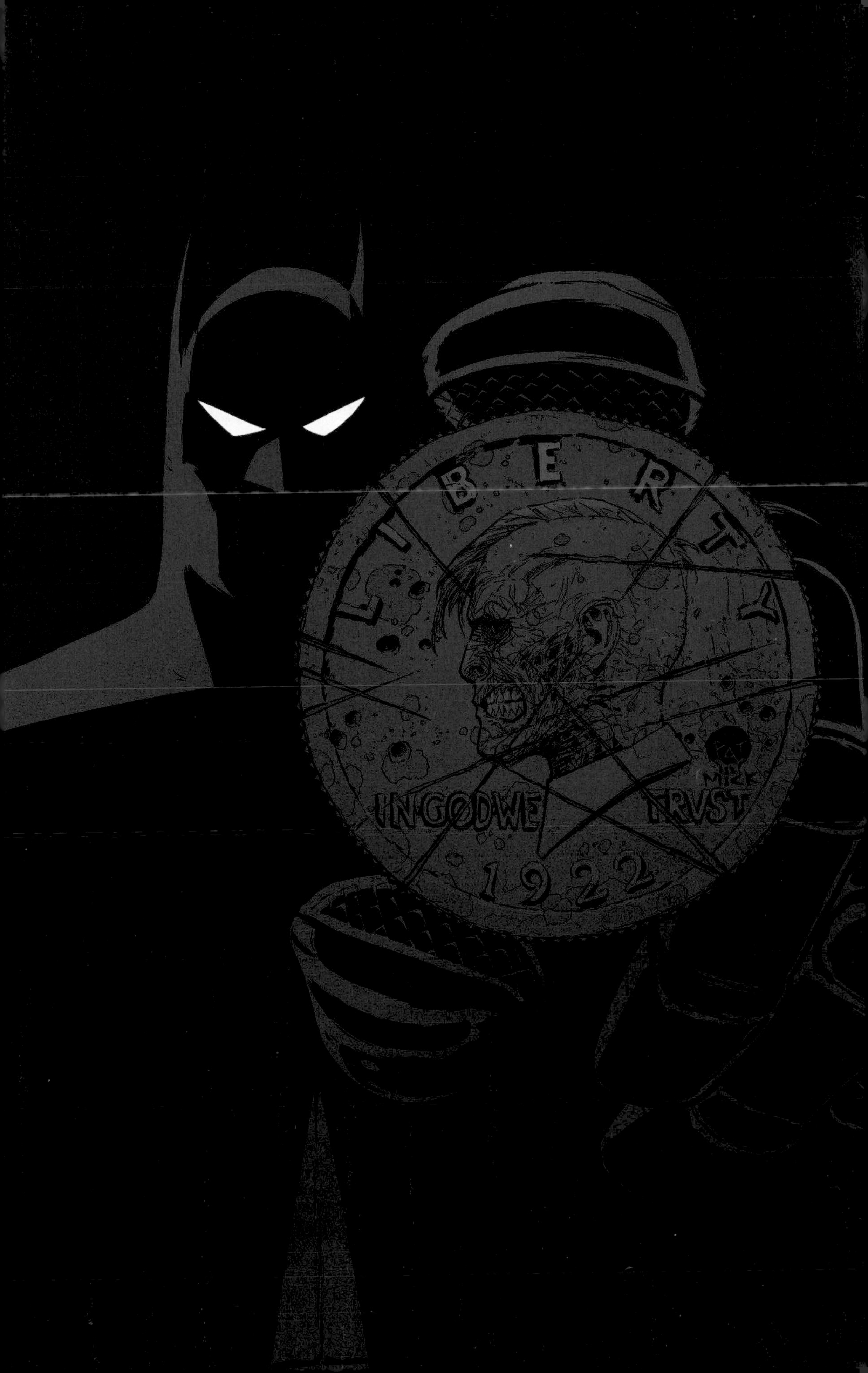
LIBERTY
IN GØD WE TRVST
1922

THE BIG BURN: SPARKS

PATRICK GLEASON penciller **MICK GRAY** inker **JOHN KALISZ** colorist cover art by **GLEASON, GRAY & KALISZ**

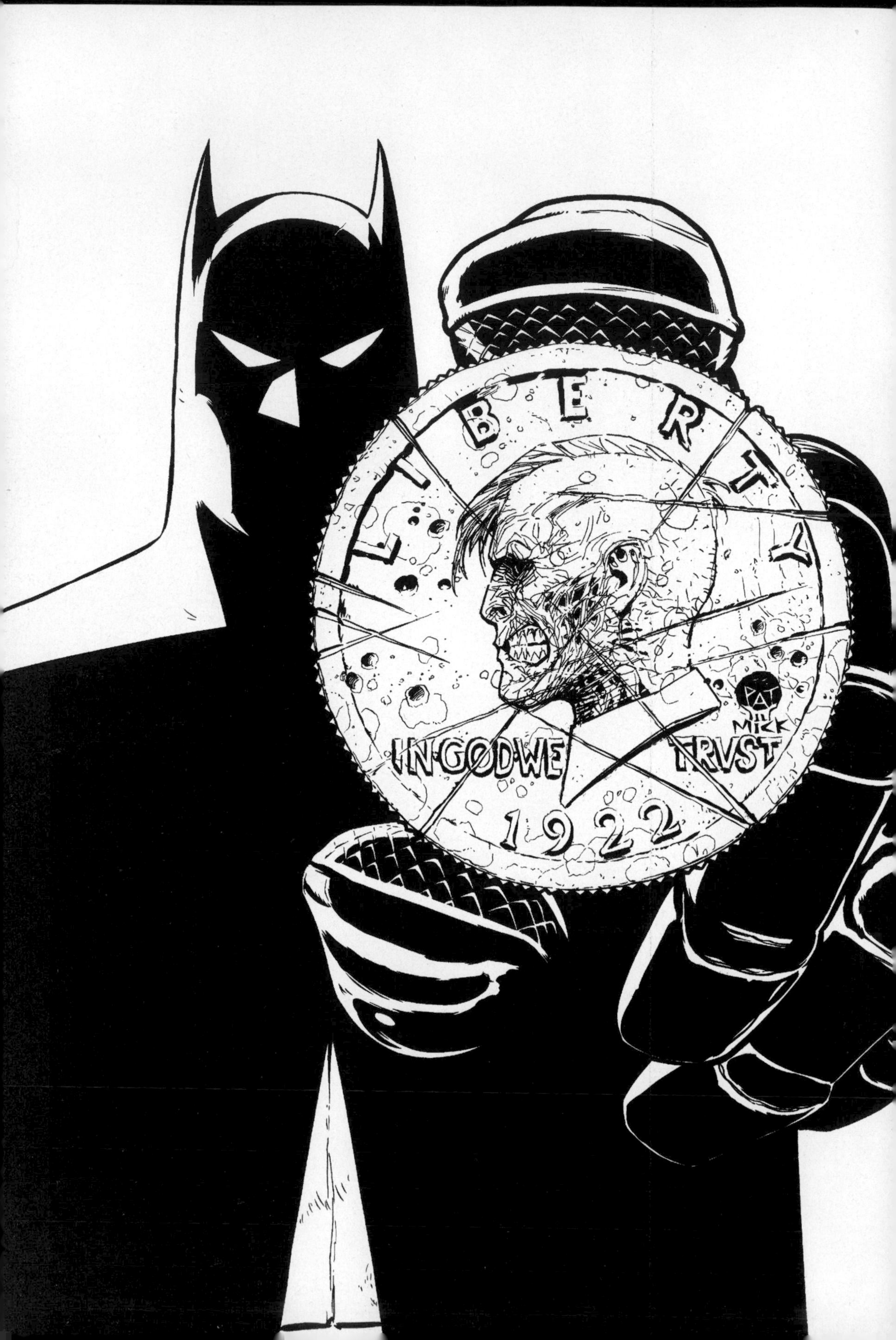
LIBERTY
INGODWE TRVST
1922
PAT
MICK

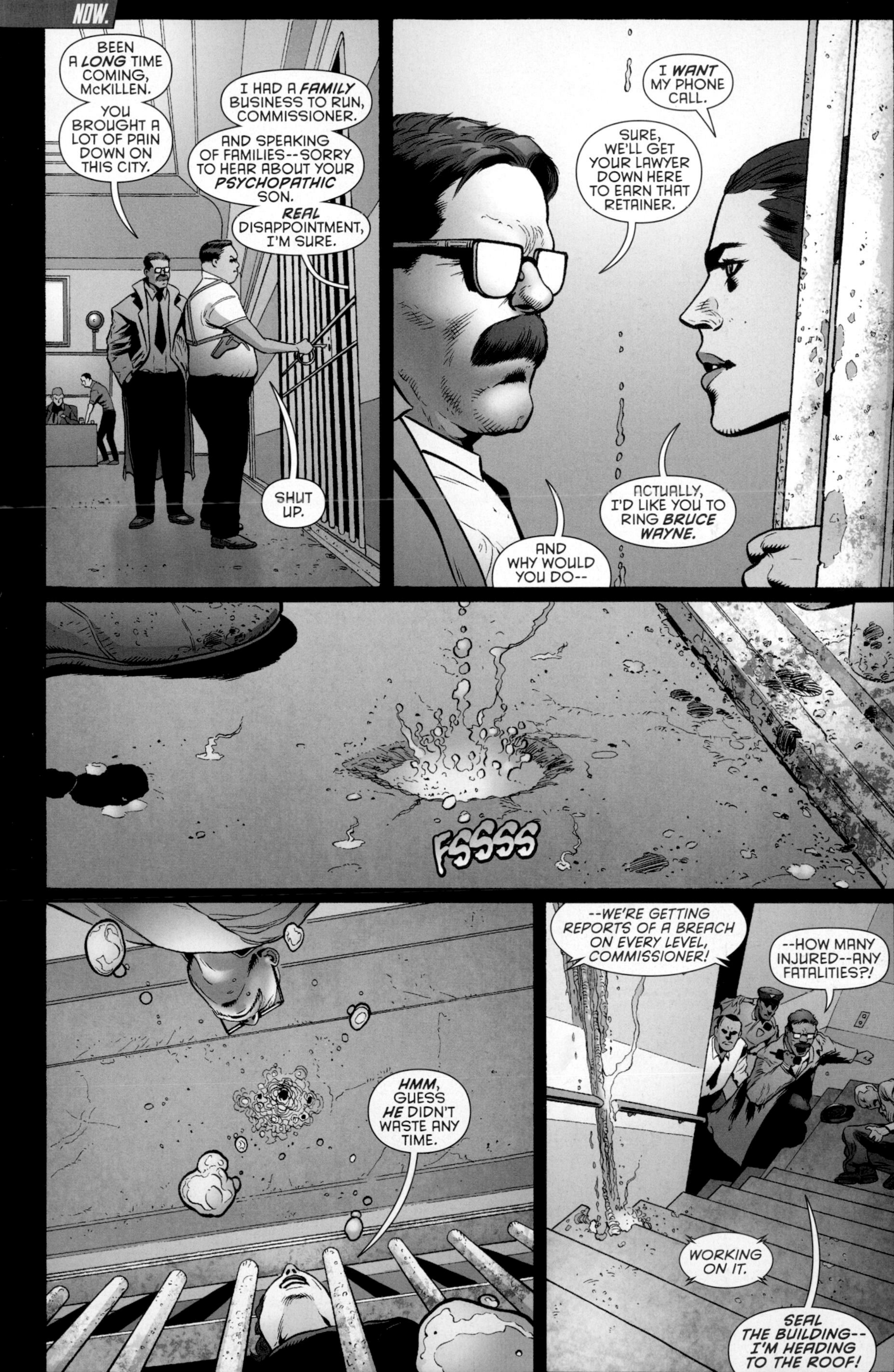
NOW.
BEEN A LONG TIME COMING, McKILLEN.
YOU BROUGHT A LOT OF PAIN DOWN ON THIS CITY.
I HAD A FAMILY BUSINESS TO RUN, COMMISSIONER.
AND SPEAKING OF FAMILIES--SORRY TO HEAR ABOUT YOUR PSYCHOPATHIC SON.
REAL DISAPPOINTMENT, I'M SURE.
SHUT UP.
I WANT MY PHONE CALL.
SURE, WE'LL GET YOUR LAWYER DOWN HERE TO EARN THAT RETAINER.
ACTUALLY, I'D LIKE YOU TO RING BRUCE WAYNE.
AND WHY WOULD YOU DO--
FSSSS
HMM, GUESS HE DIDN'T WASTE ANY TIME.
--WE'RE GETTING REPORTS OF A BREACH ON EVERY LEVEL, COMMISSIONER!
--HOW MANY INJURED--ANY FATALITIES?!
WORKING ON IT.
SEAL THE BUILDING-- I'M HEADING TO THE ROOF!

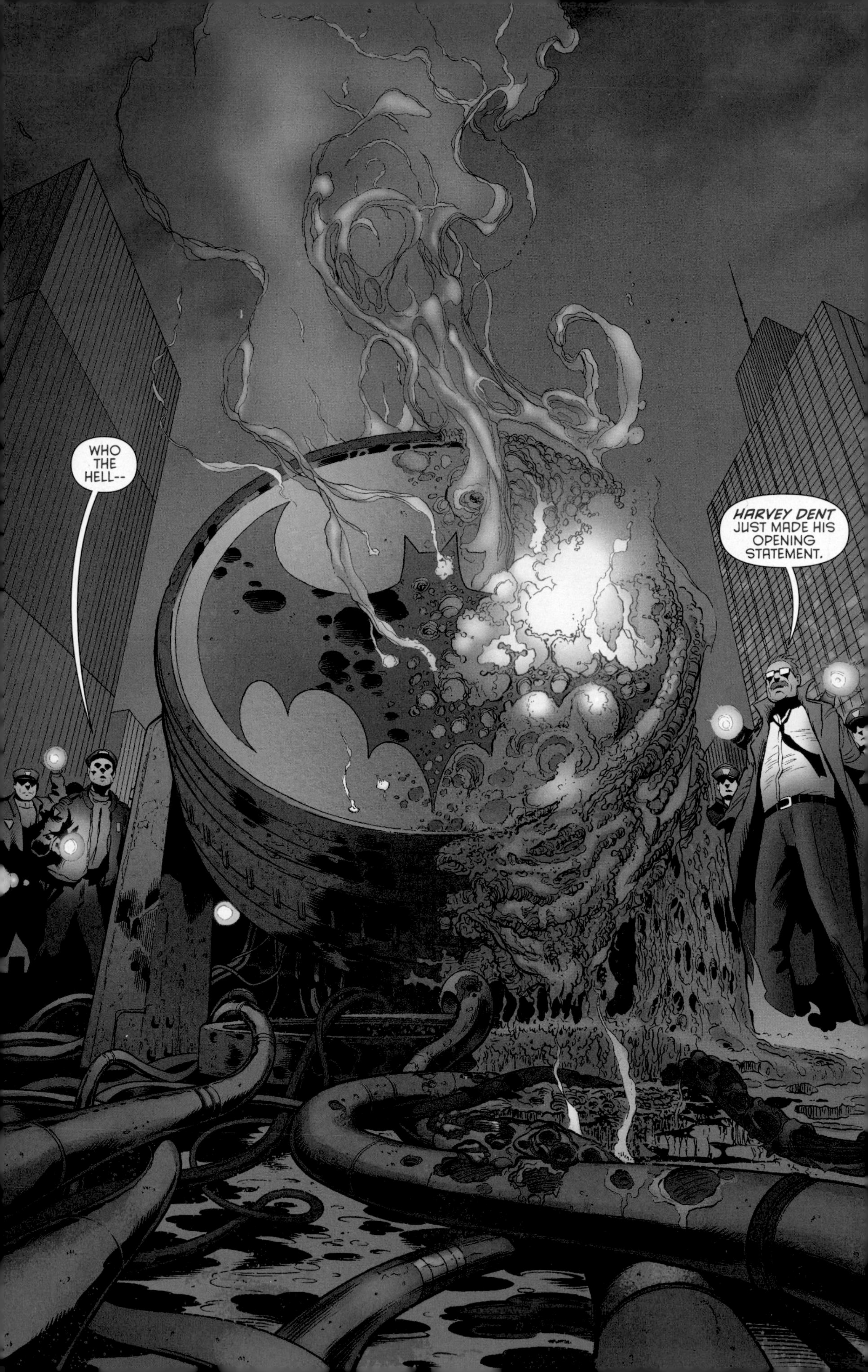
WHO THE HELL--
HARVEY DENT JUST MADE HIS OPENING STATEMENT.

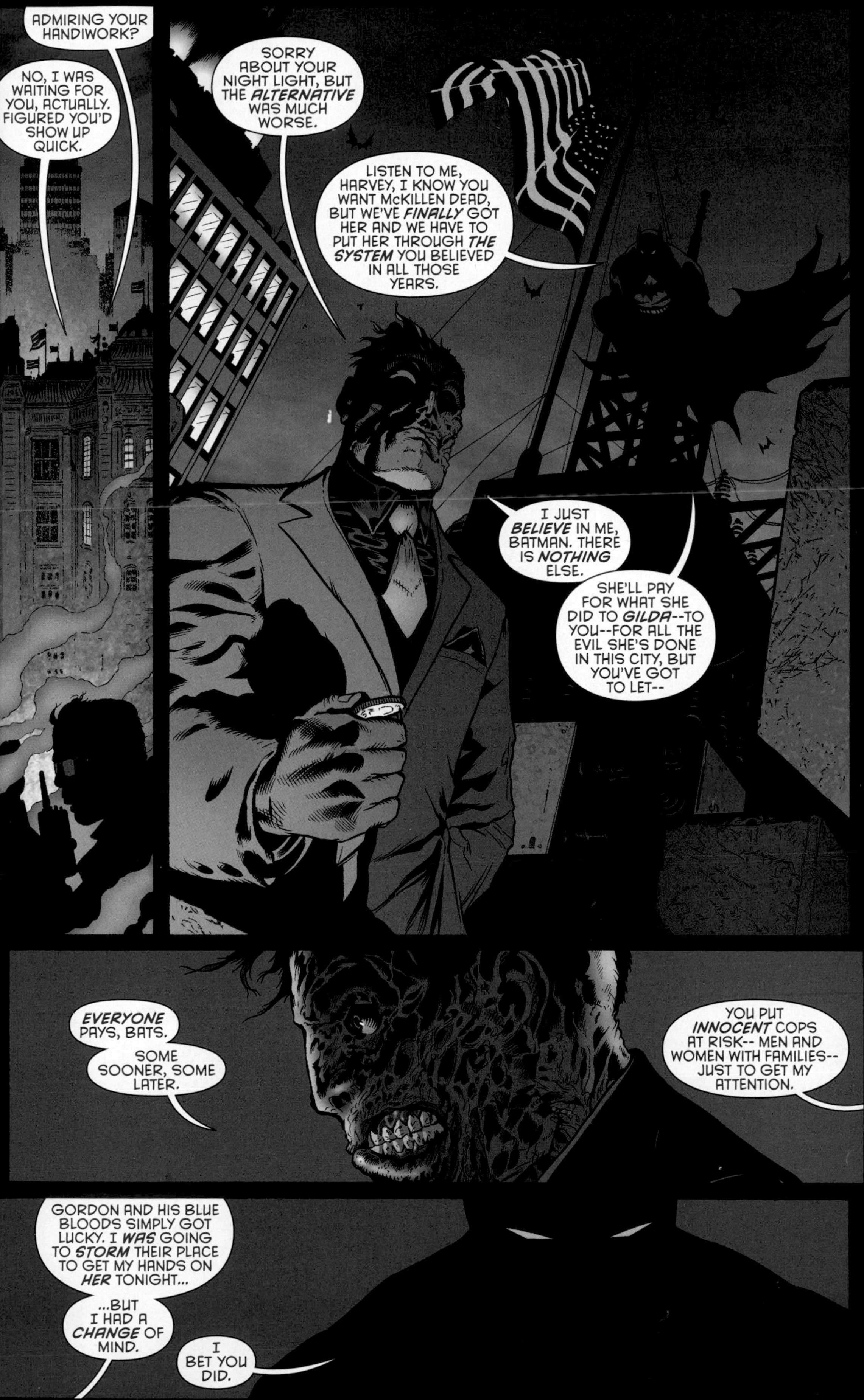
ADMIRING YOUR HANDIWORK?
NO, I WAS WAITING FOR YOU, ACTUALLY. FIGURED YOU'D SHOW UP QUICK.
SORRY ABOUT YOUR NIGHT LIGHT, BUT THE ALTERNATIVE WAS MUCH WORSE.
LISTEN TO ME, HARVEY, I KNOW YOU WANT McKILLEN DEAD, BUT WE'VE FINALLY GOT HER AND WE HAVE TO PUT HER THROUGH THE SYSTEM YOU BELIEVED IN ALL THOSE YEARS.
I JUST BELIEVE IN ME, BATMAN. THERE IS NOTHING ELSE.
SHE'LL PAY FOR WHAT SHE DID TO GILDA--TO YOU--FOR ALL THE EVIL SHE'S DONE IN THIS CITY, BUT YOU'VE GOT TO LET--
EVERYONE PAYS, BATS.
SOME SOONER, SOME LATER.
YOU PUT INNOCENT COPS AT RISK-- MEN AND WOMEN WITH FAMILIES-- JUST TO GET MY ATTENTION.
GORDON AND HIS BLUE BLOODS SIMPLY GOT LUCKY. I WAS GOING TO STORM THEIR PLACE TO GET MY HANDS ON HER TONIGHT...
...BUT I HAD A CHANGE OF MIND.
I BET YOU DID.

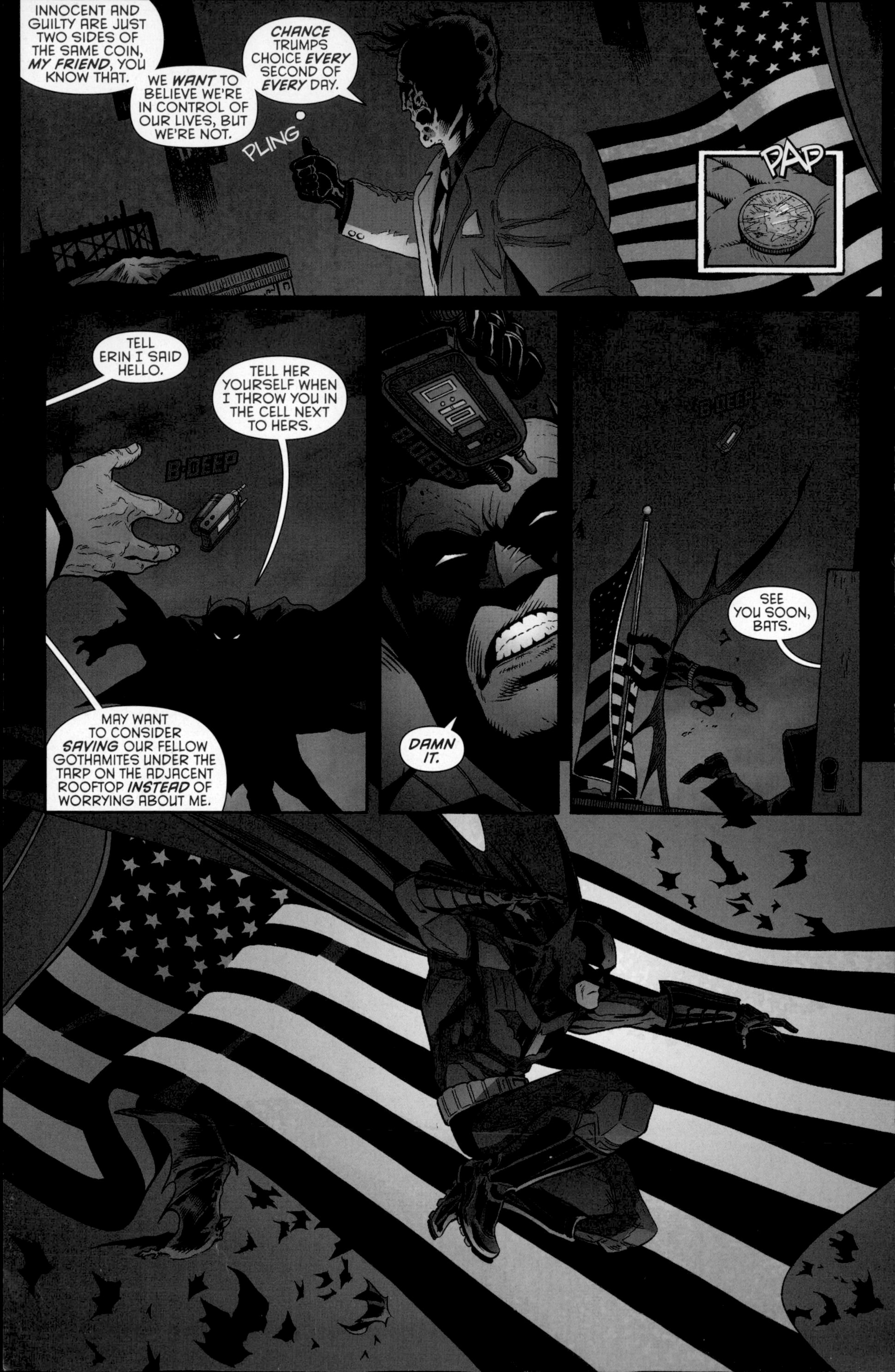
INNOCENT AND GUILTY ARE JUST TWO SIDES OF THE SAME COIN, MY FRIEND, YOU KNOW THAT.
WE WANT TO BELIEVE WE'RE IN CONTROL OF OUR LIVES, BUT WE'RE NOT.
CHANCE TRUMPS CHOICE EVERY SECOND OF EVERY DAY.
PLING
PAP
TELL ERIN I SAID HELLO.
TELL HER YOURSELF WHEN I THROW YOU IN THE CELL NEXT TO HERS.
B-DEEP
MAY WANT TO CONSIDER SAVING OUR FELLOW GOTHAMITES UNDER THE TARP ON THE ADJACENT ROOFTOP INSTEAD OF WORRYING ABOUT ME.
DAMN IT.
SEE YOU SOON, BATS.

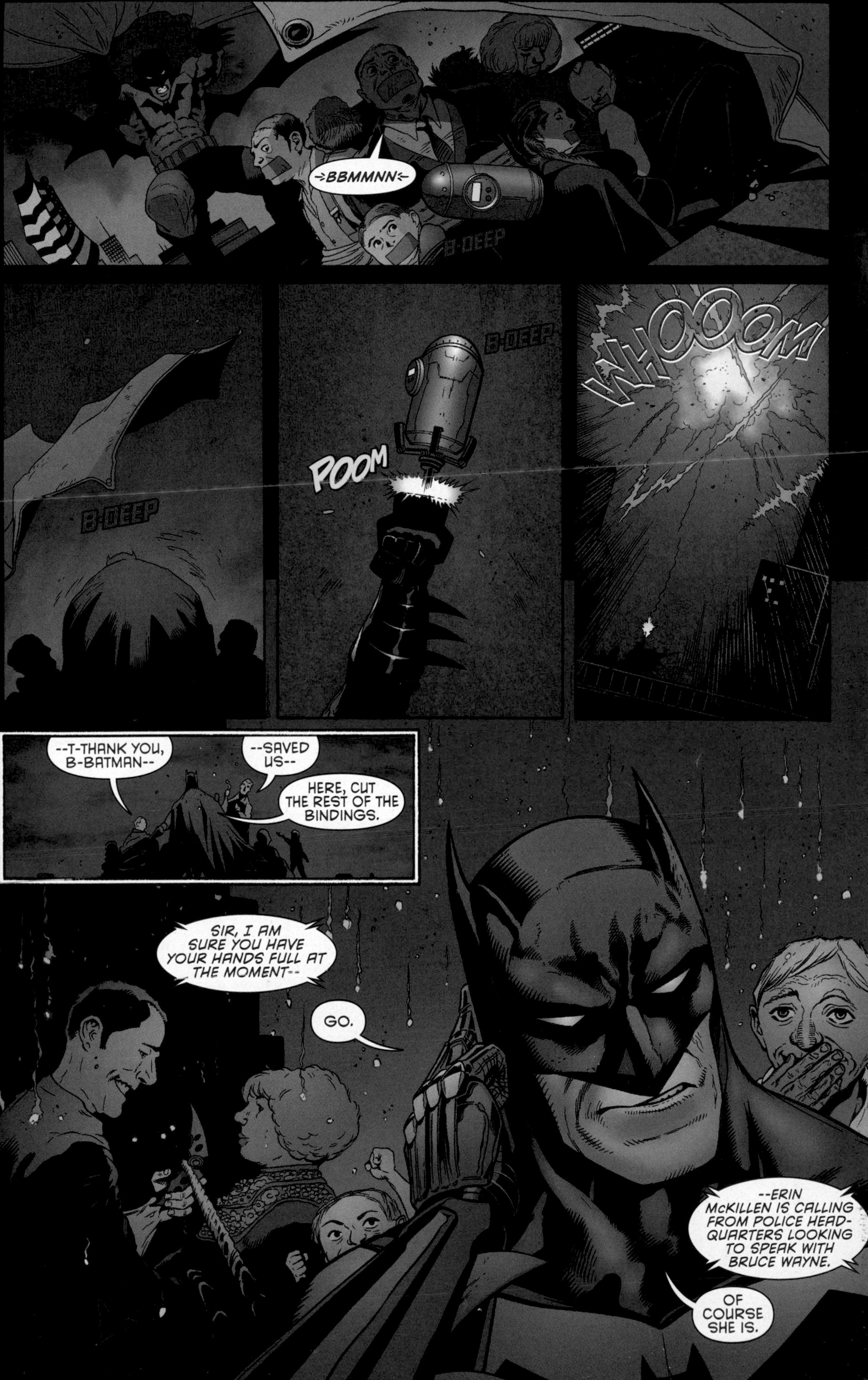

-BBMMNN-
B-DEEP
B-DEEP
B-DEEP
POOM
WHOOOM
--T-THANK YOU, B-BATMAN--
--SAVED US--
HERE, CUT THE REST OF THE BINDINGS.
SIR, I AM SURE YOU HAVE YOUR HANDS FULL AT THE MOMENT--
GO.
--ERIN McKILLEN IS CALLING FROM POLICE HEAD-QUARTERS LOOKING TO SPEAK WITH BRUCE WAYNE.
OF COURSE SHE IS.

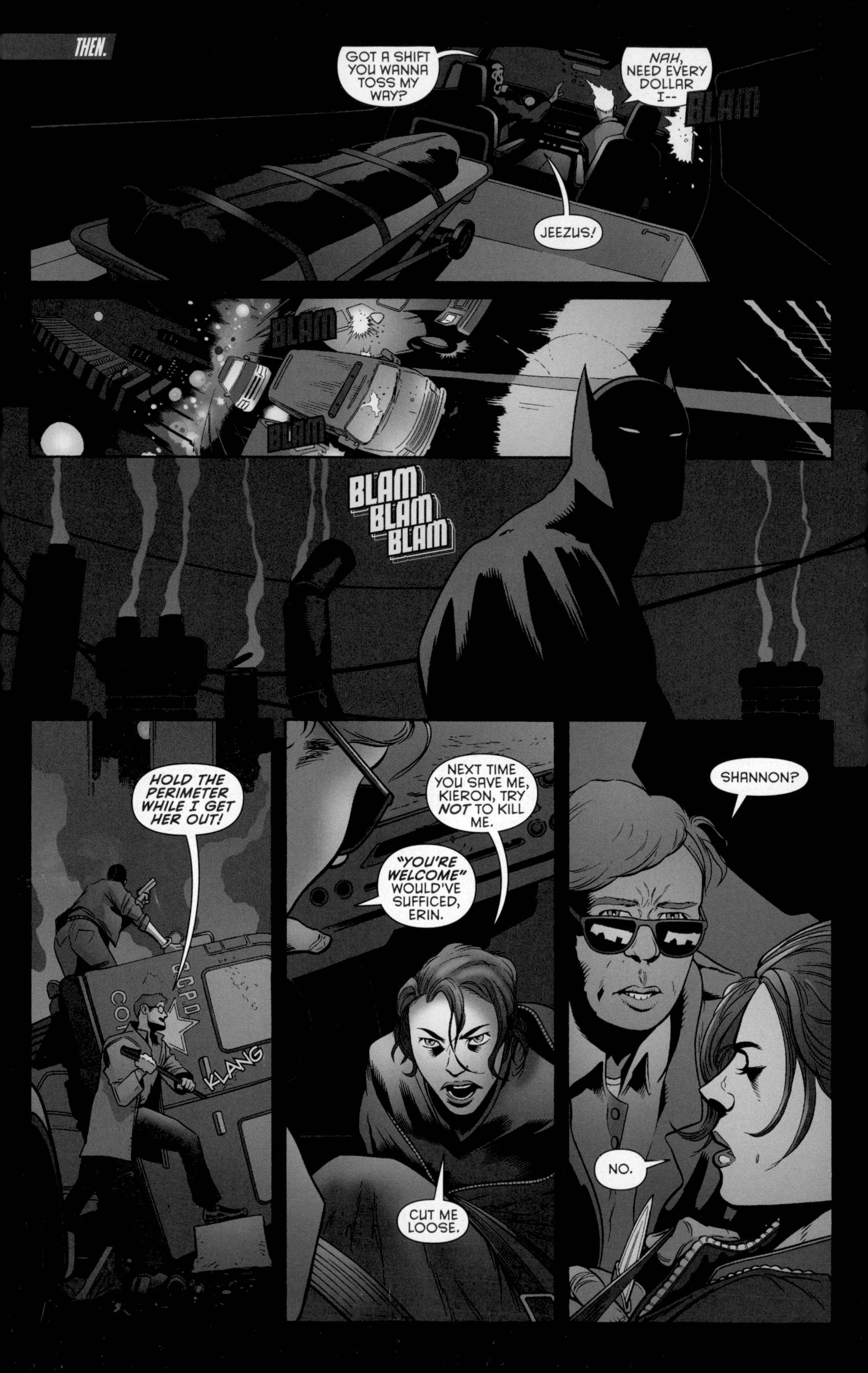
THEN.
GOT A SHIFT YOU WANNA TOSS MY WAY?
NAH, NEED EVERY DOLLAR I--
BLAM
JEEZUS!
BLAM
BLAM
BLAM BLAM BLAM
HOLD THE PERIMETER WHILE I GET HER OUT!
G.C.P.D.
KLANG
NEXT TIME YOU SAVE ME, KIERON, TRY NOT TO KILL ME.
"YOU'RE WELCOME" WOULD'VE SUFFICED, ERIN.
CUT ME LOOSE.
SHANNON?
NO.

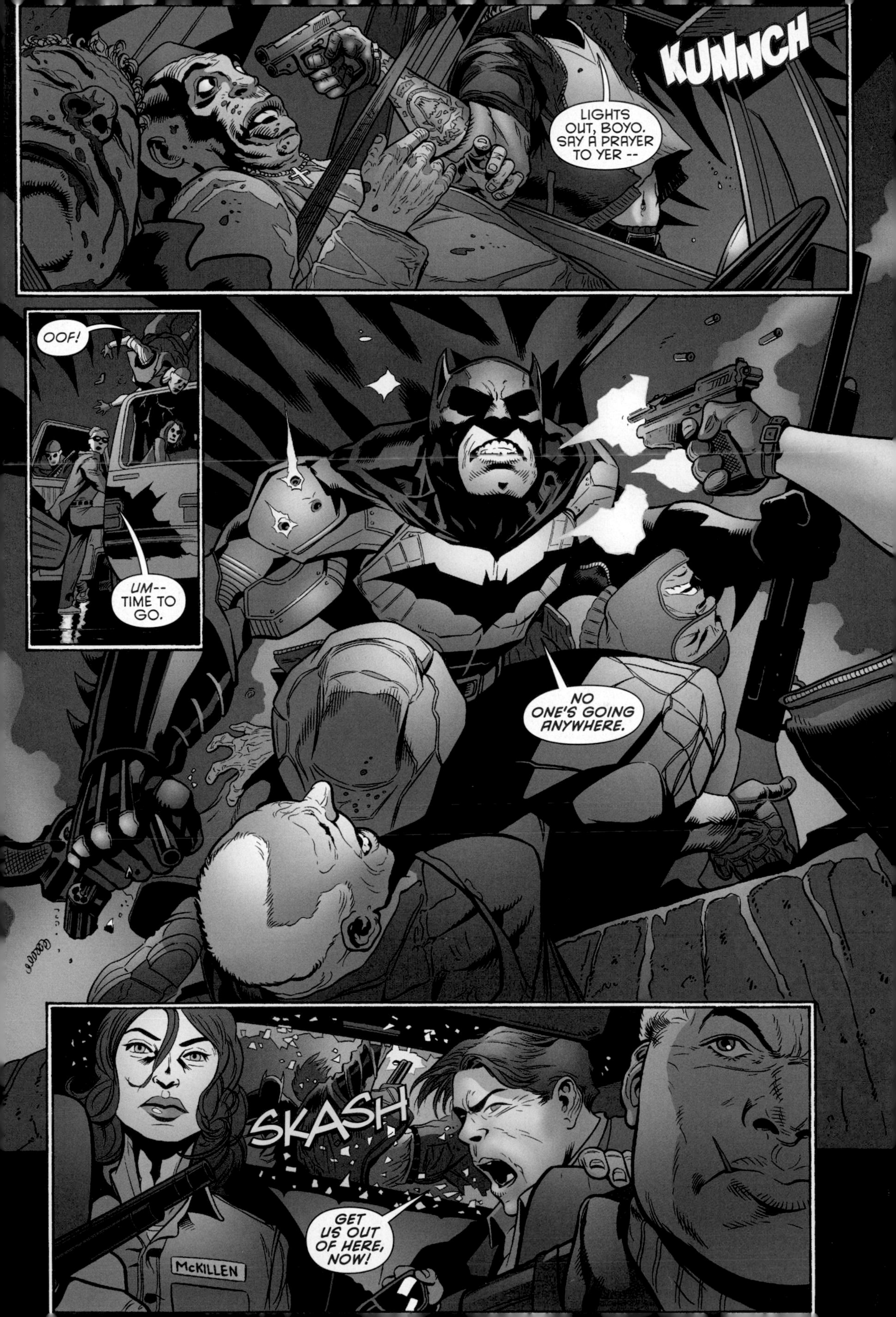
KUNNCH
LIGHTS OUT, BOYO. SAY A PRAYER TO YER --
OOF!
UM-- TIME TO GO.
NO ONE'S GOING ANYWHERE.
McKILLEN
SKASH
GET US OUT OF HERE, NOW!

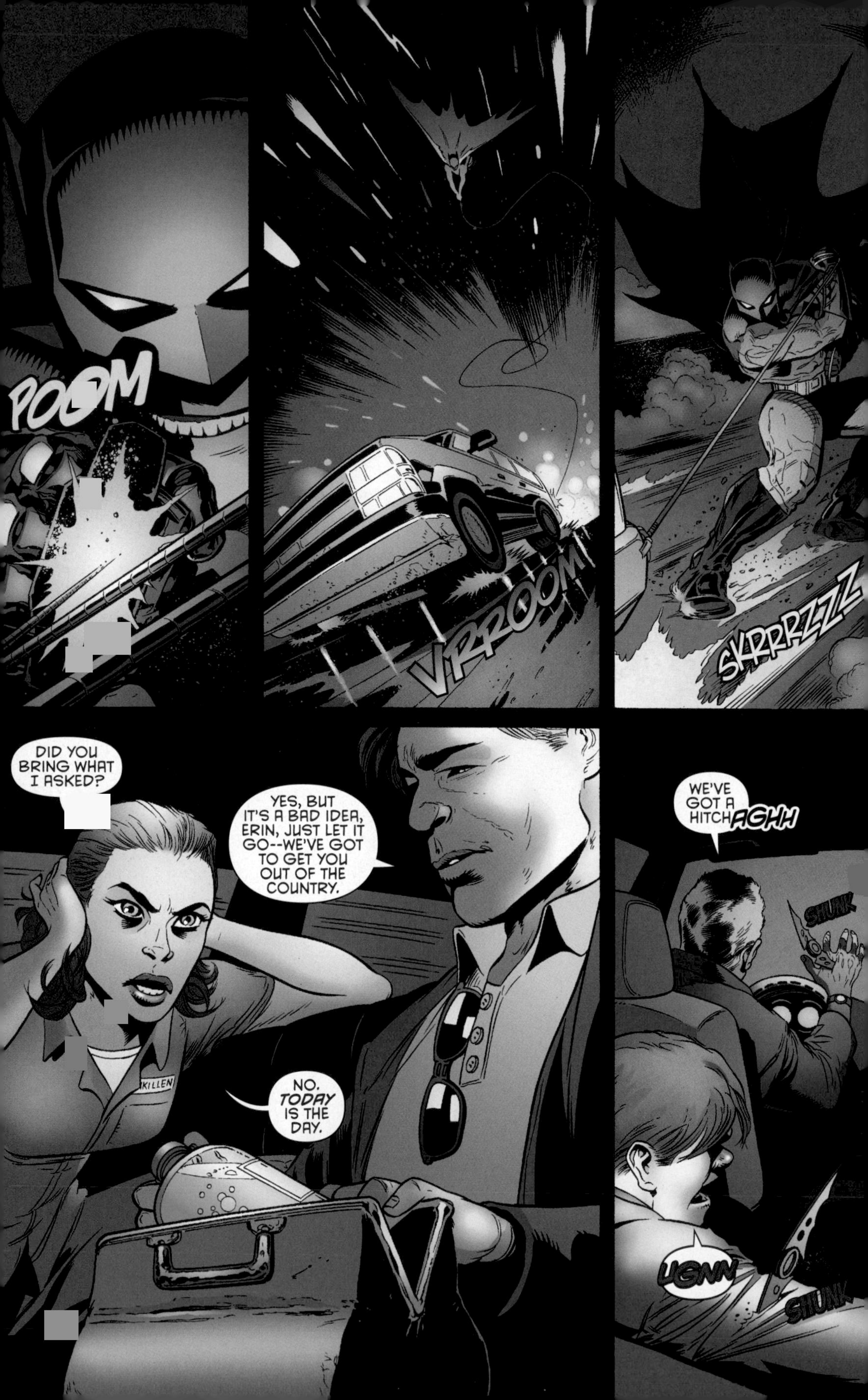
POOM
VRROOM
SKRRRZZZ
DID YOU BRING WHAT I ASKED?
YES, BUT IT'S A BAD IDEA, ERIN, JUST LET IT GO--WE'VE GOT TO GET YOU OUT OF THE COUNTRY.
NO. TODAY IS THE DAY.
KILLEN
WE'VE GOT A HITCH AGHH
SHUNK
UGNN
SHUNK

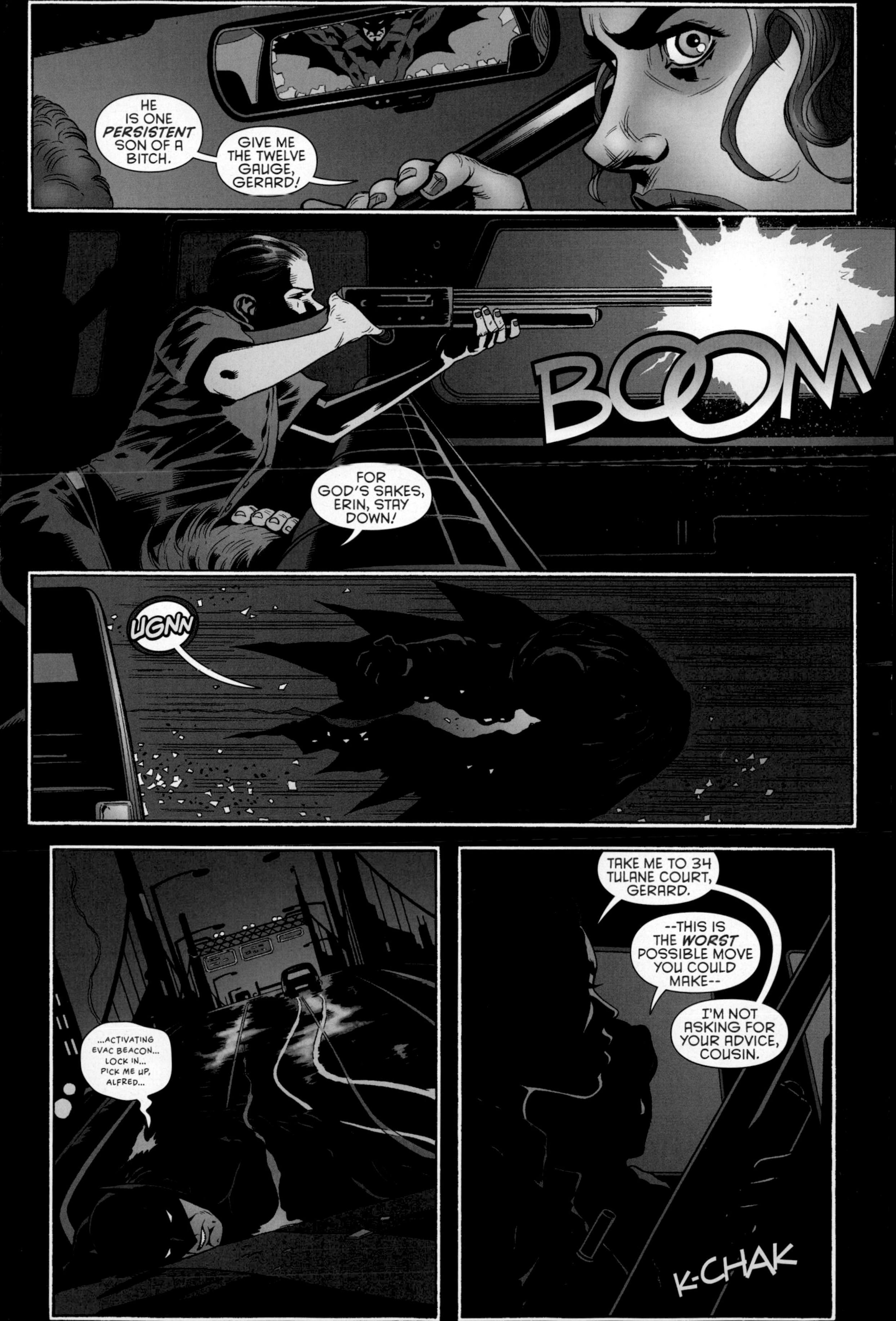
HE IS ONE *PERSISTENT* SON OF A BITCH.
GIVE ME THE TWELVE GAUGE, GERARD!
BOOM
FOR GOD'S SAKES, ERIN, STAY DOWN!
UGNN
...ACTIVATING EVAC BEACON... LOCK IN... PICK ME UP, ALFRED...
TAKE ME TO 34 TULANE COURT, GERARD.
--THIS IS THE *WORST* POSSIBLE MOVE YOU COULD MAKE--
I'M NOT ASKING FOR YOUR ADVICE, COUSIN.
K-CHAK

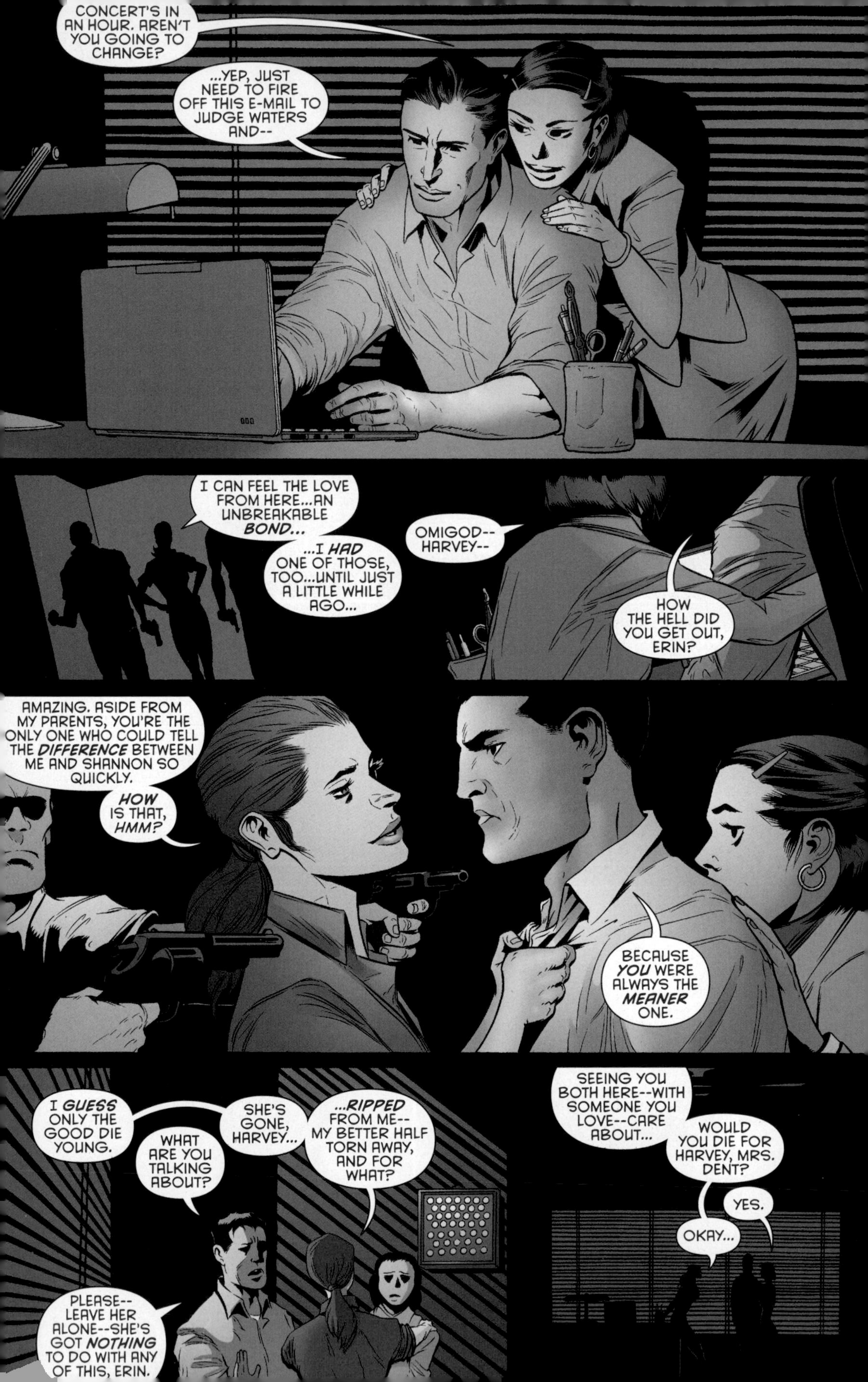
CONCERT'S IN AN HOUR. AREN'T YOU GOING TO CHANGE?
...YEP, JUST NEED TO FIRE OFF THIS E-MAIL TO JUDGE WATERS AND--
I CAN FEEL THE LOVE FROM HERE...AN UNBREAKABLE BOND...
...I HAD ONE OF THOSE, TOO...UNTIL JUST A LITTLE WHILE AGO...
OMIGOD-- HARVEY--
HOW THE HELL DID YOU GET OUT, ERIN?
AMAZING. ASIDE FROM MY PARENTS, YOU'RE THE ONLY ONE WHO COULD TELL THE DIFFERENCE BETWEEN ME AND SHANNON SO QUICKLY.
HOW IS THAT, HMM?
BECAUSE YOU WERE ALWAYS THE MEANER ONE.
I GUESS ONLY THE GOOD DIE YOUNG.
WHAT ARE YOU TALKING ABOUT?
SHE'S GONE, HARVEY...
...RIPPED FROM ME-- MY BETTER HALF TORN AWAY, AND FOR WHAT?
PLEASE-- LEAVE HER ALONE--SHE'S GOT NOTHING TO DO WITH ANY OF THIS, ERIN.
SEEING YOU BOTH HERE--WITH SOMEONE YOU LOVE--CARE ABOUT...
WOULD YOU DIE FOR HARVEY, MRS. DENT?
YES.
OKAY...

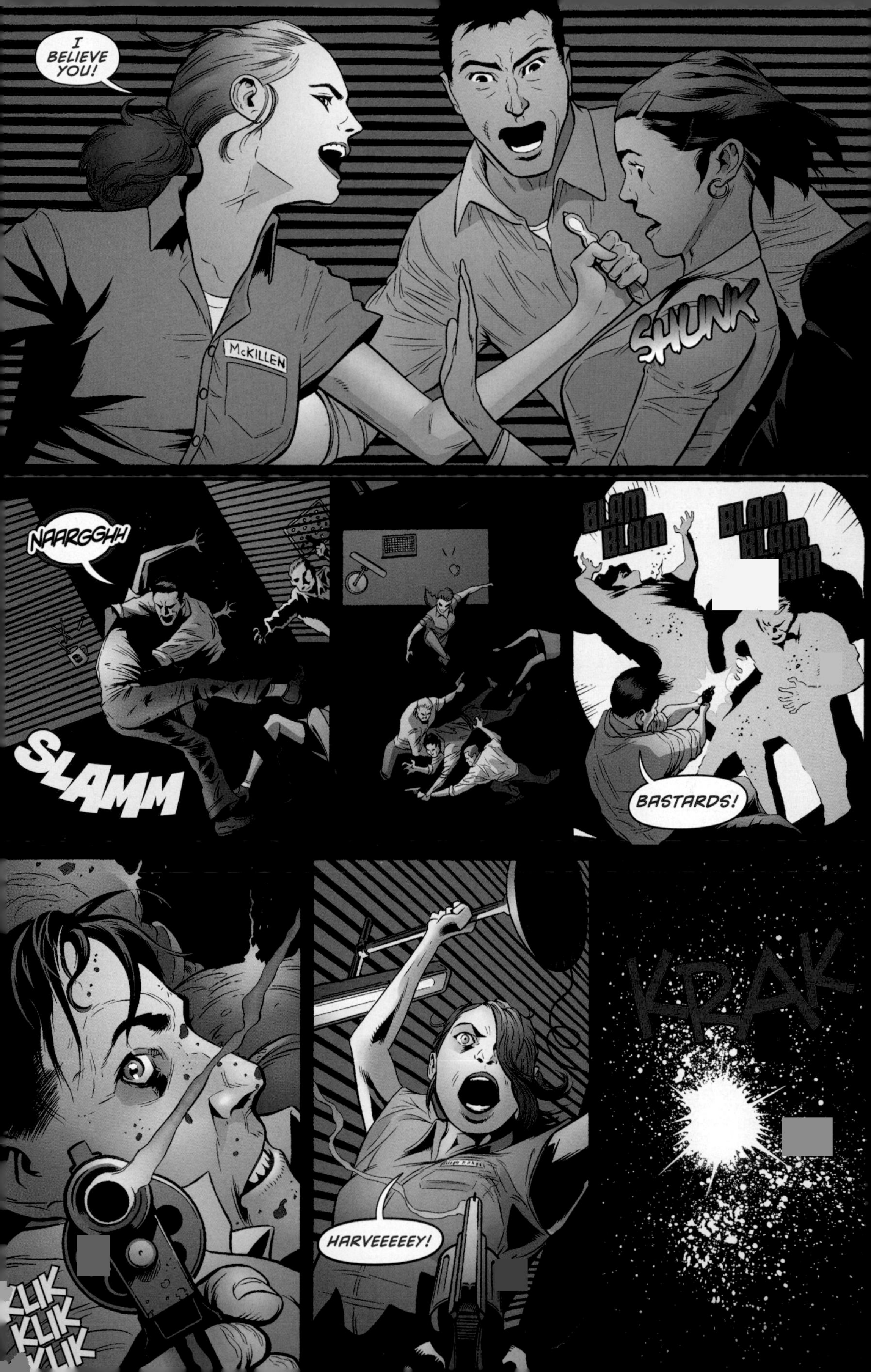

I BELIEVE YOU!
McKILLEN
SHUNK
NAARGGHH
SLAMM
BLAM BLAM
BLAM BLAM
BASTARDS!
KLIK KLIK
HARVEEEEEY!
KRAK

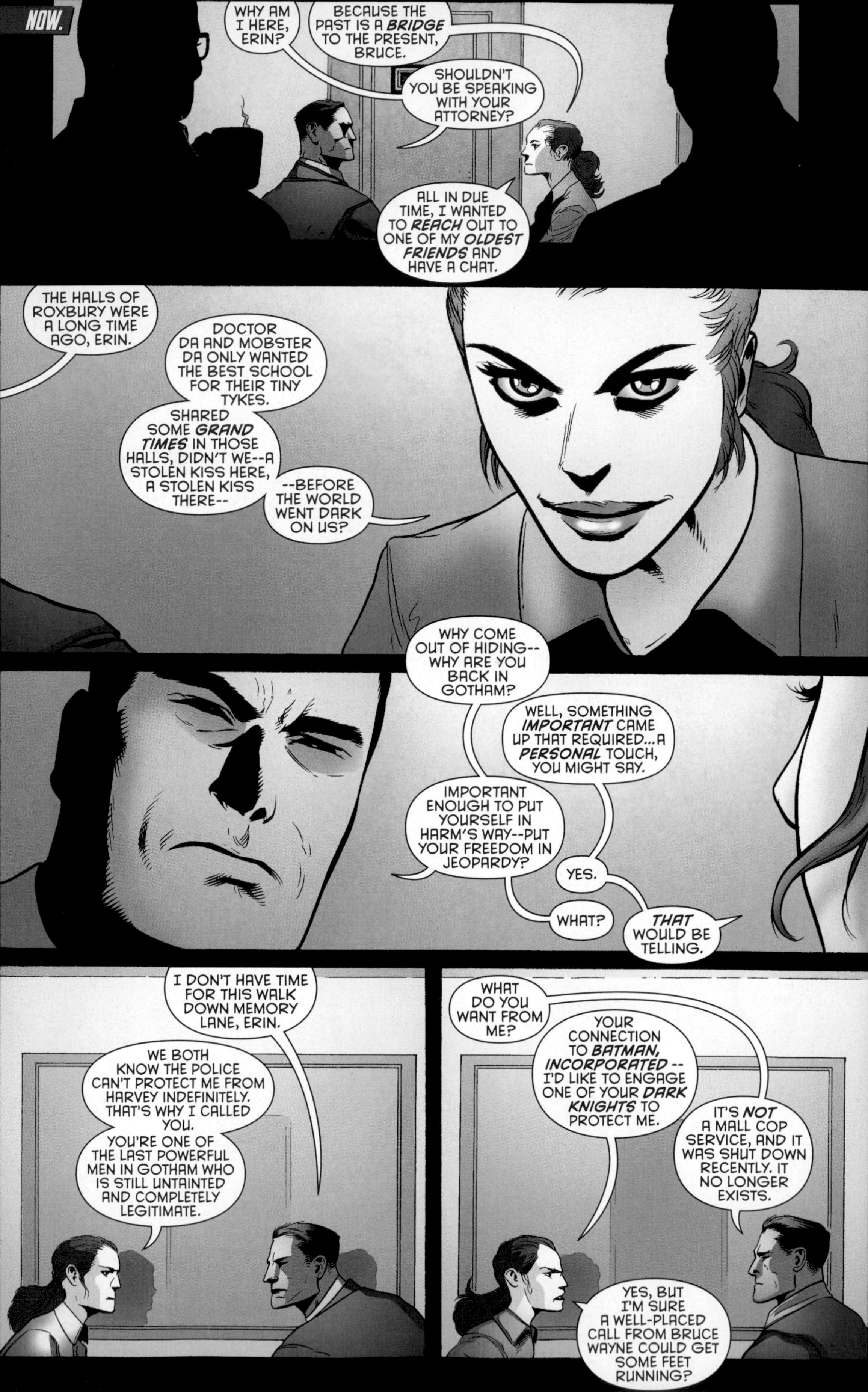
NOW.
WHY AM I HERE, ERIN?
BECAUSE THE PAST IS A *BRIDGE* TO THE PRESENT, BRUCE.
SHOULDN'T YOU BE SPEAKING WITH YOUR ATTORNEY?
ALL IN DUE TIME, I WANTED TO *REACH* OUT TO ONE OF MY *OLDEST FRIENDS* AND HAVE A CHAT.
THE HALLS OF ROXBURY WERE A LONG TIME AGO, ERIN.
DOCTOR DA AND MOBSTER DA ONLY WANTED THE BEST SCHOOL FOR THEIR TINY TYKES.
SHARED SOME *GRAND TIMES* IN THOSE HALLS, DIDN'T WE--A STOLEN KISS HERE, A STOLEN KISS THERE--
--BEFORE THE WORLD WENT DARK ON US?
WHY COME OUT OF HIDING--WHY ARE YOU BACK IN GOTHAM?
WELL, SOMETHING *IMPORTANT* CAME UP THAT REQUIRED...A *PERSONAL* TOUCH, YOU MIGHT SAY.
IMPORTANT ENOUGH TO PUT YOURSELF IN HARM'S WAY--PUT YOUR FREEDOM IN JEOPARDY?
YES.
WHAT?
THAT WOULD BE TELLING.
I DON'T HAVE TIME FOR THIS WALK DOWN MEMORY LANE, ERIN.
WE BOTH KNOW THE POLICE CAN'T PROTECT ME FROM HARVEY INDEFINITELY. THAT'S WHY I CALLED YOU.
YOU'RE ONE OF THE LAST POWERFUL MEN IN GOTHAM WHO IS STILL UNTAINTED AND COMPLETELY LEGITIMATE.
WHAT DO YOU WANT FROM ME?
YOUR CONNECTION TO *BATMAN, INCORPORATED* -- I'D LIKE TO ENGAGE ONE OF YOUR *DARK KNIGHTS* TO PROTECT ME.
IT'S *NOT* A MALL COP SERVICE, AND IT WAS SHUT DOWN RECENTLY. IT NO LONGER EXISTS.
YES, BUT I'M SURE A WELL-PLACED CALL FROM BRUCE WAYNE COULD GET SOME FEET RUNNING?

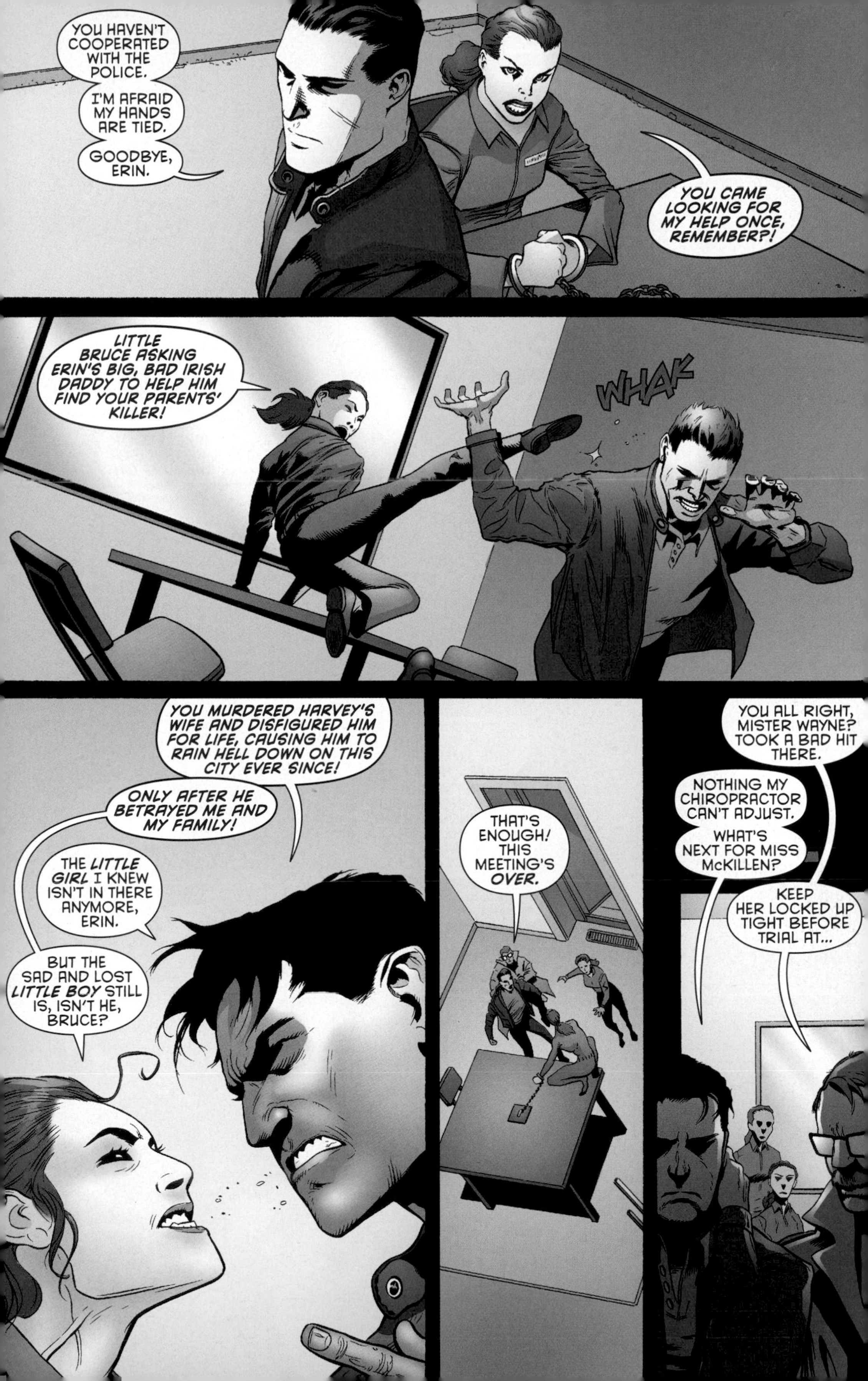
YOU HAVEN'T COOPERATED WITH THE POLICE.
I'M AFRAID MY HANDS ARE TIED.
GOODBYE, ERIN.
YOU CAME LOOKING FOR MY HELP ONCE, REMEMBER?!
LITTLE BRUCE ASKING ERIN'S BIG, BAD IRISH DADDY TO HELP HIM FIND YOUR PARENTS' KILLER!
WHAK
YOU MURDERED HARVEY'S WIFE AND DISFIGURED HIM FOR LIFE, CAUSING HIM TO RAIN HELL DOWN ON THIS CITY EVER SINCE!
ONLY AFTER HE BETRAYED ME AND MY FAMILY!
THE LITTLE GIRL I KNEW ISN'T IN THERE ANYMORE, ERIN.
BUT THE SAD AND LOST LITTLE BOY STILL IS, ISN'T HE, BRUCE?
THAT'S ENOUGH! THIS MEETING'S OVER.
YOU ALL RIGHT, MISTER WAYNE? TOOK A BAD HIT THERE.
NOTHING MY CHIROPRACTOR CAN'T ADJUST.
WHAT'S NEXT FOR MISS McKILLEN?
KEEP HER LOCKED UP TIGHT BEFORE TRIAL AT...

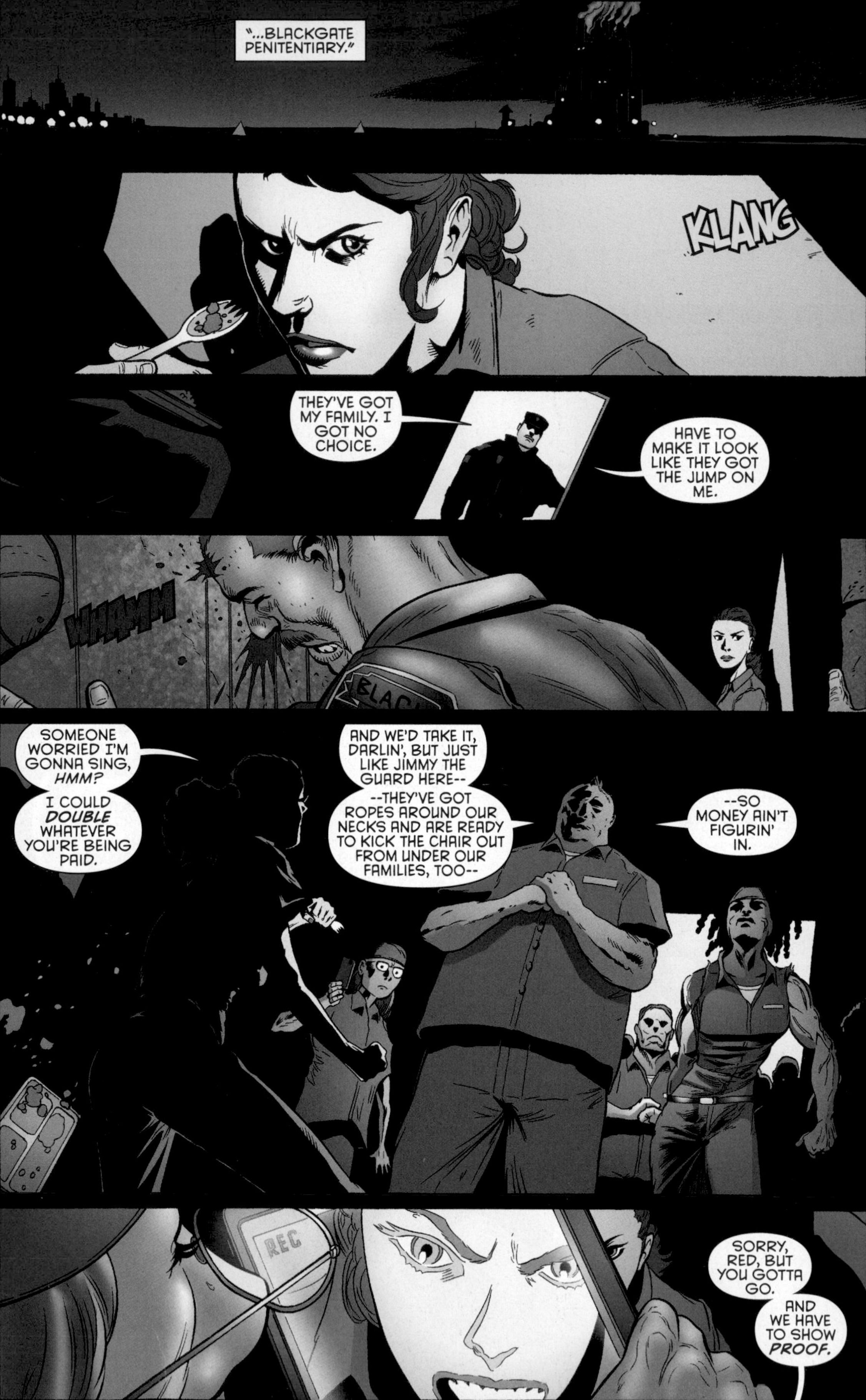
"...BLACKGATE PENITENTIARY."
KLANG
THEY'VE GOT MY FAMILY. I GOT NO CHOICE.
HAVE TO MAKE IT LOOK LIKE THEY GOT THE JUMP ON ME.
WHAMM
SOMEONE WORRIED I'M GONNA SING, HMM?
I COULD DOUBLE WHATEVER YOU'RE BEING PAID.
AND WE'D TAKE IT, DARLIN', BUT JUST LIKE JIMMY THE GUARD HERE--
--THEY'VE GOT ROPES AROUND OUR NECKS AND ARE READY TO KICK THE CHAIR OUT FROM UNDER OUR FAMILIES, TOO--
--SO MONEY AIN'T FIGURIN' IN.
REC
SORRY, RED, BUT YOU GOTTA GO.
AND WE HAVE TO SHOW PROOF.

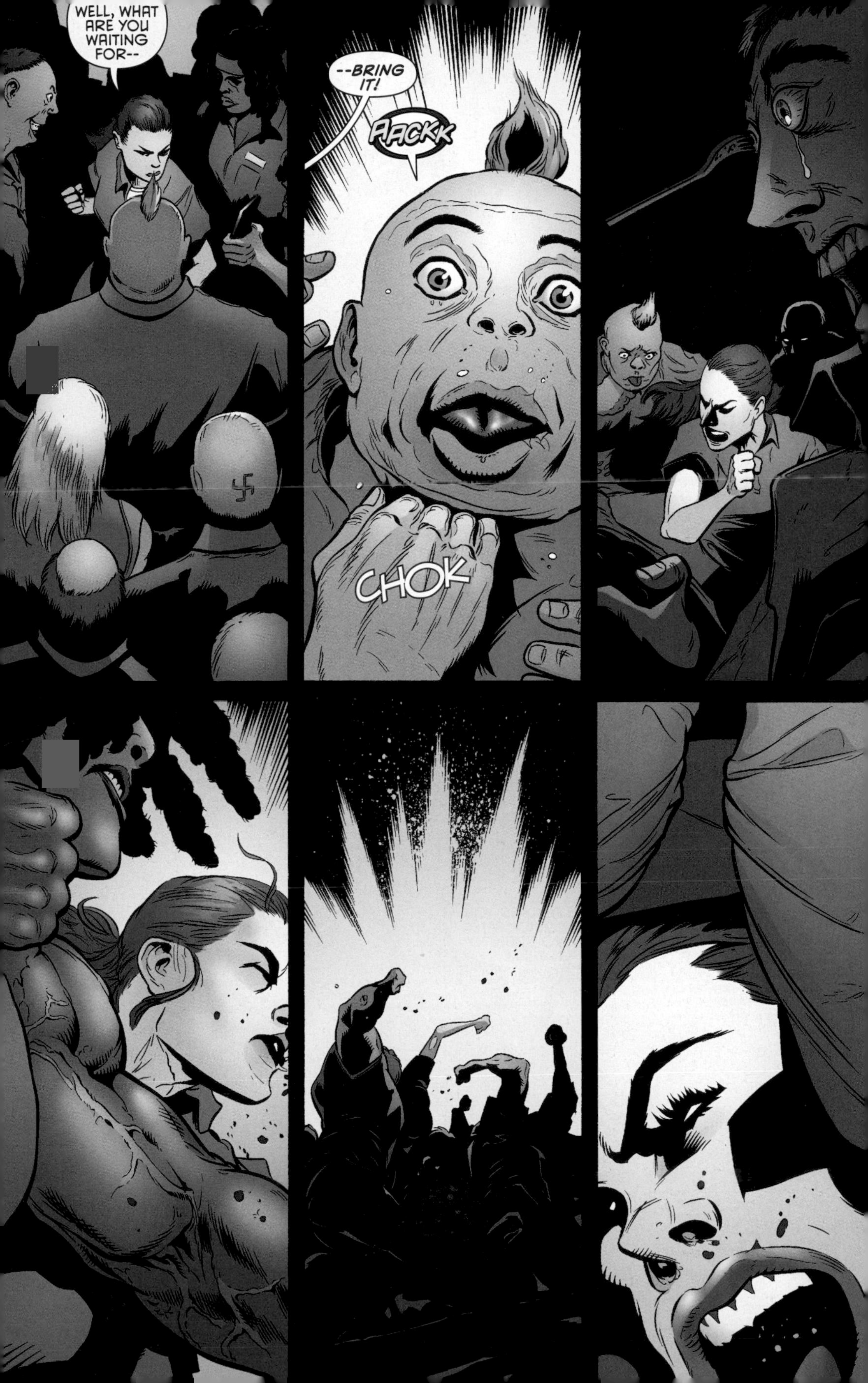
WELL, WHAT ARE YOU WAITING FOR--
--BRING IT!
AACKK
CHOK

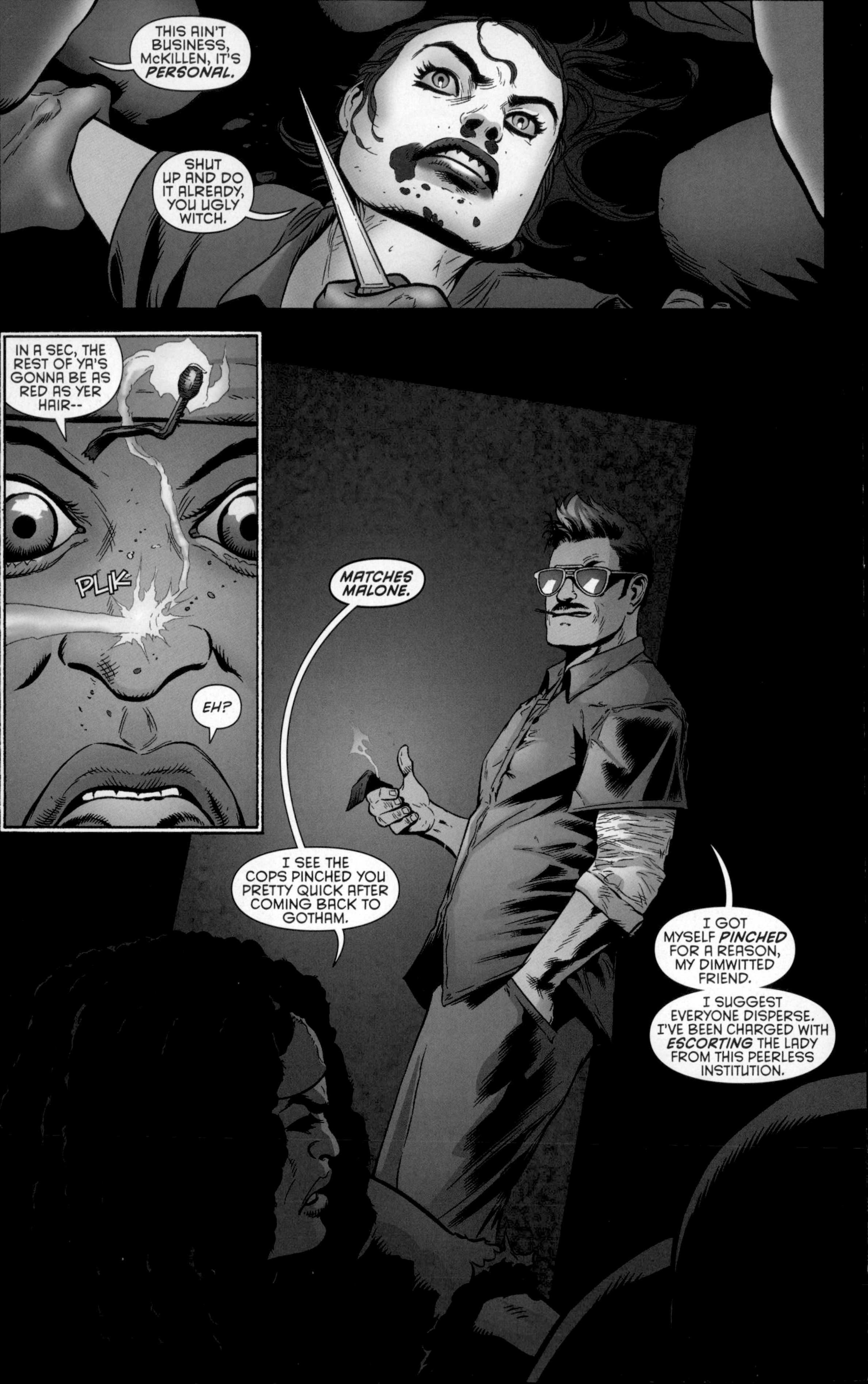
THIS AIN'T BUSINESS, McKILLEN, IT'S PERSONAL.
SHUT UP AND DO IT ALREADY, YOU UGLY WITCH.
IN A SEC, THE REST OF YA'S GONNA BE AS RED AS YER HAIR--
PLIK
EH?
MATCHES MALONE.
I SEE THE COPS PINCHED YOU PRETTY QUICK AFTER COMING BACK TO GOTHAM.
I GOT MYSELF PINCHED FOR A REASON, MY DIMWITTED FRIEND.
I SUGGEST EVERYONE DISPERSE. I'VE BEEN CHARGED WITH ESCORTING THE LADY FROM THIS PEERLESS INSTITUTION.

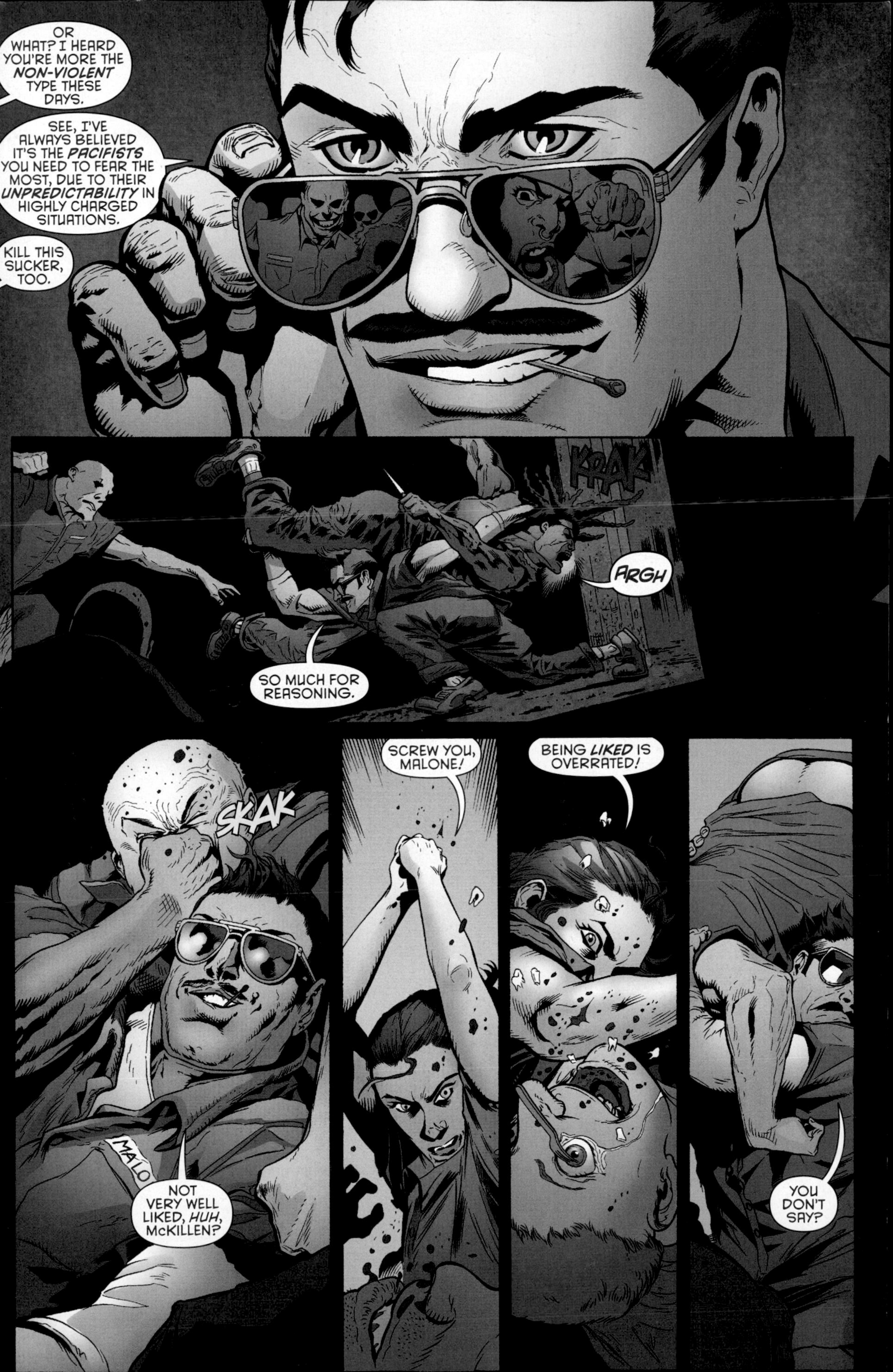

OR WHAT? I HEARD YOU'RE MORE THE NON-VIOLENT TYPE THESE DAYS.
SEE, I'VE ALWAYS BELIEVED IT'S THE PACIFISTS YOU NEED TO FEAR THE MOST, DUE TO THEIR UNPREDICTABILITY IN HIGHLY CHARGED SITUATIONS.
KILL THIS SUCKER, TOO.
KRAK
ARGH
SO MUCH FOR REASONING.
SKAK
MALO
NOT VERY WELL LIKED, HUH, McKILLEN?
SCREW YOU, MALONE!
BEING LIKED IS OVERRATED!
YOU DON'T SAY?

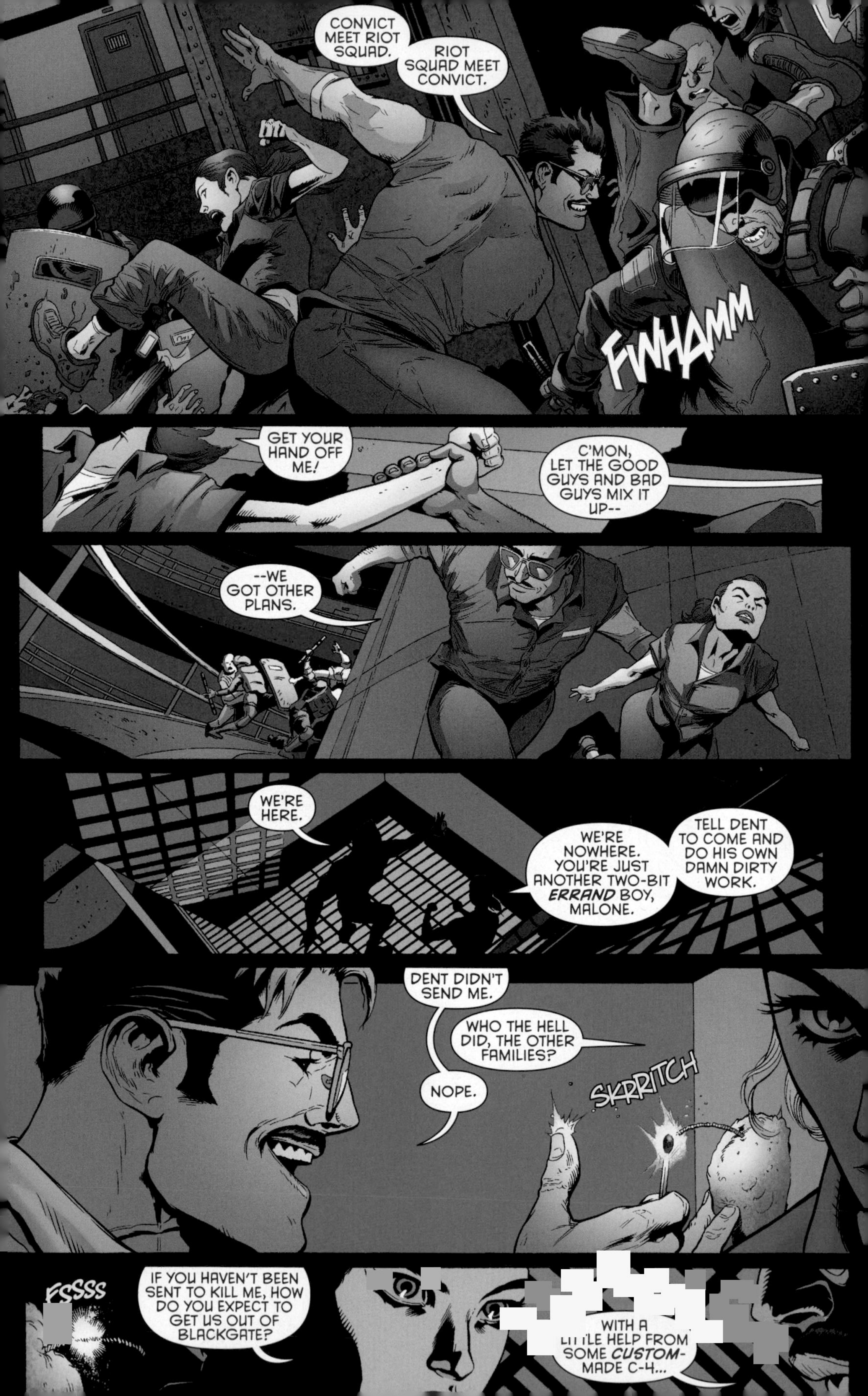

CONVICT MEET RIOT SQUAD.
RIOT SQUAD MEET CONVICT.
FWHAMM
GET YOUR HAND OFF ME!
C'MON, LET THE GOOD GUYS AND BAD GUYS MIX IT UP--
--WE GOT OTHER PLANS.
WE'RE HERE.
WE'RE NOWHERE. YOU'RE JUST ANOTHER TWO-BIT *ERRAND* BOY, MALONE.
TELL DENT TO COME AND DO HIS OWN DAMN DIRTY WORK.
DENT DIDN'T SEND ME.
WHO THE HELL DID, THE OTHER FAMILIES?
NOPE.
SKRRITCH
FSSSS
IF YOU HAVEN'T BEEN SENT TO KILL ME, HOW DO YOU EXPECT TO GET US OUT OF BLACKGATE?
WITH A LITTLE HELP FROM SOME *CUSTOM*-MADE C-4...

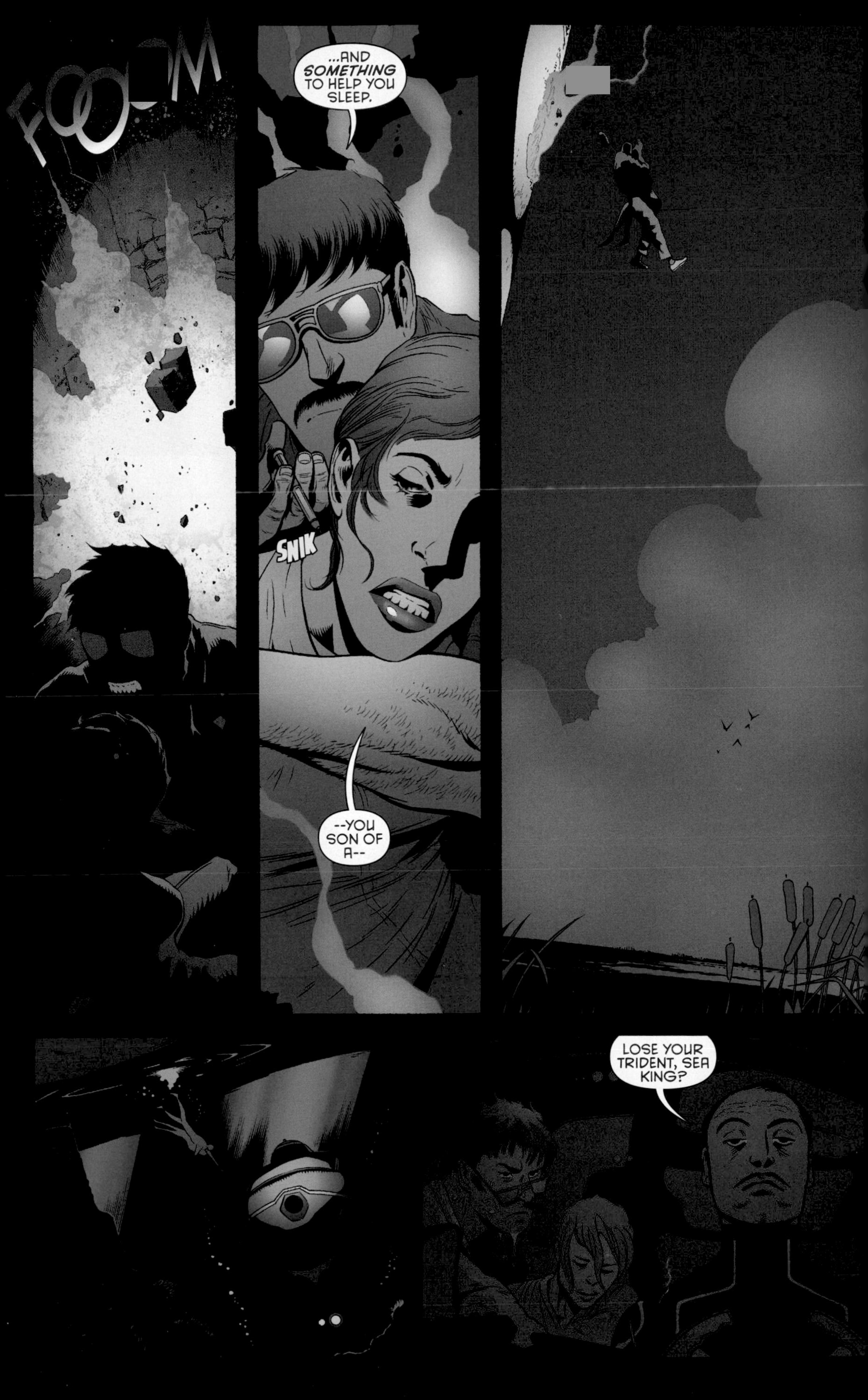
...AND SOMETHING TO HELP YOU SLEEP.
SNIK
--YOU SON OF A--
LOSE YOUR TRIDENT, SEA KING?

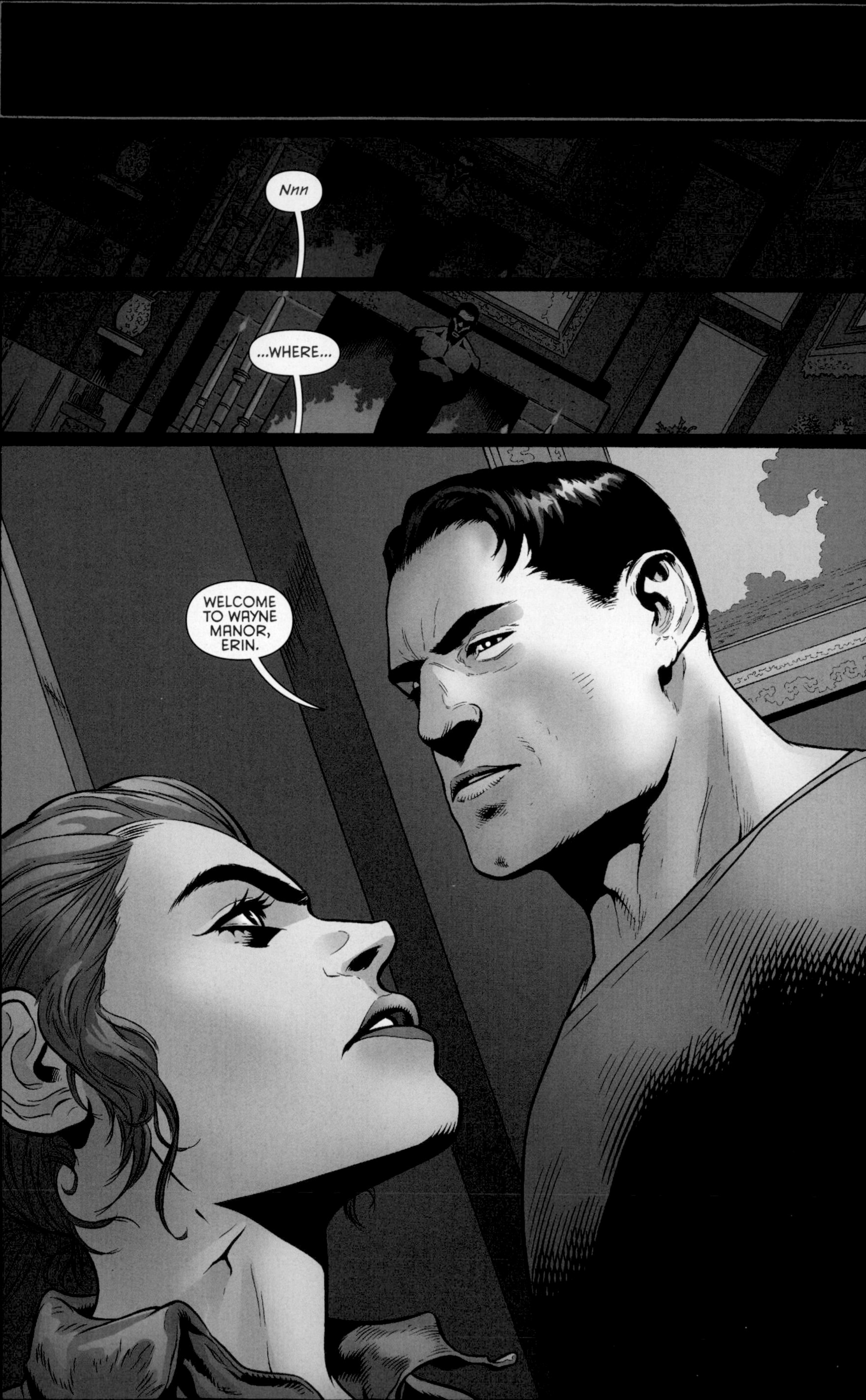
Nnn
...WHERE...
WELCOME TO WAYNE MANOR, ERIN.

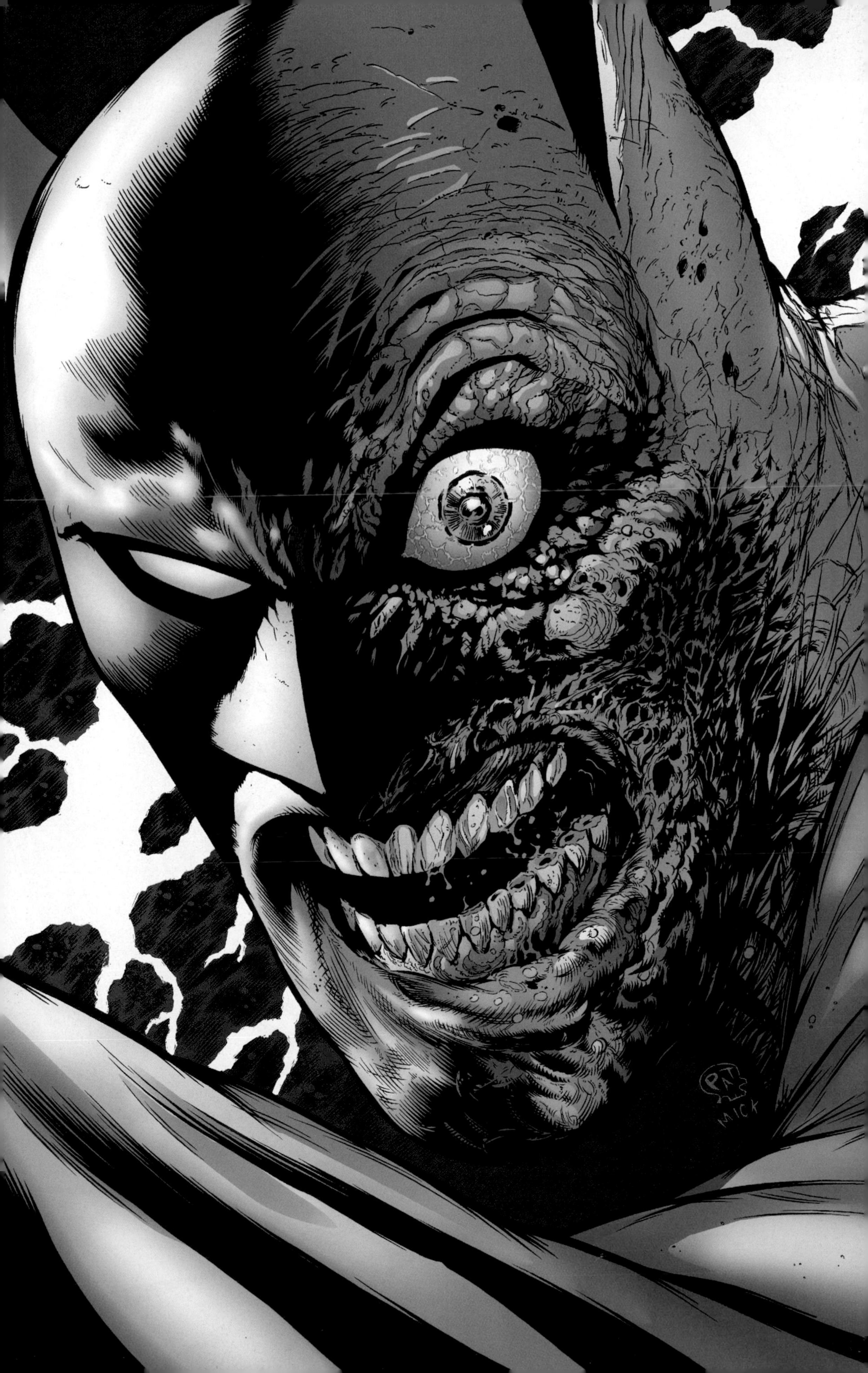

THE BIG BURN: IGNITION

PATRICK GLEASON penciller MICK GRAY with KEITH CHAMPAGNE inkers JOHN KALISZ colorist cover art by GLEASON, GRAY & KALISZ

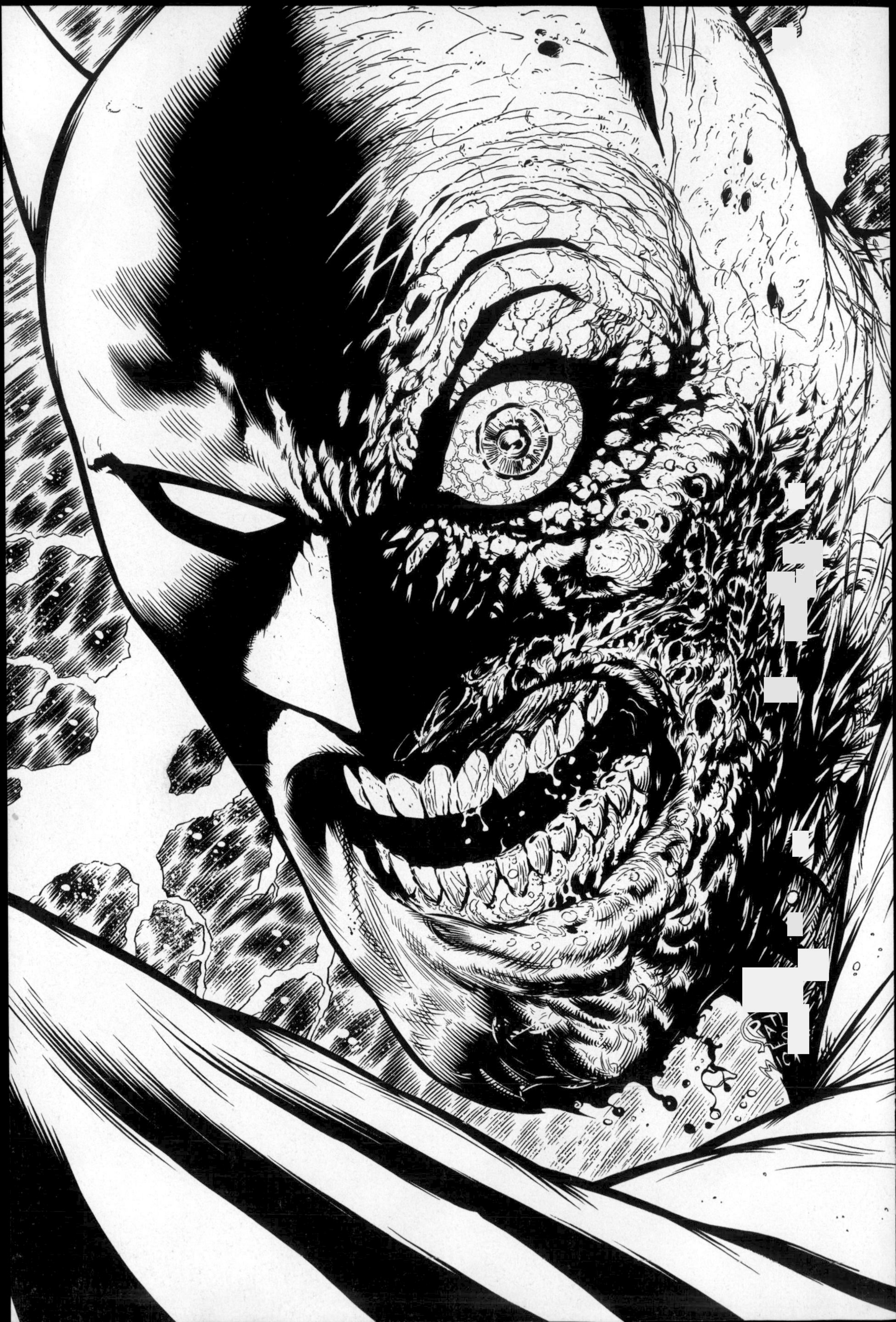

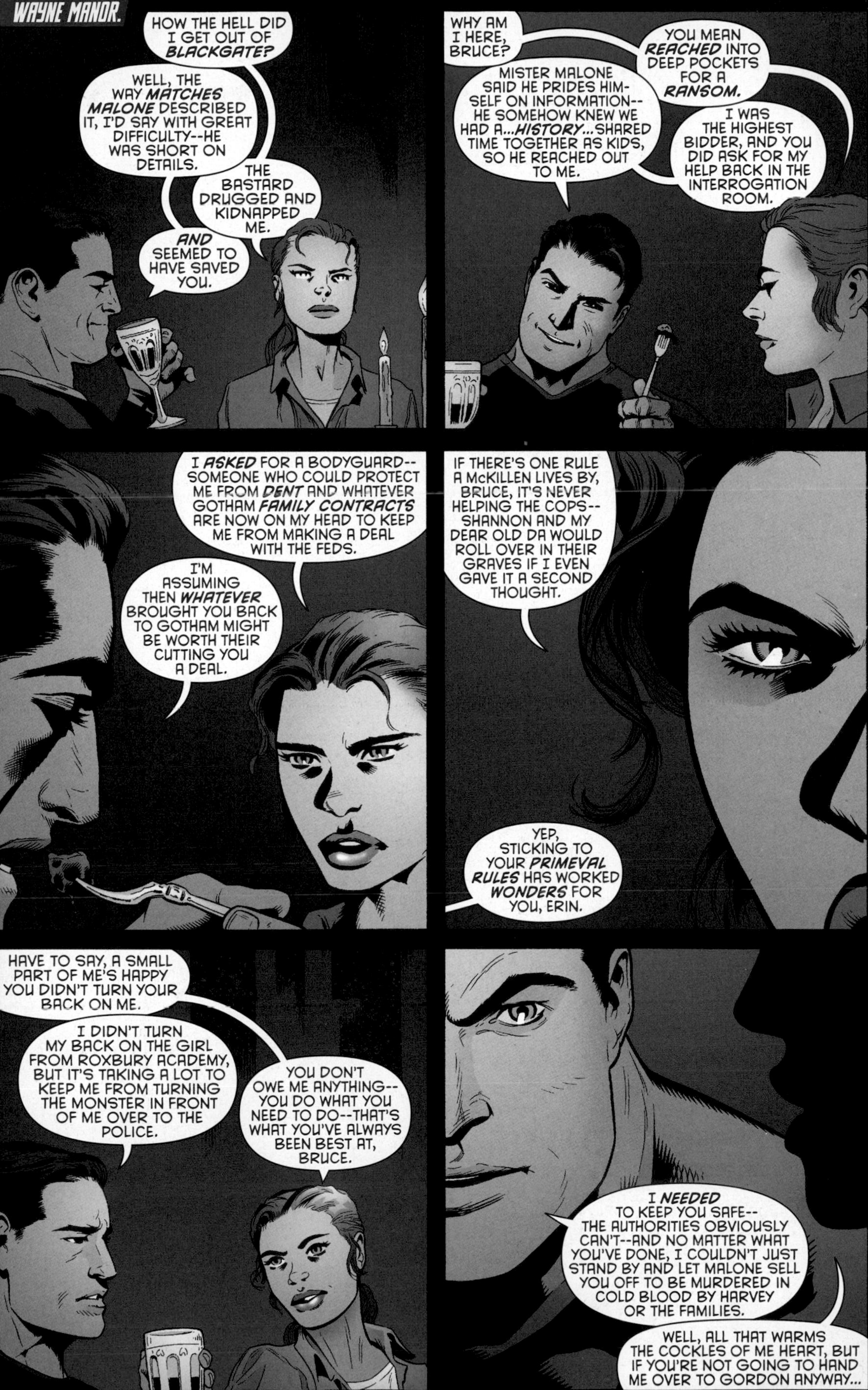
WAYNE MANOR.
HOW THE HELL DID I GET OUT OF BLACKGATE?
WELL, THE WAY MATCHES MALONE DESCRIBED IT, I'D SAY WITH GREAT DIFFICULTY--HE WAS SHORT ON DETAILS.
THE BASTARD DRUGGED AND KIDNAPPED ME.
AND SEEMED TO HAVE SAVED YOU.
WHY AM I HERE, BRUCE?
MISTER MALONE SAID HE PRIDES HIMSELF ON INFORMATION-- HE SOMEHOW KNEW WE HAD A...HISTORY...SHARED TIME TOGETHER AS KIDS, SO HE REACHED OUT TO ME.
YOU MEAN REACHED INTO DEEP POCKETS FOR A RANSOM.
I WAS THE HIGHEST BIDDER, AND YOU DID ASK FOR MY HELP BACK IN THE INTERROGATION ROOM.
I ASKED FOR A BODYGUARD-- SOMEONE WHO COULD PROTECT ME FROM DENT AND WHATEVER GOTHAM FAMILY CONTRACTS ARE NOW ON MY HEAD TO KEEP ME FROM MAKING A DEAL WITH THE FEDS.
I'M ASSUMING THEN WHATEVER BROUGHT YOU BACK TO GOTHAM MIGHT BE WORTH THEIR CUTTING YOU A DEAL.
IF THERE'S ONE RULE A McKILLEN LIVES BY, BRUCE, IT'S NEVER HELPING THE COPS-- SHANNON AND MY DEAR OLD DA WOULD ROLL OVER IN THEIR GRAVES IF I EVEN GAVE IT A SECOND THOUGHT.
YEP, STICKING TO YOUR PRIMEVAL RULES HAS WORKED WONDERS FOR YOU, ERIN.
HAVE TO SAY, A SMALL PART OF ME'S HAPPY YOU DIDN'T TURN YOUR BACK ON ME.
I DIDN'T TURN MY BACK ON THE GIRL FROM ROXBURY ACADEMY, BUT IT'S TAKING A LOT TO KEEP ME FROM TURNING THE MONSTER IN FRONT OF ME OVER TO THE POLICE.
YOU DON'T OWE ME ANYTHING-- YOU DO WHAT YOU NEED TO DO--THAT'S WHAT YOU'VE ALWAYS BEEN BEST AT, BRUCE.
I NEEDED TO KEEP YOU SAFE-- THE AUTHORITIES OBVIOUSLY CAN'T--AND NO MATTER WHAT YOU'VE DONE, I COULDN'T JUST STAND BY AND LET MALONE SELL YOU OFF TO BE MURDERED IN COLD BLOOD BY HARVEY OR THE FAMILIES.
WELL, ALL THAT WARMS THE COCKLES OF ME HEART, BUT IF YOU'RE NOT GOING TO HAND ME OVER TO GORDON ANYWAY...

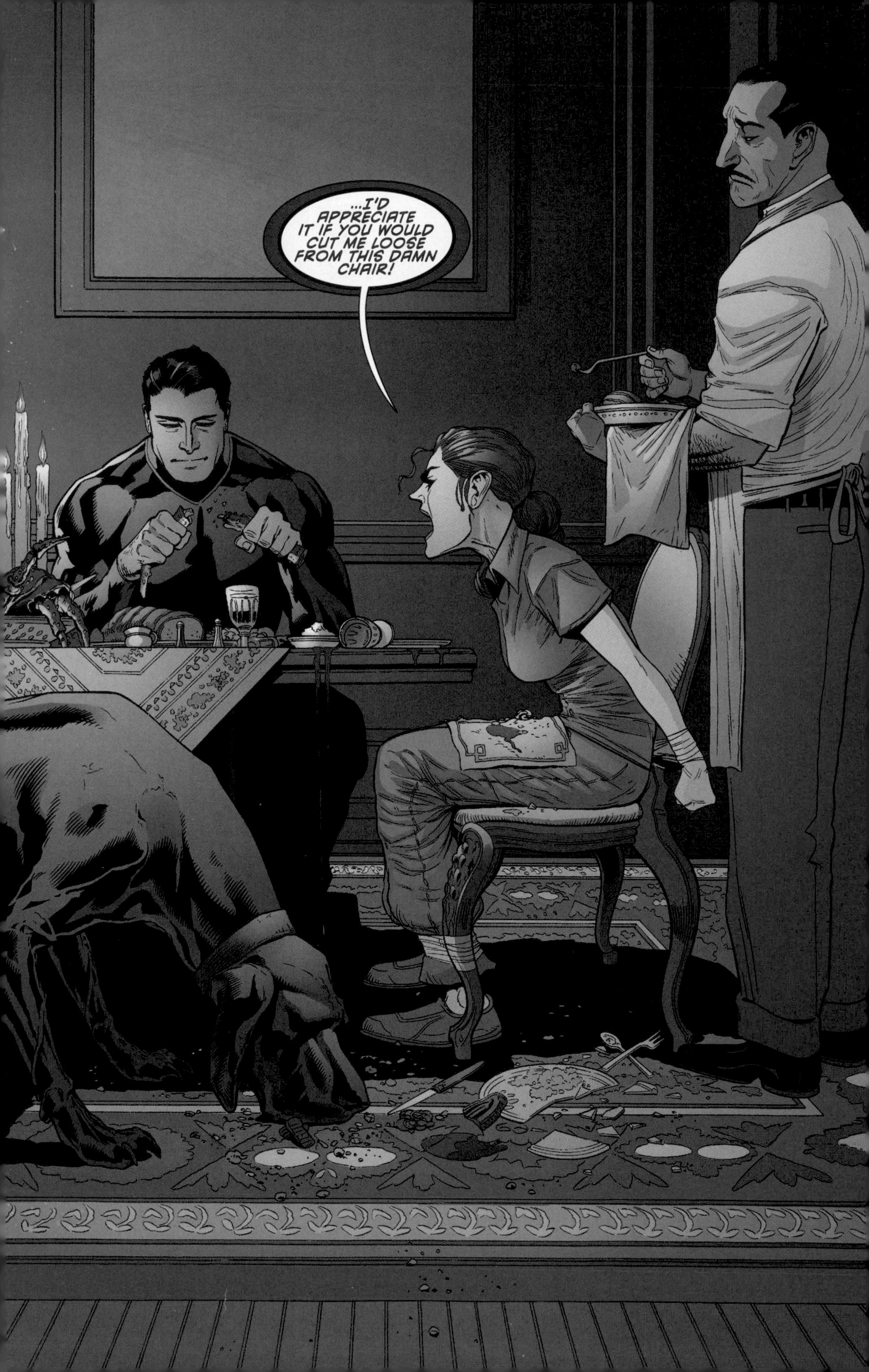
...I'D APPRECIATE IT IF YOU WOULD CUT ME LOOSE FROM THIS DAMN CHAIR!

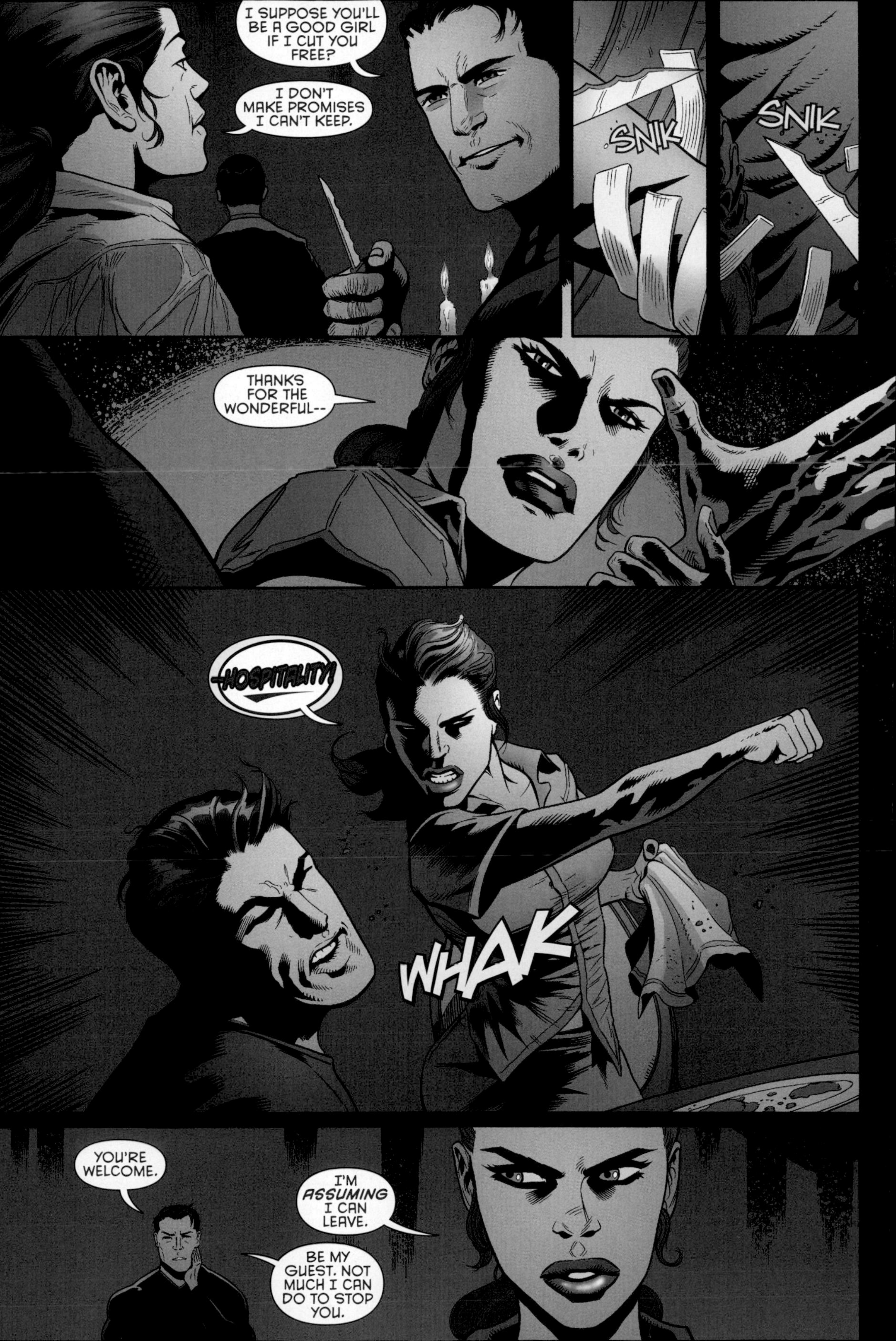

I SUPPOSE YOU'LL BE A GOOD GIRL IF I CUT YOU FREE?
I DON'T MAKE PROMISES I CAN'T KEEP.
SNIK
SNIK
THANKS FOR THE WONDERFUL--
-HOSPITALITY!
WHAK
YOU'RE WELCOME.
I'M ASSUMING I CAN LEAVE.
BE MY GUEST. NOT MUCH I CAN DO TO STOP YOU.

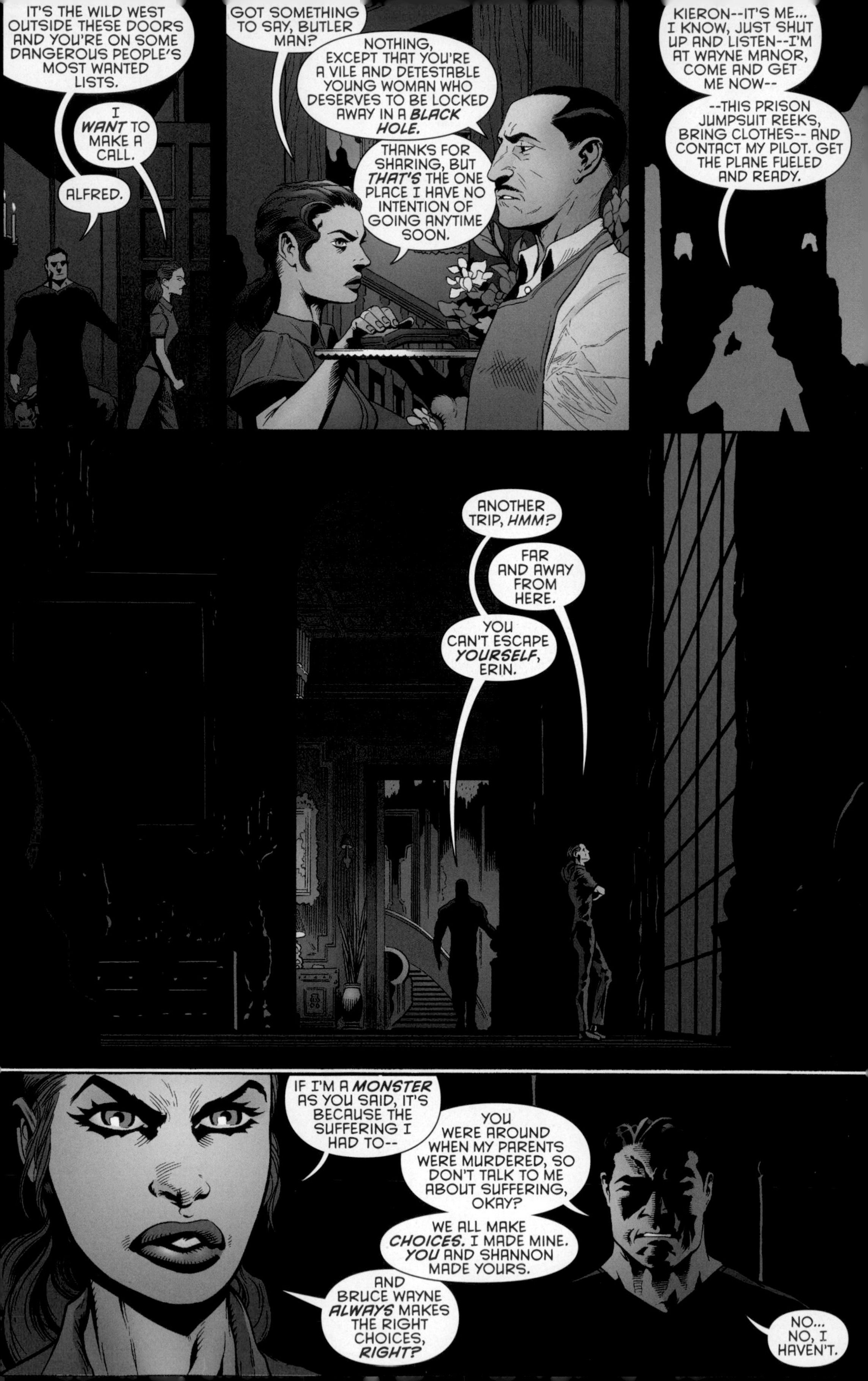
IT'S THE WILD WEST OUTSIDE THESE DOORS AND YOU'RE ON SOME DANGEROUS PEOPLE'S MOST WANTED LISTS.
I *WANT* TO MAKE A CALL.
ALFRED.
GOT SOMETHING TO SAY, BUTLER MAN?
NOTHING, EXCEPT THAT YOU'RE A VILE AND DETESTABLE YOUNG WOMAN WHO DESERVES TO BE LOCKED AWAY IN A *BLACK HOLE.*
THANKS FOR SHARING, BUT *THAT'S* THE ONE PLACE I HAVE NO INTENTION OF GOING ANYTIME SOON.
KIERON--IT'S ME... I KNOW, JUST SHUT UP AND LISTEN--I'M AT WAYNE MANOR, COME AND GET ME NOW--
--THIS PRISON JUMPSUIT REEKS, BRING CLOTHES-- AND CONTACT MY PILOT. GET THE PLANE FUELED AND READY.
ANOTHER TRIP, *HMM?*
FAR AND AWAY FROM HERE.
YOU CAN'T ESCAPE *YOURSELF,* ERIN.
IF I'M A *MONSTER* AS YOU SAID, IT'S BECAUSE THE SUFFERING I HAD TO--
YOU WERE AROUND WHEN MY PARENTS WERE MURDERED, SO DON'T TALK TO ME ABOUT SUFFERING, OKAY?
WE ALL MAKE *CHOICES.* I MADE MINE. *YOU* AND SHANNON MADE YOURS.
AND BRUCE WAYNE *ALWAYS* MAKES THE RIGHT CHOICES, *RIGHT?*
NO... NO, I HAVEN'T.

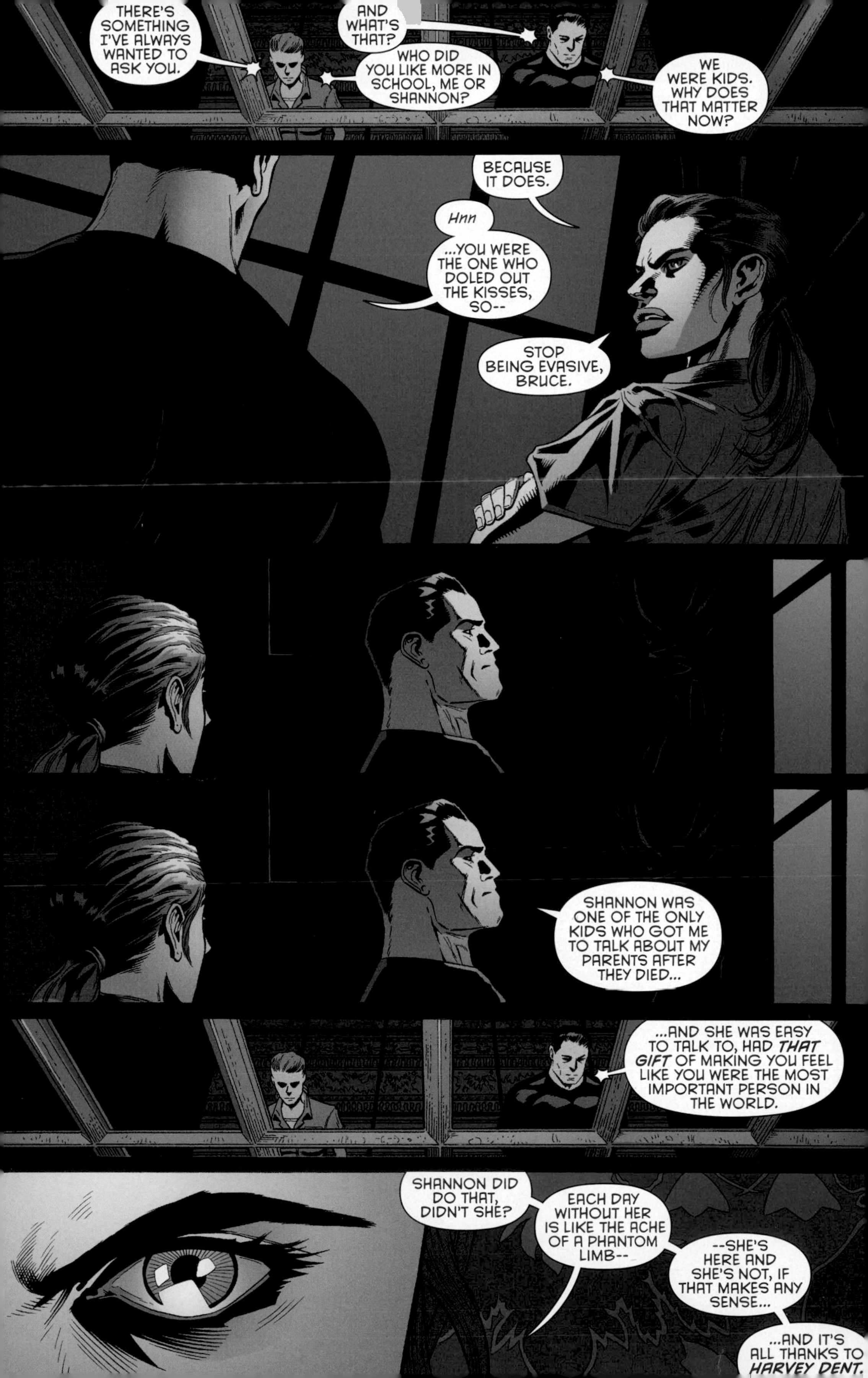
THERE'S SOMETHING I'VE ALWAYS WANTED TO ASK YOU.
AND WHAT'S THAT?
WHO DID YOU LIKE MORE IN SCHOOL, ME OR SHANNON?
WE WERE KIDS. WHY DOES THAT MATTER NOW?
BECAUSE IT DOES.
Hnn
...YOU WERE THE ONE WHO DOLED OUT THE KISSES, SO--
STOP BEING EVASIVE, BRUCE.
SHANNON WAS ONE OF THE ONLY KIDS WHO GOT ME TO TALK ABOUT MY PARENTS AFTER THEY DIED...
...AND SHE WAS EASY TO TALK TO, HAD THAT GIFT OF MAKING YOU FEEL LIKE YOU WERE THE MOST IMPORTANT PERSON IN THE WORLD.
SHANNON DID DO THAT, DIDN'T SHE?
EACH DAY WITHOUT HER IS LIKE THE ACHE OF A PHANTOM LIMB--
--SHE'S HERE AND SHE'S NOT, IF THAT MAKES ANY SENSE...
...AND IT'S ALL THANKS TO HARVEY DENT.

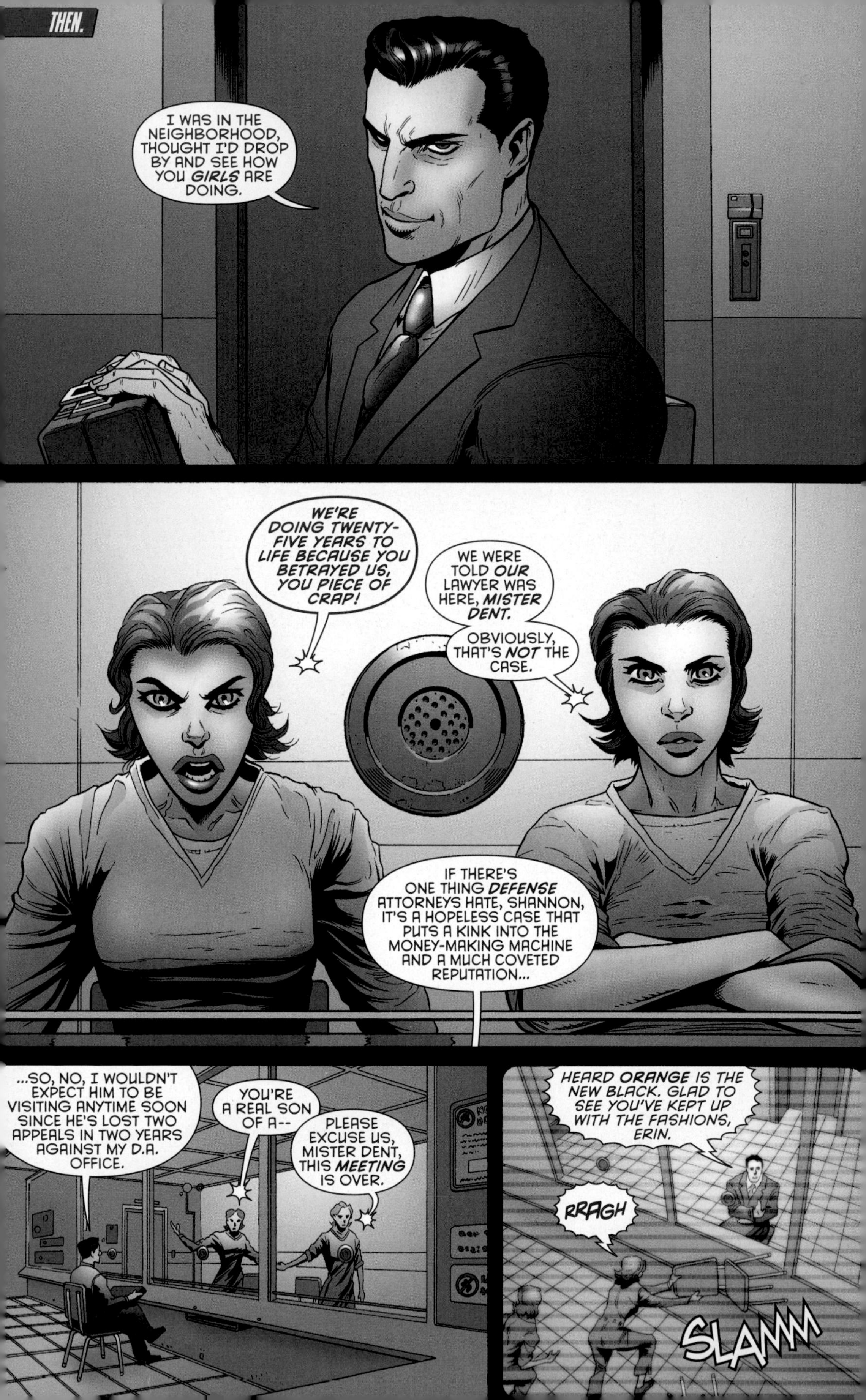
THEN.
I WAS IN THE NEIGHBORHOOD, THOUGHT I'D DROP BY AND SEE HOW YOU GIRLS ARE DOING.
WE'RE DOING TWENTY-FIVE YEARS TO LIFE BECAUSE YOU BETRAYED US, YOU PIECE OF CRAP!
WE WERE TOLD OUR LAWYER WAS HERE, MISTER DENT.
OBVIOUSLY, THAT'S NOT THE CASE.
IF THERE'S ONE THING DEFENSE ATTORNEYS HATE, SHANNON, IT'S A HOPELESS CASE THAT PUTS A KINK INTO THE MONEY-MAKING MACHINE AND A MUCH COVETED REPUTATION...
...SO, NO, I WOULDN'T EXPECT HIM TO BE VISITING ANYTIME SOON SINCE HE'S LOST TWO APPEALS IN TWO YEARS AGAINST MY D.A. OFFICE.
YOU'RE A REAL SON OF A--
PLEASE EXCUSE US, MISTER DENT, THIS MEETING IS OVER.
HEARD ORANGE IS THE NEW BLACK. GLAD TO SEE YOU'VE KEPT UP WITH THE FASHIONS, ERIN.
RRAGH
SLAMM

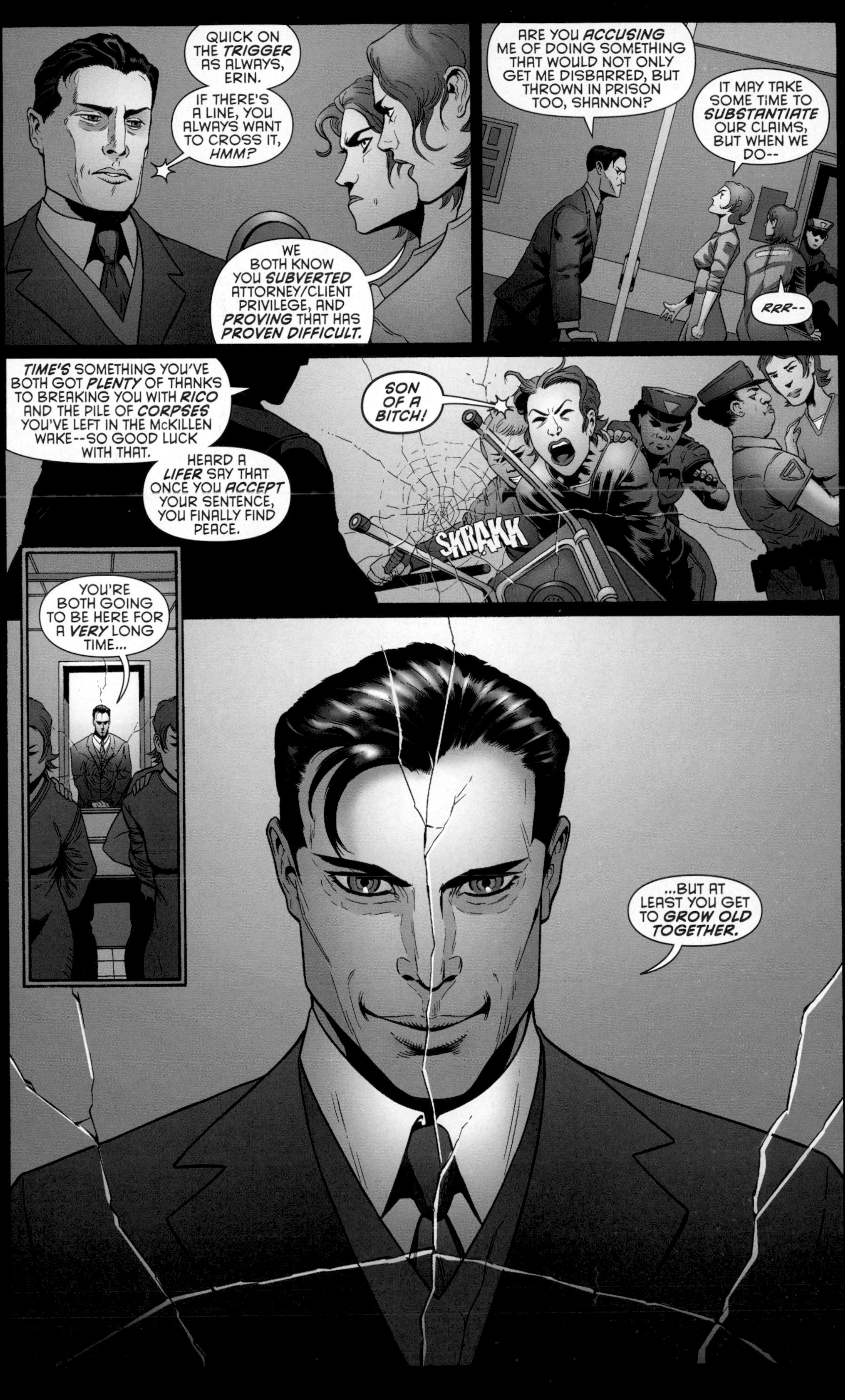
QUICK ON THE TRIGGER AS ALWAYS, ERIN.
IF THERE'S A LINE, YOU ALWAYS WANT TO CROSS IT, HMM?
WE BOTH KNOW YOU SUBVERTED ATTORNEY/CLIENT PRIVILEGE, AND PROVING THAT HAS PROVEN DIFFICULT.
ARE YOU ACCUSING ME OF DOING SOMETHING THAT WOULD NOT ONLY GET ME DISBARRED, BUT THROWN IN PRISON TOO, SHANNON?
IT MAY TAKE SOME TIME TO SUBSTANTIATE OUR CLAIMS, BUT WHEN WE DO--
RRR--
TIME'S SOMETHING YOU'VE BOTH GOT PLENTY OF THANKS TO BREAKING YOU WITH RICO AND THE PILE OF CORPSES YOU'VE LEFT IN THE McKILLEN WAKE--SO GOOD LUCK WITH THAT.
HEARD A LIFER SAY THAT ONCE YOU ACCEPT YOUR SENTENCE, YOU FINALLY FIND PEACE.
SON OF A BITCH!
SKRAKK
YOU'RE BOTH GOING TO BE HERE FOR A VERY LONG TIME...
...BUT AT LEAST YOU GET TO GROW OLD TOGETHER.

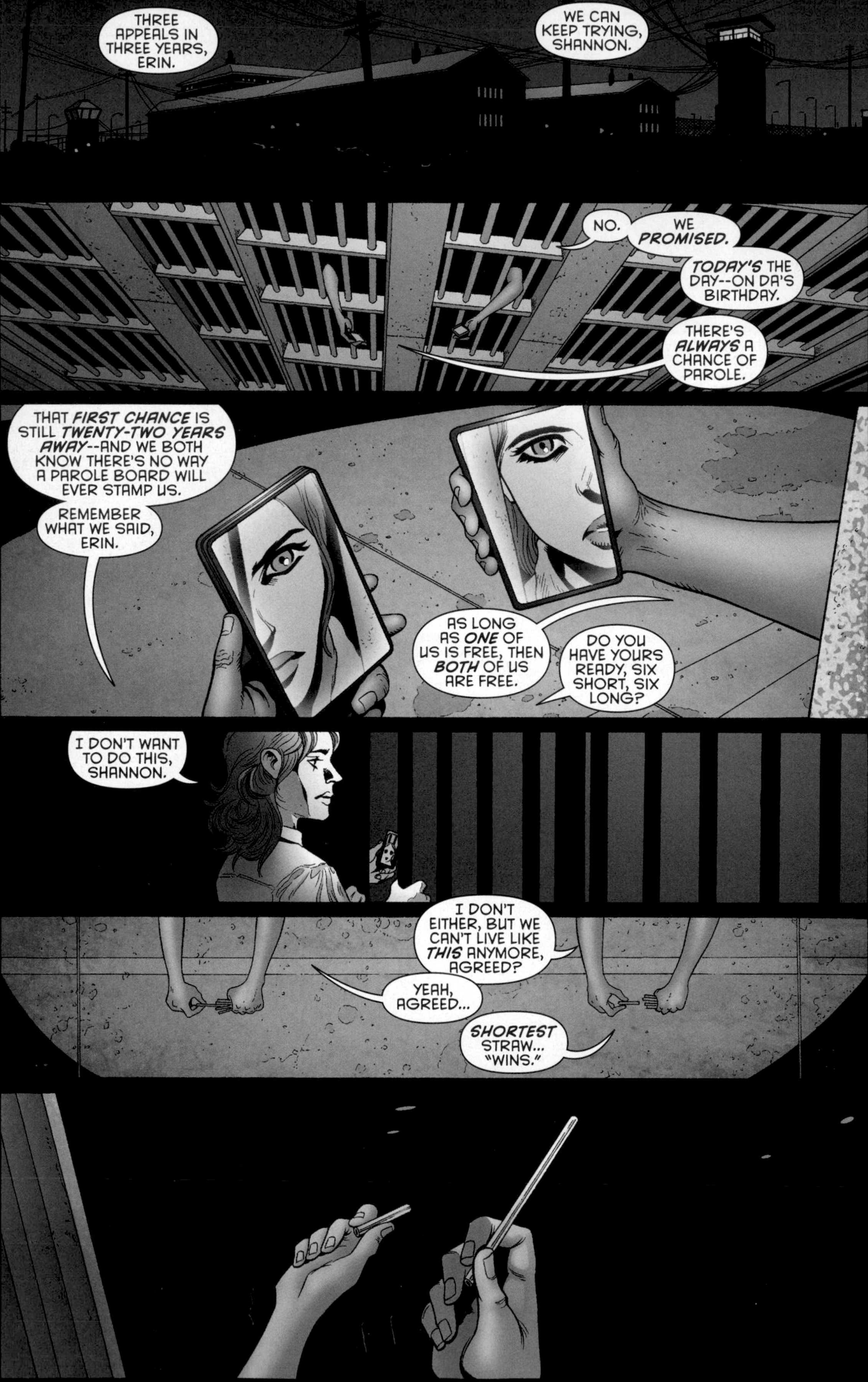
THREE APPEALS IN THREE YEARS, ERIN.
WE CAN KEEP TRYING, SHANNON.
NO.
WE PROMISED.
TODAY'S THE DAY--ON DA'S BIRTHDAY.
THERE'S ALWAYS A CHANCE OF PAROLE.
THAT FIRST CHANCE IS STILL TWENTY-TWO YEARS AWAY--AND WE BOTH KNOW THERE'S NO WAY A PAROLE BOARD WILL EVER STAMP US.
REMEMBER WHAT WE SAID, ERIN.
AS LONG AS ONE OF US IS FREE, THEN BOTH OF US ARE FREE.
DO YOU HAVE YOURS READY, SIX SHORT, SIX LONG?
I DON'T WANT TO DO THIS, SHANNON.
I DON'T EITHER, BUT WE CAN'T LIVE LIKE THIS ANYMORE, AGREED?
YEAH, AGREED...
SHORTEST STRAW... "WINS."

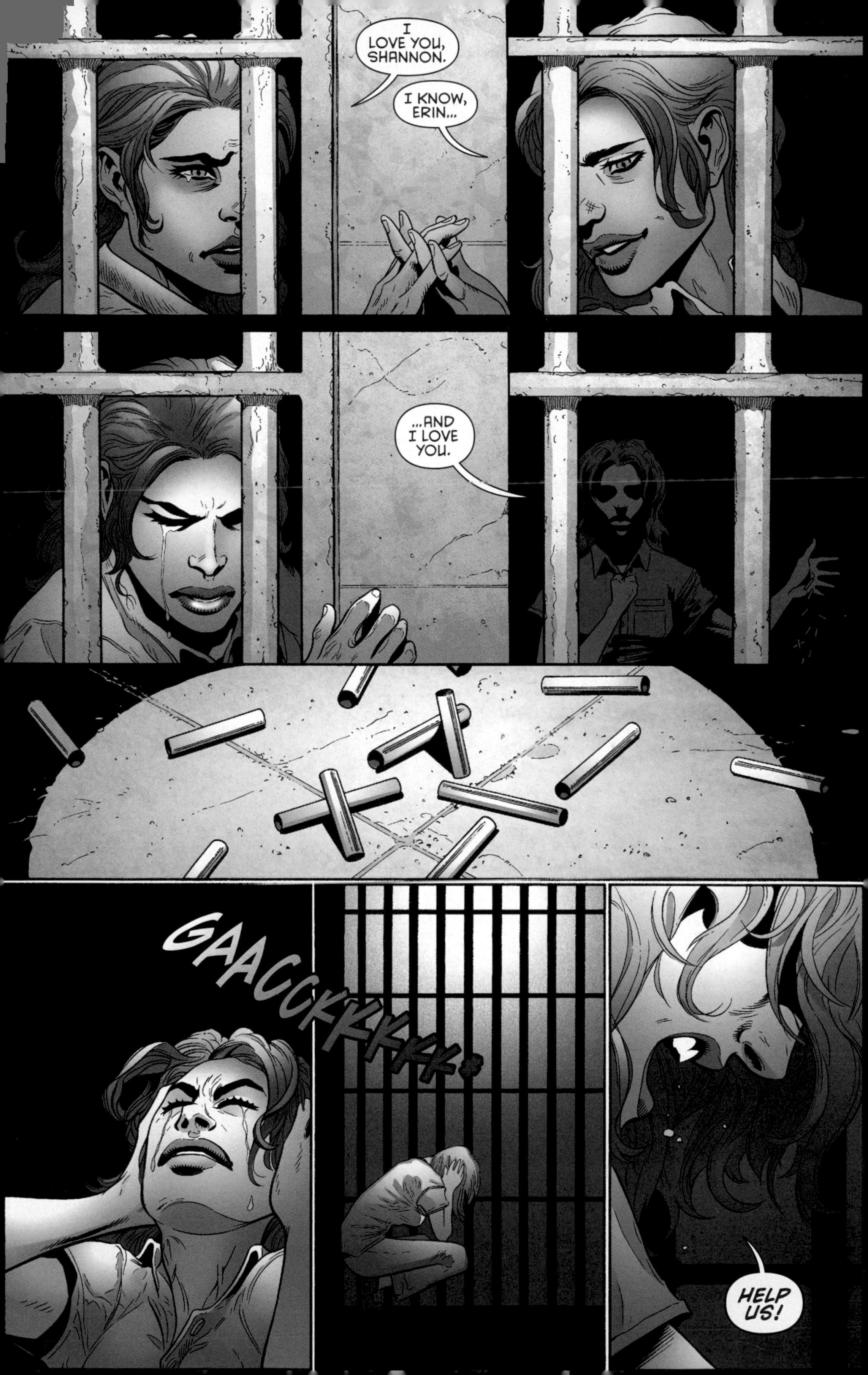
I LOVE YOU, SHANNON.
I KNOW, ERIN...
...AND I LOVE YOU.
GAACCKKKKK!
HELP US!

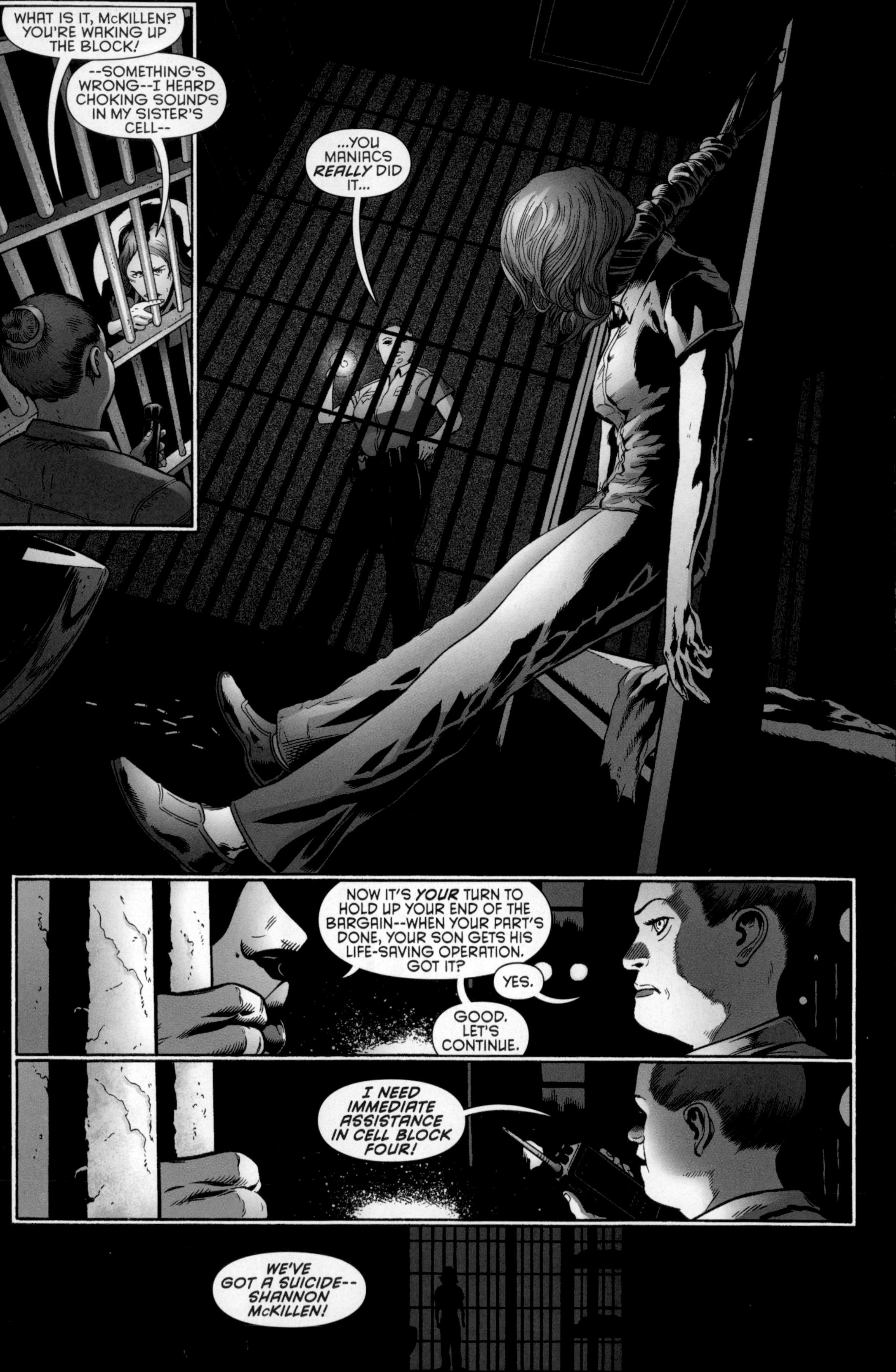
WHAT IS IT, McKILLEN? YOU'RE WAKING UP THE BLOCK!
--SOMETHING'S WRONG--I HEARD CHOKING SOUNDS IN MY SISTER'S CELL--
...YOU MANIACS *REALLY* DID IT...
NOW IT'S *YOUR* TURN TO HOLD UP YOUR END OF THE BARGAIN--WHEN YOUR PART'S DONE, YOUR SON GETS HIS LIFE-SAVING OPERATION. GOT IT?
YES.
GOOD. LET'S CONTINUE.
I NEED IMMEDIATE ASSISTANCE IN CELL BLOCK FOUR!
WE'VE GOT A SUICIDE-- SHANNON McKILLEN!

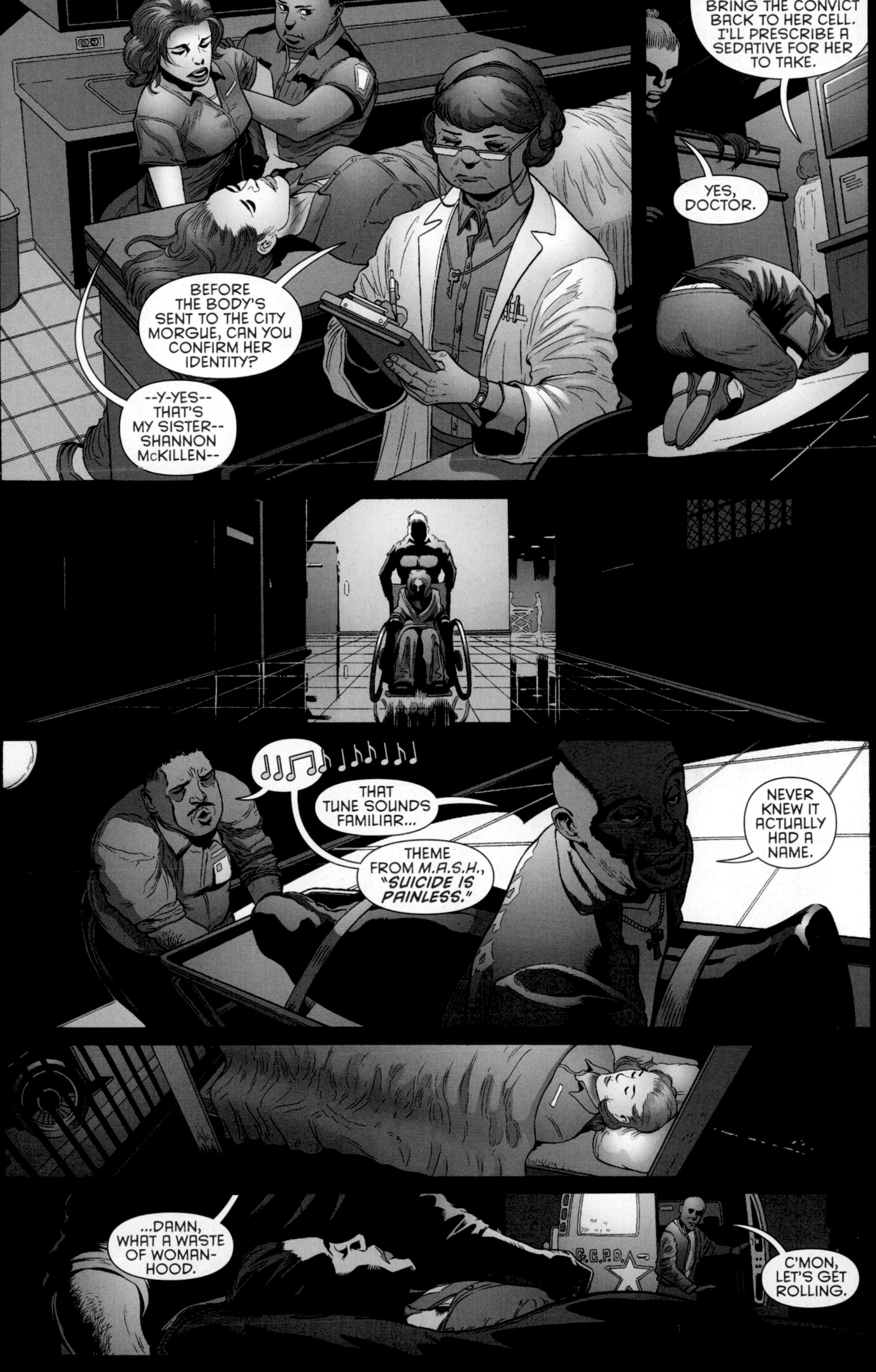
BEFORE THE BODY'S SENT TO THE CITY MORGUE, CAN YOU CONFIRM HER IDENTITY?
--Y-YES-- THAT'S MY SISTER-- SHANNON McKILLEN--
GUARD, GET A WHEELCHAIR AND BRING THE CONVICT BACK TO HER CELL. I'LL PRESCRIBE A SEDATIVE FOR HER TO TAKE.
YES, DOCTOR.
THAT TUNE SOUNDS FAMILIAR...
THEME FROM M.A.S.H., "SUICIDE IS PAINLESS."
NEVER KNEW IT ACTUALLY HAD A NAME.
...DAMN, WHAT A WASTE OF WOMAN-HOOD.
G.C.P.D.
C'MON, LET'S GET ROLLING.

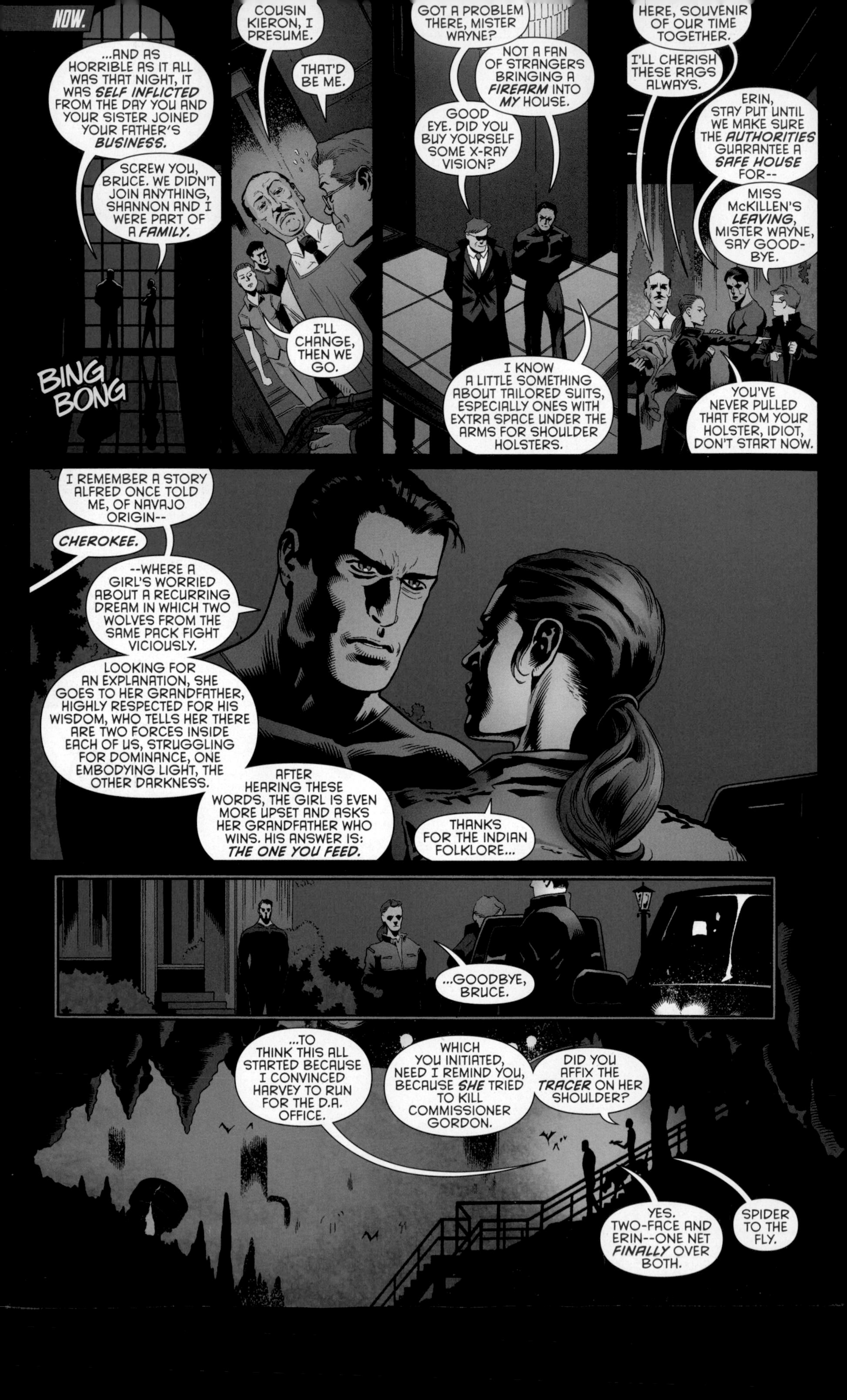
NOW.
...AND AS HORRIBLE AS IT ALL WAS THAT NIGHT, IT WAS SELF INFLICTED FROM THE DAY YOU AND YOUR SISTER JOINED YOUR FATHER'S BUSINESS.
SCREW YOU, BRUCE. WE DIDN'T JOIN ANYTHING, SHANNON AND I WERE PART OF A FAMILY.
BING BONG
COUSIN KIERON, I PRESUME.
THAT'D BE ME.
I'LL CHANGE, THEN WE GO.
GOT A PROBLEM THERE, MISTER WAYNE?
NOT A FAN OF STRANGERS BRINGING A FIREARM INTO MY HOUSE.
GOOD EYE. DID YOU BUY YOURSELF SOME X-RAY VISION?
I KNOW A LITTLE SOMETHING ABOUT TAILORED SUITS, ESPECIALLY ONES WITH EXTRA SPACE UNDER THE ARMS FOR SHOULDER HOLSTERS.
HERE, SOUVENIR OF OUR TIME TOGETHER.
I'LL CHERISH THESE RAGS ALWAYS.
ERIN, STAY PUT UNTIL WE MAKE SURE THE AUTHORITIES GUARANTEE A SAFE HOUSE FOR--
MISS McKILLEN'S LEAVING, MISTER WAYNE, SAY GOOD-BYE.
YOU'VE NEVER PULLED THAT FROM YOUR HOLSTER, IDIOT, DON'T START NOW.
I REMEMBER A STORY ALFRED ONCE TOLD ME, OF NAVAJO ORIGIN--
CHEROKEE.
--WHERE A GIRL'S WORRIED ABOUT A RECURRING DREAM IN WHICH TWO WOLVES FROM THE SAME PACK FIGHT VICIOUSLY.
LOOKING FOR AN EXPLANATION, SHE GOES TO HER GRANDFATHER, HIGHLY RESPECTED FOR HIS WISDOM, WHO TELLS HER THERE ARE TWO FORCES INSIDE EACH OF US, STRUGGLING FOR DOMINANCE, ONE EMBODYING LIGHT, THE OTHER DARKNESS.
AFTER HEARING THESE WORDS, THE GIRL IS EVEN MORE UPSET AND ASKS HER GRANDFATHER WHO WINS. HIS ANSWER IS: THE ONE YOU FEED.
THANKS FOR THE INDIAN FOLKLORE...
...GOODBYE, BRUCE.
...TO THINK THIS ALL STARTED BECAUSE I CONVINCED HARVEY TO RUN FOR THE D.A. OFFICE.
WHICH YOU INITIATED, NEED I REMIND YOU, BECAUSE SHE TRIED TO KILL COMMISSIONER GORDON.
DID YOU AFFIX THE TRACER ON HER SHOULDER?
YES. TWO-FACE AND ERIN--ONE NET FINALLY OVER BOTH.
SPIDER TO THE FLY.

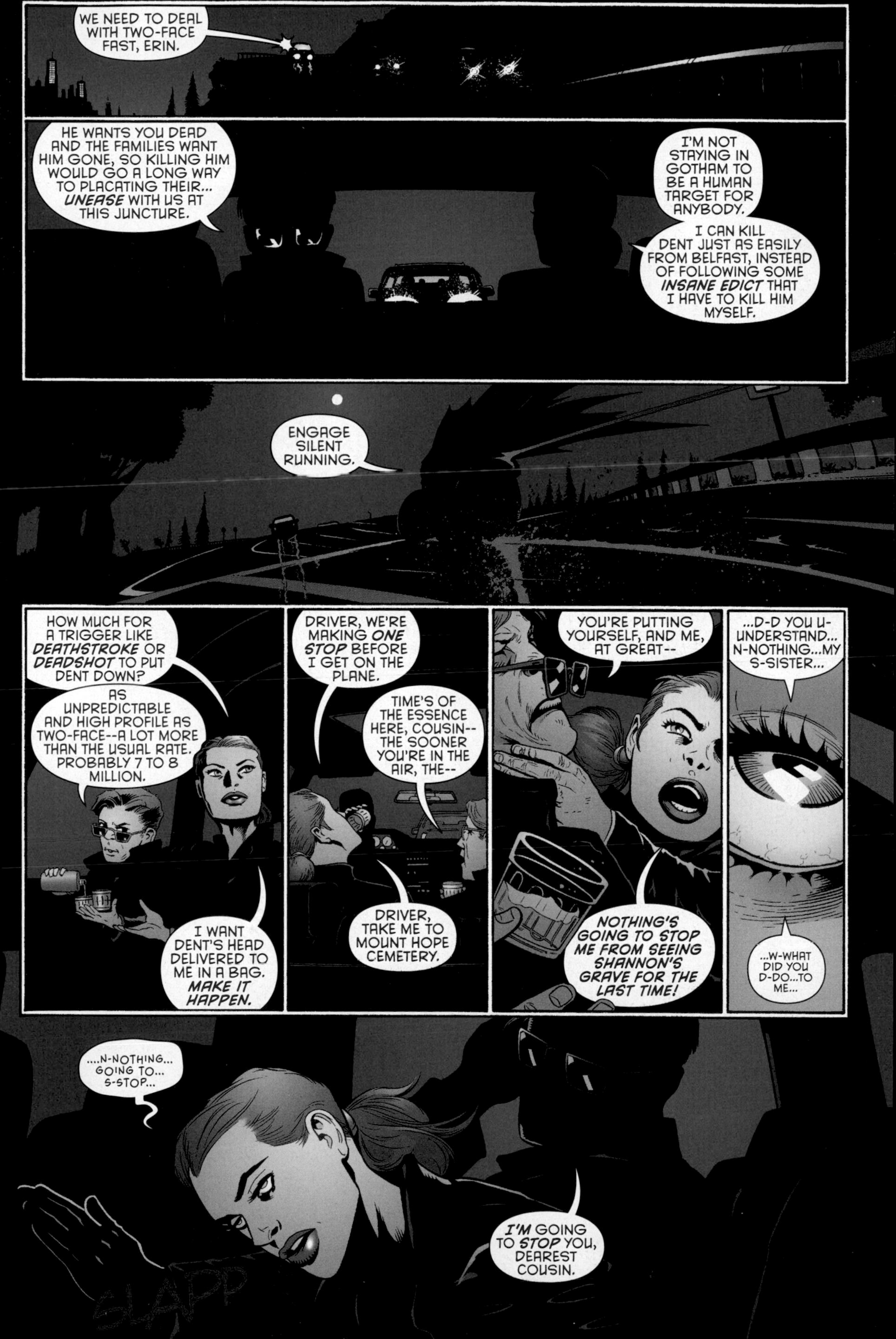

WE NEED TO DEAL WITH TWO-FACE FAST, ERIN.
HE WANTS YOU DEAD AND THE FAMILIES WANT HIM GONE, SO KILLING HIM WOULD GO A LONG WAY TO PLACATING THEIR... UNEASE WITH US AT THIS JUNCTURE.
I'M NOT STAYING IN GOTHAM TO BE A HUMAN TARGET FOR ANYBODY.
I CAN KILL DENT JUST AS EASILY FROM BELFAST, INSTEAD OF FOLLOWING SOME INSANE EDICT THAT I HAVE TO KILL HIM MYSELF.
ENGAGE SILENT RUNNING.
HOW MUCH FOR A TRIGGER LIKE DEATHSTROKE OR DEADSHOT TO PUT DENT DOWN?
AS UNPREDICTABLE AND HIGH PROFILE AS TWO-FACE--A LOT MORE THAN THE USUAL RATE. PROBABLY 7 TO 8 MILLION.
I WANT DENT'S HEAD DELIVERED TO ME IN A BAG. MAKE IT HAPPEN.
DRIVER, WE'RE MAKING ONE STOP BEFORE I GET ON THE PLANE.
TIME'S OF THE ESSENCE HERE, COUSIN--THE SOONER YOU'RE IN THE AIR, THE--
DRIVER, TAKE ME TO MOUNT HOPE CEMETERY.
YOU'RE PUTTING YOURSELF, AND ME, AT GREAT--
NOTHING'S GOING TO STOP ME FROM SEEING SHANNON'S GRAVE FOR THE LAST TIME!
...D-D YOU U-UNDERSTAND... N-NOTHING...MY S-SISTER...
...W-WHAT DID YOU D-DO...TO ME...
....N-NOTHING... GOING TO... S-STOP...
I'M GOING TO STOP YOU, DEAREST COUSIN.
SLAPP

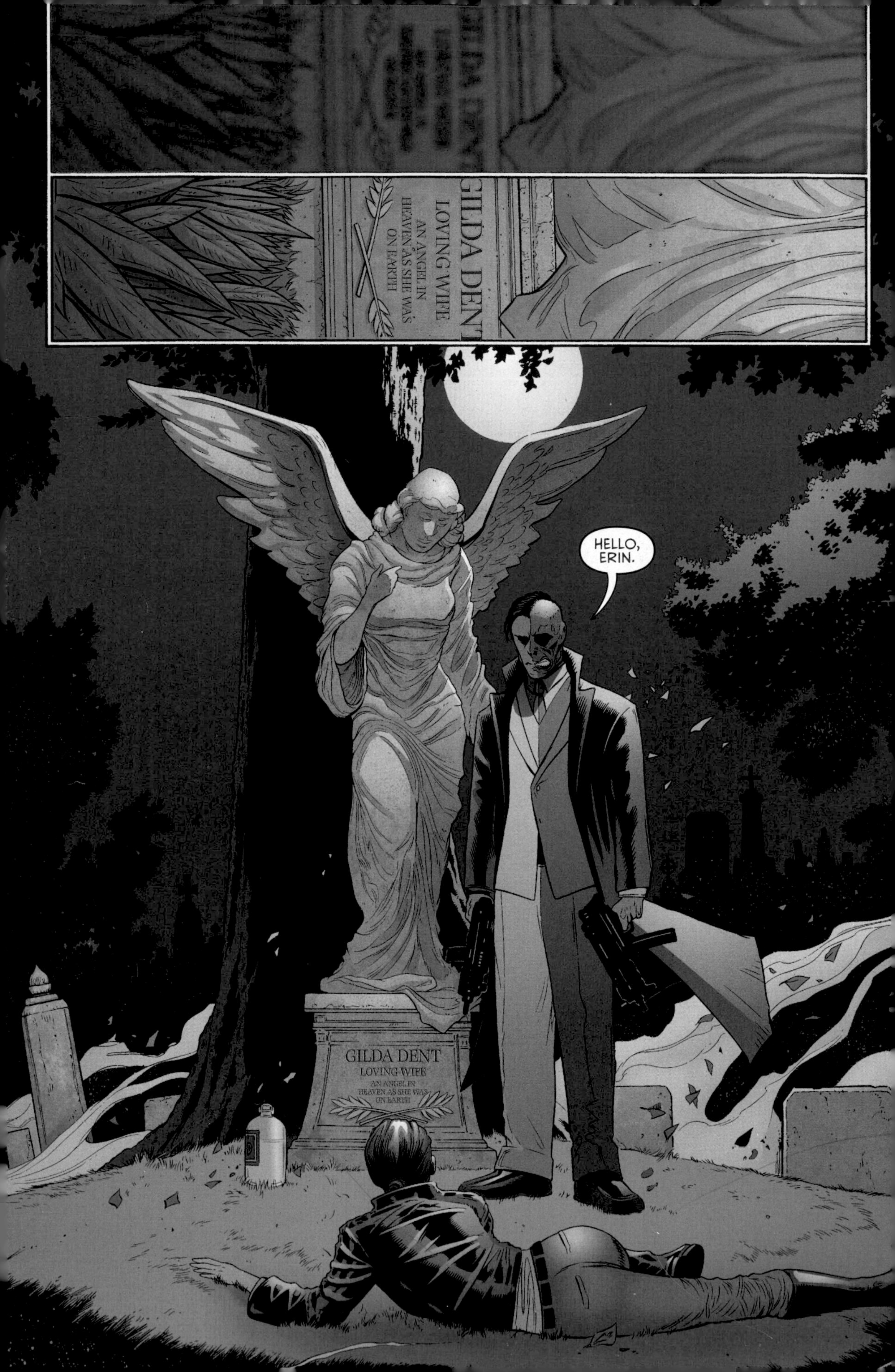
GILDA DENT
LOVING WIFE
AN ANGEL IN HEAVEN AS SHE WAS ON EARTH
HELLO, ERIN.
GILDA DENT
LOVING WIFE
AN ANGEL IN HEAVEN AS SHE WAS ON EARTH

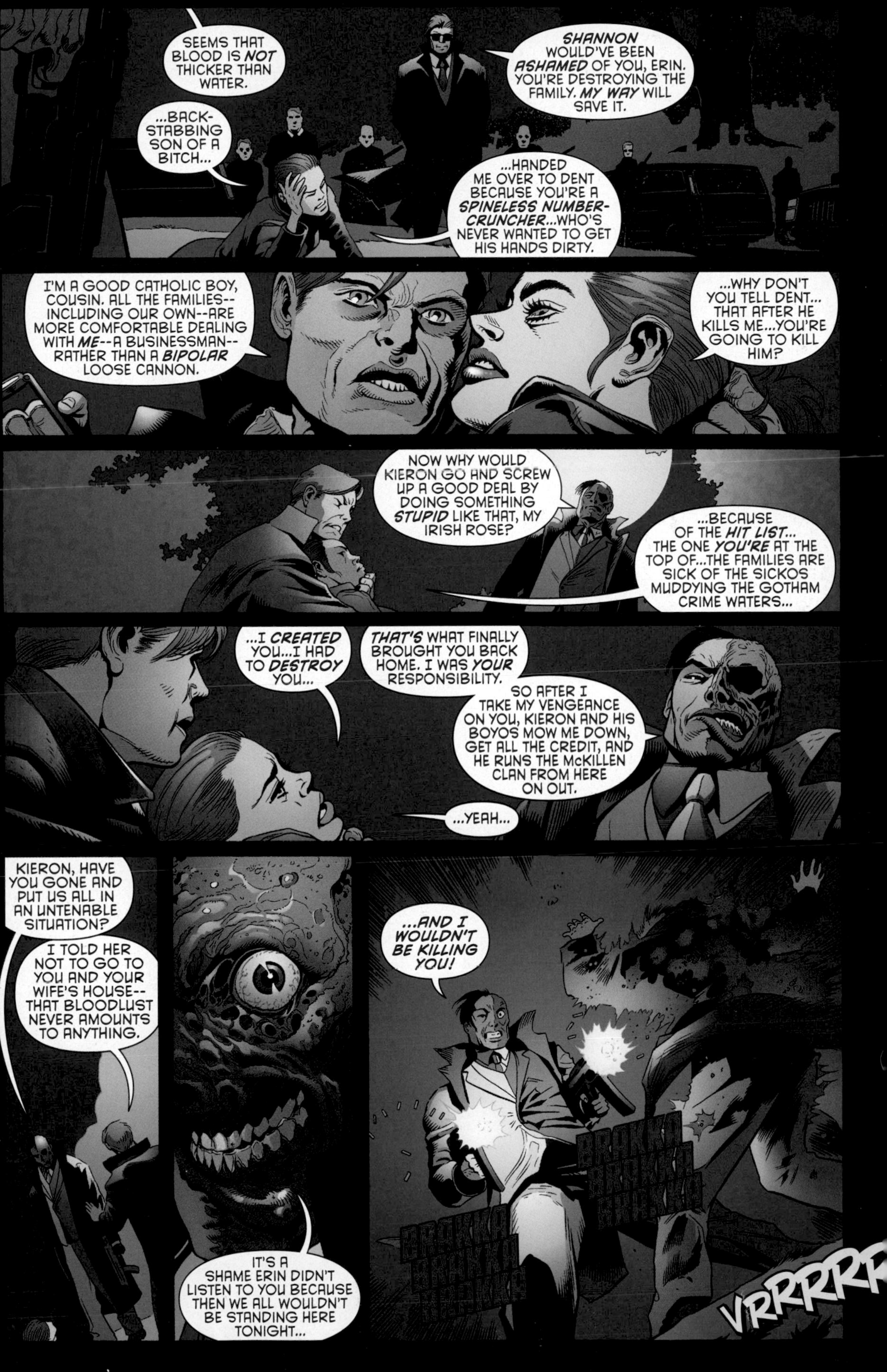
SEEMS THAT BLOOD IS NOT THICKER THAN WATER.
...BACK-STABBING SON OF A BITCH...
SHANNON WOULD'VE BEEN ASHAMED OF YOU, ERIN. YOU'RE DESTROYING THE FAMILY. MY WAY WILL SAVE IT.
...HANDED ME OVER TO DENT BECAUSE YOU'RE A SPINELESS NUMBER-CRUNCHER...WHO'S NEVER WANTED TO GET HIS HANDS DIRTY.
I'M A GOOD CATHOLIC BOY, COUSIN. ALL THE FAMILIES--INCLUDING OUR OWN--ARE MORE COMFORTABLE DEALING WITH ME--A BUSINESSMAN--RATHER THAN A BIPOLAR LOOSE CANNON.
...WHY DON'T YOU TELL DENT... THAT AFTER HE KILLS ME...YOU'RE GOING TO KILL HIM?
NOW WHY WOULD KIERON GO AND SCREW UP A GOOD DEAL BY DOING SOMETHING STUPID LIKE THAT, MY IRISH ROSE?
...BECAUSE OF THE HIT LIST... THE ONE YOU'RE AT THE TOP OF...THE FAMILIES ARE SICK OF THE SICKOS MUDDYING THE GOTHAM CRIME WATERS...
...I CREATED YOU...I HAD TO DESTROY YOU...
THAT'S WHAT FINALLY BROUGHT YOU BACK HOME. I WAS YOUR RESPONSIBILITY.
SO AFTER I TAKE MY VENGEANCE ON YOU, KIERON AND HIS BOYOS MOW ME DOWN, GET ALL THE CREDIT, AND HE RUNS THE McKILLEN CLAN FROM HERE ON OUT.
...YEAH...
KIERON, HAVE YOU GONE AND PUT US ALL IN AN UNTENABLE SITUATION?
I TOLD HER NOT TO GO TO YOU AND YOUR WIFE'S HOUSE--THAT BLOODLUST NEVER AMOUNTS TO ANYTHING.
IT'S A SHAME ERIN DIDN'T LISTEN TO YOU BECAUSE THEN WE ALL WOULDN'T BE STANDING HERE TONIGHT...
...AND I WOULDN'T BE KILLING YOU!
VRRRRR

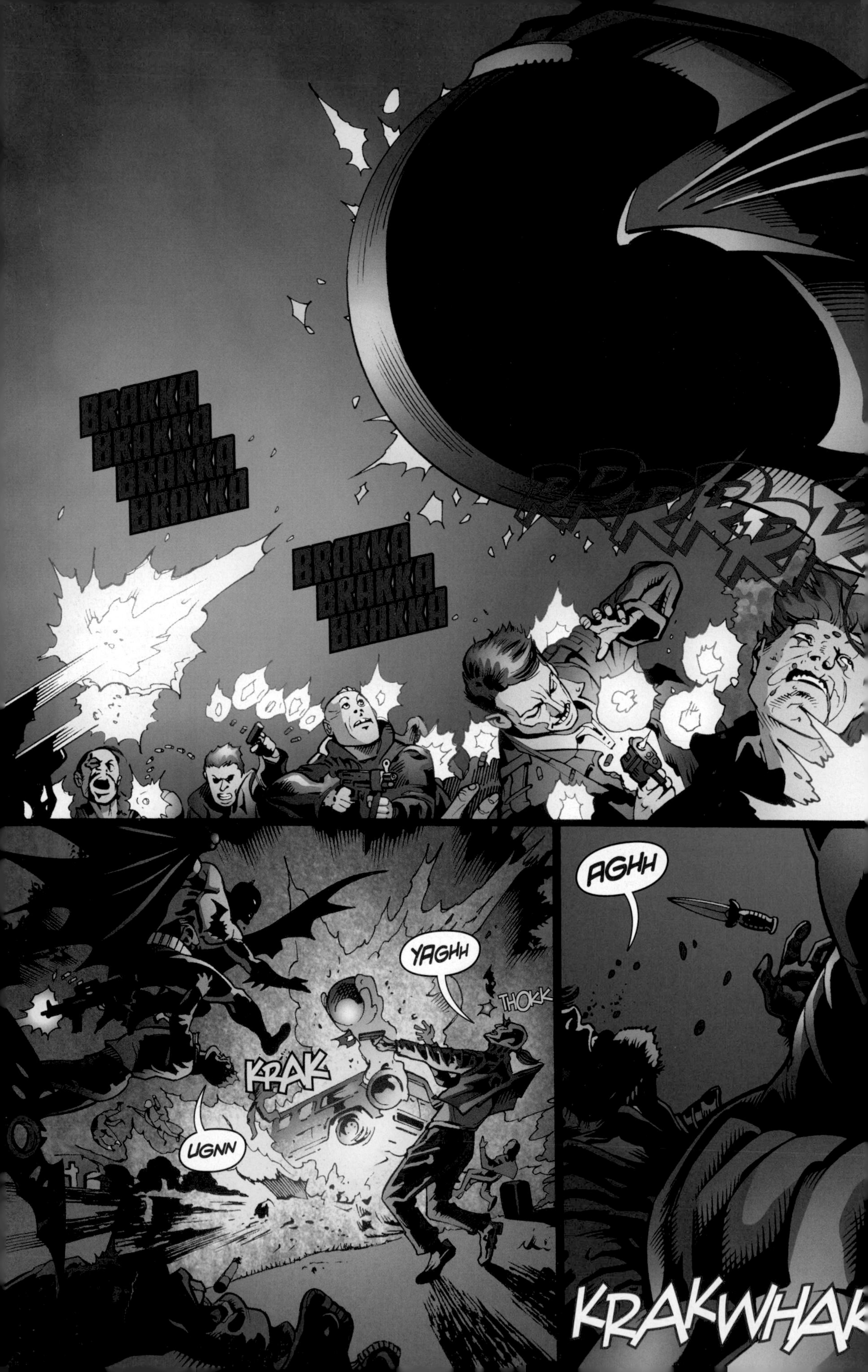
BRAKKA BRAKKA BRAKKA BRAKKA
BRAKKA BRAKKA BRAKKA
YAGHH
THOKK
KRAK
UGNN
AGHH
KRAKWHAK

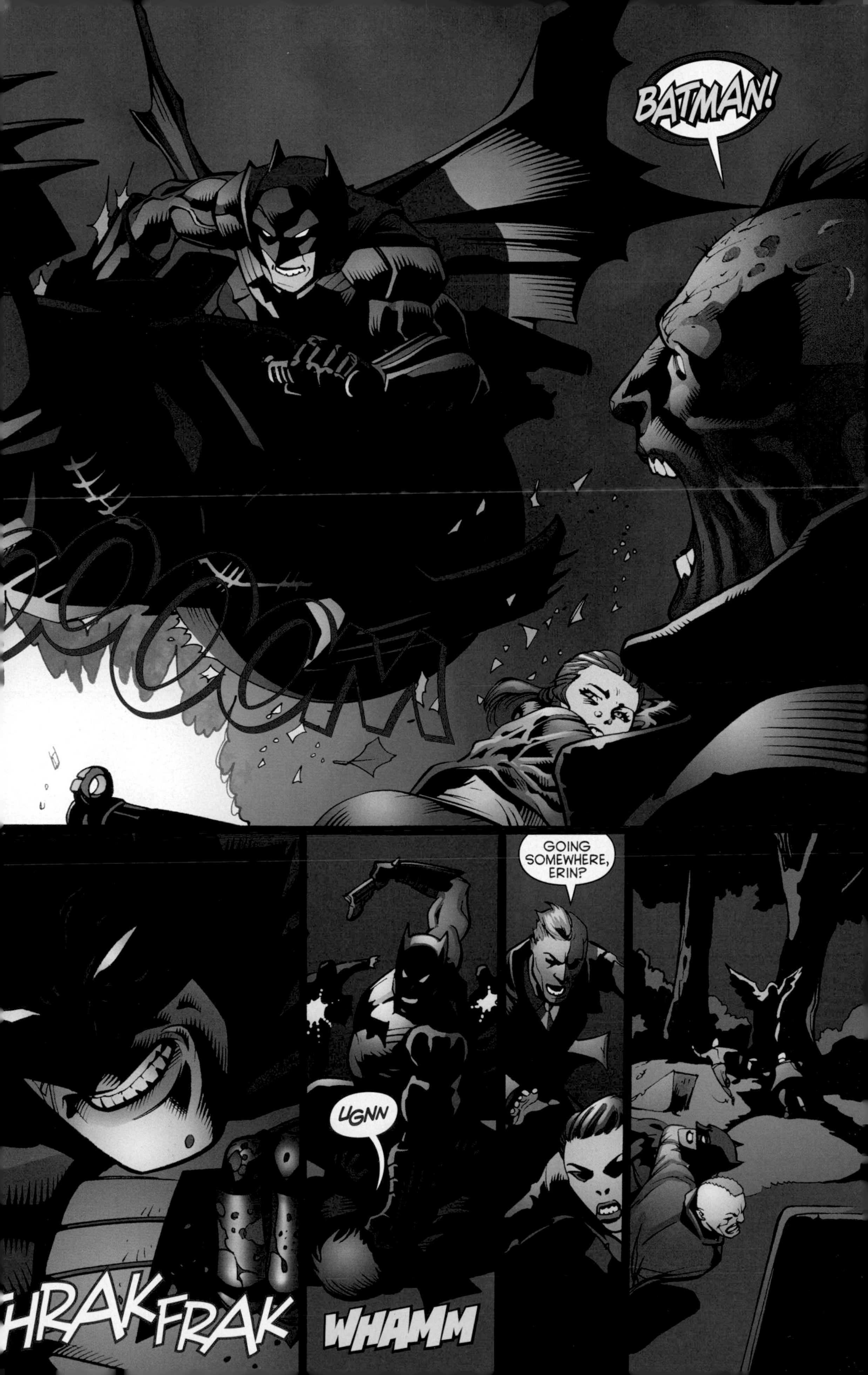
BATMAN!
BOOOOOM
GOING SOMEWHERE, ERIN?
UGNN
THRAK FRAK
WHAMM

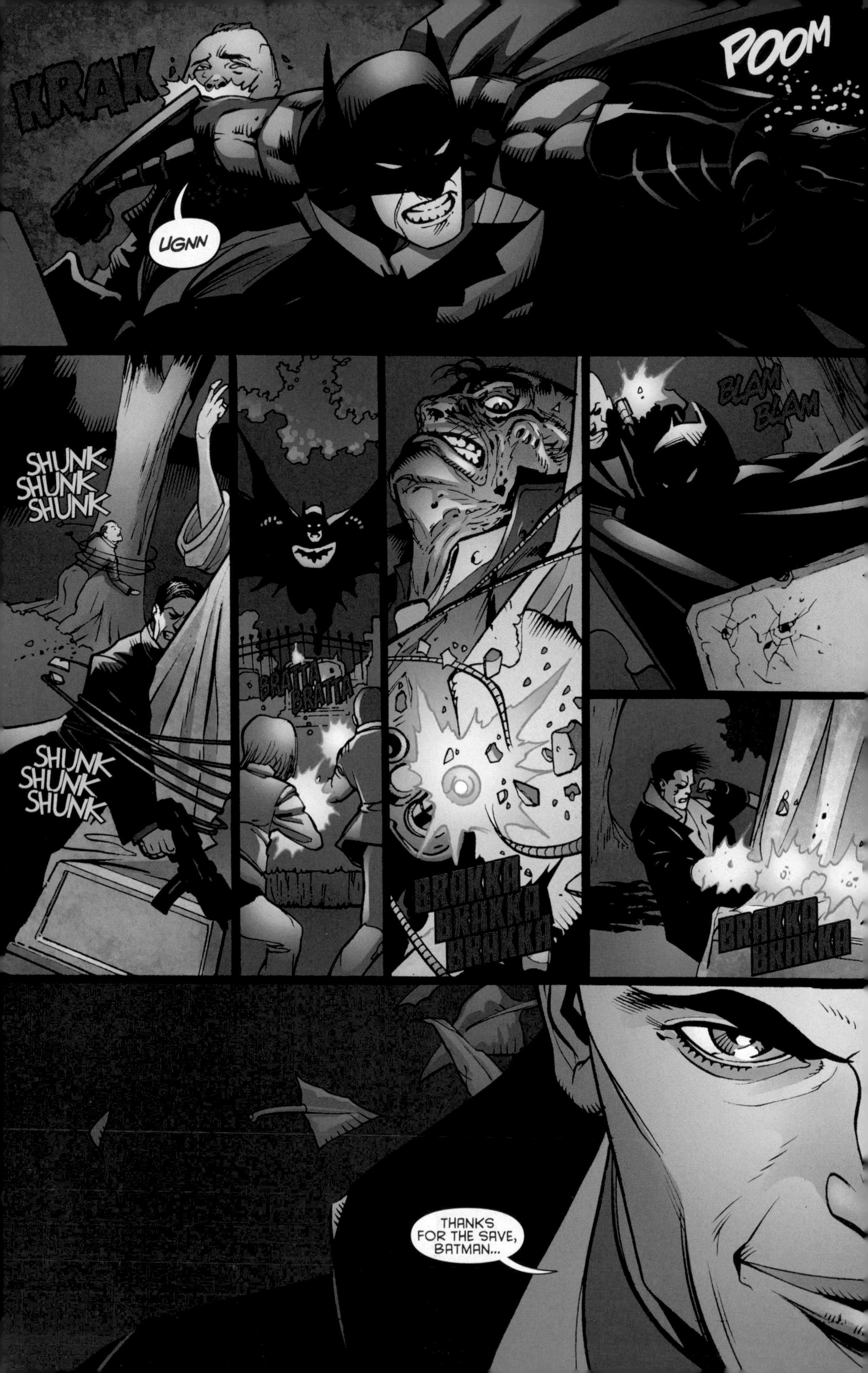
KRAK
POOM
UGNN
SHUNK SHUNK SHUNK
SHUNK SHUNK SHUNK
BRATTA BRATTA
BRAKKA BRAKKA BRAKKA
BLAM BLAM
BRAKKA BRAKKA
THANKS FOR THE SAVE, BATMAN...

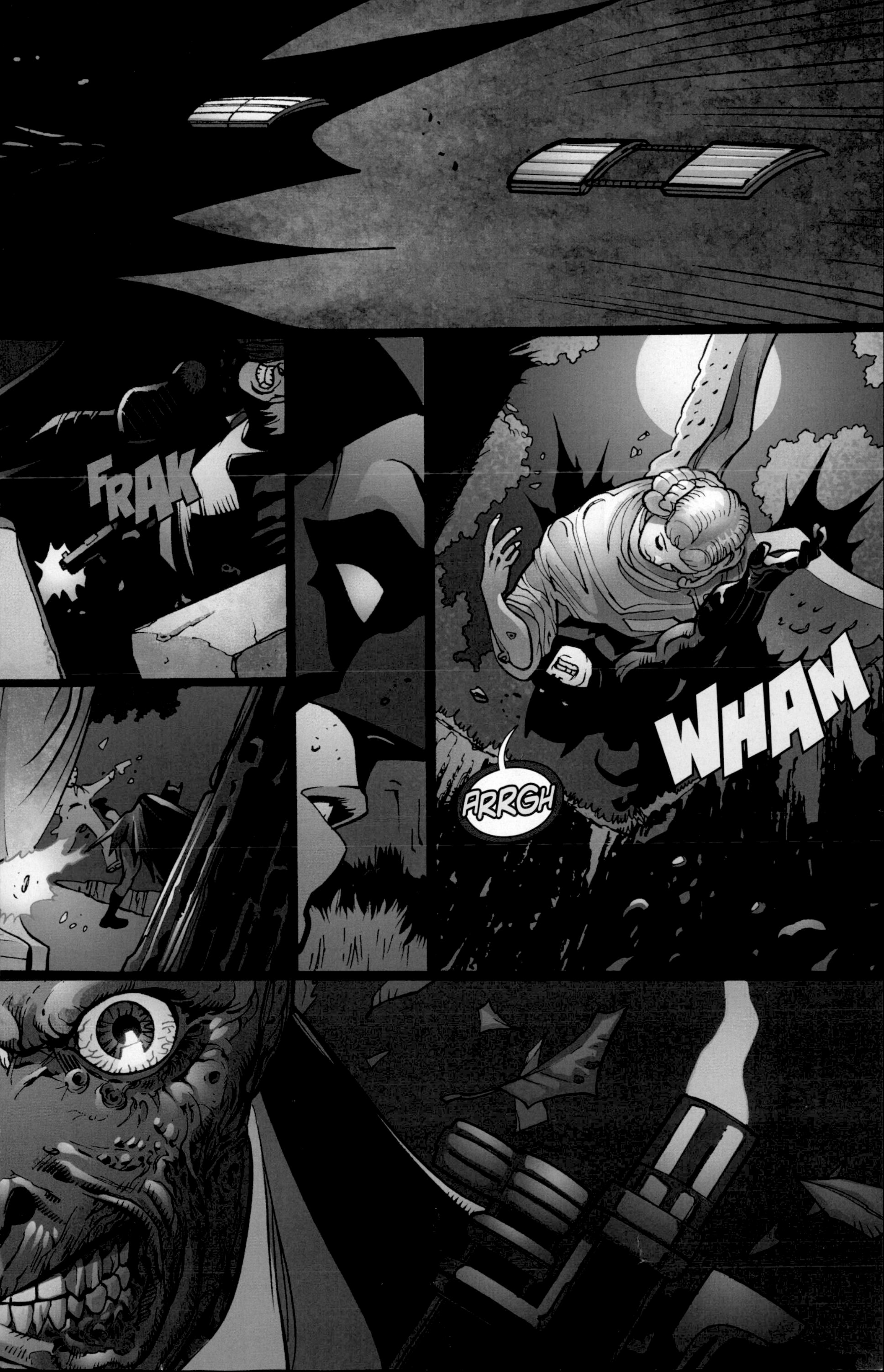
FRAK
ARRGH
WHAM

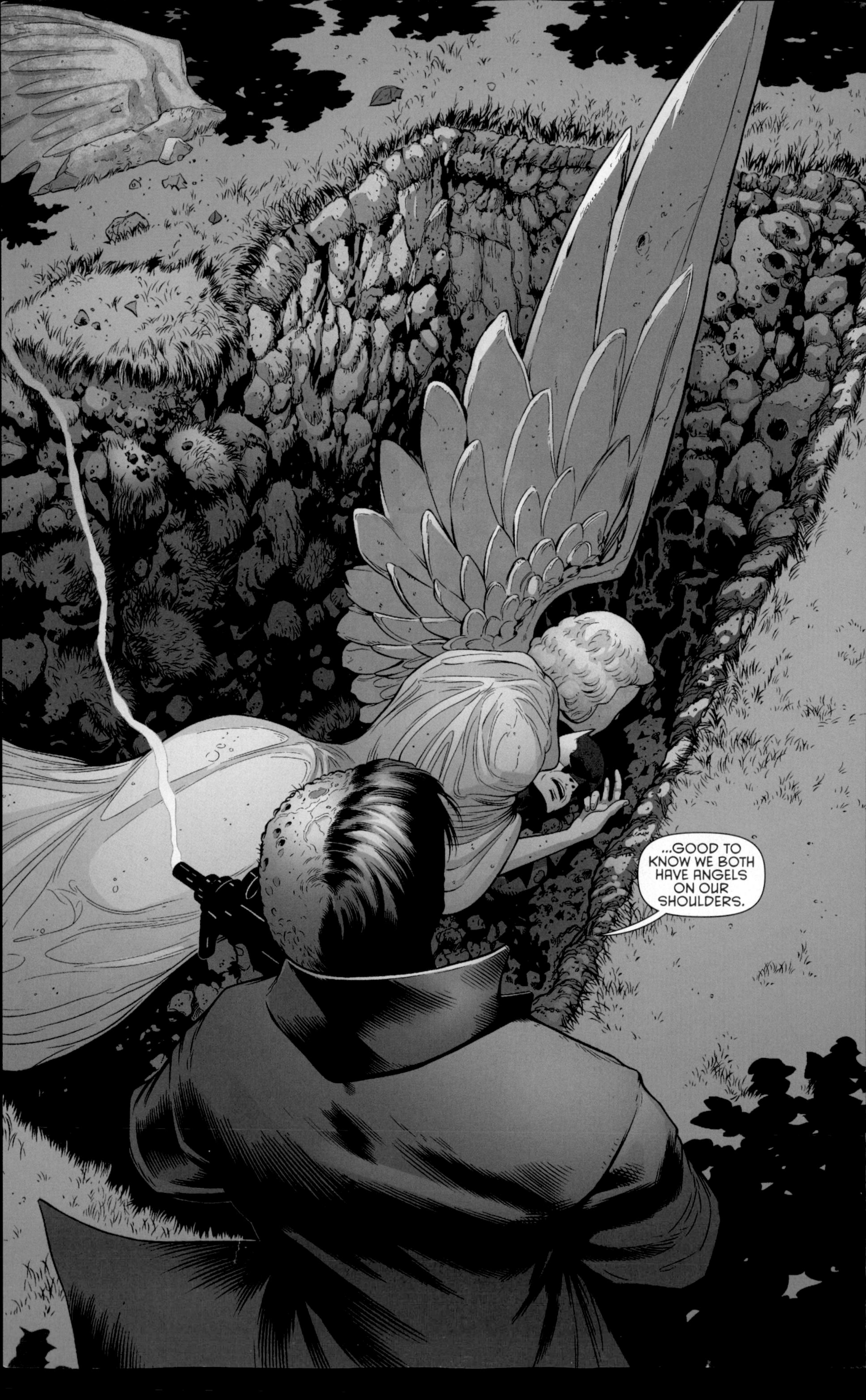
...GOOD TO KNOW WE BOTH HAVE ANGELS ON OUR SHOULDERS.

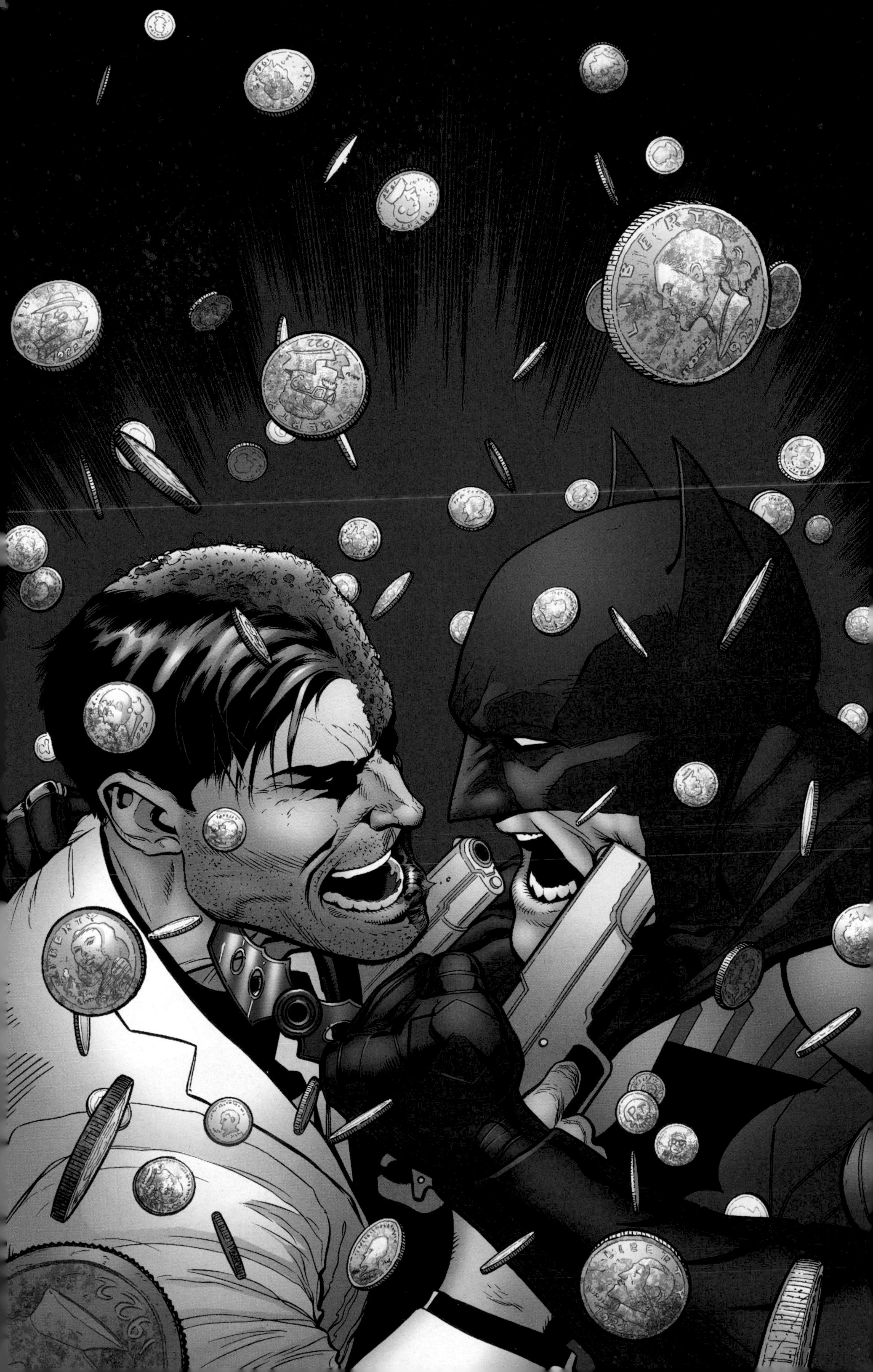
LIBERTY
1922

THE BIG BURN: ABLAZE

PATRICK GLEASON penciller **MICK GRAY** inker **JOHN KALISZ** colorist cover art by **GLEASON, GRAY & KALISZ**

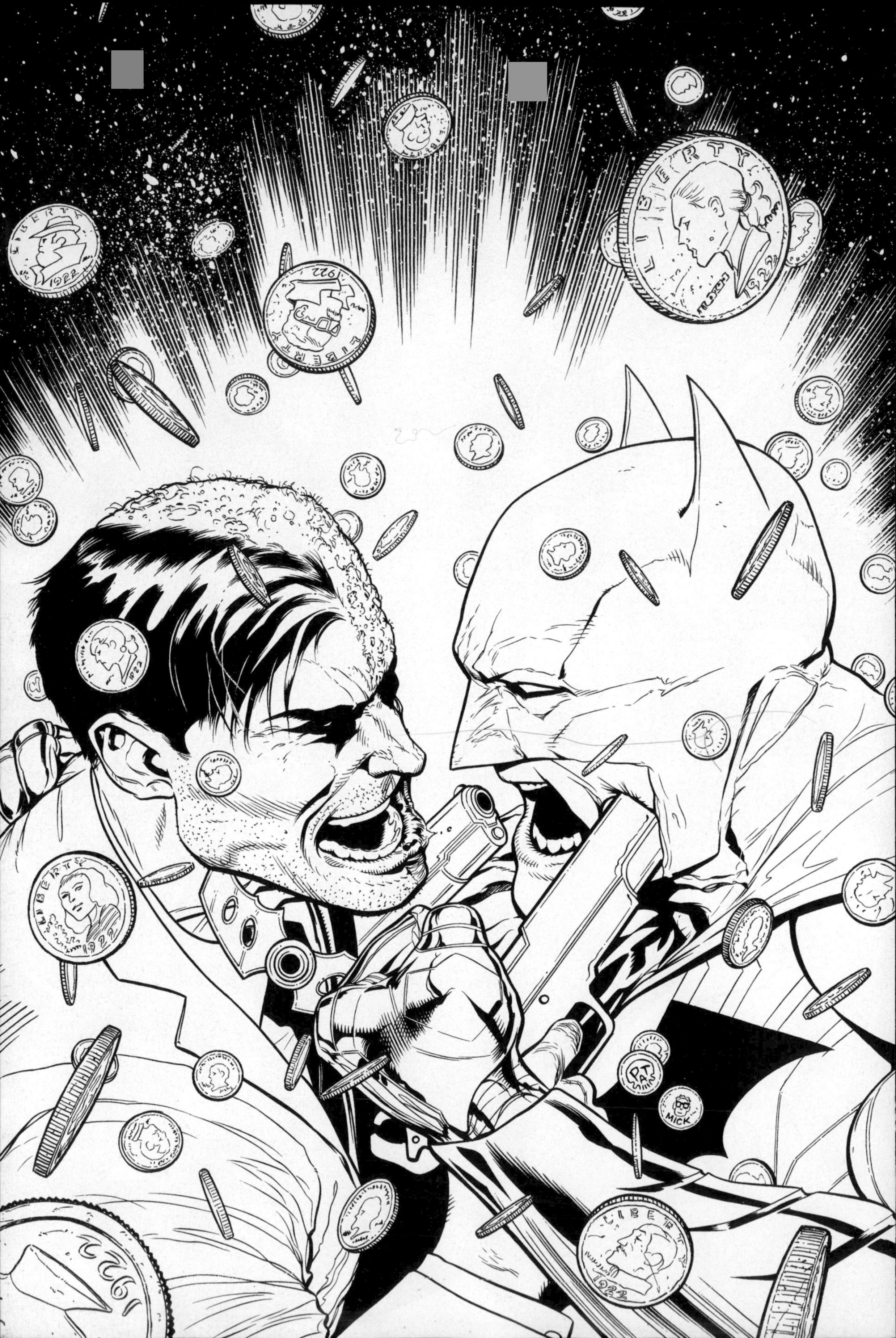
LIBERTY
1922
PAT
MICK

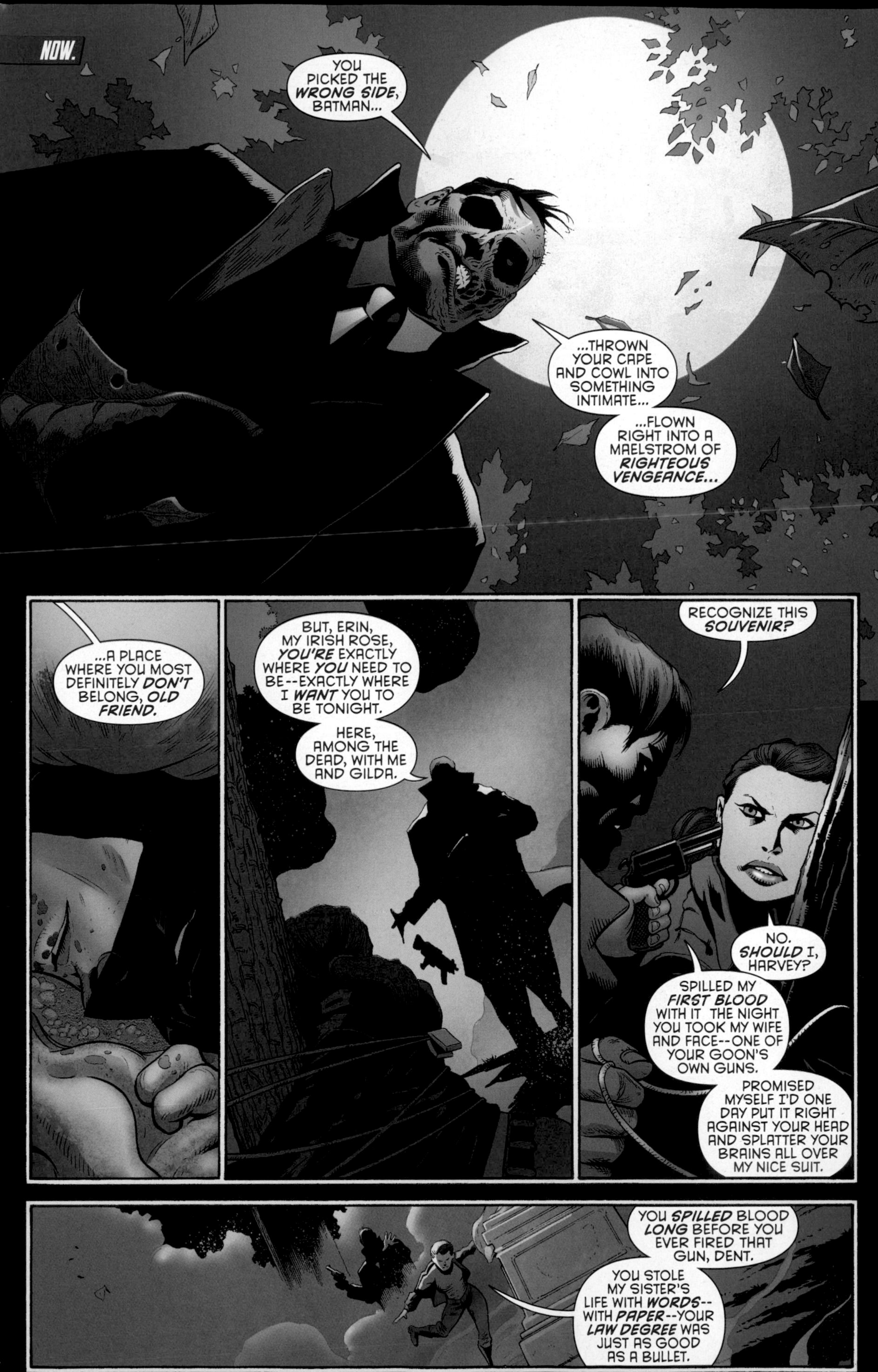
NOW.
YOU PICKED THE WRONG SIDE, BATMAN...
...THROWN YOUR CAPE AND COWL INTO SOMETHING INTIMATE...
...FLOWN RIGHT INTO A MAELSTROM OF RIGHTEOUS VENGEANCE...
...A PLACE WHERE YOU MOST DEFINITELY DON'T BELONG, OLD FRIEND.
BUT, ERIN, MY IRISH ROSE, YOU'RE EXACTLY WHERE YOU NEED TO BE--EXACTLY WHERE I WANT YOU TO BE TONIGHT.
HERE, AMONG THE DEAD, WITH ME AND GILDA.
RECOGNIZE THIS SOUVENIR?
NO. SHOULD I, HARVEY?
SPILLED MY FIRST BLOOD WITH IT THE NIGHT YOU TOOK MY WIFE AND FACE--ONE OF YOUR GOON'S OWN GUNS.
PROMISED MYSELF I'D ONE DAY PUT IT RIGHT AGAINST YOUR HEAD AND SPLATTER YOUR BRAINS ALL OVER MY NICE SUIT.
YOU SPILLED BLOOD LONG BEFORE YOU EVER FIRED THAT GUN, DENT.
YOU STOLE MY SISTER'S LIFE WITH WORDS--WITH PAPER--YOUR LAW DEGREE WAS JUST AS GOOD AS A BULLET.

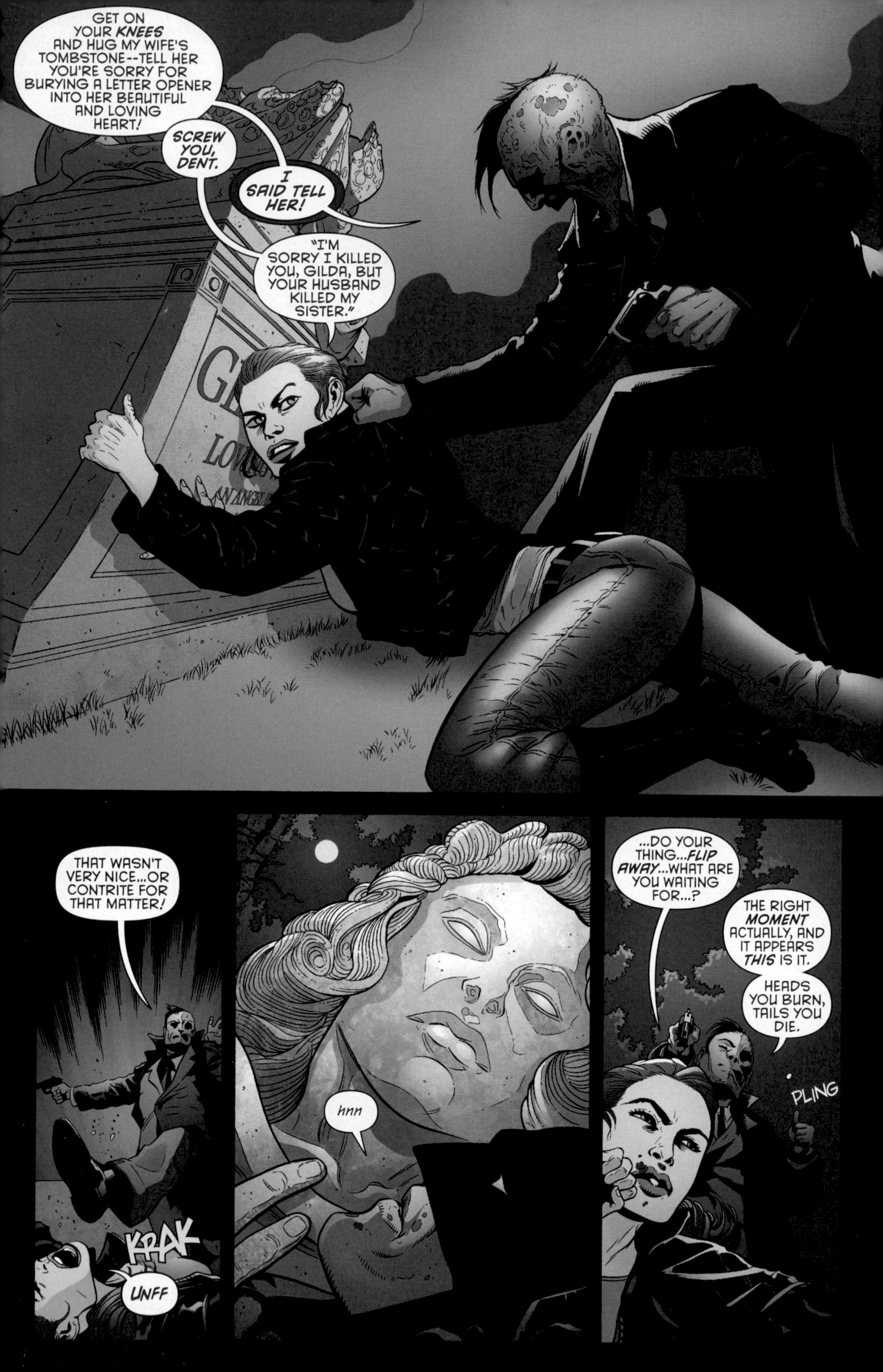
GET ON YOUR KNEES AND HUG MY WIFE'S TOMBSTONE--TELL HER YOU'RE SORRY FOR BURYING A LETTER OPENER INTO HER BEAUTIFUL AND LOVING HEART!
SCREW YOU, DENT.
I SAID TELL HER!
"I'M SORRY I KILLED YOU, GILDA, BUT YOUR HUSBAND KILLED MY SISTER."
THAT WASN'T VERY NICE...OR CONTRITE FOR THAT MATTER!
KRAK
UNFF
hnn
...DO YOUR THING...FLIP AWAY...WHAT ARE YOU WAITING FOR...?
THE RIGHT MOMENT ACTUALLY, AND IT APPEARS THIS IS IT.
HEADS YOU BURN, TAILS YOU DIE.
PLING

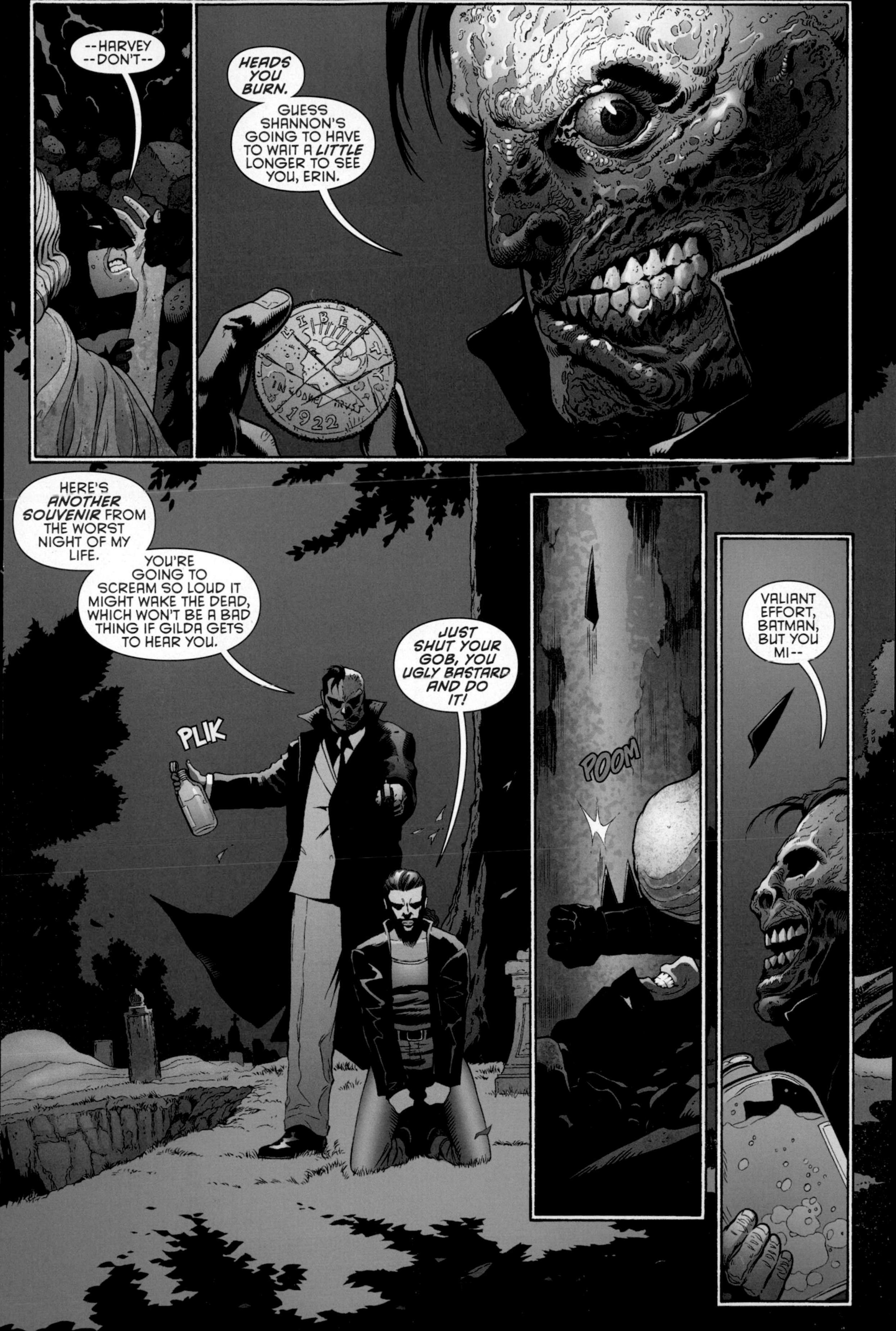
--HARVEY --DON'T--
HEADS YOU BURN.
GUESS SHANNON'S GOING TO HAVE TO WAIT A LITTLE LONGER TO SEE YOU, ERIN.
LIBERTY
IN GOD WE TRUST
1922
HERE'S ANOTHER SOUVENIR FROM THE WORST NIGHT OF MY LIFE.
YOU'RE GOING TO SCREAM SO LOUD IT MIGHT WAKE THE DEAD, WHICH WON'T BE A BAD THING IF GILDA GETS TO HEAR YOU.
JUST SHUT YOUR GOB, YOU UGLY BASTARD AND DO IT!
PLIK
POOM
VALIANT EFFORT, BATMAN, BUT YOU MI--

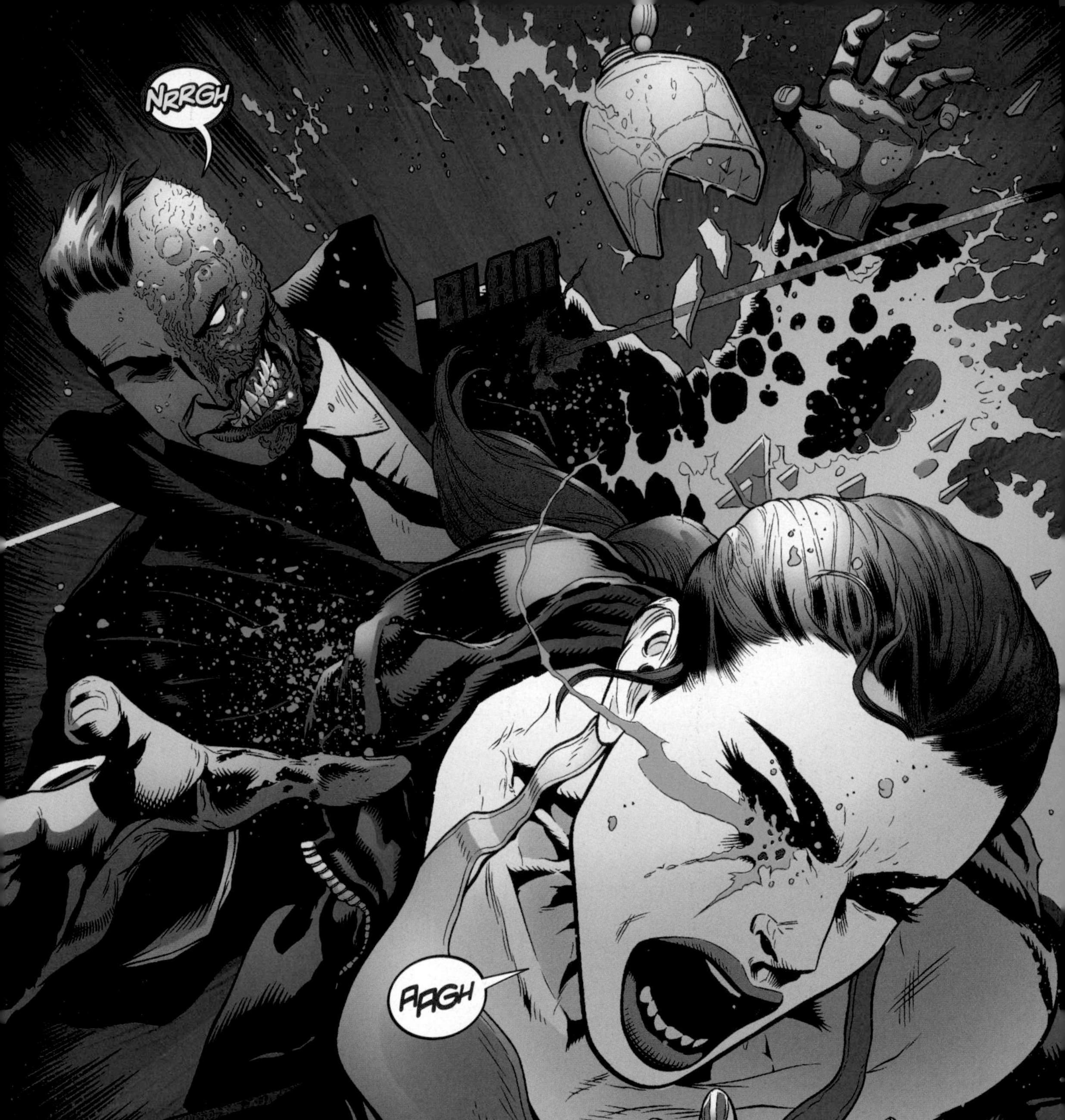
NRRGH
BLAM
AAGH

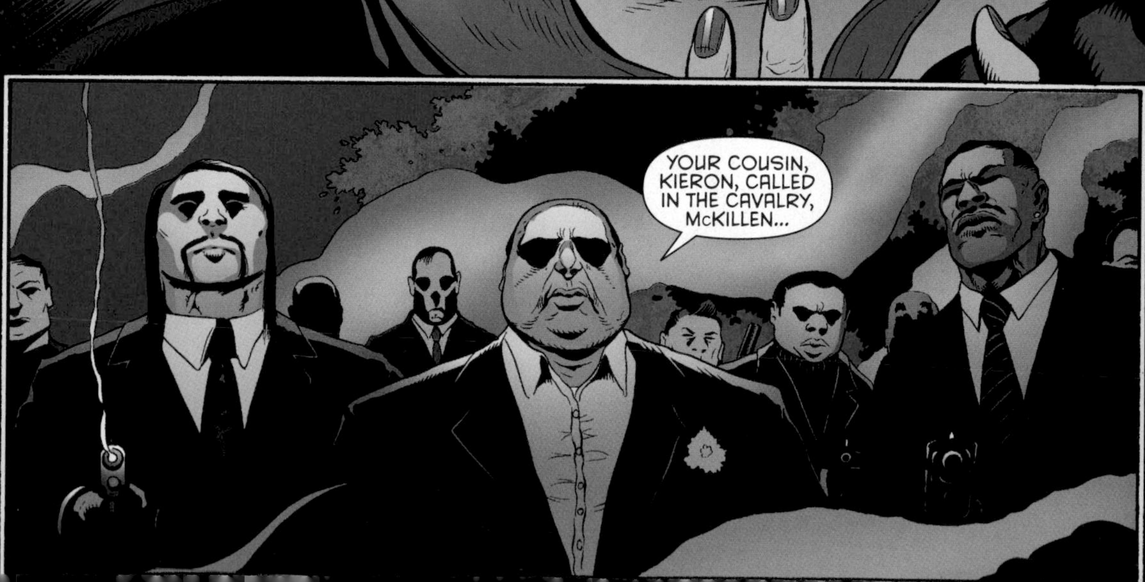
YOUR COUSIN, KIERON, CALLED IN THE CAVALRY, McKILLEN...

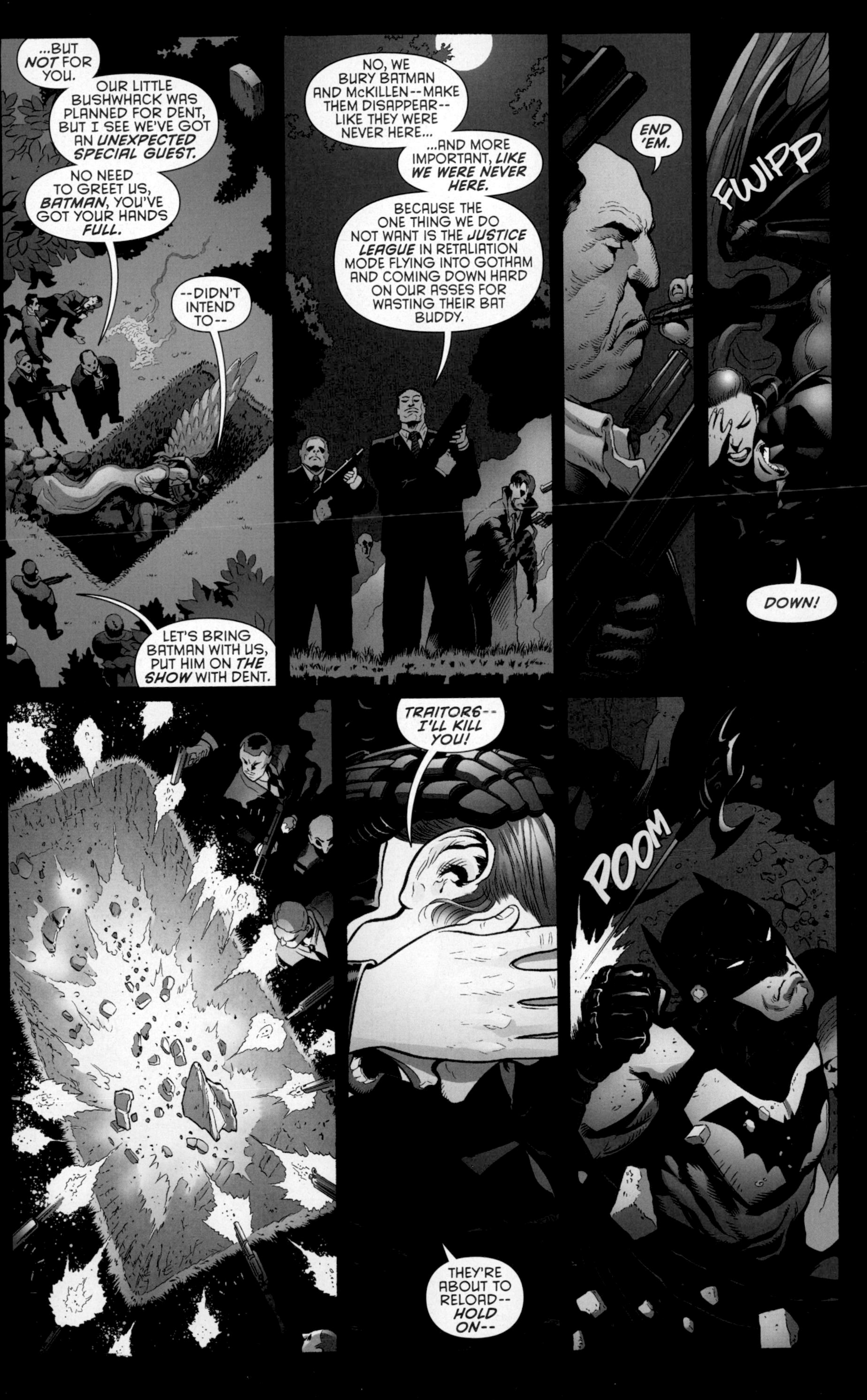

...BUT NOT FOR YOU.
OUR LITTLE BUSHWHACK WAS PLANNED FOR DENT, BUT I SEE WE'VE GOT AN UNEXPECTED SPECIAL GUEST.
NO NEED TO GREET US, BATMAN, YOU'VE GOT YOUR HANDS FULL.
--DIDN'T INTEND TO--
LET'S BRING BATMAN WITH US, PUT HIM ON THE SHOW WITH DENT.
NO, WE BURY BATMAN AND McKILLEN--MAKE THEM DISAPPEAR--LIKE THEY WERE NEVER HERE...
...AND MORE IMPORTANT, LIKE WE WERE NEVER HERE.
BECAUSE THE ONE THING WE DO NOT WANT IS THE JUSTICE LEAGUE IN RETALIATION MODE FLYING INTO GOTHAM AND COMING DOWN HARD ON OUR ASSES FOR WASTING THEIR BAT BUDDY.
END 'EM.
FWIPP
DOWN!
TRAITORS--I'LL KILL YOU!
THEY'RE ABOUT TO RELOAD--HOLD ON--
POOM

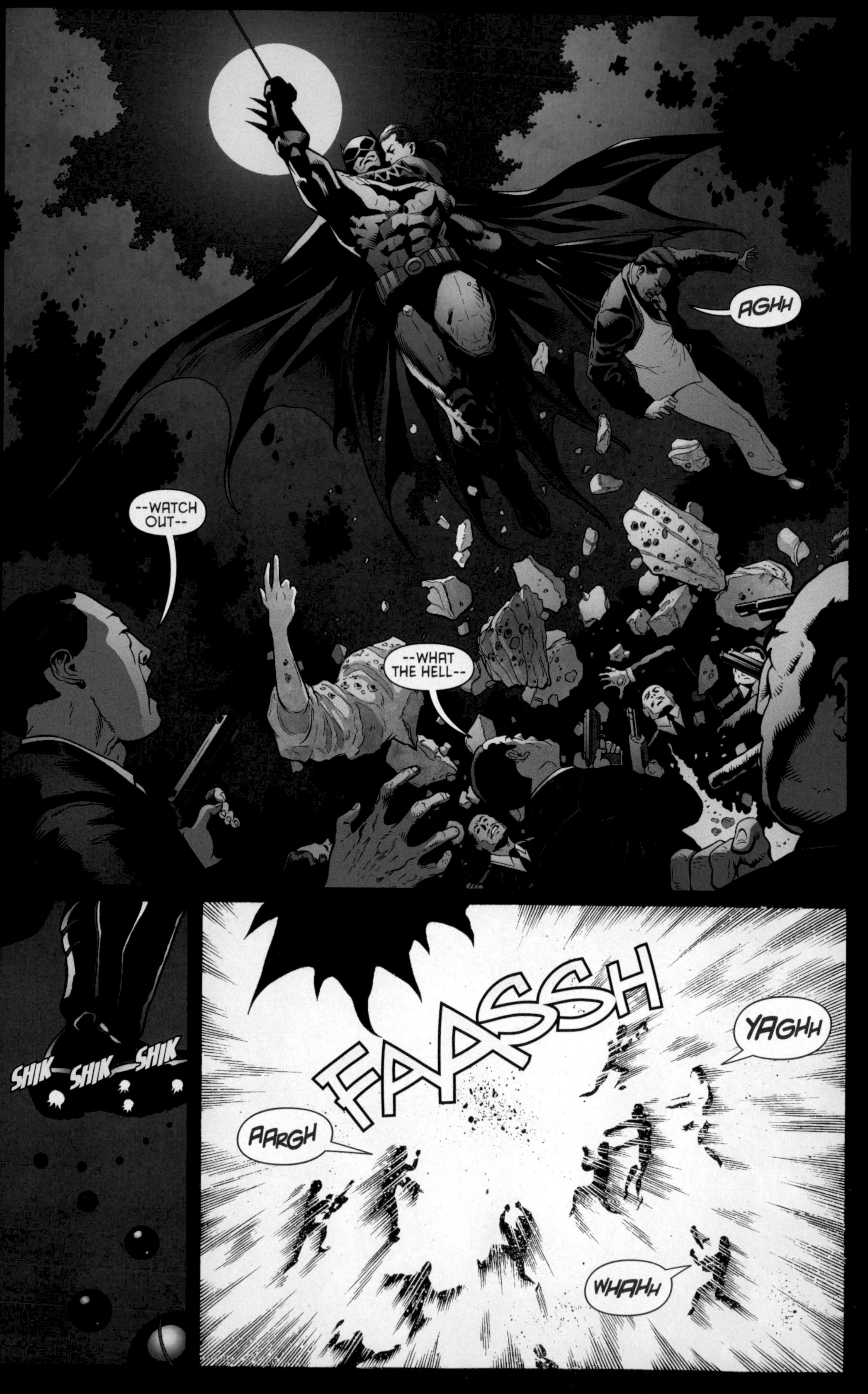
AGHH
--WATCH OUT--
--WHAT THE HELL--
SHIK—SHIK—SHIK
FAASSH
YAGHH
AARGH
WHAHH

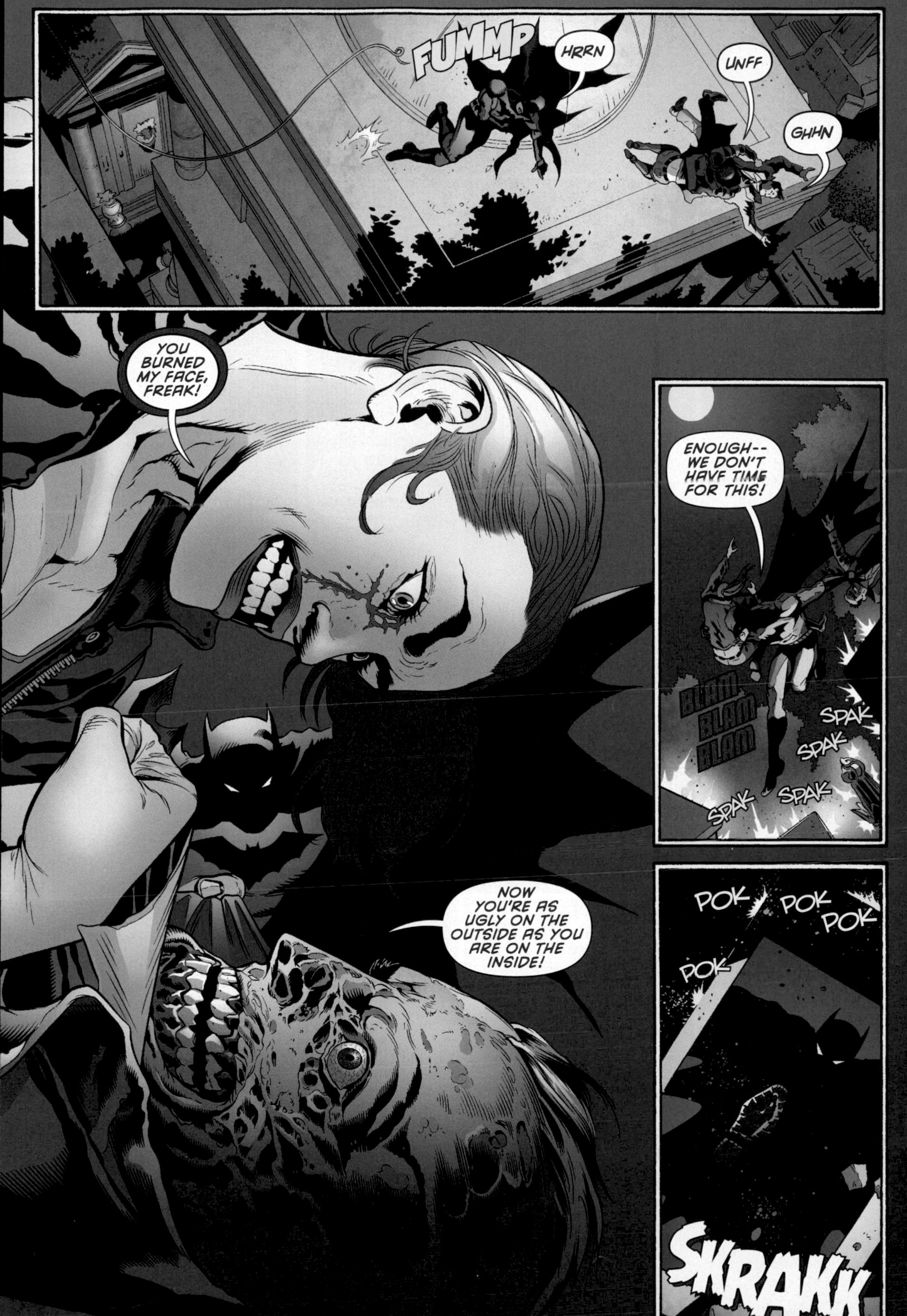
FUMMP
HRRN
UNFF
GHHN
YOU BURNED MY FACE, FREAK!
NOW YOU'RE AS UGLY ON THE OUTSIDE AS YOU ARE ON THE INSIDE!
ENOUGH-- WE DON'T HAVE TIME FOR THIS!
BLAM BLAM BLAM
SPAK
SPAK
SPAK
SPAK
POK
POK
POK
POK
SKRAKK

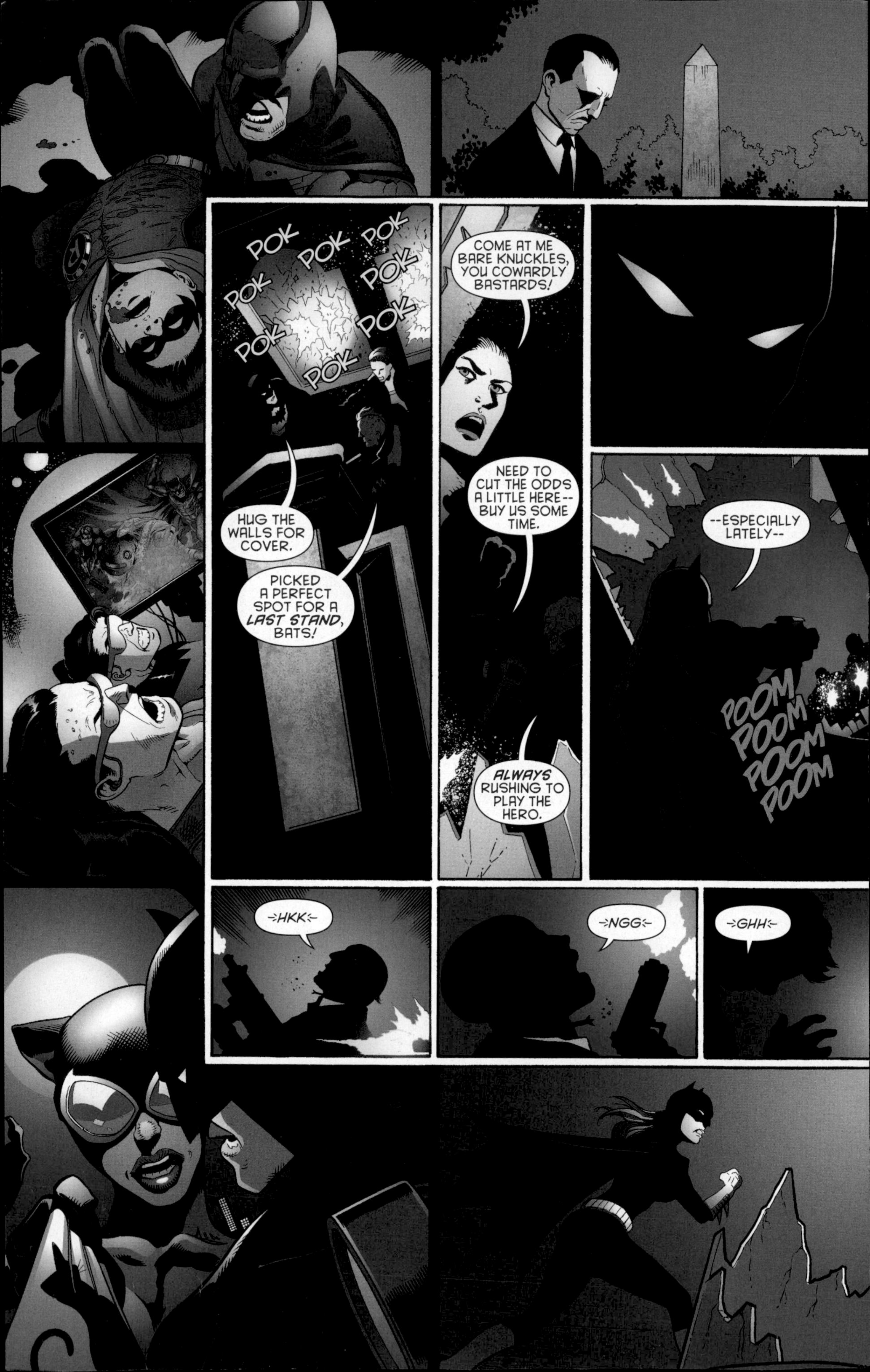
POK POK POK POK POK POK POK POK POK
HUG THE WALLS FOR COVER.
PICKED A PERFECT SPOT FOR A LAST STAND, BATS!
COME AT ME BARE KNUCKLES, YOU COWARDLY BASTARDS!
NEED TO CUT THE ODDS A LITTLE HERE-- BUY US SOME TIME.
ALWAYS RUSHING TO PLAY THE HERO.
--ESPECIALLY LATELY--
POOM POOM POOM POOM
HKK
NGG
GHH

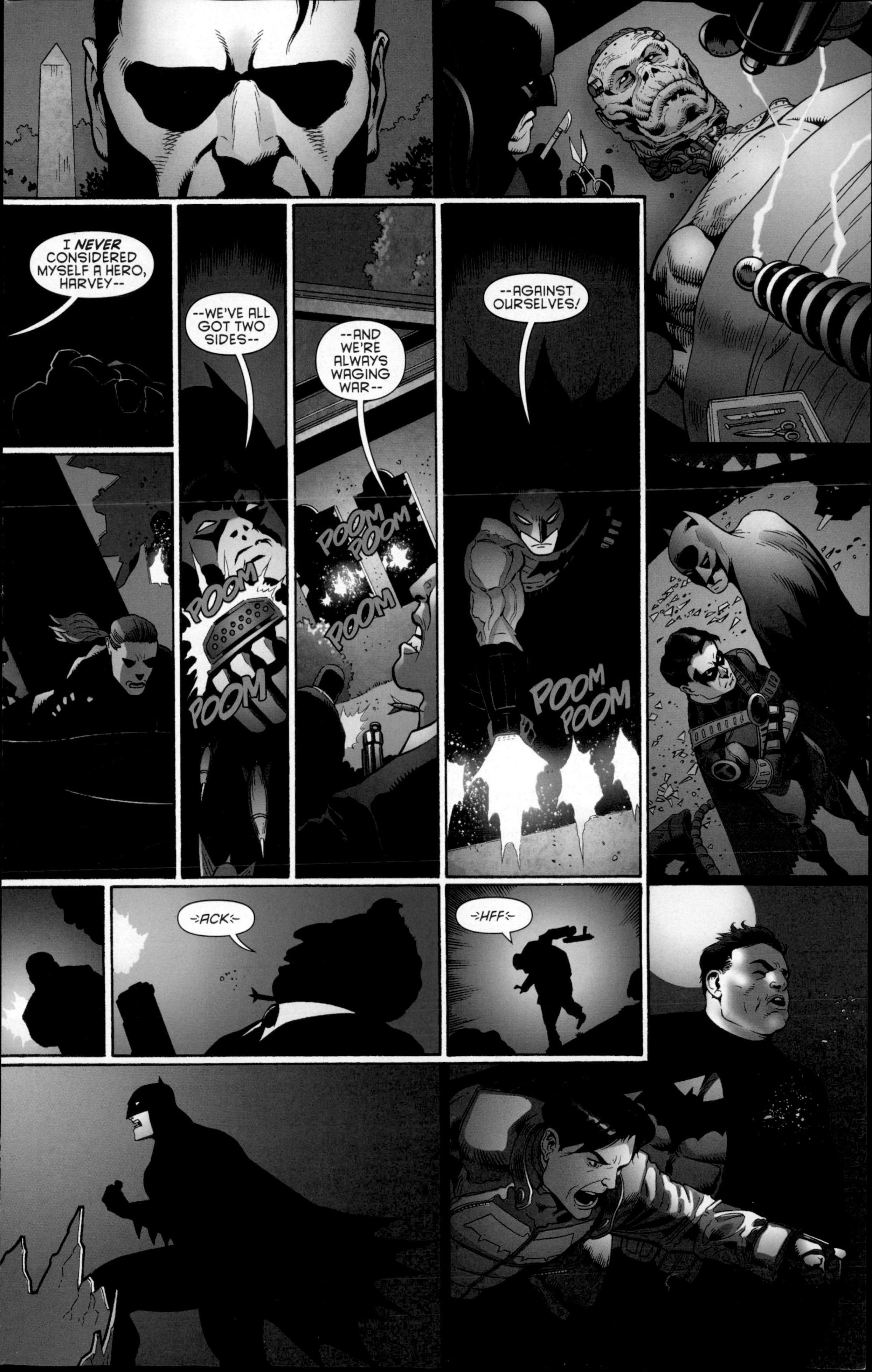
I NEVER CONSIDERED MYSELF A HERO, HARVEY--
--WE'VE ALL GOT TWO SIDES--
--AND WE'RE ALWAYS WAGING WAR--
--AGAINST OURSELVES!
POOM
POOM
POOM POOM
POOM
POOM POOM
ACK
HFF

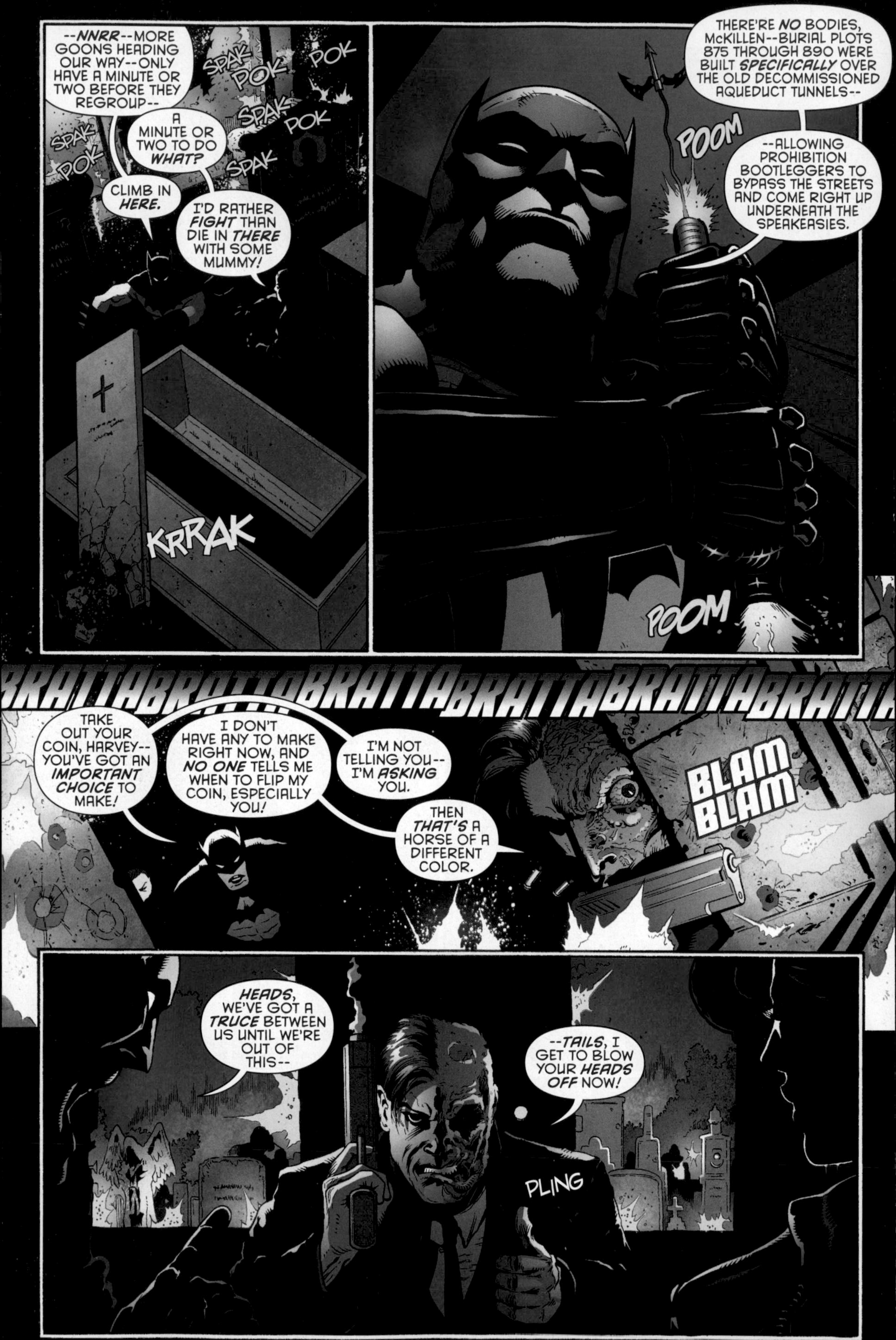

--NNRR--MORE GOONS HEADING OUR WAY--ONLY HAVE A MINUTE OR TWO BEFORE THEY REGROUP--
SPAK POK SPAK POK SPAK SPAK POK SPAK POK
A MINUTE OR TWO TO DO WHAT?
CLIMB IN HERE.
I'D RATHER FIGHT THAN DIE IN THERE WITH SOME MUMMY!
KRRAK
THERE'RE NO BODIES, McKILLEN--BURIAL PLOTS 875 THROUGH 890 WERE BUILT SPECIFICALLY OVER THE OLD DECOMMISSIONED AQUEDUCT TUNNELS--
POOM
--ALLOWING PROHIBITION BOOTLEGGERS TO BYPASS THE STREETS AND COME RIGHT UP UNDERNEATH THE SPEAKEASIES.
POOM
BRATTABRATTABRATTABRATTABRATTABRATTA
TAKE OUT YOUR COIN, HARVEY--YOU'VE GOT AN IMPORTANT CHOICE TO MAKE!
I DON'T HAVE ANY TO MAKE RIGHT NOW, AND NO ONE TELLS ME WHEN TO FLIP MY COIN, ESPECIALLY YOU!
I'M NOT TELLING YOU--I'M ASKING YOU.
THEN THAT'S A HORSE OF A DIFFERENT COLOR.
BLAM BLAM
HEADS, WE'VE GOT A TRUCE BETWEEN US UNTIL WE'RE OUT OF THIS--
--TAILS, I GET TO BLOW YOUR HEADS OFF NOW!
PLING

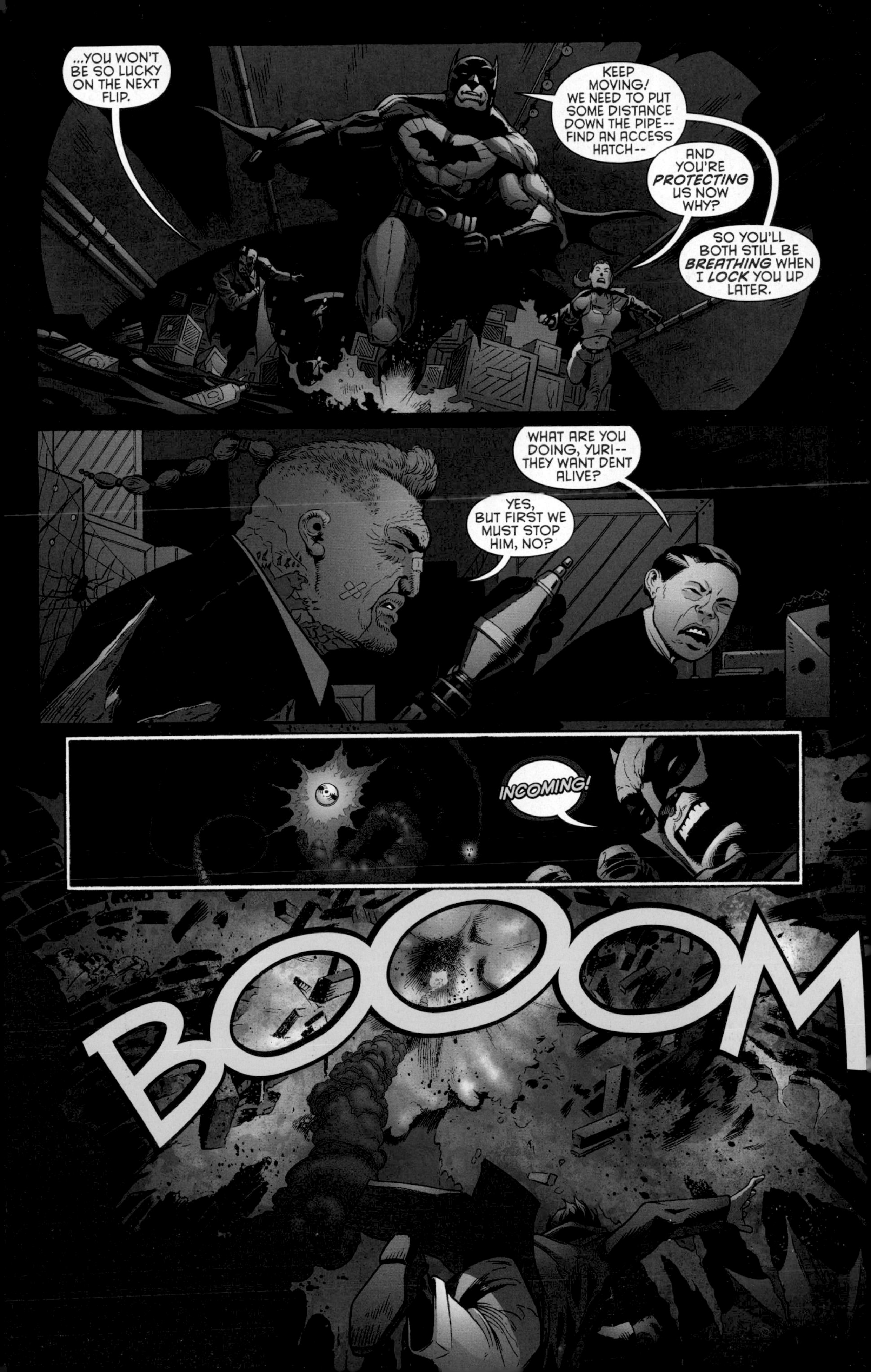
...YOU WON'T BE SO LUCKY ON THE NEXT FLIP.
KEEP MOVING! WE NEED TO PUT SOME DISTANCE DOWN THE PIPE-- FIND AN ACCESS HATCH--
AND YOU'RE PROTECTING US NOW WHY?
SO YOU'LL BOTH STILL BE BREATHING WHEN I LOCK YOU UP LATER.
WHAT ARE YOU DOING, YURI-- THEY WANT DENT ALIVE?
YES, BUT FIRST WE MUST STOP HIM, NO?
INCOMING!
BOOOOM

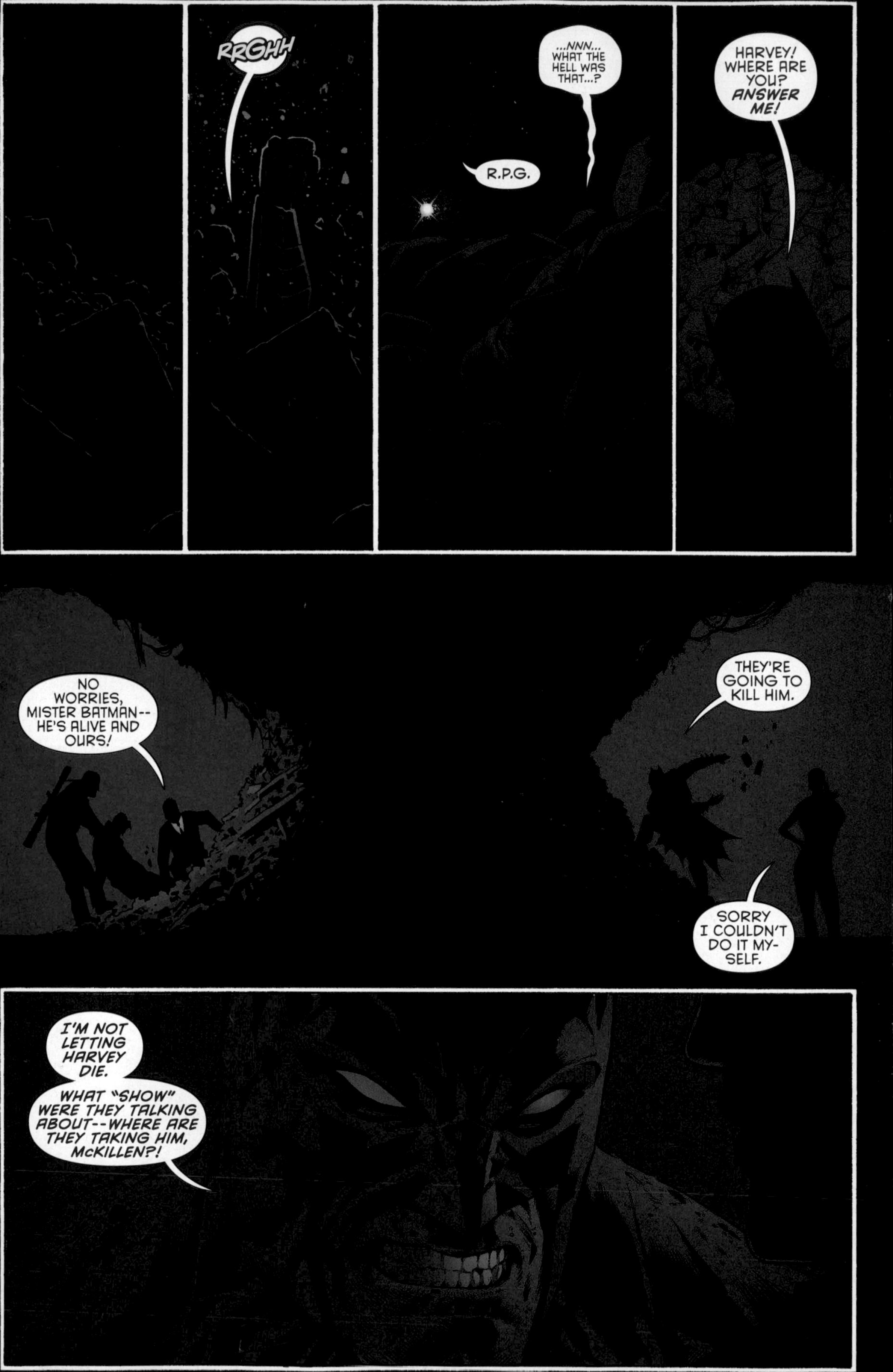
RRGHH
...NNN... WHAT THE HELL WAS THAT...?
R.P.G.
HARVEY! WHERE ARE YOU? ANSWER ME!
NO WORRIES, MISTER BATMAN-- HE'S ALIVE AND OURS!
THEY'RE GOING TO KILL HIM.
SORRY I COULDN'T DO IT MY-SELF.
I'M NOT LETTING HARVEY DIE.
WHAT "SHOW" WERE THEY TALKING ABOUT--WHERE ARE THEY TAKING HIM, McKILLEN?!

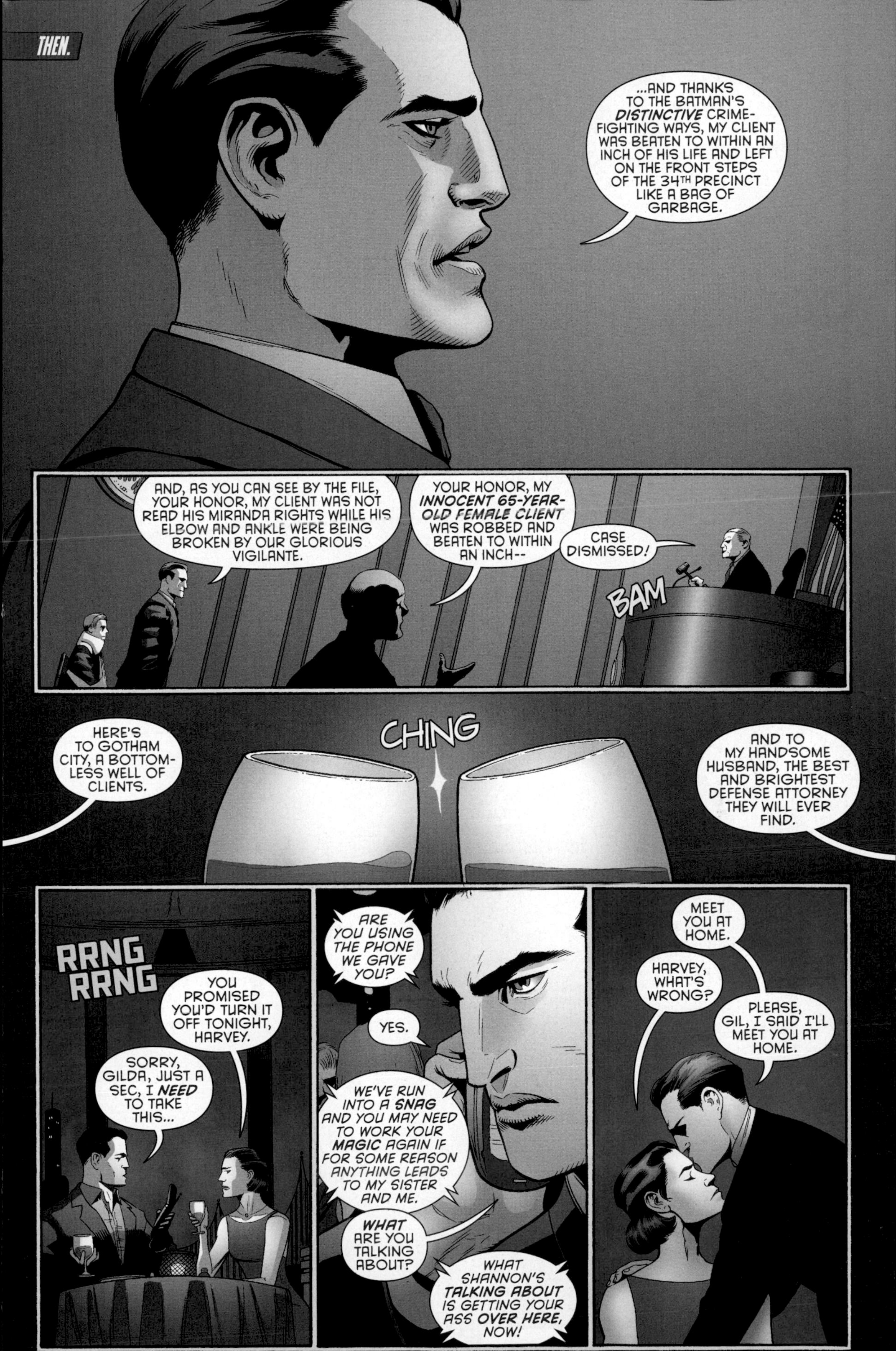
THEN.
...AND THANKS TO THE BATMAN'S DISTINCTIVE CRIME-FIGHTING WAYS, MY CLIENT WAS BEATEN TO WITHIN AN INCH OF HIS LIFE AND LEFT ON THE FRONT STEPS OF THE 34TH PRECINCT LIKE A BAG OF GARBAGE.
AND, AS YOU CAN SEE BY THE FILE, YOUR HONOR, MY CLIENT WAS NOT READ HIS MIRANDA RIGHTS WHILE HIS ELBOW AND ANKLE WERE BEING BROKEN BY OUR GLORIOUS VIGILANTE.
YOUR HONOR, MY INNOCENT 65-YEAR-OLD FEMALE CLIENT WAS ROBBED AND BEATEN TO WITHIN AN INCH--
CASE DISMISSED!
BAM
HERE'S TO GOTHAM CITY, A BOTTOMLESS WELL OF CLIENTS.
CHING
AND TO MY HANDSOME HUSBAND, THE BEST AND BRIGHTEST DEFENSE ATTORNEY THEY WILL EVER FIND.
RRNG RRNG
YOU PROMISED YOU'D TURN IT OFF TONIGHT, HARVEY.
SORRY, GILDA, JUST A SEC, I NEED TO TAKE THIS...
ARE YOU USING THE PHONE WE GAVE YOU?
YES.
WE'VE RUN INTO A SNAG AND YOU MAY NEED TO WORK YOUR MAGIC AGAIN IF FOR SOME REASON ANYTHING LEADS TO MY SISTER AND ME.
WHAT ARE YOU TALKING ABOUT?
WHAT SHANNON'S TALKING ABOUT IS GETTING YOUR ASS OVER HERE, NOW!
MEET YOU AT HOME.
HARVEY, WHAT'S WRONG?
PLEASE, GIL, I SAID I'LL MEET YOU AT HOME.

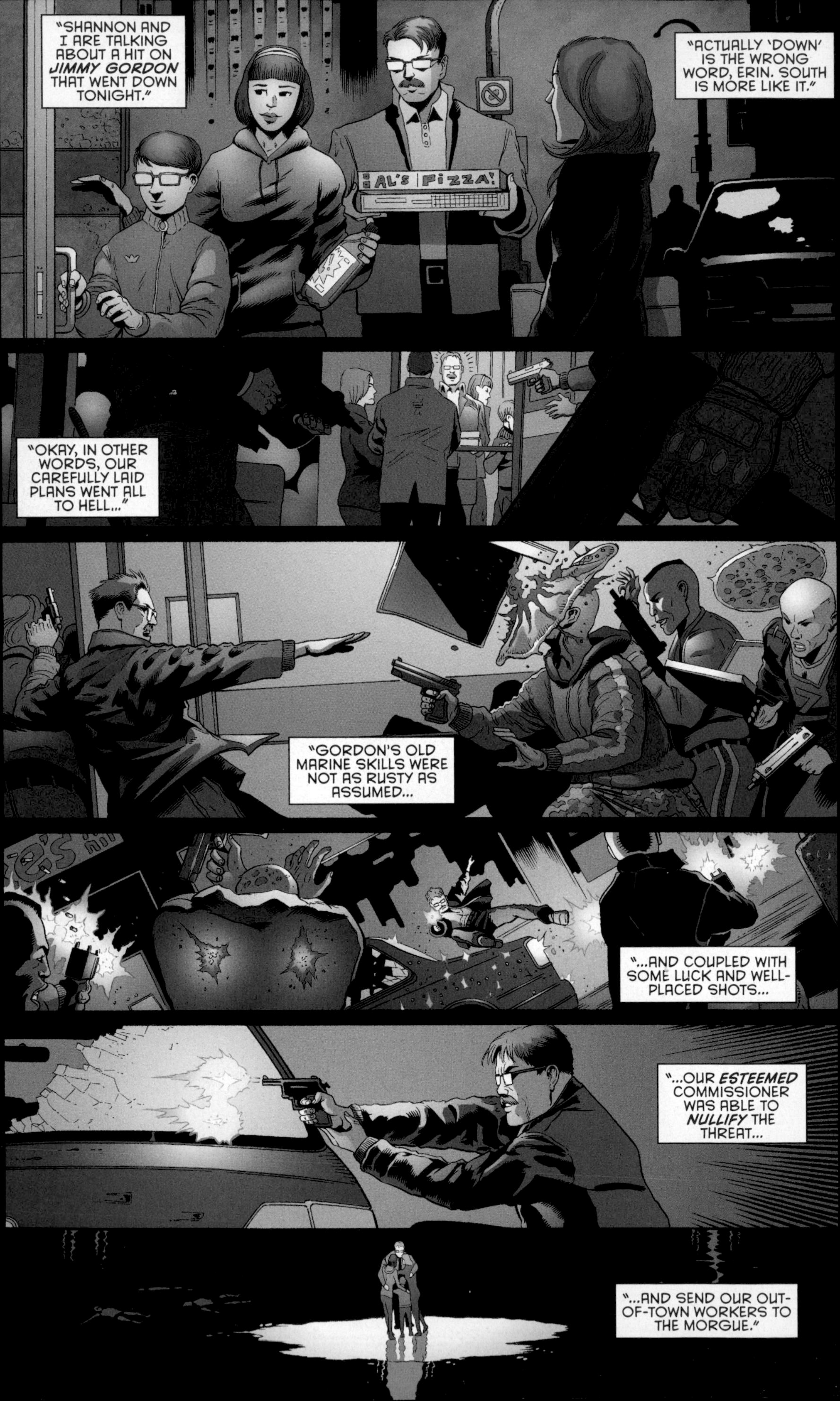
"SHANNON AND I ARE TALKING ABOUT A HIT ON *JIMMY GORDON* THAT WENT DOWN TONIGHT."
"ACTUALLY 'DOWN' IS THE WRONG WORD, ERIN. SOUTH IS MORE LIKE IT."
AL'S PIZZA!
"OKAY, IN OTHER WORDS, OUR CAREFULLY LAID PLANS WENT ALL TO HELL..."
"GORDON'S OLD MARINE SKILLS WERE NOT AS RUSTY AS ASSUMED...
"...AND COUPLED WITH SOME LUCK AND WELL-PLACED SHOTS...
"...OUR *ESTEEMED* COMMISSIONER WAS ABLE TO *NULLIFY* THE THREAT...
"...AND SEND OUR OUT-OF-TOWN WORKERS TO THE MORGUE."

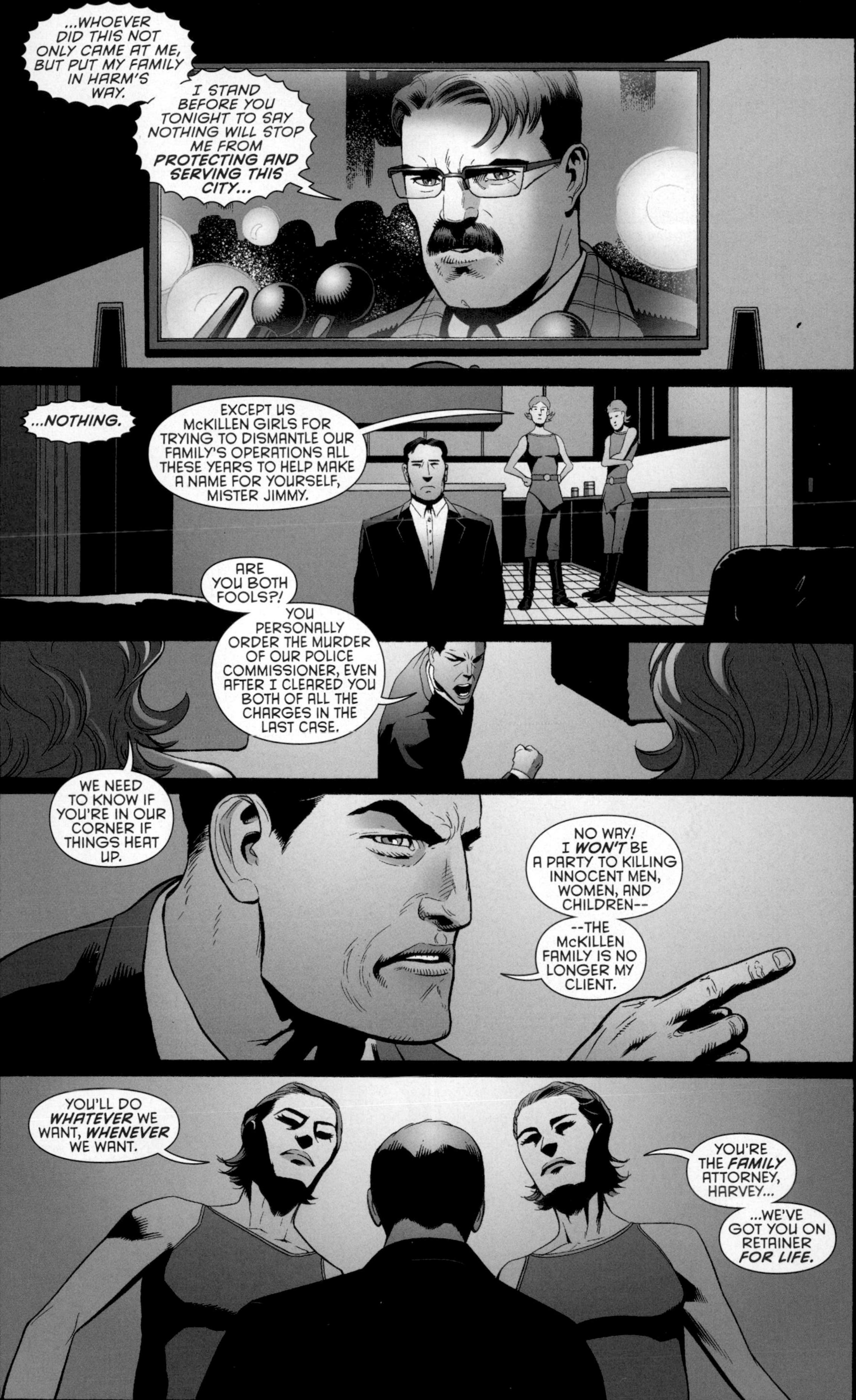
...WHOEVER DID THIS NOT ONLY CAME AT ME, BUT PUT MY FAMILY IN HARM'S WAY.
I STAND BEFORE YOU TONIGHT TO SAY NOTHING WILL STOP ME FROM PROTECTING AND SERVING THIS CITY...
...NOTHING.
EXCEPT US McKILLEN GIRLS FOR TRYING TO DISMANTLE OUR FAMILY'S OPERATIONS ALL THESE YEARS TO HELP MAKE A NAME FOR YOURSELF, MISTER JIMMY.
ARE YOU BOTH FOOLS?!
YOU PERSONALLY ORDER THE MURDER OF OUR POLICE COMMISSIONER, EVEN AFTER I CLEARED YOU BOTH OF ALL THE CHARGES IN THE LAST CASE.
WE NEED TO KNOW IF YOU'RE IN OUR CORNER IF THINGS HEAT UP.
NO WAY! I WON'T BE A PARTY TO KILLING INNOCENT MEN, WOMEN, AND CHILDREN--
--THE McKILLEN FAMILY IS NO LONGER MY CLIENT.
YOU'LL DO WHATEVER WE WANT, WHENEVER WE WANT.
YOU'RE THE FAMILY ATTORNEY, HARVEY...
...WE'VE GOT YOU ON RETAINER FOR LIFE.

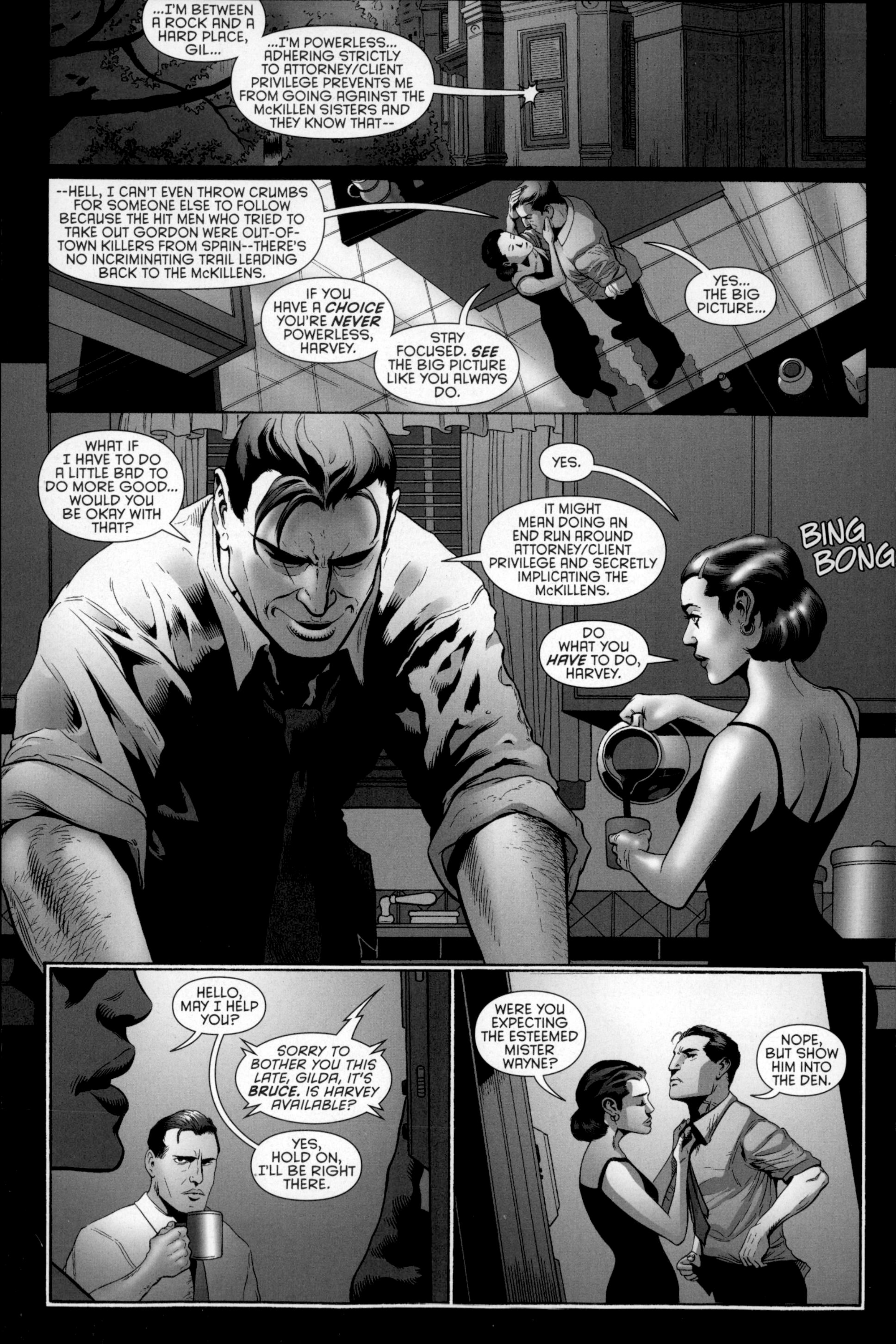
...I'M BETWEEN A ROCK AND A HARD PLACE, GIL...
...I'M POWERLESS... ADHERING STRICTLY TO ATTORNEY/CLIENT PRIVILEGE PREVENTS ME FROM GOING AGAINST THE McKILLEN SISTERS AND THEY KNOW THAT--
--HELL, I CAN'T EVEN THROW CRUMBS FOR SOMEONE ELSE TO FOLLOW BECAUSE THE HIT MEN WHO TRIED TO TAKE OUT GORDON WERE OUT-OF-TOWN KILLERS FROM SPAIN--THERE'S NO INCRIMINATING TRAIL LEADING BACK TO THE McKILLENS.
IF YOU HAVE A CHOICE YOU'RE NEVER POWERLESS, HARVEY.
STAY FOCUSED. SEE THE BIG PICTURE LIKE YOU ALWAYS DO.
YES... THE BIG PICTURE...
WHAT IF I HAVE TO DO A LITTLE BAD TO DO MORE GOOD... WOULD YOU BE OKAY WITH THAT?
YES.
IT MIGHT MEAN DOING AN END RUN AROUND ATTORNEY/CLIENT PRIVILEGE AND SECRETLY IMPLICATING THE McKILLENS.
DO WHAT YOU HAVE TO DO, HARVEY.
BING BONG
HELLO, MAY I HELP YOU?
SORRY TO BOTHER YOU THIS LATE, GILDA, IT'S BRUCE. IS HARVEY AVAILABLE?
YES, HOLD ON, I'LL BE RIGHT THERE.
WERE YOU EXPECTING THE ESTEEMED MISTER WAYNE?
NOPE, BUT SHOW HIM INTO THE DEN.

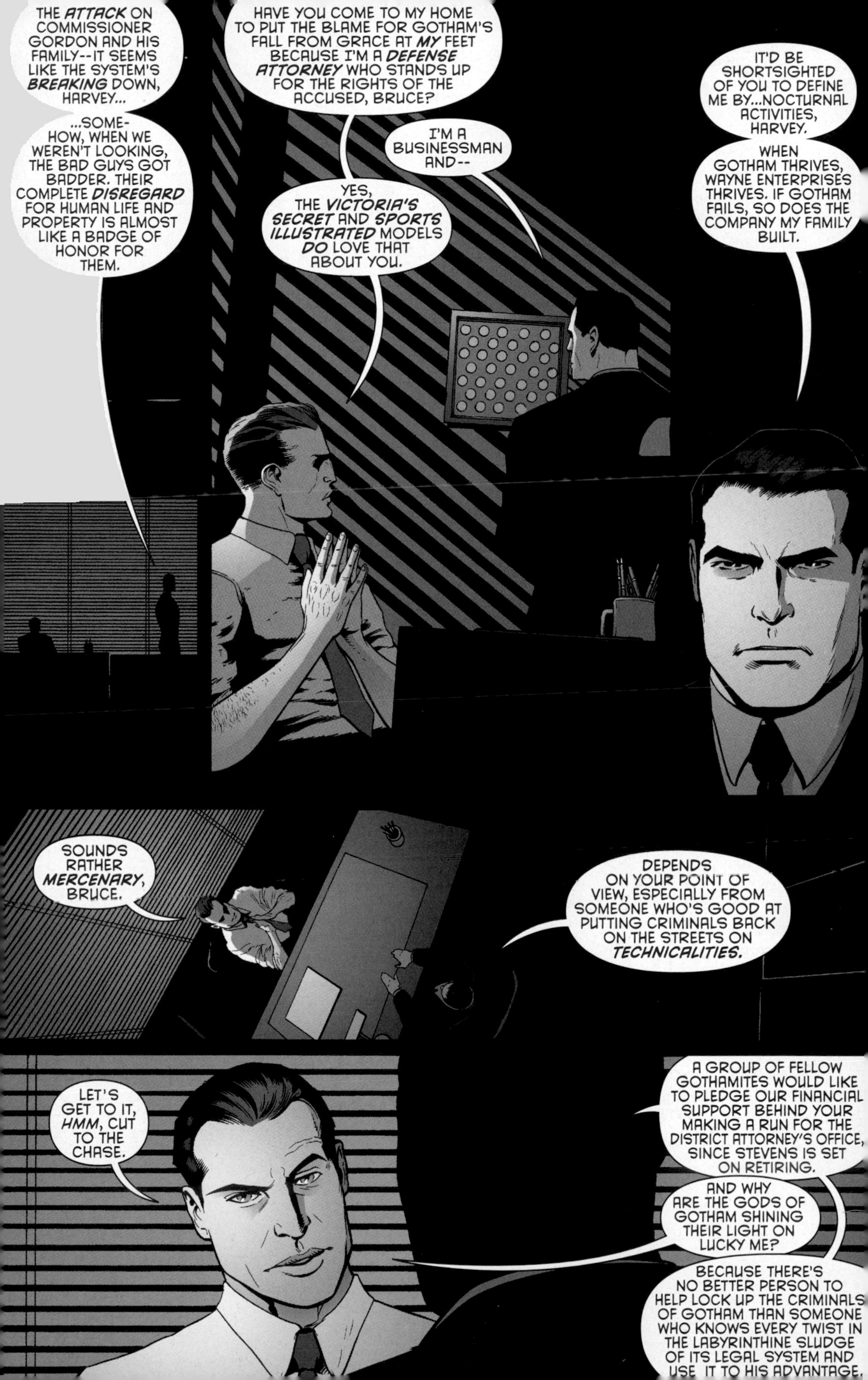
THE ATTACK ON COMMISSIONER GORDON AND HIS FAMILY--IT SEEMS LIKE THE SYSTEM'S BREAKING DOWN, HARVEY...
...SOME-HOW, WHEN WE WEREN'T LOOKING, THE BAD GUYS GOT BADDER. THEIR COMPLETE DISREGARD FOR HUMAN LIFE AND PROPERTY IS ALMOST LIKE A BADGE OF HONOR FOR THEM.
HAVE YOU COME TO MY HOME TO PUT THE BLAME FOR GOTHAM'S FALL FROM GRACE AT MY FEET BECAUSE I'M A DEFENSE ATTORNEY WHO STANDS UP FOR THE RIGHTS OF THE ACCUSED, BRUCE?
I'M A BUSINESSMAN AND--
YES, THE VICTORIA'S SECRET AND SPORTS ILLUSTRATED MODELS DO LOVE THAT ABOUT YOU.
IT'D BE SHORTSIGHTED OF YOU TO DEFINE ME BY...NOCTURNAL ACTIVITIES, HARVEY.
WHEN GOTHAM THRIVES, WAYNE ENTERPRISES THRIVES. IF GOTHAM FAILS, SO DOES THE COMPANY MY FAMILY BUILT.
SOUNDS RATHER MERCENARY, BRUCE.
DEPENDS ON YOUR POINT OF VIEW, ESPECIALLY FROM SOMEONE WHO'S GOOD AT PUTTING CRIMINALS BACK ON THE STREETS ON TECHNICALITIES.
LET'S GET TO IT, HMM, CUT TO THE CHASE.
A GROUP OF FELLOW GOTHAMITES WOULD LIKE TO PLEDGE OUR FINANCIAL SUPPORT BEHIND YOUR MAKING A RUN FOR THE DISTRICT ATTORNEY'S OFFICE, SINCE STEVENS IS SET ON RETIRING.
AND WHY ARE THE GODS OF GOTHAM SHINING THEIR LIGHT ON LUCKY ME?
BECAUSE THERE'S NO BETTER PERSON TO HELP LOCK UP THE CRIMINALS OF GOTHAM THAN SOMEONE WHO KNOWS EVERY TWIST IN THE LABYRINTHINE SLUDGE OF ITS LEGAL SYSTEM AND USE IT TO HIS ADVANTAGE.

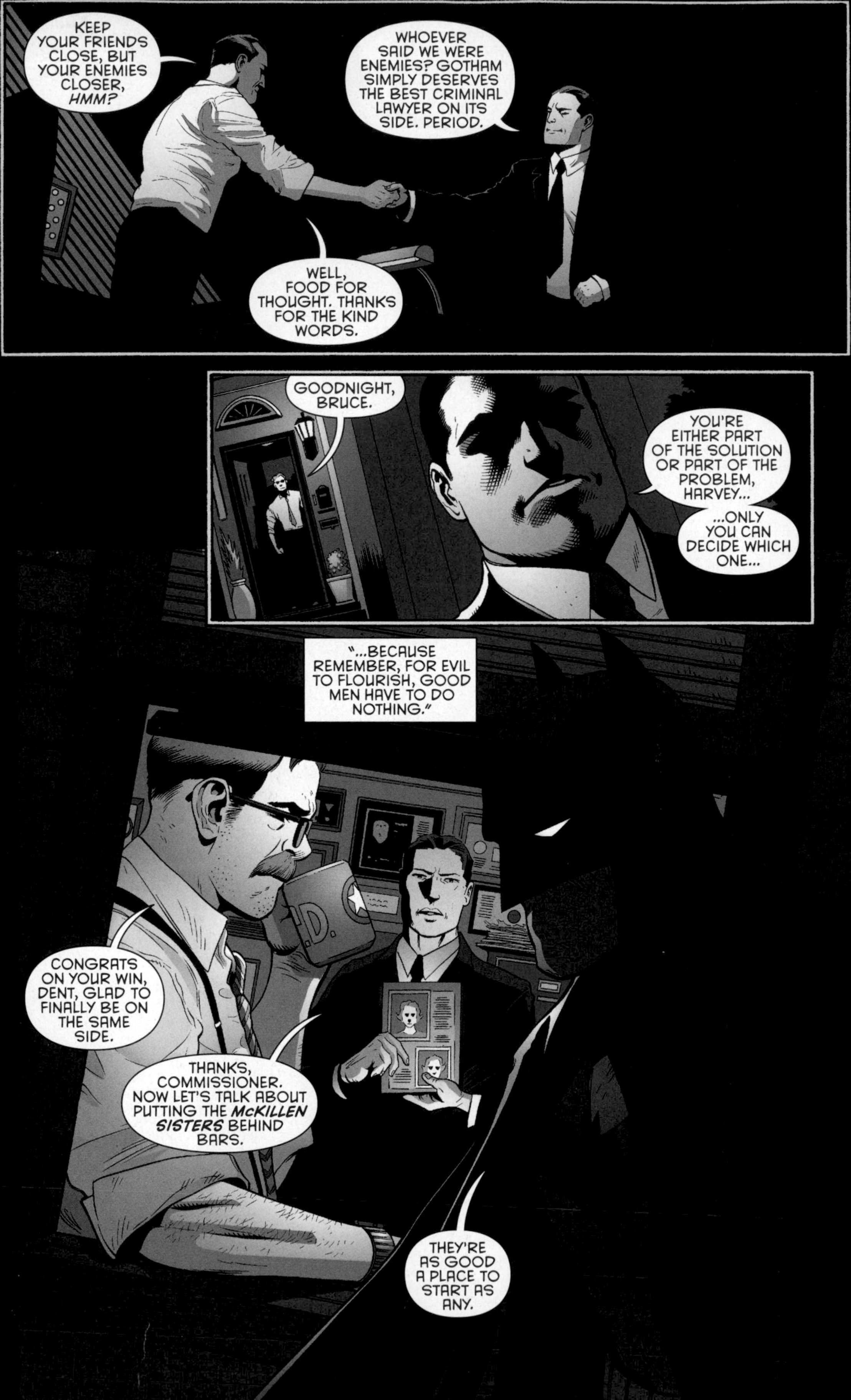
KEEP YOUR FRIENDS CLOSE, BUT YOUR ENEMIES CLOSER, *HMM?*
WHOEVER SAID WE WERE ENEMIES? GOTHAM SIMPLY DESERVES THE BEST CRIMINAL LAWYER ON ITS SIDE. PERIOD.
WELL, FOOD FOR THOUGHT. THANKS FOR THE KIND WORDS.
GOODNIGHT, BRUCE.
YOU'RE EITHER PART OF THE SOLUTION OR PART OF THE PROBLEM, HARVEY...
...ONLY YOU CAN DECIDE WHICH ONE...
"...BECAUSE REMEMBER, FOR EVIL TO FLOURISH, GOOD MEN HAVE TO DO NOTHING."
CONGRATS ON YOUR WIN, DENT, GLAD TO FINALLY BE ON THE SAME SIDE.
THANKS, COMMISSIONER. NOW LET'S TALK ABOUT PUTTING THE ***McKILLEN SISTERS*** BEHIND BARS.
THEY'RE AS GOOD A PLACE TO START AS ANY.

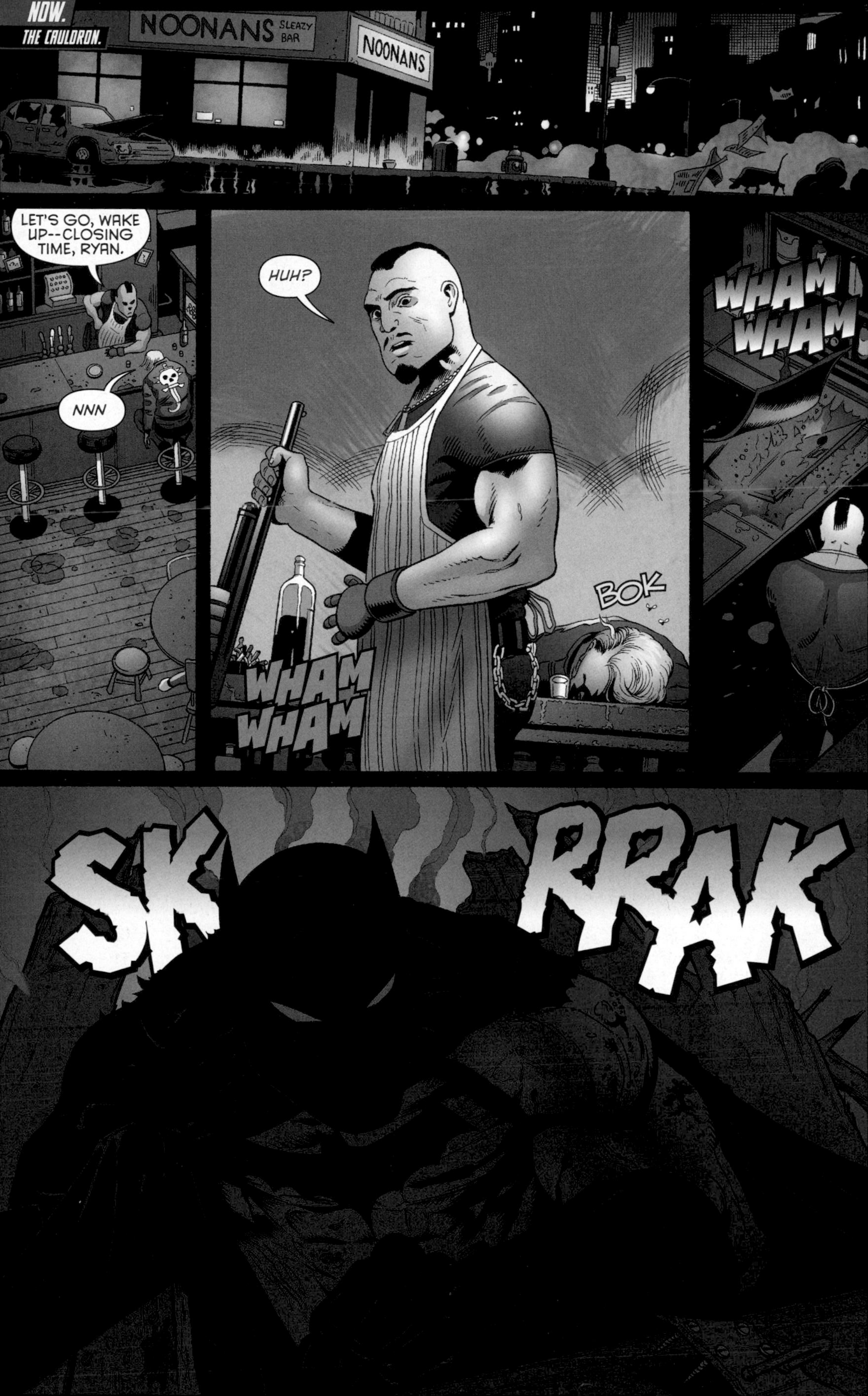
NOW.
THE CAULDRON.
NOONANS SLEAZY BAR
NOONANS
LET'S GO, WAKE UP--CLOSING TIME, RYAN.
NNN
HUH?
BOK
WHAM WHAM
WHAM WHAM
SK RRAK

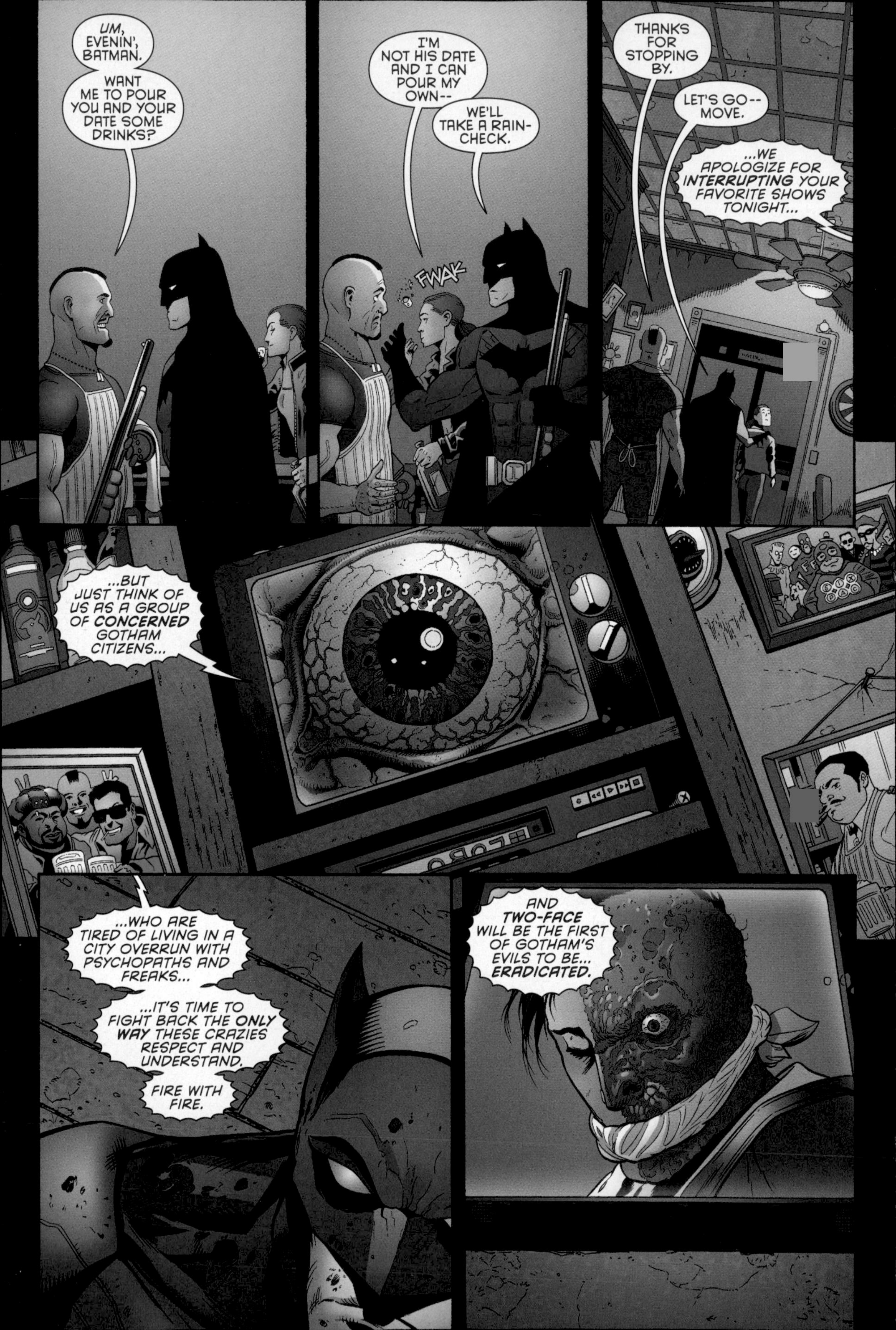
UM, EVENIN', BATMAN.
WANT ME TO POUR YOU AND YOUR DATE SOME DRINKS?
I'M NOT HIS DATE AND I CAN POUR MY OWN--
FWAK
WE'LL TAKE A RAIN-CHECK.
THANKS FOR STOPPING BY.
LET'S GO-- MOVE.
...WE APOLOGIZE FOR INTERRUPTING YOUR FAVORITE SHOWS TONIGHT...
...BUT JUST THINK OF US AS A GROUP OF CONCERNED GOTHAM CITIZENS...
...WHO ARE TIRED OF LIVING IN A CITY OVERRUN WITH PSYCHOPATHS AND FREAKS...
...IT'S TIME TO FIGHT BACK THE ONLY WAY THESE CRAZIES RESPECT AND UNDERSTAND.
FIRE WITH FIRE.
AND TWO-FACE WILL BE THE FIRST OF GOTHAM'S EVILS TO BE... ERADICATED.

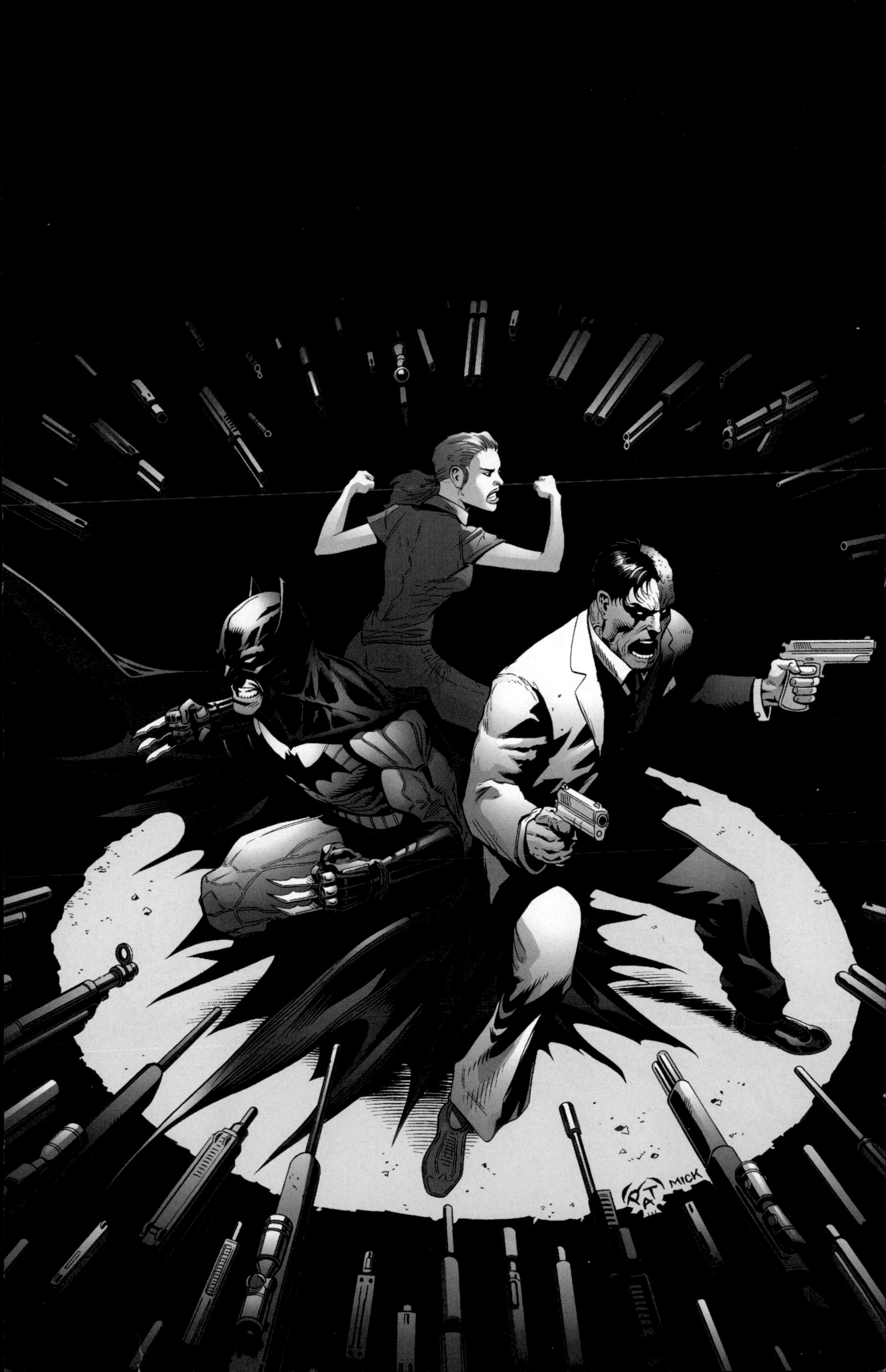

THE BIG BURN: INFERNO

PATRICK GLEASON penciller **MICK GRAY** with **PATRICK GLEASON** inkers **JOHN KALISZ** colorist cover art by **GLEASON, GRAY & KALISZ**

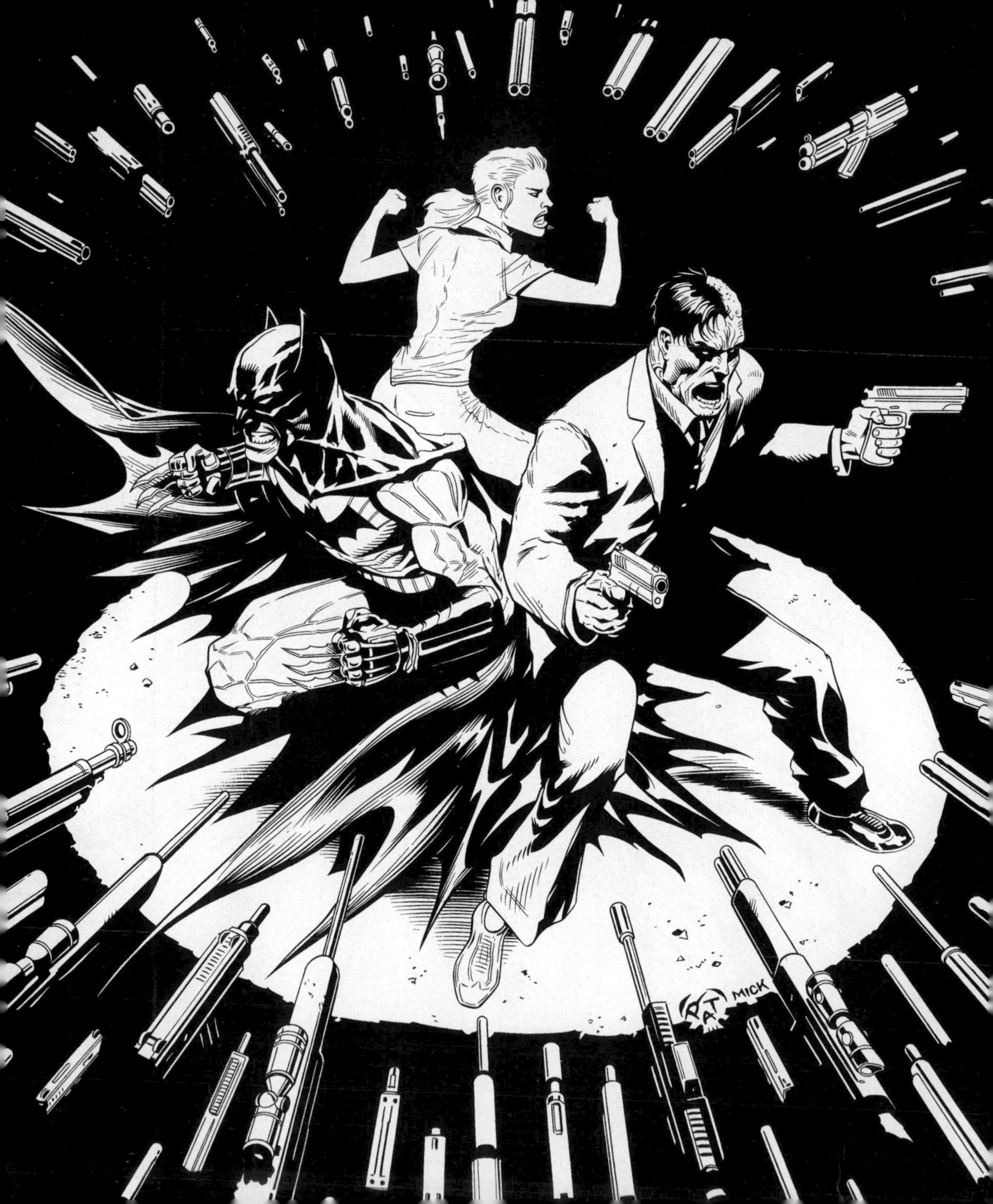
PAT
MICK

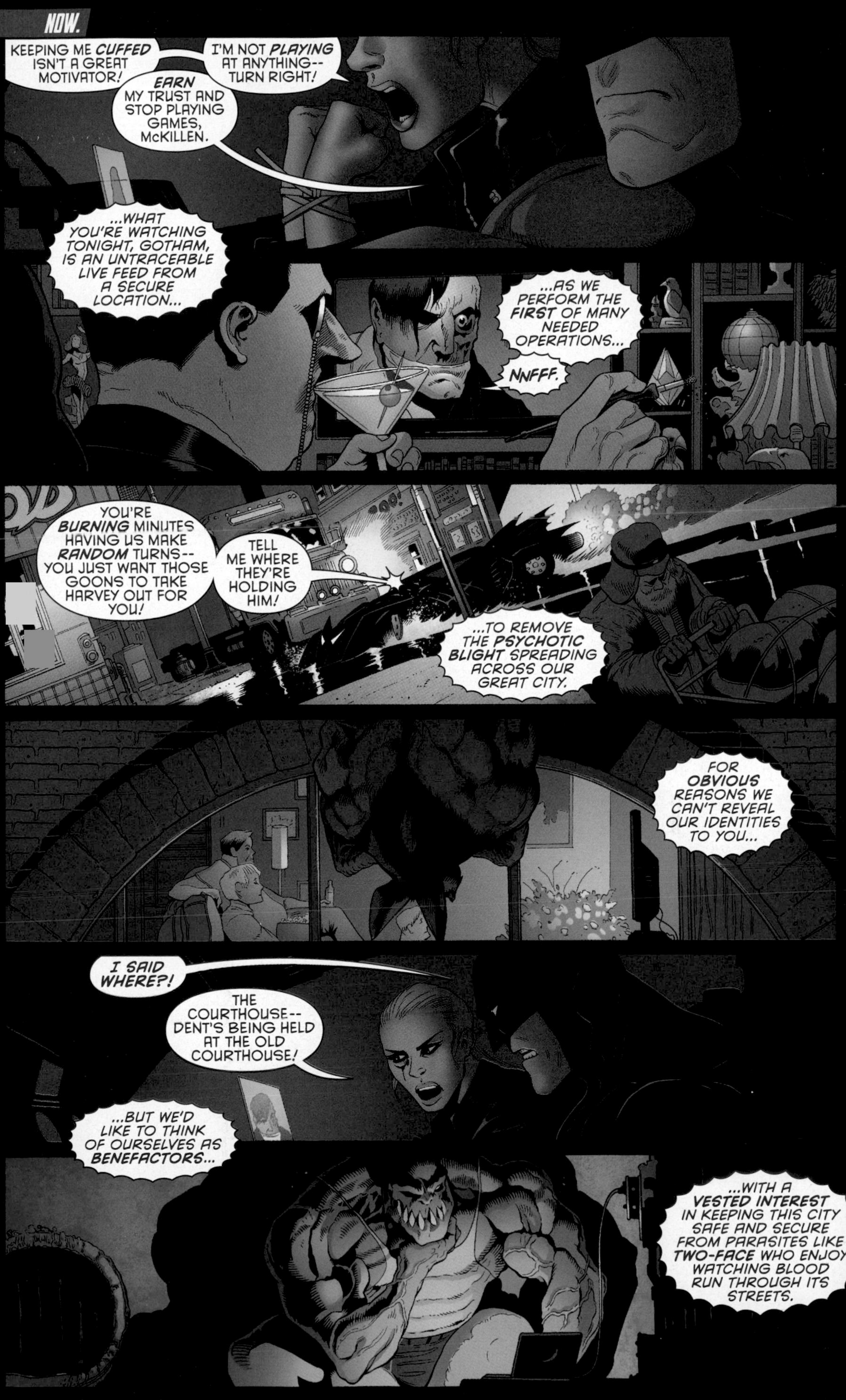
NOW.
KEEPING ME CUFFED ISN'T A GREAT MOTIVATOR!
I'M NOT PLAYING AT ANYTHING-- TURN RIGHT!
EARN MY TRUST AND STOP PLAYING GAMES, McKILLEN.
...WHAT YOU'RE WATCHING TONIGHT, GOTHAM, IS AN UNTRACEABLE LIVE FEED FROM A SECURE LOCATION...
...AS WE PERFORM THE FIRST OF MANY NEEDED OPERATIONS...
NNFFF.
YOU'RE BURNING MINUTES HAVING US MAKE RANDOM TURNS-- YOU JUST WANT THOSE GOONS TO TAKE HARVEY OUT FOR YOU!
TELL ME WHERE THEY'RE HOLDING HIM!
...TO REMOVE THE PSYCHOTIC BLIGHT SPREADING ACROSS OUR GREAT CITY.
FOR OBVIOUS REASONS WE CAN'T REVEAL OUR IDENTITIES TO YOU...
I SAID WHERE?!
THE COURTHOUSE-- DENT'S BEING HELD AT THE OLD COURTHOUSE!
...BUT WE'D LIKE TO THINK OF OURSELVES AS BENEFACTORS...
...WITH A VESTED INTEREST IN KEEPING THIS CITY SAFE AND SECURE FROM PARASITES LIKE TWO-FACE WHO ENJOY WATCHING BLOOD RUN THROUGH ITS STREETS.

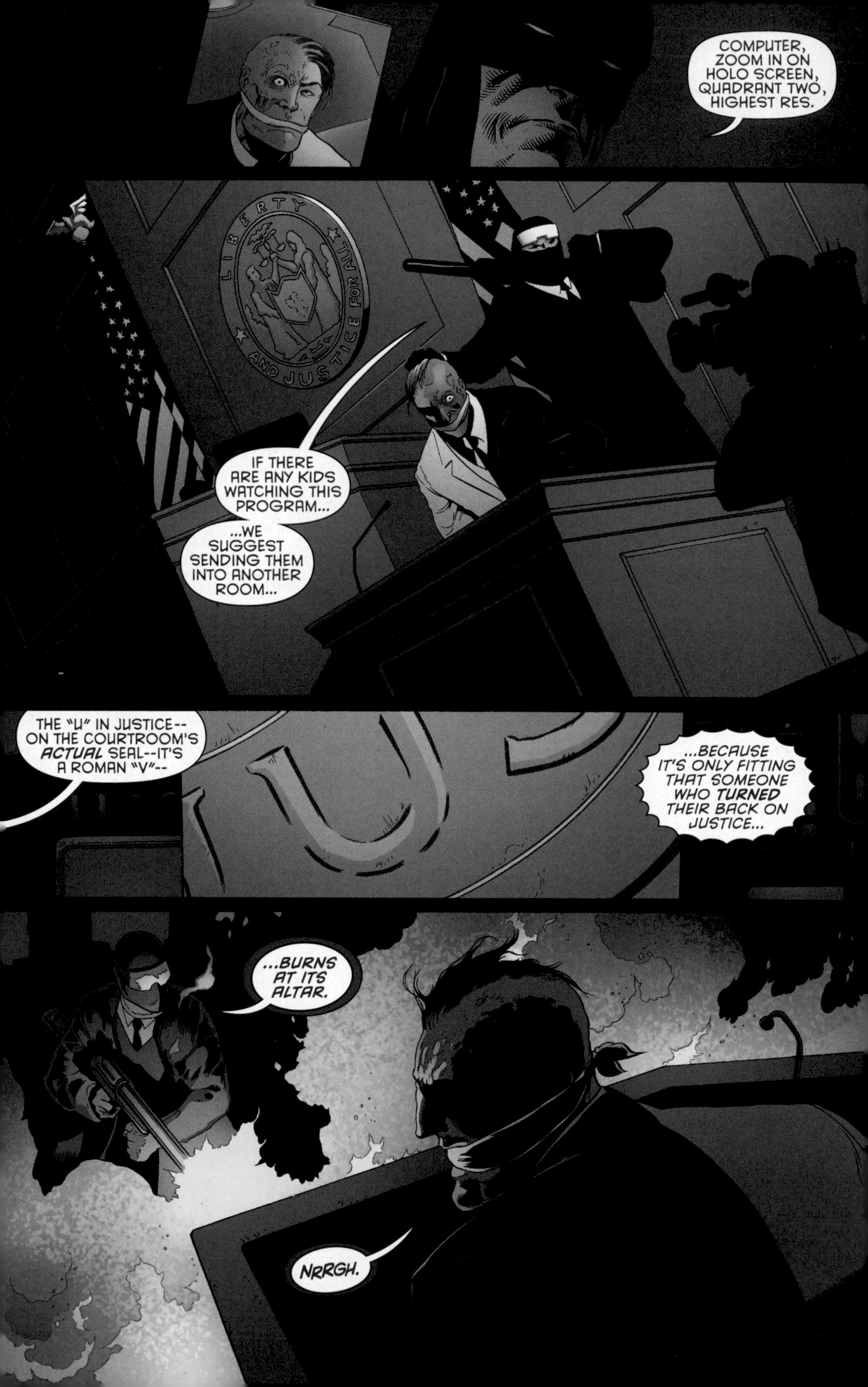
COMPUTER, ZOOM IN ON HOLO SCREEN, QUADRANT TWO, HIGHEST RES.
LIBERTY AND JUSTICE FOR ALL
IF THERE ARE ANY KIDS WATCHING THIS PROGRAM...
...WE SUGGEST SENDING THEM INTO ANOTHER ROOM...
THE "U" IN JUSTICE--ON THE COURTROOM'S ACTUAL SEAL--IT'S A ROMAN "V"--
...BECAUSE IT'S ONLY FITTING THAT SOMEONE WHO TURNED THEIR BACK ON JUSTICE...
...BURNS AT ITS ALTAR.
NRRGH.

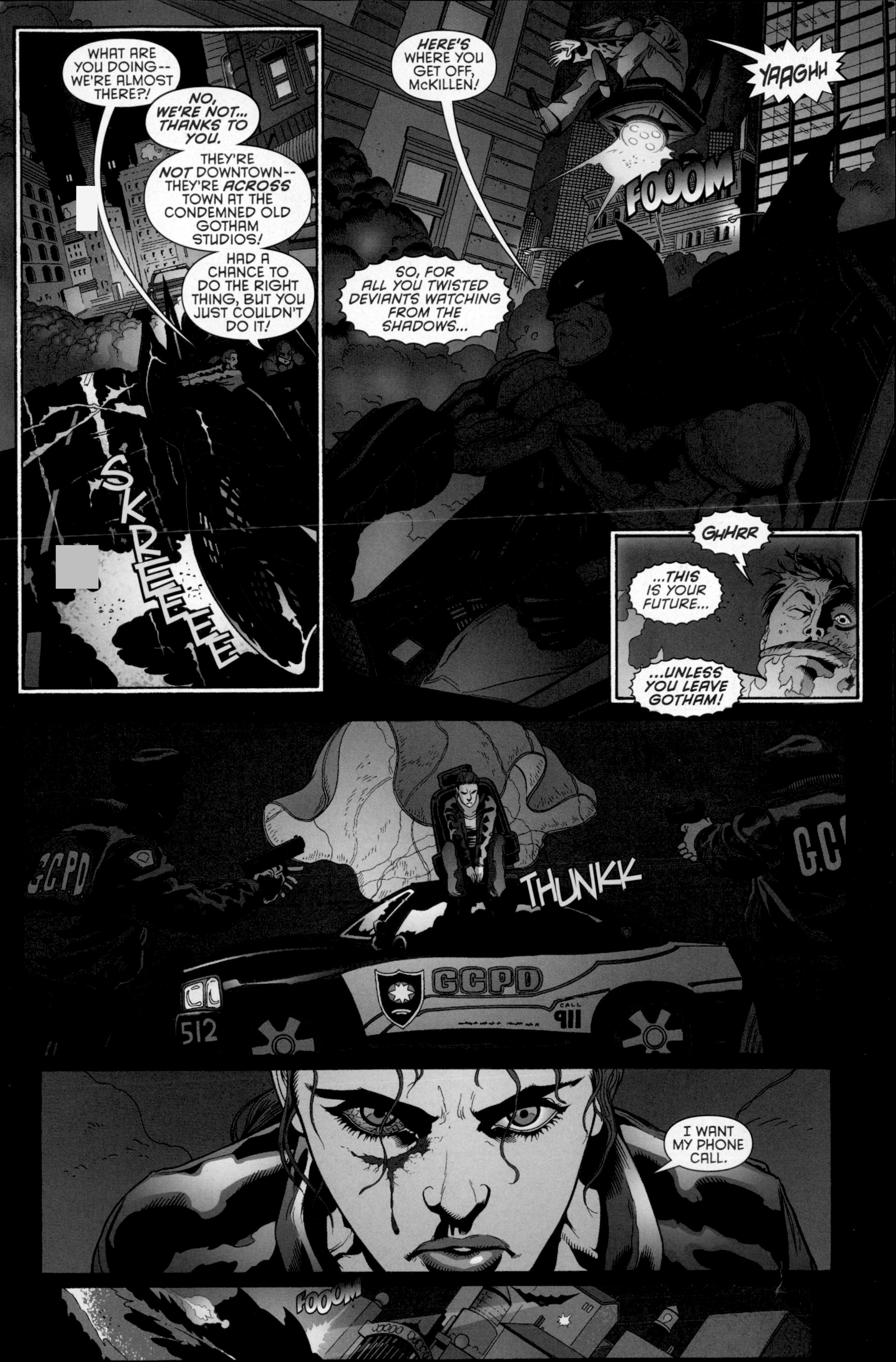

WHAT ARE YOU DOING-- WE'RE ALMOST THERE?!
NO, WE'RE NOT... THANKS TO YOU.
THEY'RE NOT DOWNTOWN-- THEY'RE ACROSS TOWN AT THE CONDEMNED OLD GOTHAM STUDIOS!
HAD A CHANCE TO DO THE RIGHT THING, BUT YOU JUST COULDN'T DO IT!
SKREEEEE
HERE'S WHERE YOU GET OFF, McKILLEN!
YAAGHH
FOOOM
SO, FOR ALL YOU TWISTED DEVIANTS WATCHING FROM THE SHADOWS...
GHHRR
...THIS IS YOUR FUTURE...
...UNLESS YOU LEAVE GOTHAM!
G.C.PD
G.C
THUNKK
GCPD
512
CALL 911
I WANT MY PHONE CALL.
FOOOM

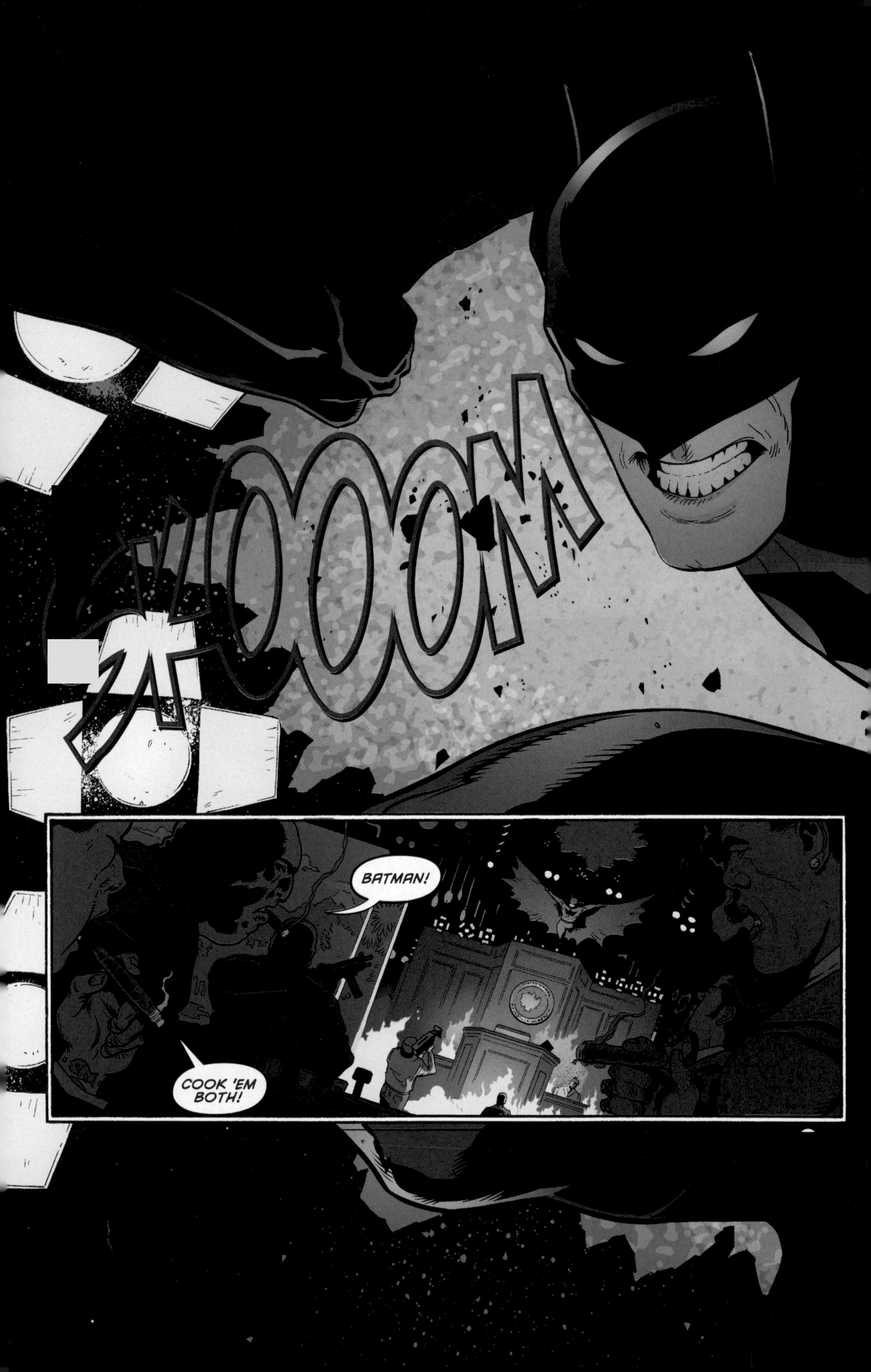

FWOOOM
BATMAN!
COOK 'EM BOTH!

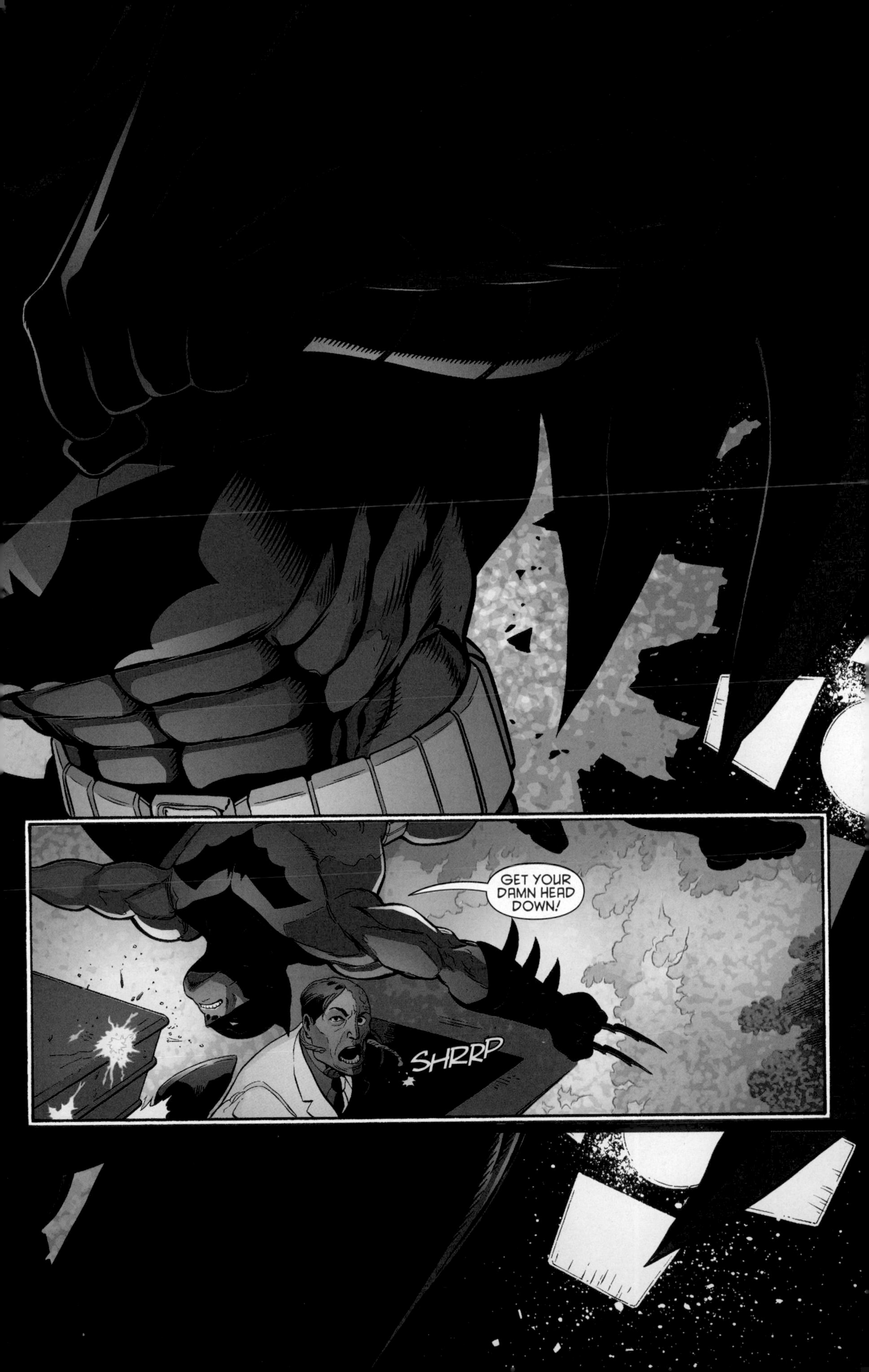
GET YOUR DAMN HEAD DOWN!
SHRRP

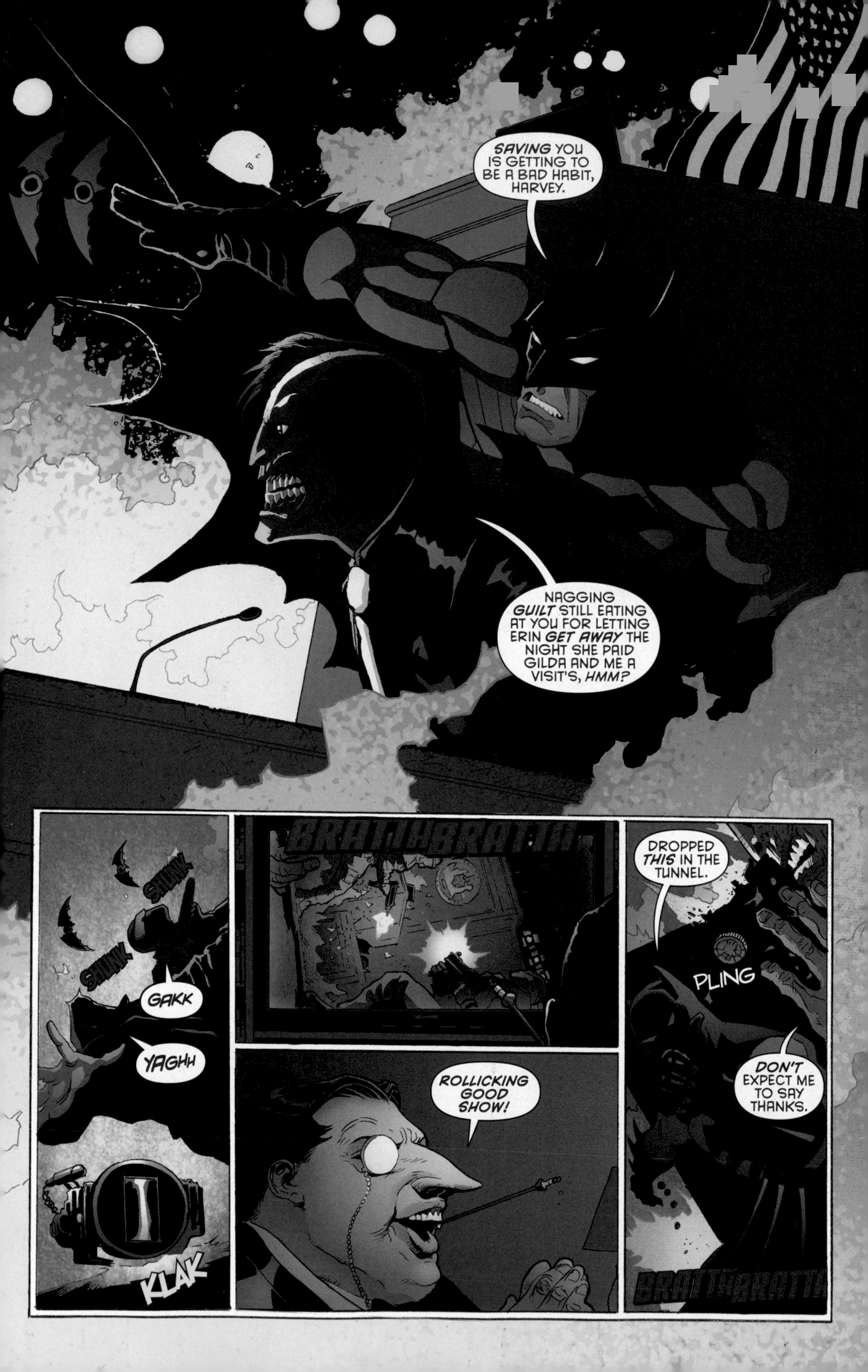
SAVING YOU IS GETTING TO BE A BAD HABIT, HARVEY.
NAGGING GUILT STILL EATING AT YOU FOR LETTING ERIN GET AWAY THE NIGHT SHE PAID GILDA AND ME A VISIT'S, HMM?
SHINK
SHINK
GAKK
YAGHH
KLAK
ROLLICKING GOOD SHOW!
DROPPED THIS IN THE TUNNEL.
PLING
DON'T EXPECT ME TO SAY THANKS.

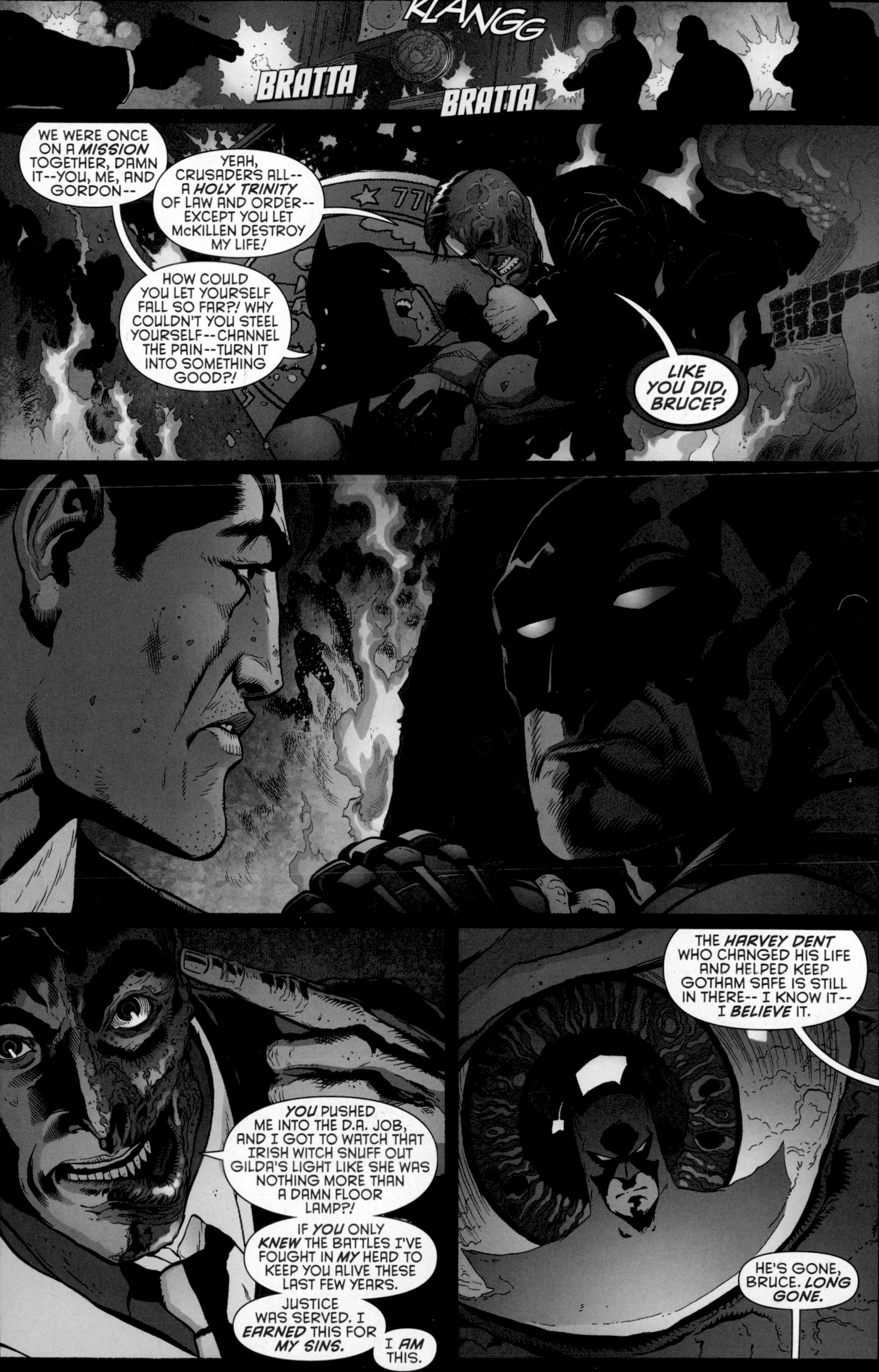
KLANGG
BRATTA
BRATTA
WE WERE ONCE ON A MISSION TOGETHER, DAMN IT--YOU, ME, AND GORDON--
YEAH, CRUSADER'S ALL-- A HOLY TRINITY OF LAW AND ORDER-- EXCEPT YOU LET McKILLEN DESTROY MY LIFE!
HOW COULD YOU LET YOURSELF FALL SO FAR?! WHY COULDN'T YOU STEEL YOURSELF--CHANNEL THE PAIN--TURN IT INTO SOMETHING GOOD?!
LIKE YOU DID, BRUCE?
YOU PUSHED ME INTO THE D.A. JOB, AND I GOT TO WATCH THAT IRISH WITCH SNUFF OUT GILDA'S LIGHT LIKE SHE WAS NOTHING MORE THAN A DAMN FLOOR LAMP?!
IF YOU ONLY KNEW THE BATTLES I'VE FOUGHT IN MY HEAD TO KEEP YOU ALIVE THESE LAST FEW YEARS.
JUSTICE WAS SERVED. I EARNED THIS FOR MY SINS.
I AM THIS.
THE HARVEY DENT WHO CHANGED HIS LIFE AND HELPED KEEP GOTHAM SAFE IS STILL IN THERE-- I KNOW IT-- I BELIEVE IT.
HE'S GONE, BRUCE. LONG GONE.

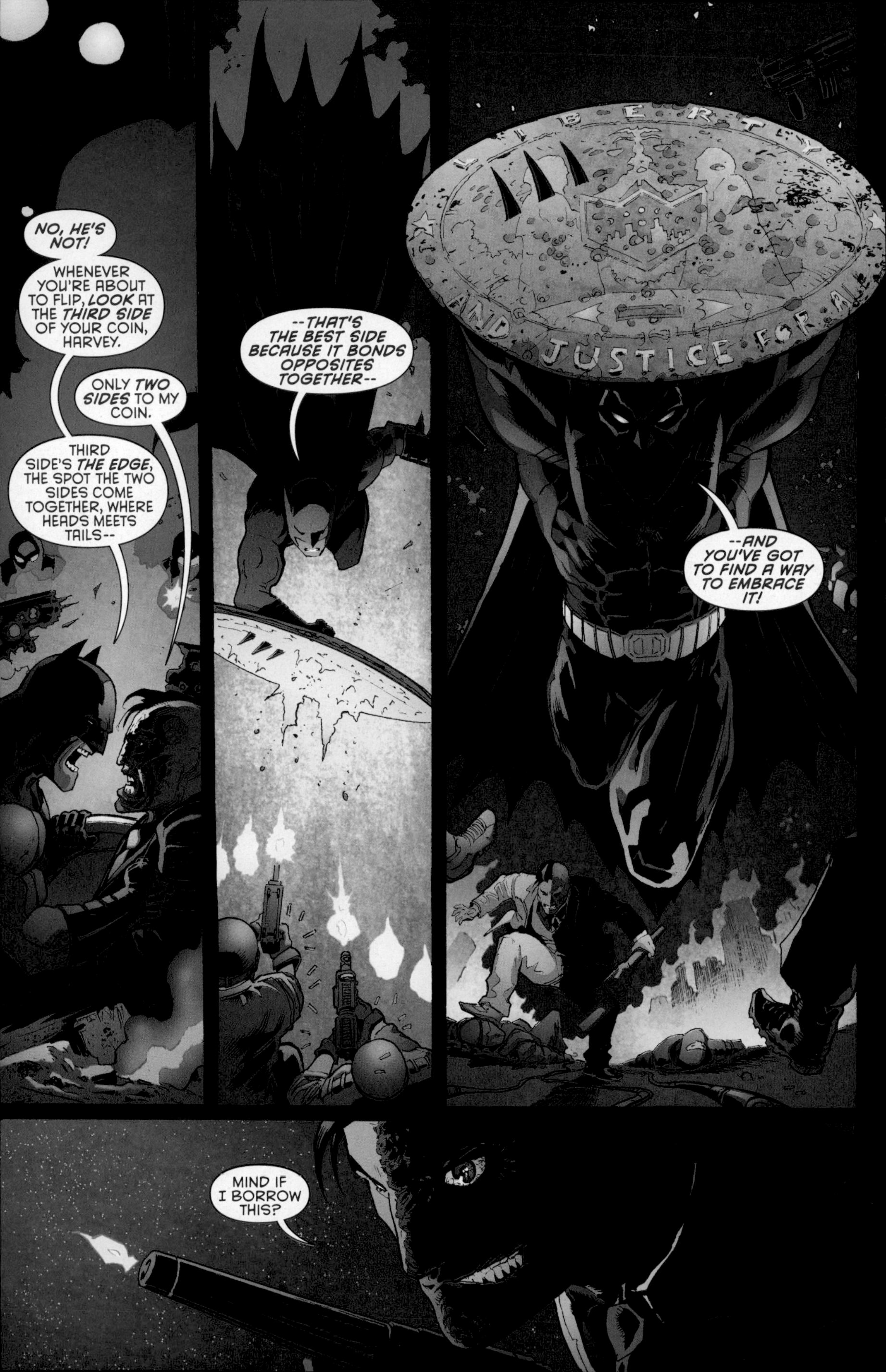
NO, HE'S NOT!
WHENEVER YOU'RE ABOUT TO FLIP, LOOK AT THE THIRD SIDE OF YOUR COIN, HARVEY.
ONLY TWO SIDES TO MY COIN.
THIRD SIDE'S THE EDGE, THE SPOT THE TWO SIDES COME TOGETHER, WHERE HEADS MEETS TAILS--
--THAT'S THE BEST SIDE BECAUSE IT BONDS OPPOSITES TOGETHER--
LIBERTY
AND JUSTICE FOR ALL
--AND YOU'VE GOT TO FIND A WAY TO EMBRACE IT!
MIND IF I BORROW THIS?

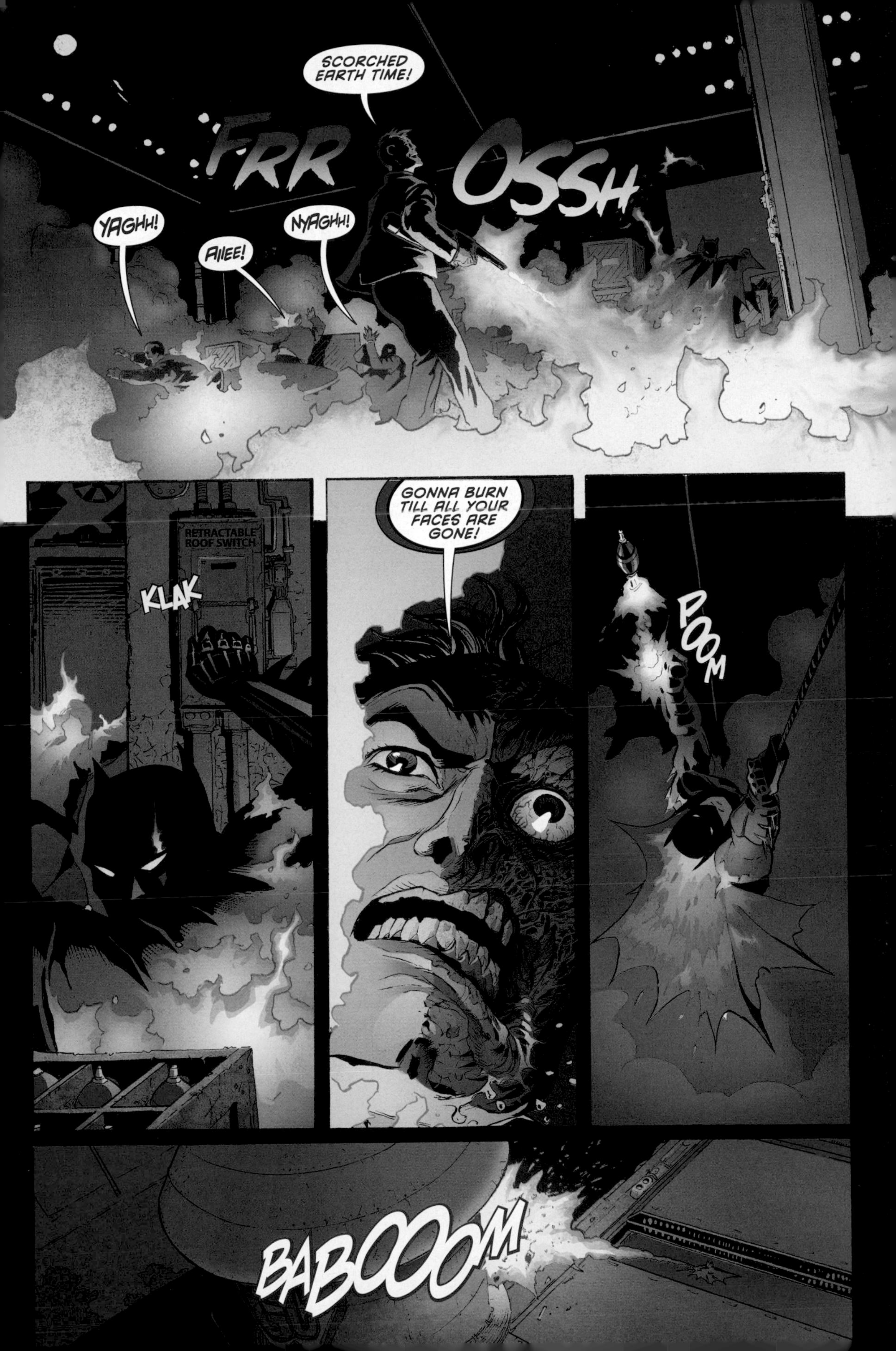
SCORCHED EARTH TIME!
FRR OSSH
YAGHH!
AIIEE!
NYAGHH!
RETRACTABLE ROOF SWITCH
KLAK
GONNA BURN TILL ALL YOUR FACES ARE GONE!
POOM
BABOOOM

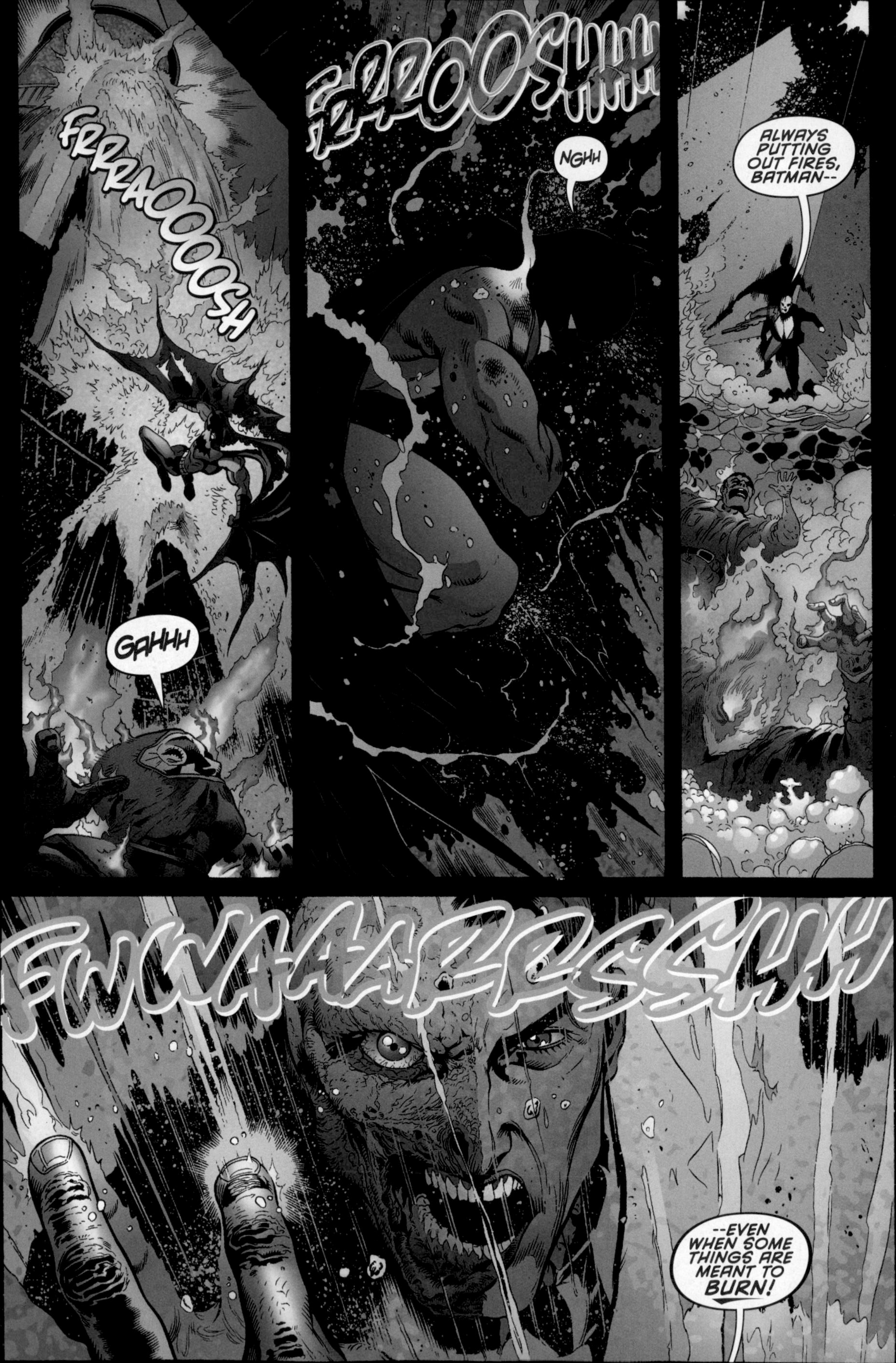
FRRRAOOOOOSH
GAHHH
FRRROOOSHHH
NGHH
ALWAYS PUTTING OUT FIRES, BATMAN--
FWAAARRSSHH
--EVEN WHEN SOME THINGS ARE MEANT TO BURN!

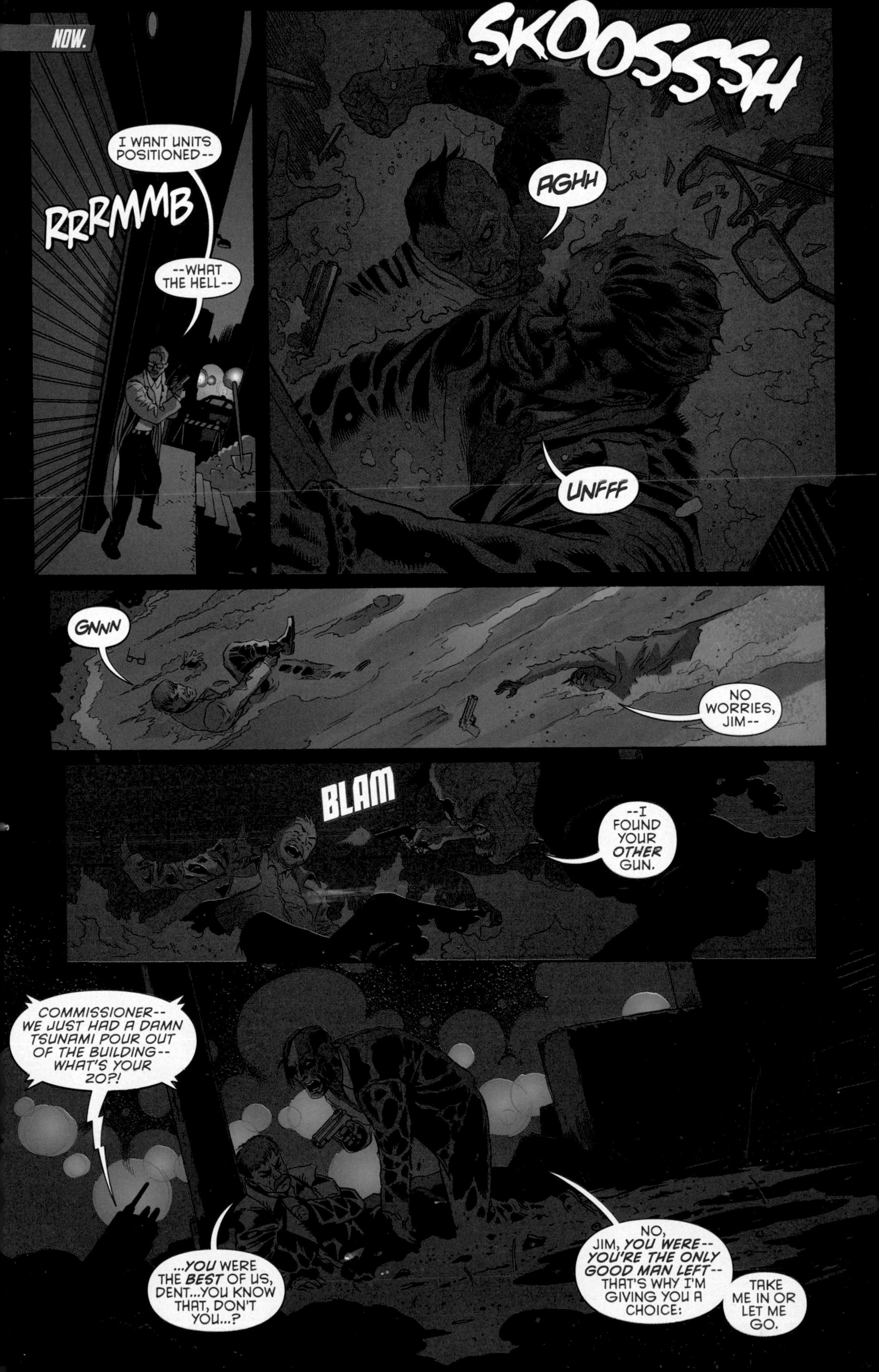
NOW.
SKOOSSSH
I WANT UNITS POSITIONED--
RRRMMMB
--WHAT THE HELL--
AGHH
UNFFF
GNNN
NO WORRIES, JIM--
BLAM
--I FOUND YOUR OTHER GUN.
COMMISSIONER-- WE JUST HAD A DAMN TSUNAMI POUR OUT OF THE BUILDING-- WHAT'S YOUR 20?!
...YOU WERE THE BEST OF US, DENT...YOU KNOW THAT, DON'T YOU...?
NO, JIM, YOU WERE-- YOU'RE THE ONLY GOOD MAN LEFT-- THAT'S WHY I'M GIVING YOU A CHOICE:
TAKE ME IN OR LET ME GO.

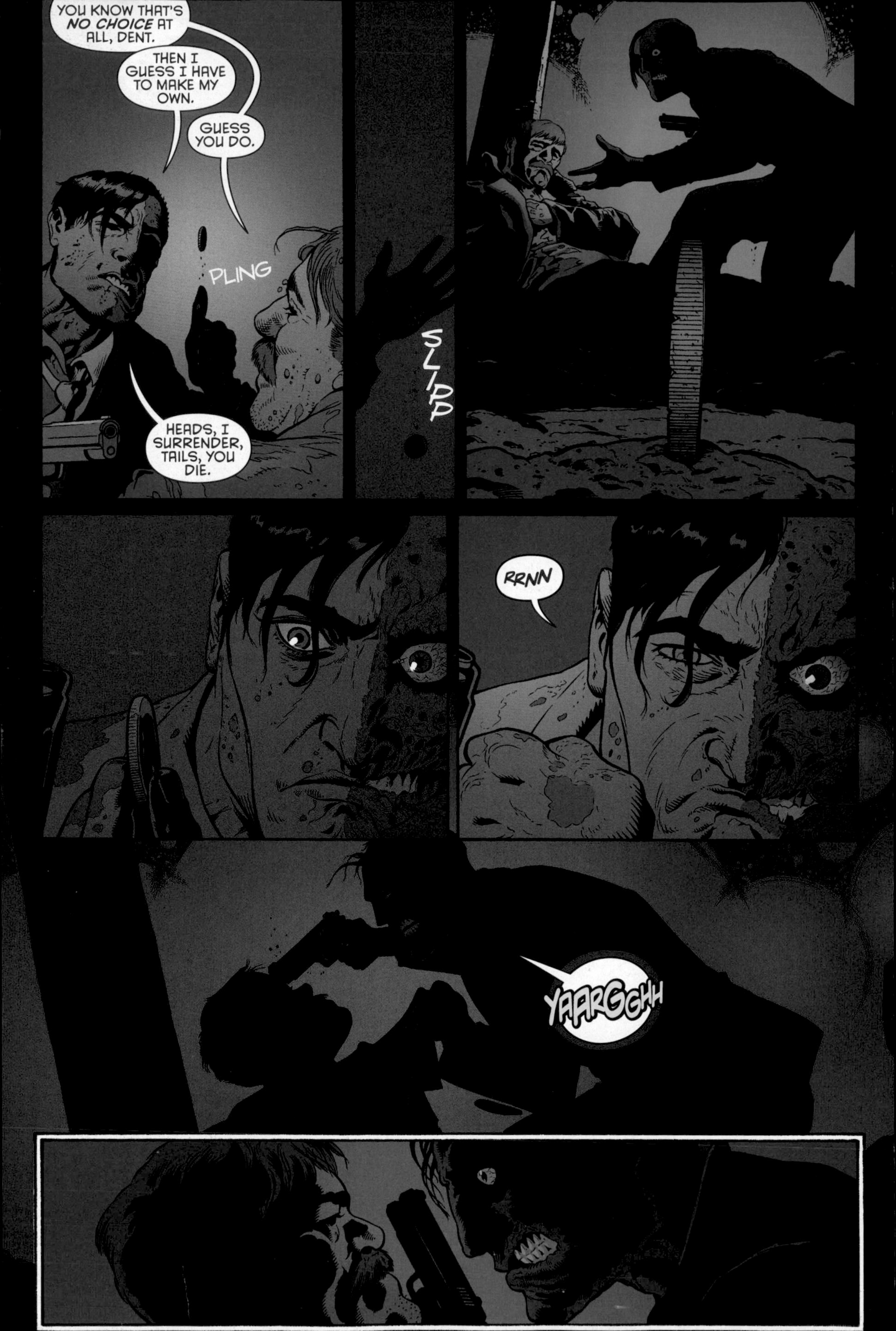
YOU KNOW THAT'S NO CHOICE AT ALL, DENT.
THEN I GUESS I HAVE TO MAKE MY OWN.
GUESS YOU DO.
PLING
HEADS, I SURRENDER, TAILS, YOU DIE.
SLIPP
RRNN
YAARGGHH

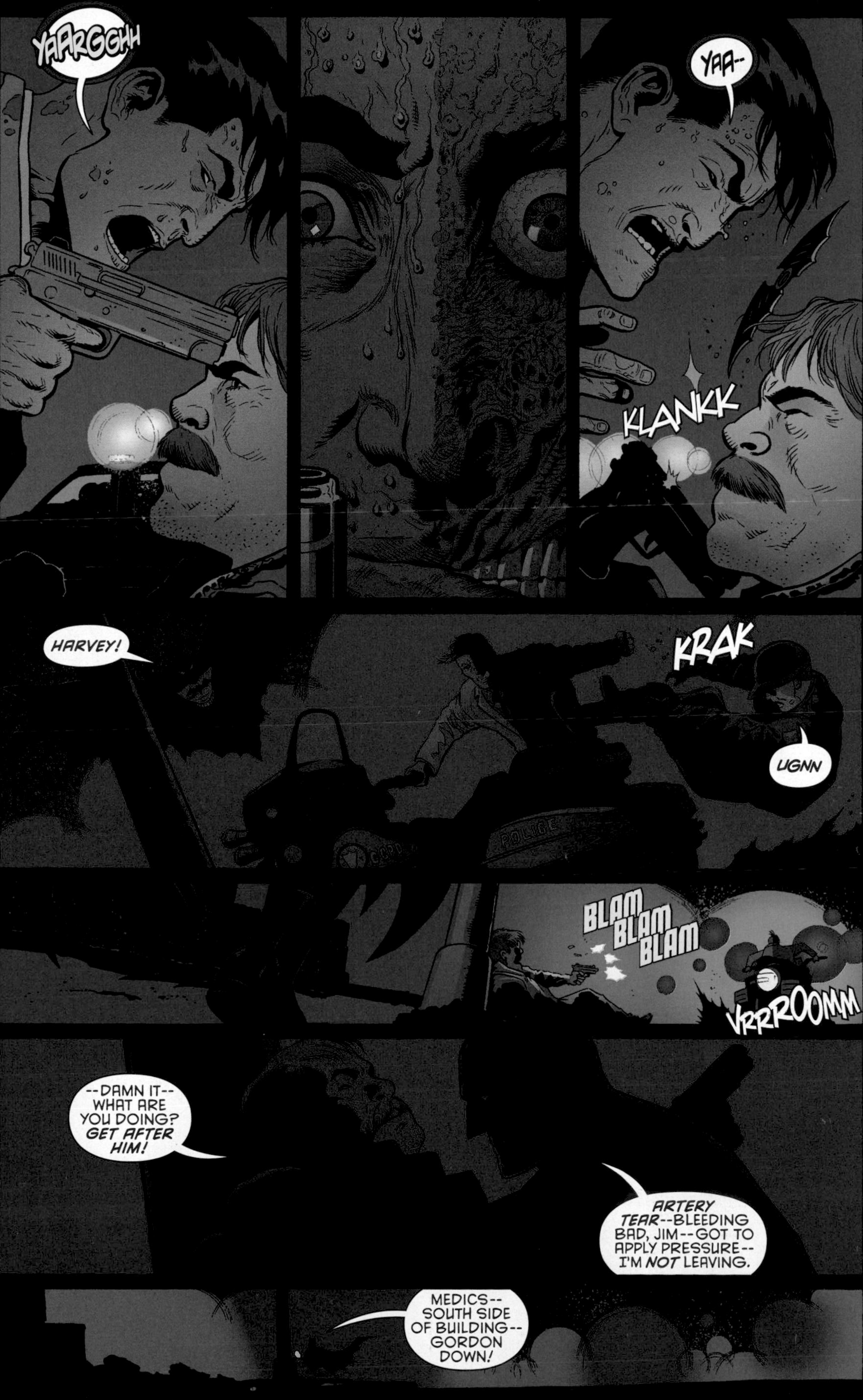
YAARGGHH
YAA--
KLANKK
HARVEY!
KRAK
UGNN
BLAM BLAM BLAM
VRRROOMM
--DAMN IT--WHAT ARE YOU DOING? GET AFTER HIM!
ARTERY TEAR--BLEEDING BAD, JIM--GOT TO APPLY PRESSURE--I'M NOT LEAVING.
MEDICS--SOUTH SIDE OF BUILDING--GORDON DOWN!

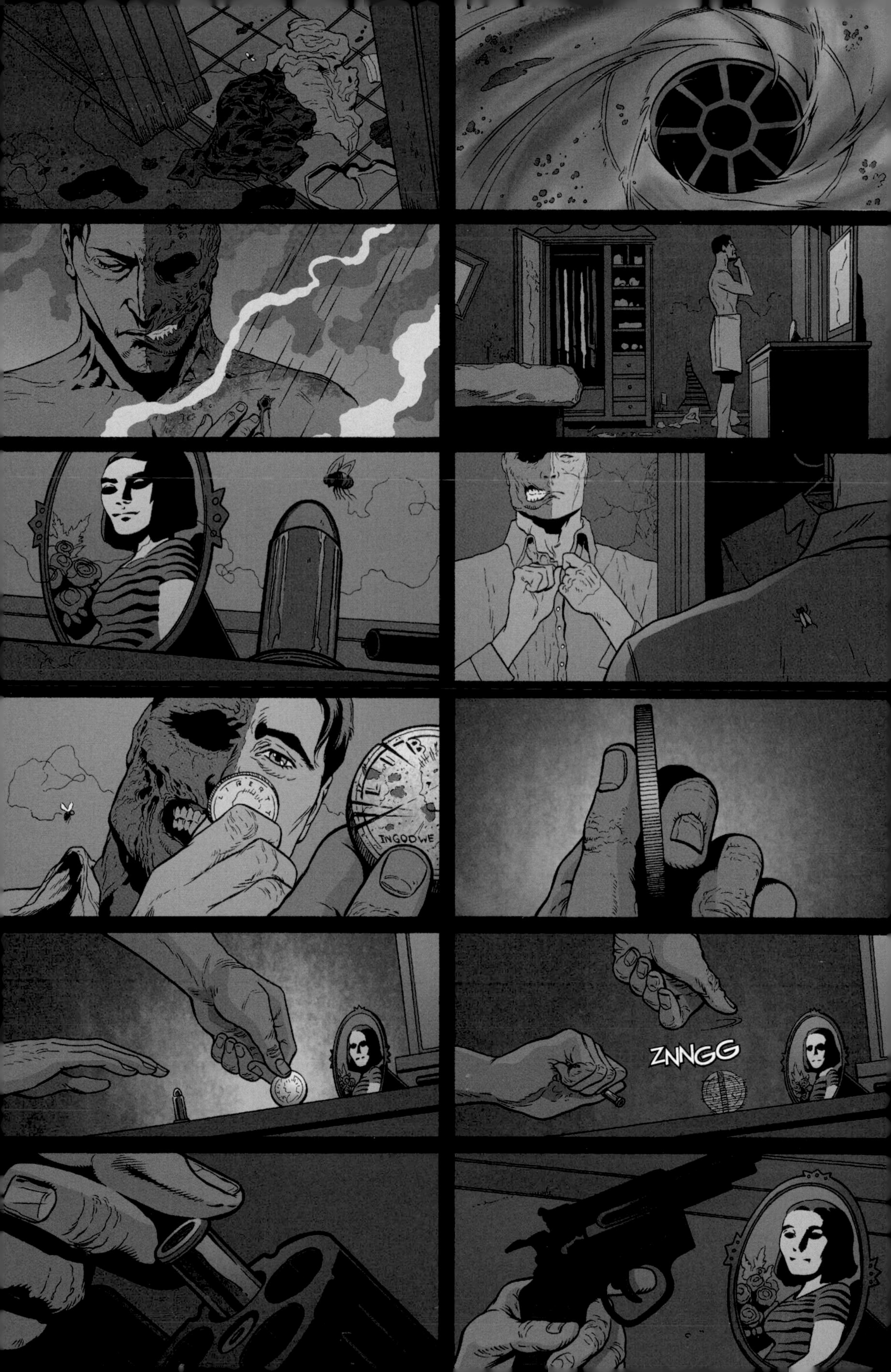
ZNNGG

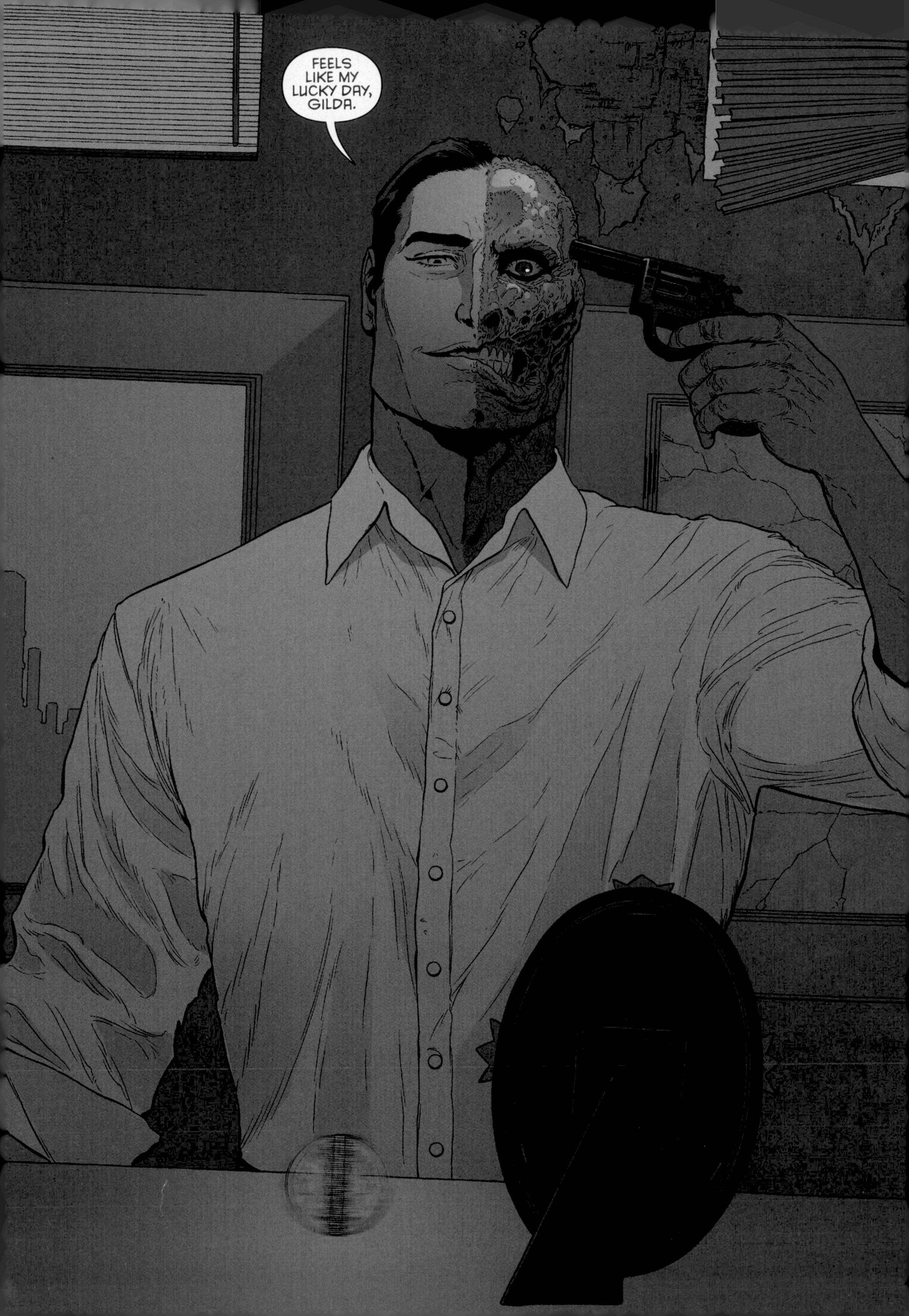
FEELS LIKE MY LUCKY DAY, GILDA.

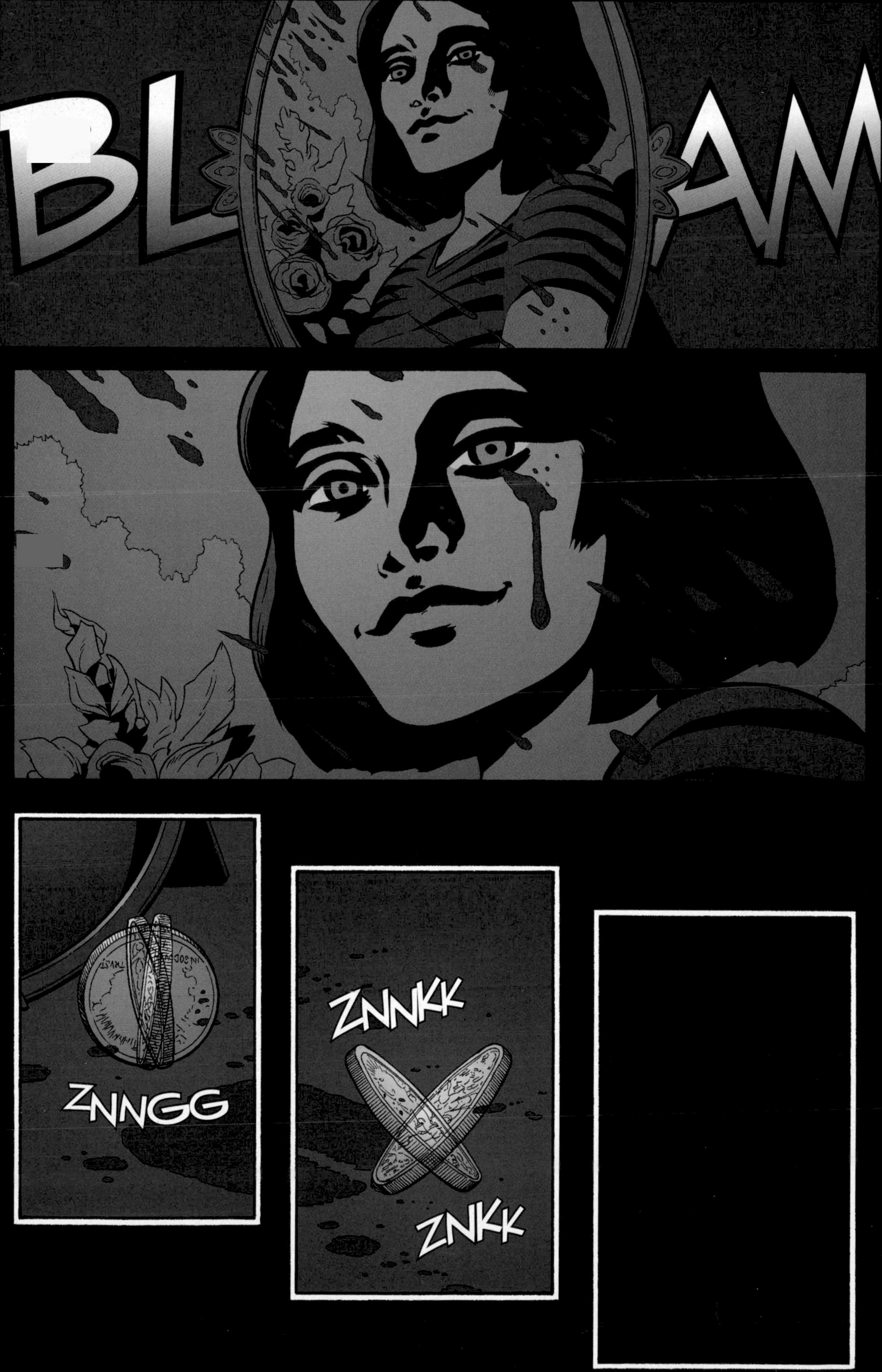
BL
AM
ZNNGG
ZNNKK
ZNKK

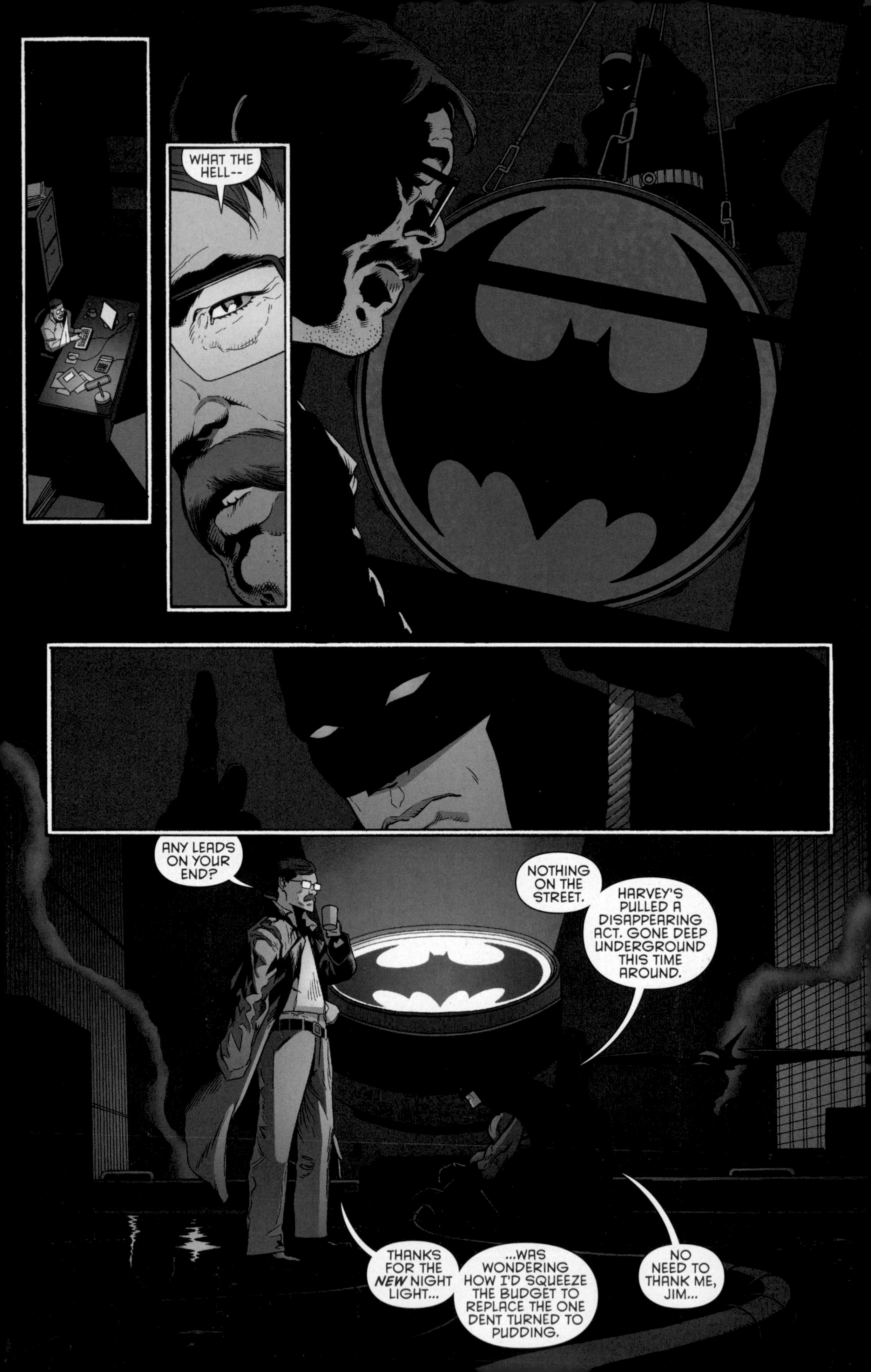
WHAT THE HELL--
ANY LEADS ON YOUR END?
NOTHING ON THE STREET.
HARVEY'S PULLED A DISAPPEARING ACT. GONE DEEP UNDERGROUND THIS TIME AROUND.
THANKS FOR THE *NEW* NIGHT LIGHT...
...WAS WONDERING HOW I'D SQUEEZE THE BUDGET TO REPLACE THE ONE DENT TURNED TO PUDDING.
NO NEED TO THANK ME, JIM...

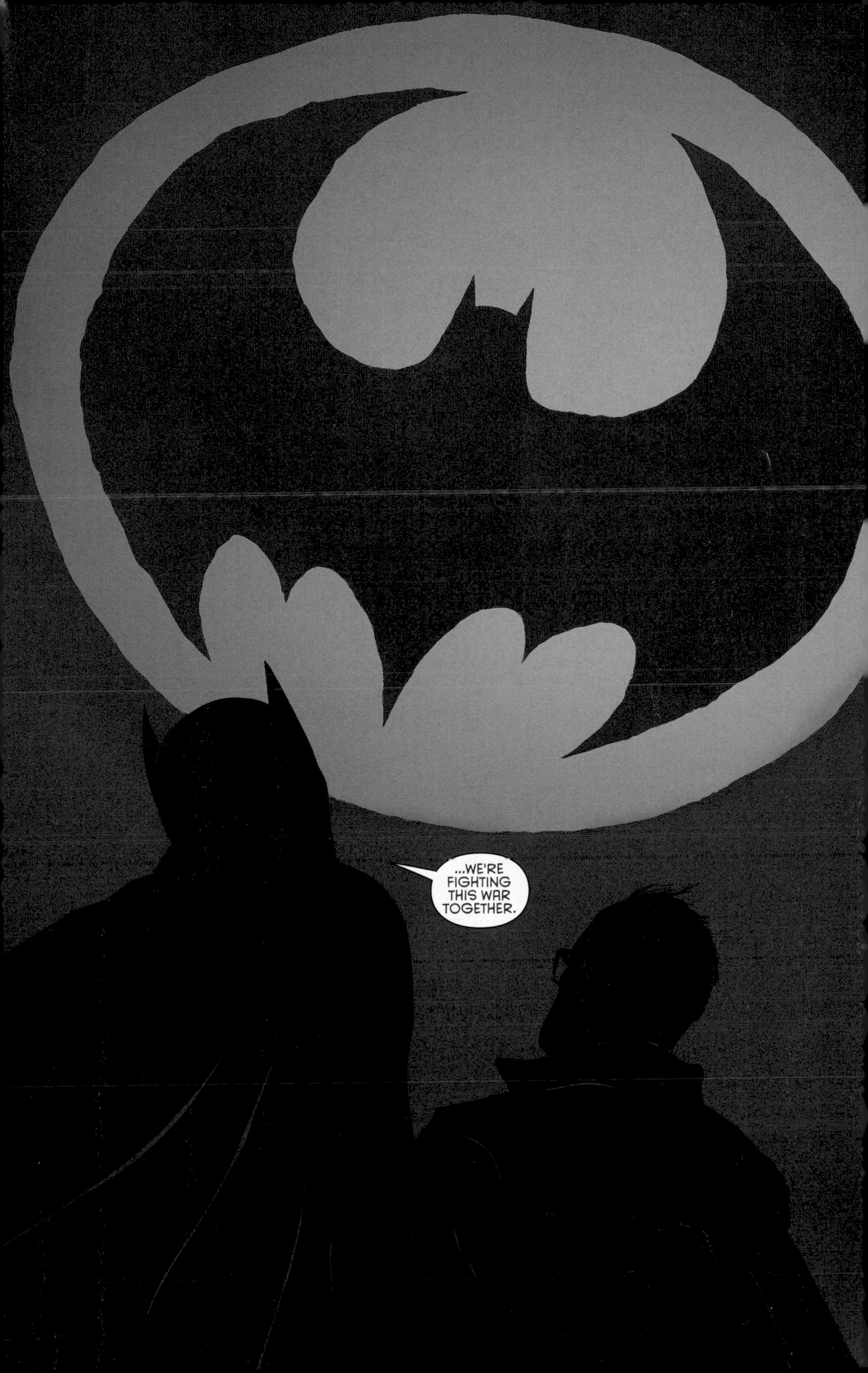
...WE'RE FIGHTING THIS WAR TOGETHER.

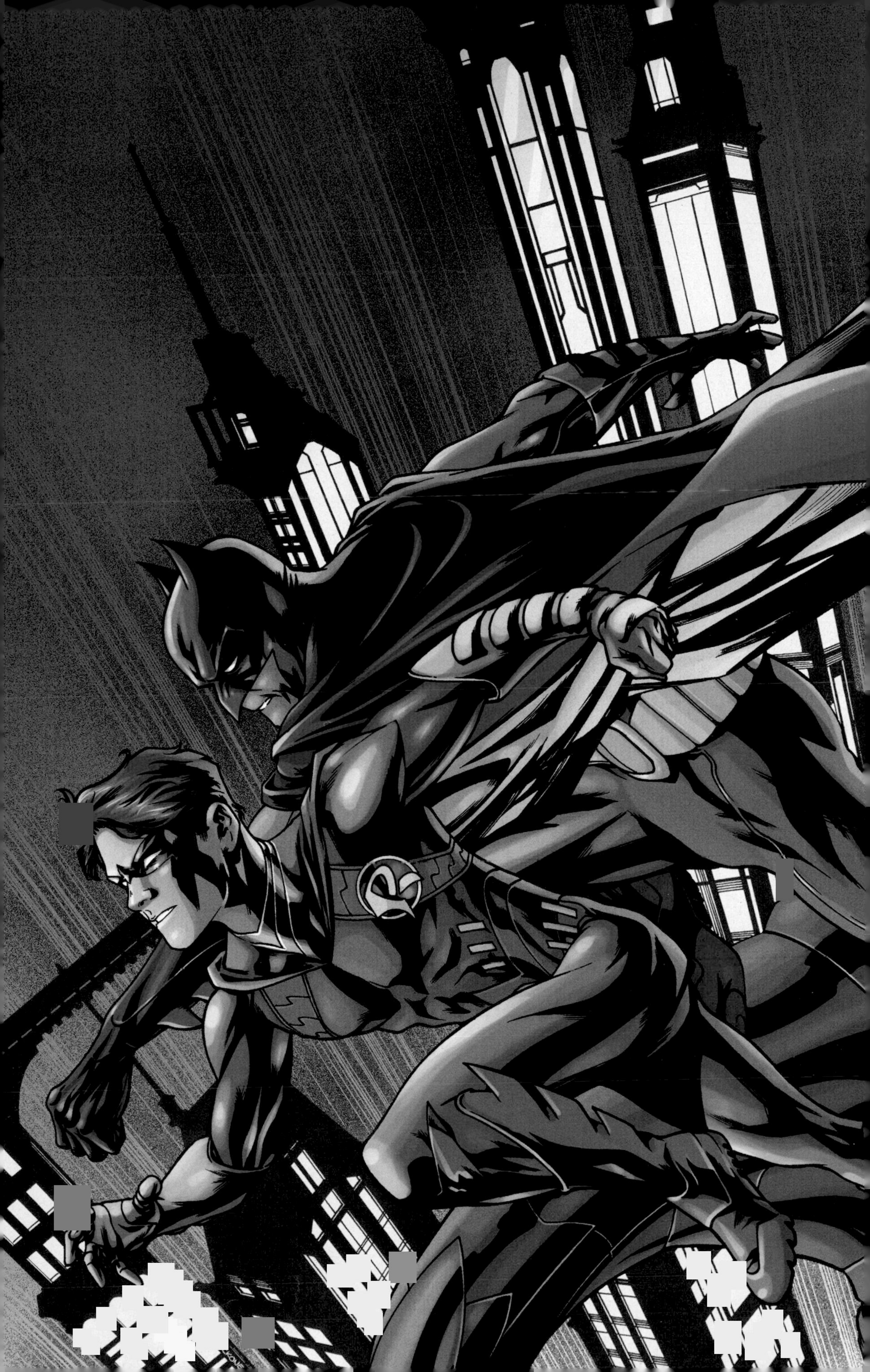

BATMAN AND ROBIN: WEEK ONE

DOUG MAHNKE with **PATRICK GLEASON** pencillers

CHRISTIAN ALAMY, KEITH CHAMPAGNE, TOM NGUYEN, MARK IRWIN, MICK GRAY & MAHNKE inkers

TONY AVIÑA colorist cover art by **MIKE MCKONE & CRIS PETER**

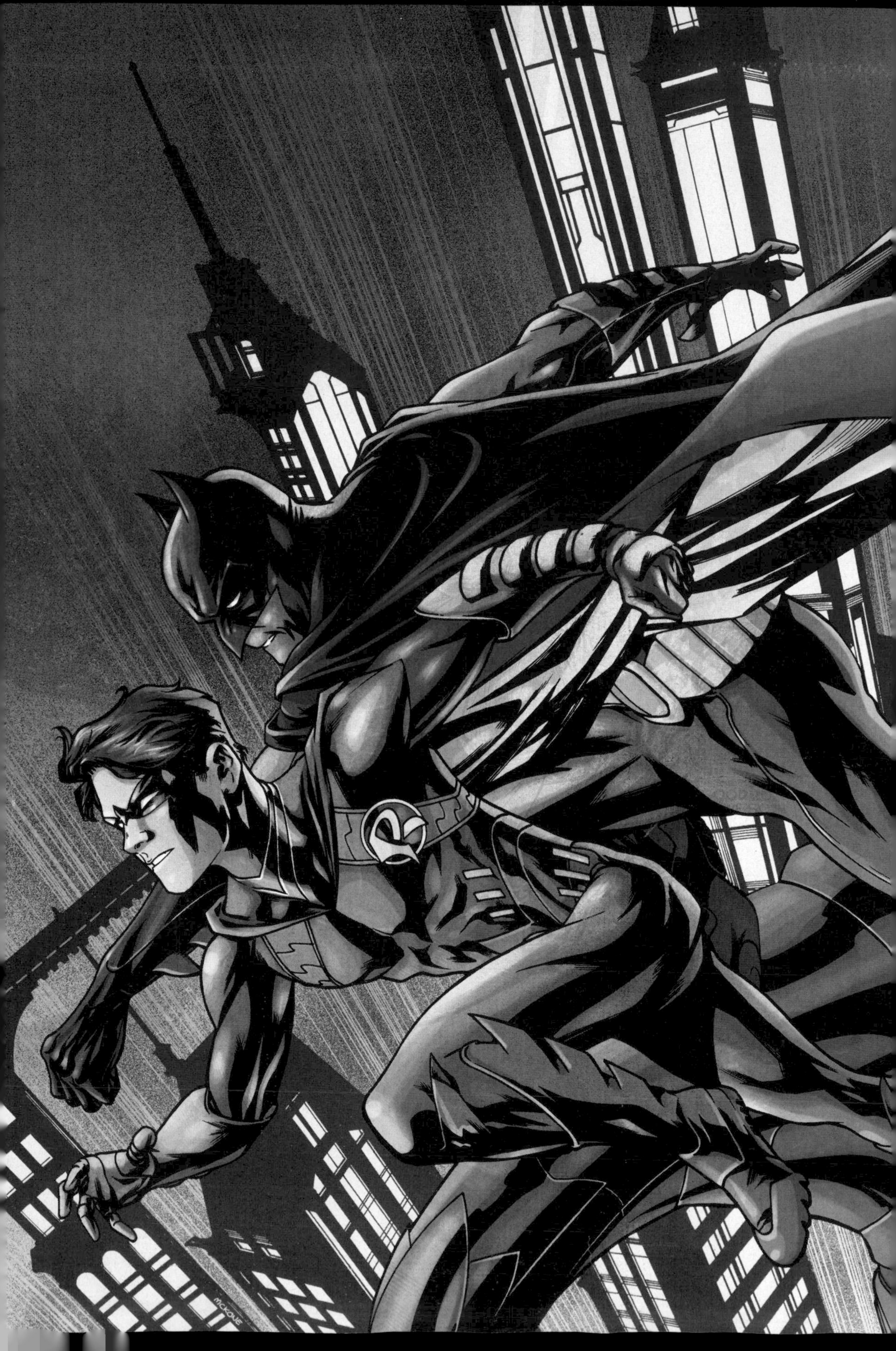

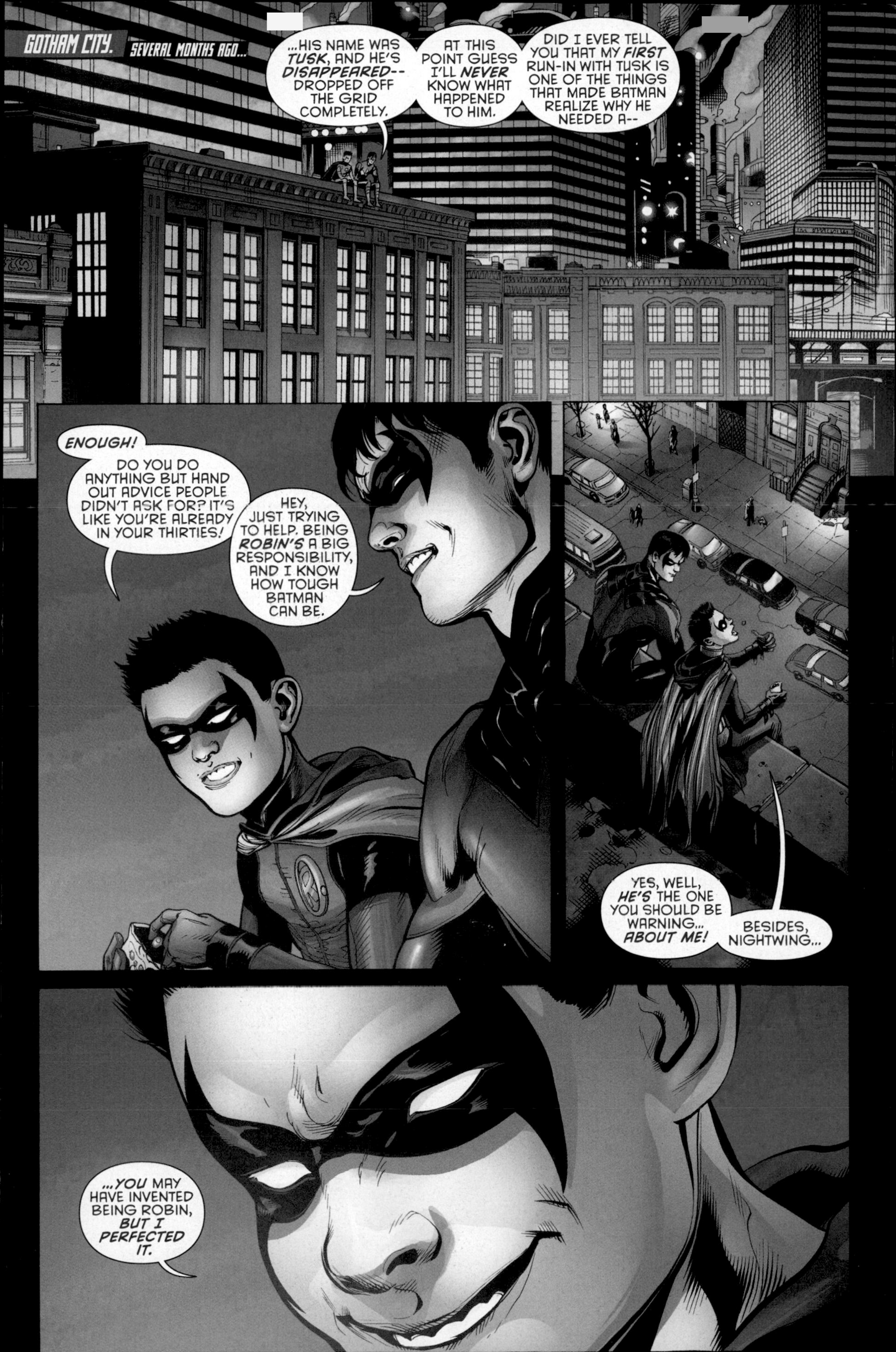
GOTHAM CITY.
SEVERAL MONTHS AGO...
...HIS NAME WAS TUSK, AND HE'S DISAPPEARED--DROPPED OFF THE GRID COMPLETELY.
AT THIS POINT GUESS I'LL NEVER KNOW WHAT HAPPENED TO HIM.
DID I EVER TELL YOU THAT MY FIRST RUN-IN WITH TUSK IS ONE OF THE THINGS THAT MADE BATMAN REALIZE WHY HE NEEDED A--
ENOUGH!
DO YOU DO ANYTHING BUT HAND OUT ADVICE PEOPLE DIDN'T ASK FOR? IT'S LIKE YOU'RE ALREADY IN YOUR THIRTIES!
HEY, JUST TRYING TO HELP. BEING ROBIN'S A BIG RESPONSIBILITY, AND I KNOW HOW TOUGH BATMAN CAN BE.
YES, WELL, HE'S THE ONE YOU SHOULD BE WARNING... ABOUT ME!
BESIDES, NIGHTWING...
...YOU MAY HAVE INVENTED BEING ROBIN, BUT I PERFECTED IT.

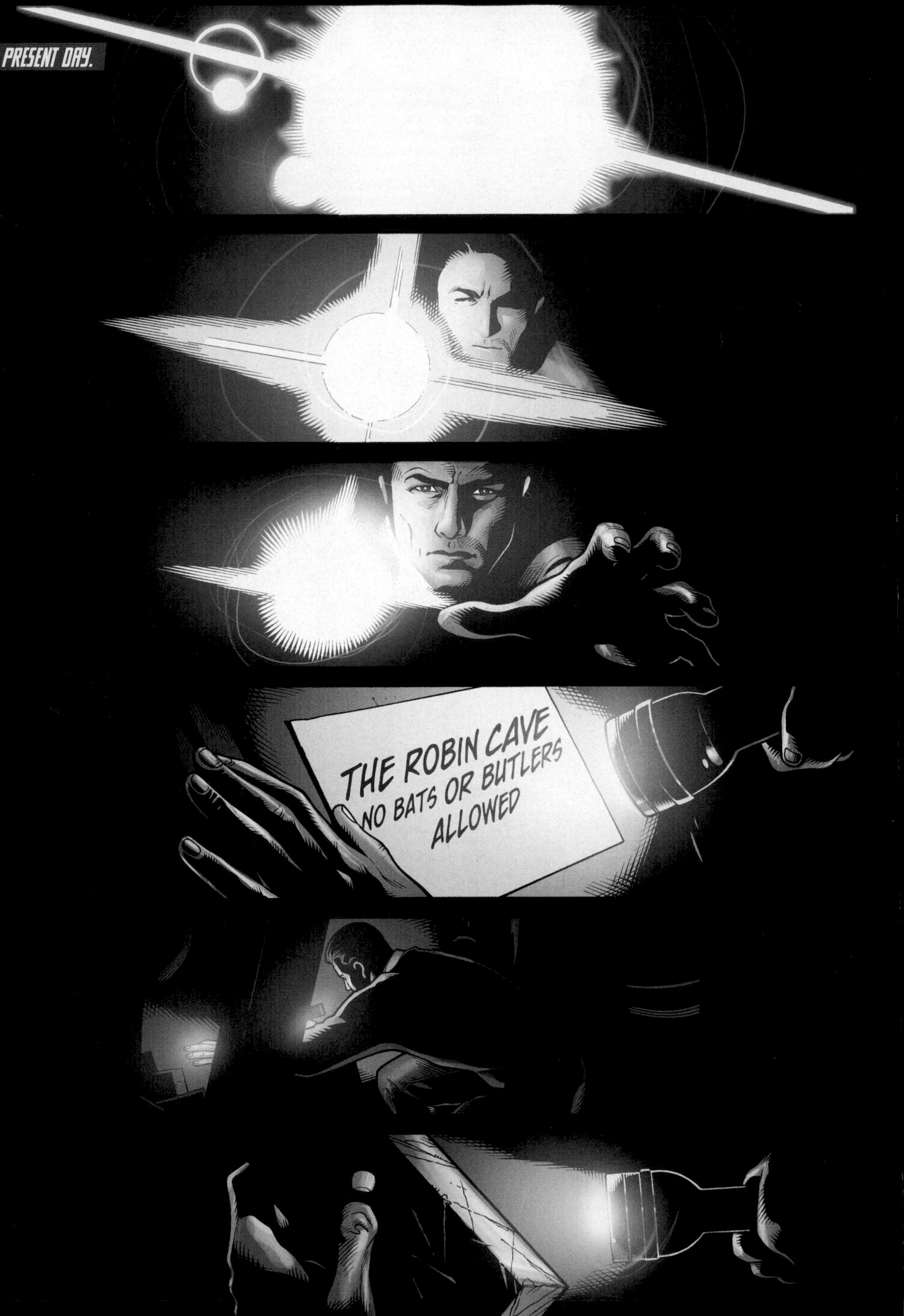
PRESENT DAY.
THE ROBIN CAVE
NO BATS OR BUTLERS ALLOWED

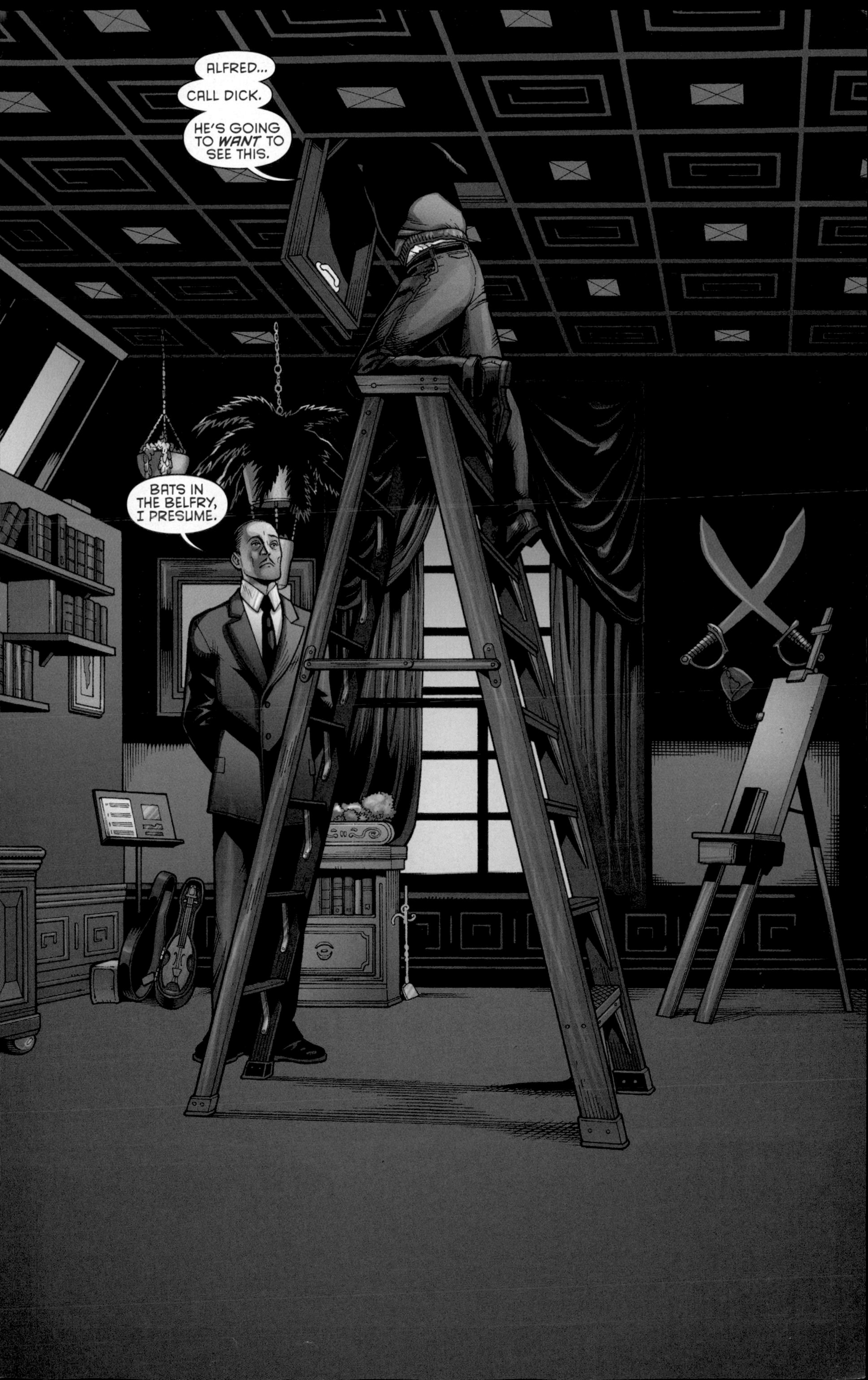
ALFRED...
CALL DICK.
HE'S GOING TO *WANT* TO SEE THIS.
BATS IN THE BELFRY, I PRESUME.

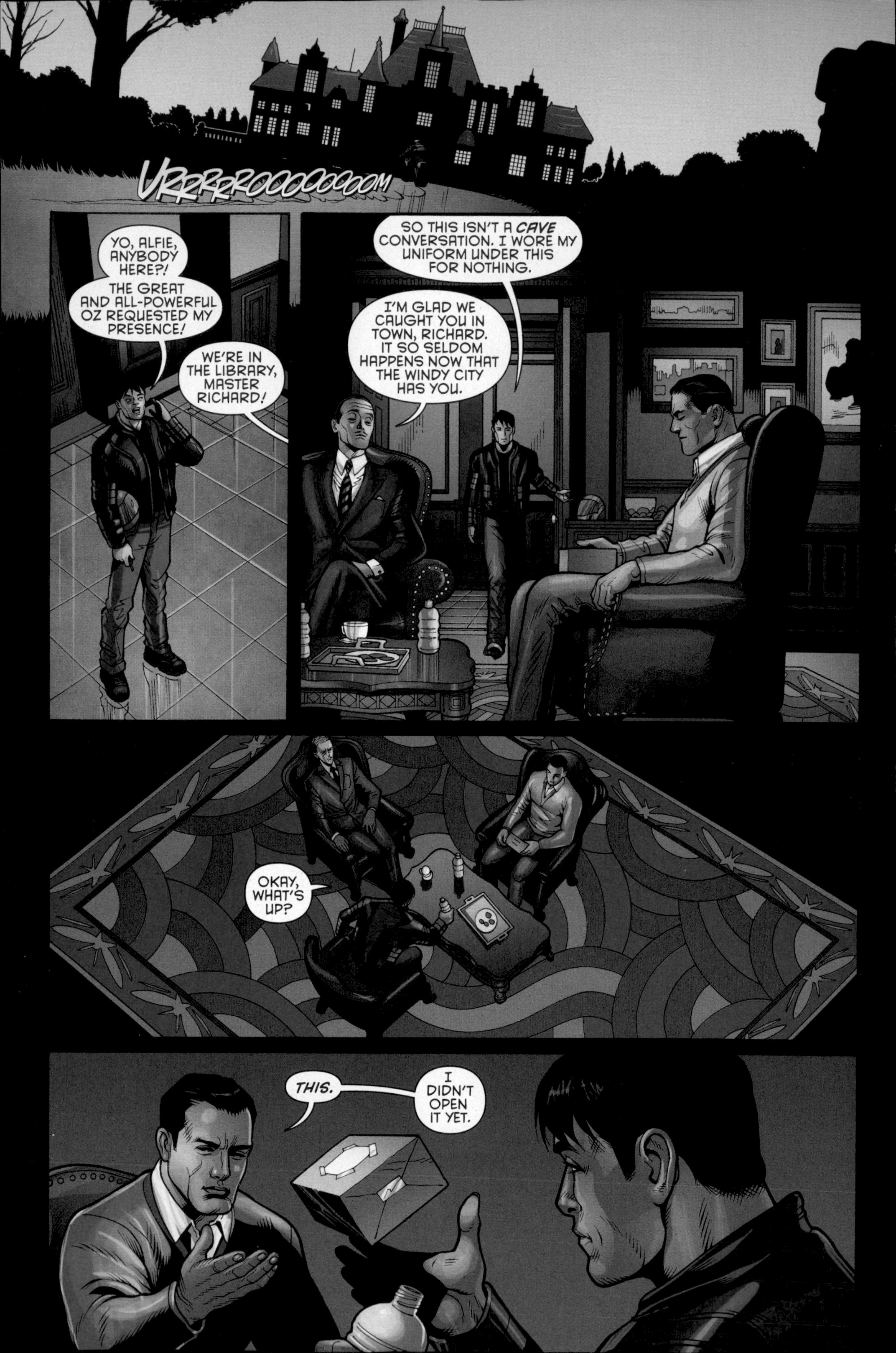
URRRRROOOOOOOOOM
YO, ALFIE, ANYBODY HERE?!
THE GREAT AND ALL-POWERFUL OZ REQUESTED MY PRESENCE!
WE'RE IN THE LIBRARY, MASTER RICHARD!
SO THIS ISN'T A *CAVE* CONVERSATION. I WORE MY UNIFORM UNDER THIS FOR NOTHING.
I'M GLAD WE CAUGHT YOU IN TOWN, RICHARD. IT SO SELDOM HAPPENS NOW THAT THE WINDY CITY HAS YOU.
OKAY, WHAT'S UP?
THIS.
I DIDN'T OPEN IT YET.

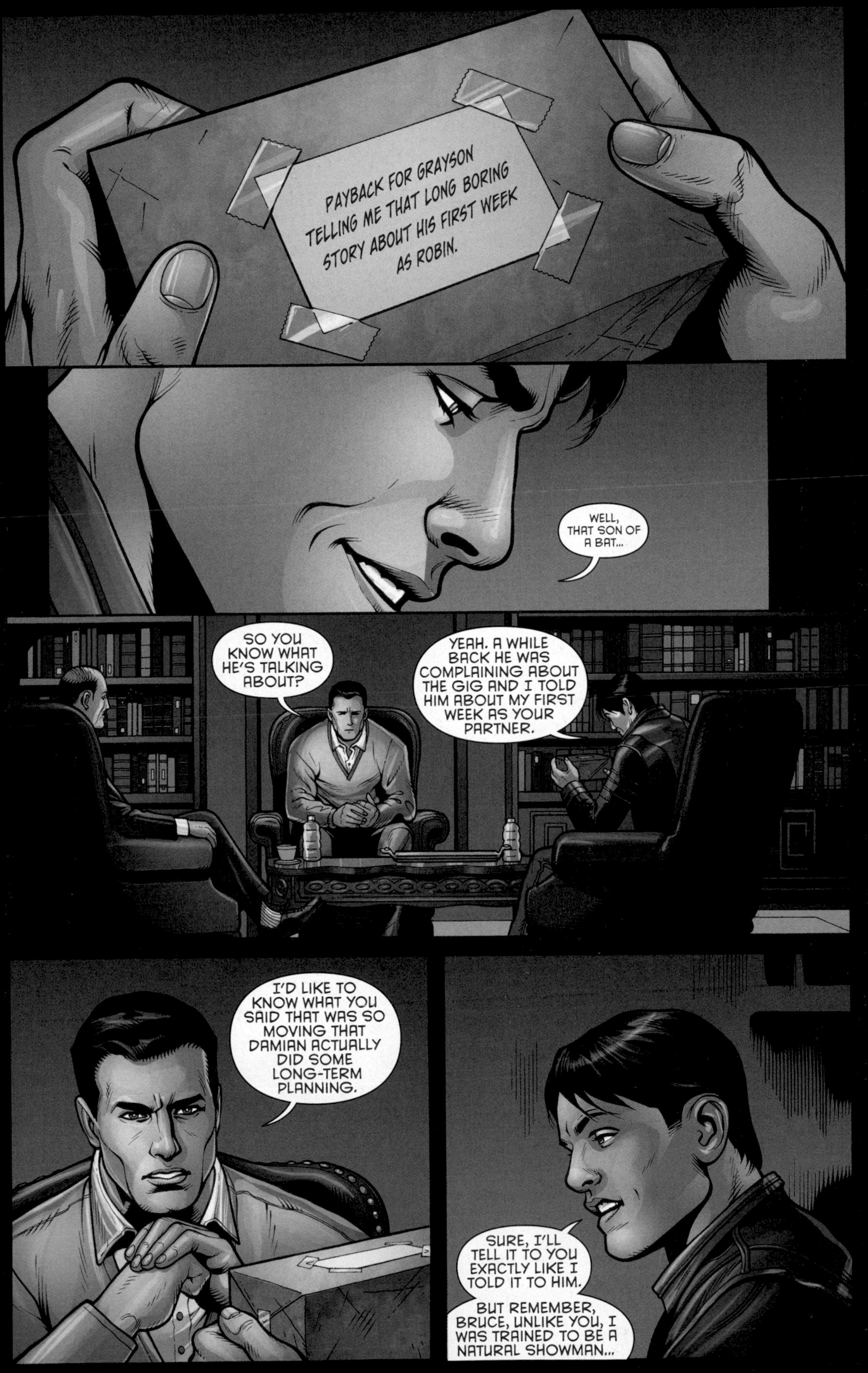
PAYBACK FOR GRAYSON TELLING ME THAT LONG BORING STORY ABOUT HIS FIRST WEEK AS ROBIN.
WELL, THAT SON OF A BAT...
SO YOU KNOW WHAT HE'S TALKING ABOUT?
YEAH. A WHILE BACK HE WAS COMPLAINING ABOUT THE GIG AND I TOLD HIM ABOUT MY FIRST WEEK AS YOUR PARTNER.
I'D LIKE TO KNOW WHAT YOU SAID THAT WAS SO MOVING THAT DAMIAN ACTUALLY DID SOME LONG-TERM PLANNING.
SURE, I'LL TELL IT TO YOU EXACTLY LIKE I TOLD IT TO HIM.
BUT REMEMBER, BRUCE, UNLIKE YOU, I WAS TRAINED TO BE A NATURAL SHOWMAN...

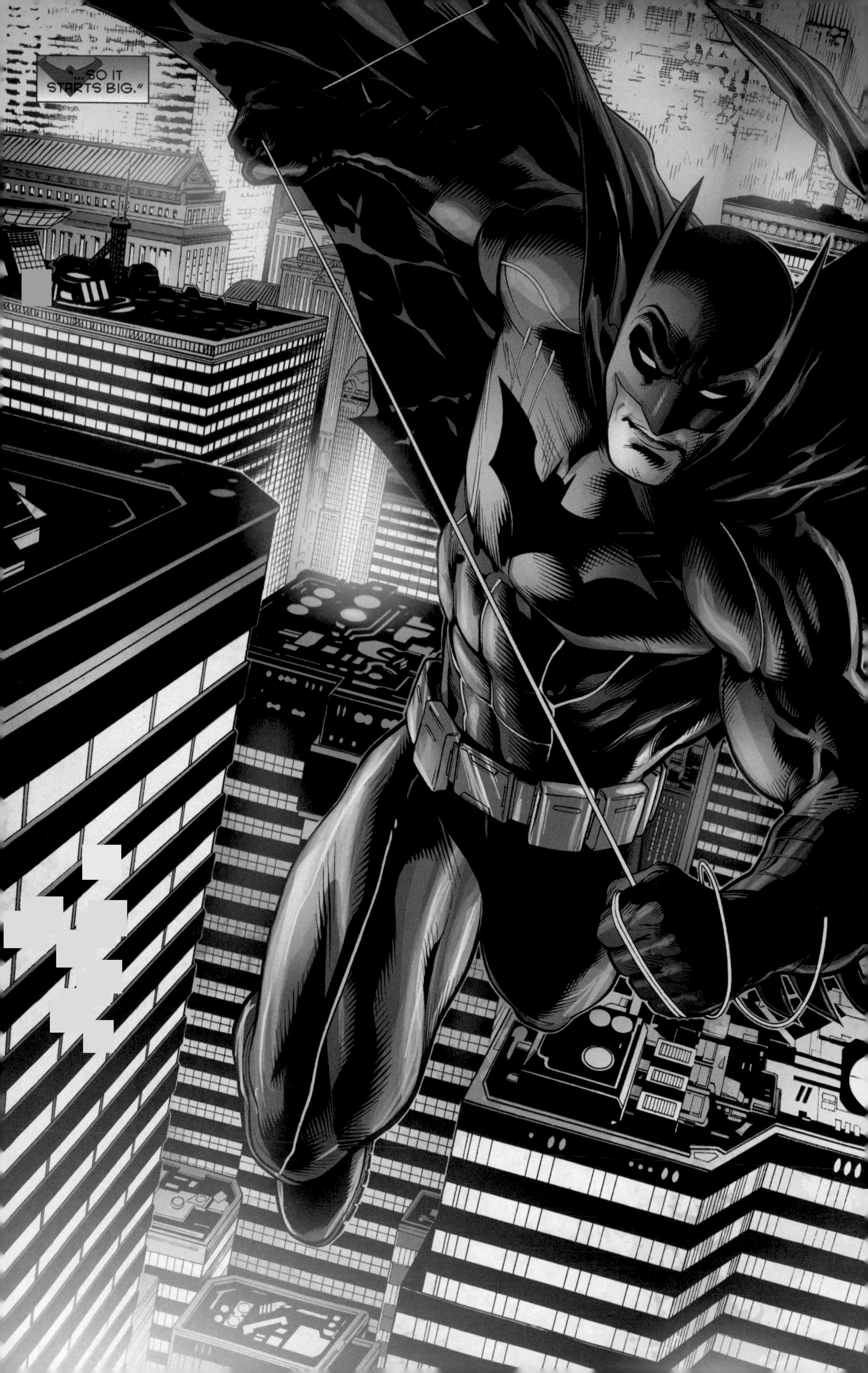
"...SO IT STARTS BIG."

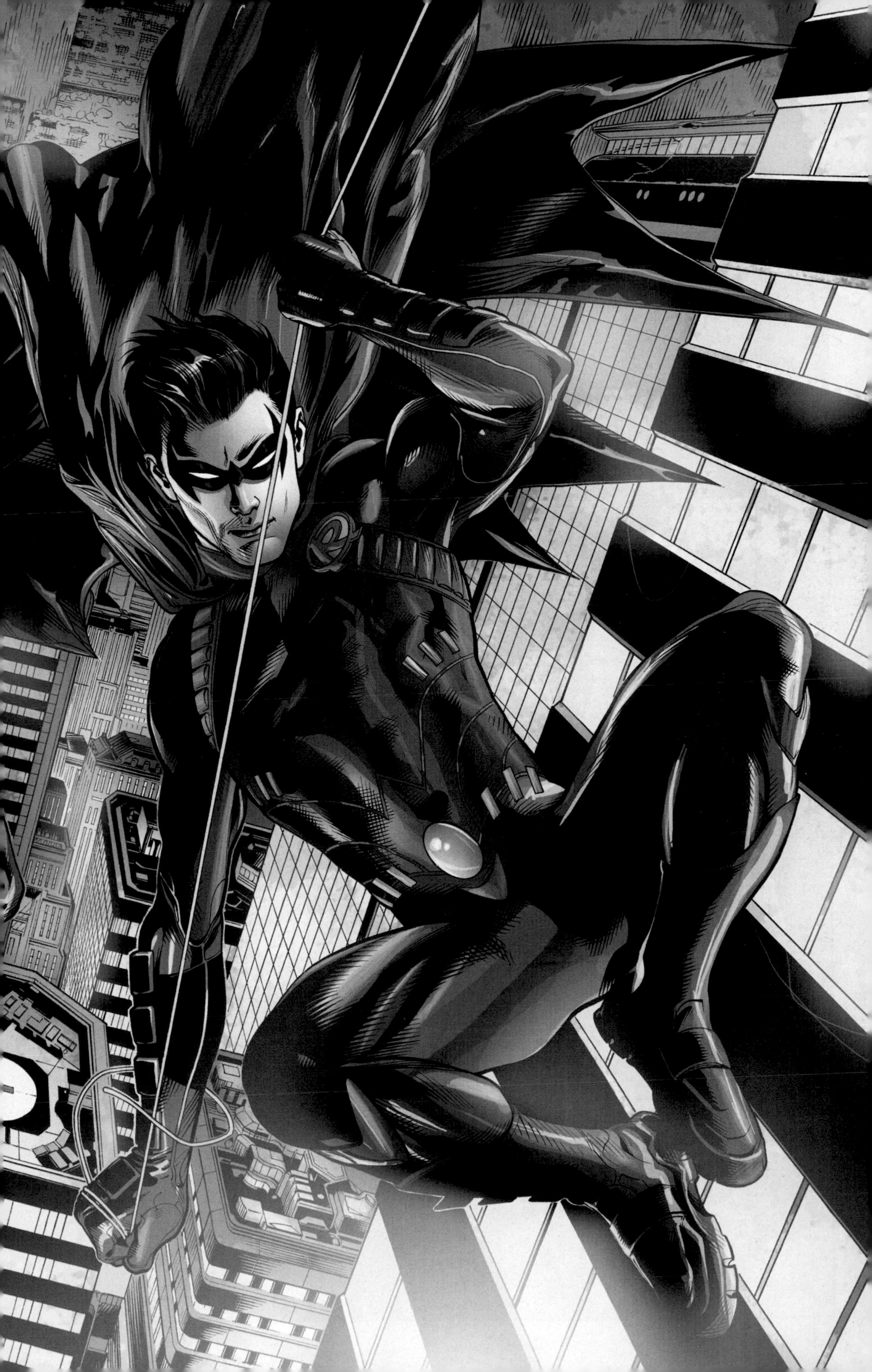

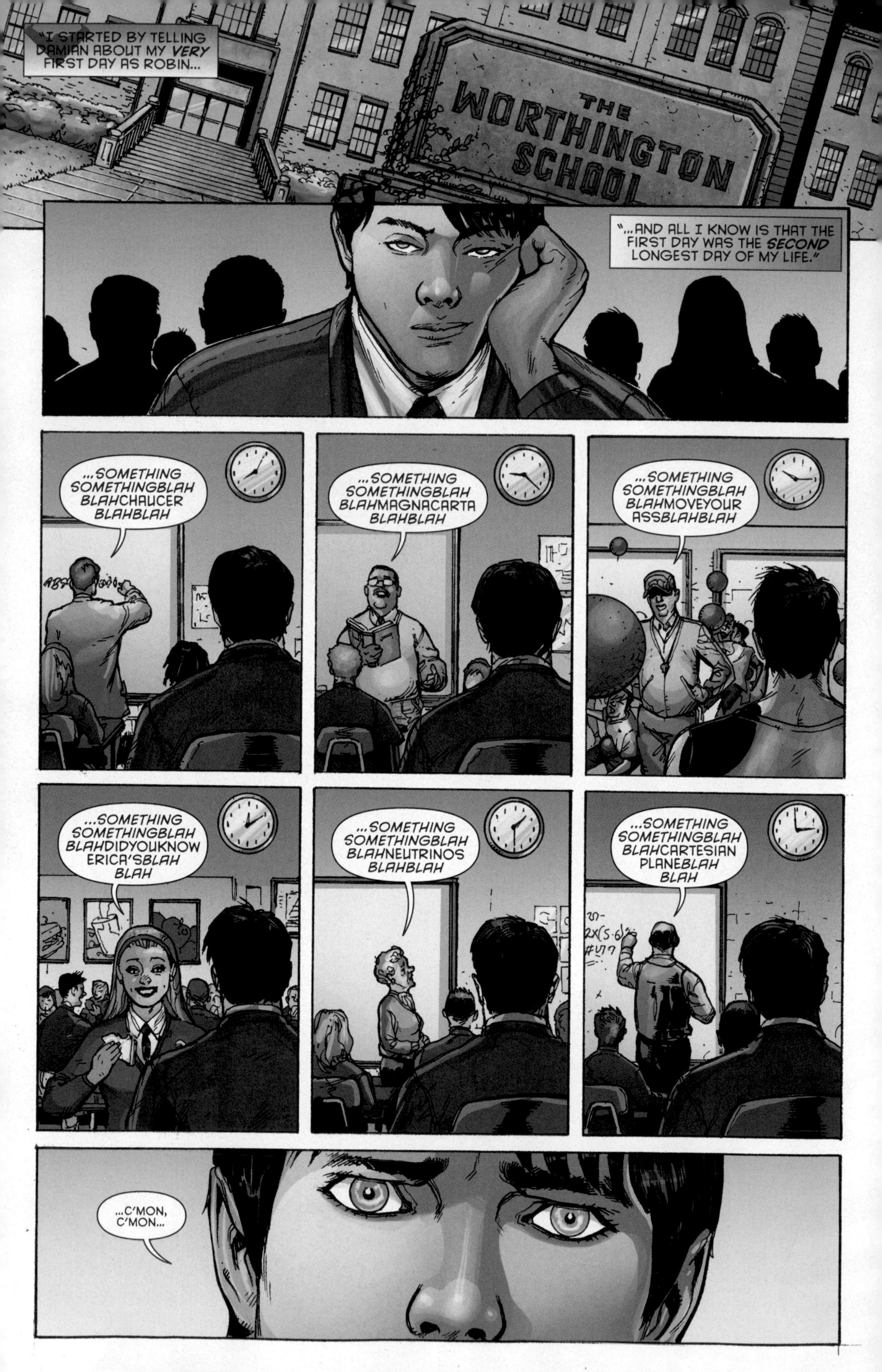
"I STARTED BY TELLING DAMIAN ABOUT MY *VERY* FIRST DAY AS ROBIN...
THE WORTHINGTON SCHOOL
"...AND ALL I KNOW IS THAT THE FIRST DAY WAS THE *SECOND* LONGEST DAY OF MY LIFE."
...SOMETHING SOMETHINGBLAH BLAHCHAUCER BLAHBLAH
...SOMETHING SOMETHINGBLAH BLAHMAGNACARTA BLAHBLAH
...SOMETHING SOMETHINGBLAH BLAHMOVEYOUR ASSBLAHBLAH
...SOMETHING SOMETHINGBLAH BLAHDIDYOUKNOW ERICA'SBLAH BLAH
...SOMETHING SOMETHINGBLAH BLAHNEUTRINOS BLAHBLAH
...SOMETHING SOMETHINGBLAH BLAHCARTESIAN PLANEBLAH BLAH
...C'MON, C'MON...

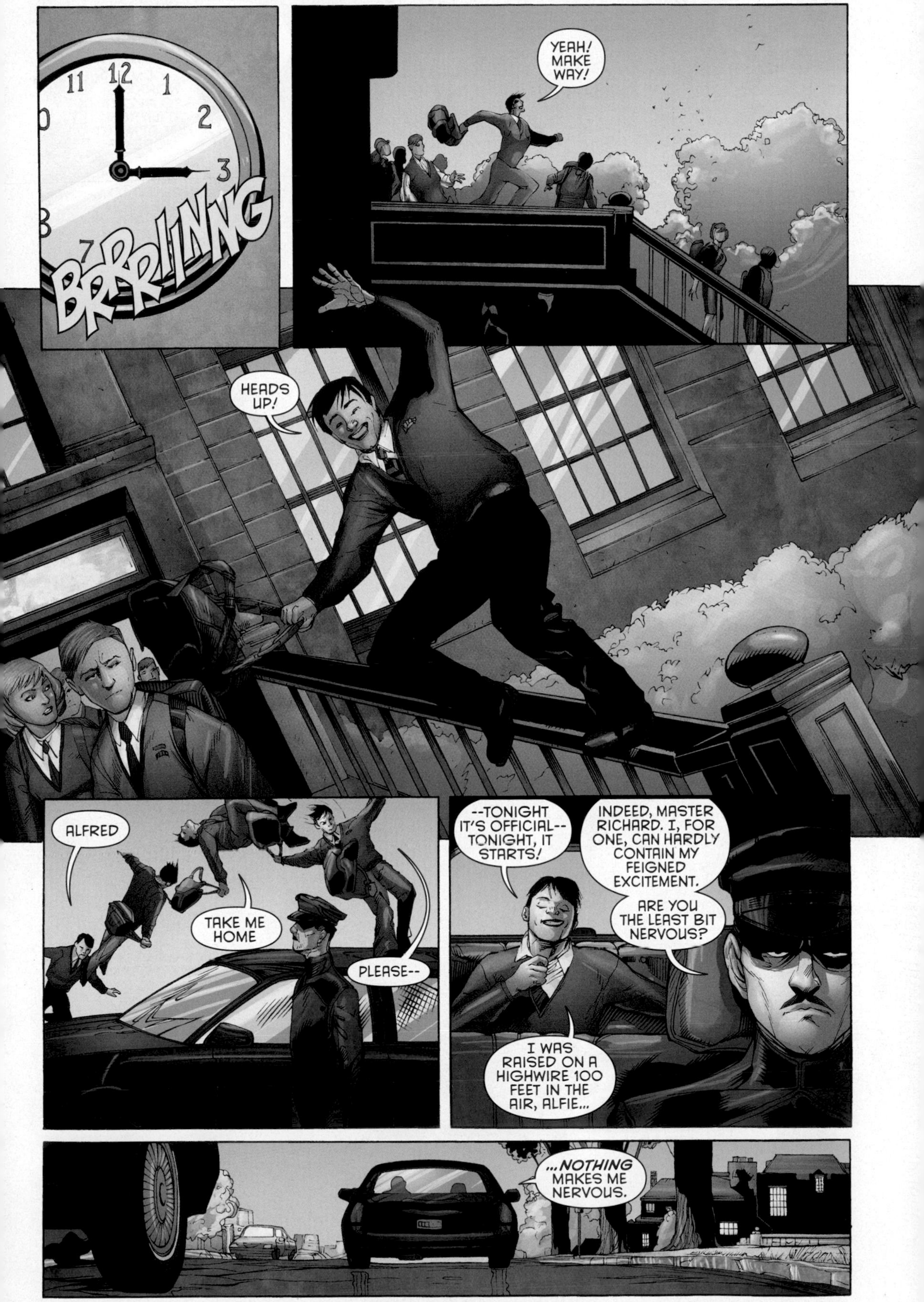
BRRRIINNG
YEAH! MAKE WAY!
HEADS UP!
ALFRED
TAKE ME HOME
PLEASE--
--TONIGHT IT'S OFFICIAL-- TONIGHT, IT STARTS!
INDEED, MASTER RICHARD. I, FOR ONE, CAN HARDLY CONTAIN MY FEIGNED EXCITEMENT.
ARE YOU THE LEAST BIT NERVOUS?
I WAS RAISED ON A HIGHWIRE 100 FEET IN THE AIR, ALFIE...
...NOTHING MAKES ME NERVOUS.

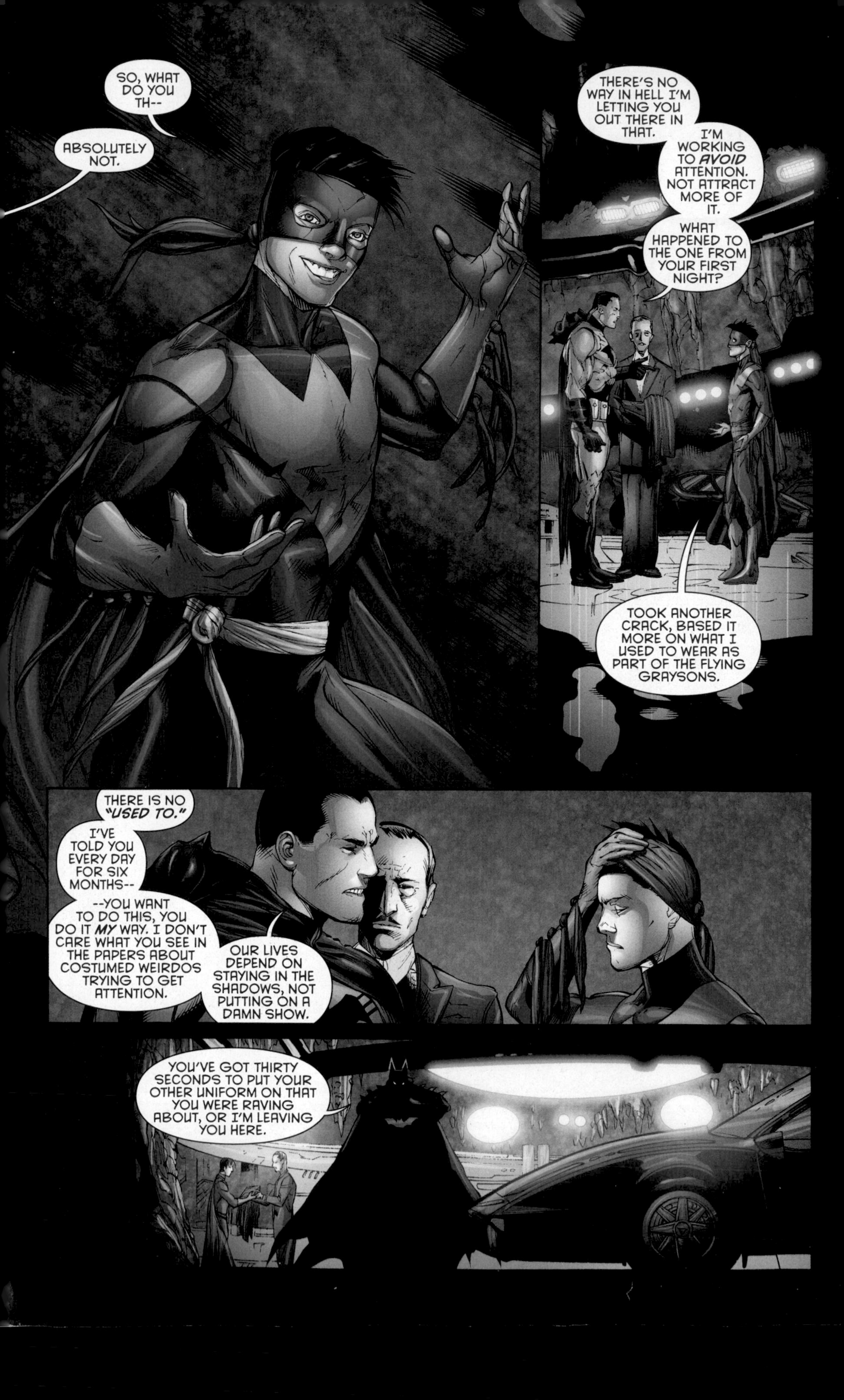
SO, WHAT DO YOU TH--
ABSOLUTELY NOT.
THERE'S NO WAY IN HELL I'M LETTING YOU OUT THERE IN THAT.
I'M WORKING TO AVOID ATTENTION. NOT ATTRACT MORE OF IT.
WHAT HAPPENED TO THE ONE FROM YOUR FIRST NIGHT?
TOOK ANOTHER CRACK, BASED IT MORE ON WHAT I USED TO WEAR AS PART OF THE FLYING GRAYSONS.
THERE IS NO "USED TO."
I'VE TOLD YOU EVERY DAY FOR SIX MONTHS--
--YOU WANT TO DO THIS, YOU DO IT MY WAY. I DON'T CARE WHAT YOU SEE IN THE PAPERS ABOUT COSTUMED WEIRDOS TRYING TO GET ATTENTION.
OUR LIVES DEPEND ON STAYING IN THE SHADOWS, NOT PUTTING ON A DAMN SHOW.
YOU'VE GOT THIRTY SECONDS TO PUT YOUR OTHER UNIFORM ON THAT YOU WERE RAVING ABOUT, OR I'M LEAVING YOU HERE.

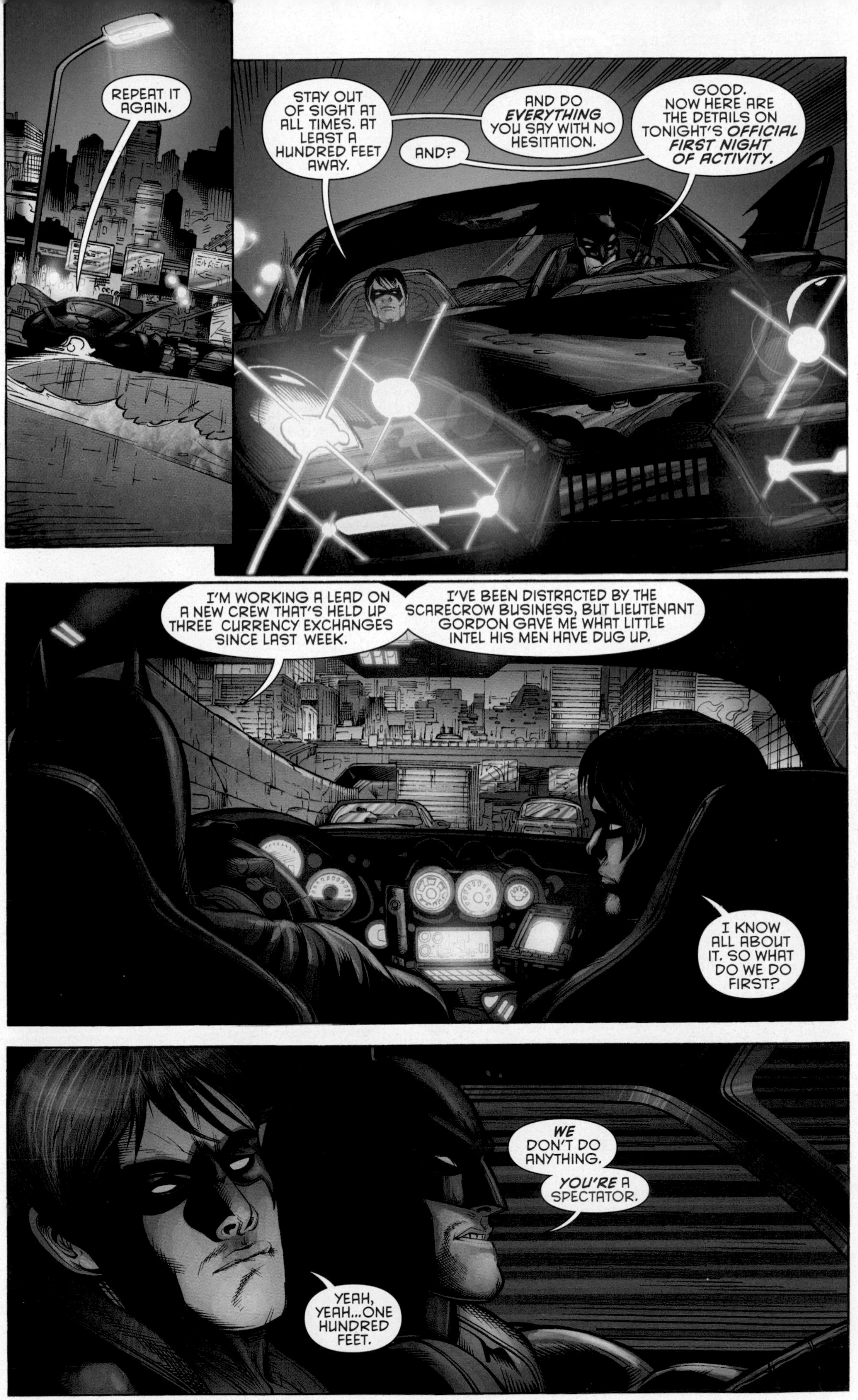
REPEAT IT AGAIN.
STAY OUT OF SIGHT AT ALL TIMES. AT LEAST A HUNDRED FEET AWAY.
AND?
AND DO *EVERYTHING* YOU SAY WITH NO HESITATION.
GOOD. NOW HERE ARE THE DETAILS ON TONIGHT'S *OFFICIAL FIRST NIGHT OF ACTIVITY.*
I'M WORKING A LEAD ON A NEW CREW THAT'S HELD UP THREE CURRENCY EXCHANGES SINCE LAST WEEK.
I'VE BEEN DISTRACTED BY THE SCARECROW BUSINESS, BUT LIEUTENANT GORDON GAVE ME WHAT LITTLE INTEL HIS MEN HAVE DUG UP.
I KNOW ALL ABOUT IT. SO WHAT DO WE DO FIRST?
WE DON'T DO ANYTHING.
YOU'RE A SPECTATOR.
YEAH, YEAH...ONE HUNDRED FEET.

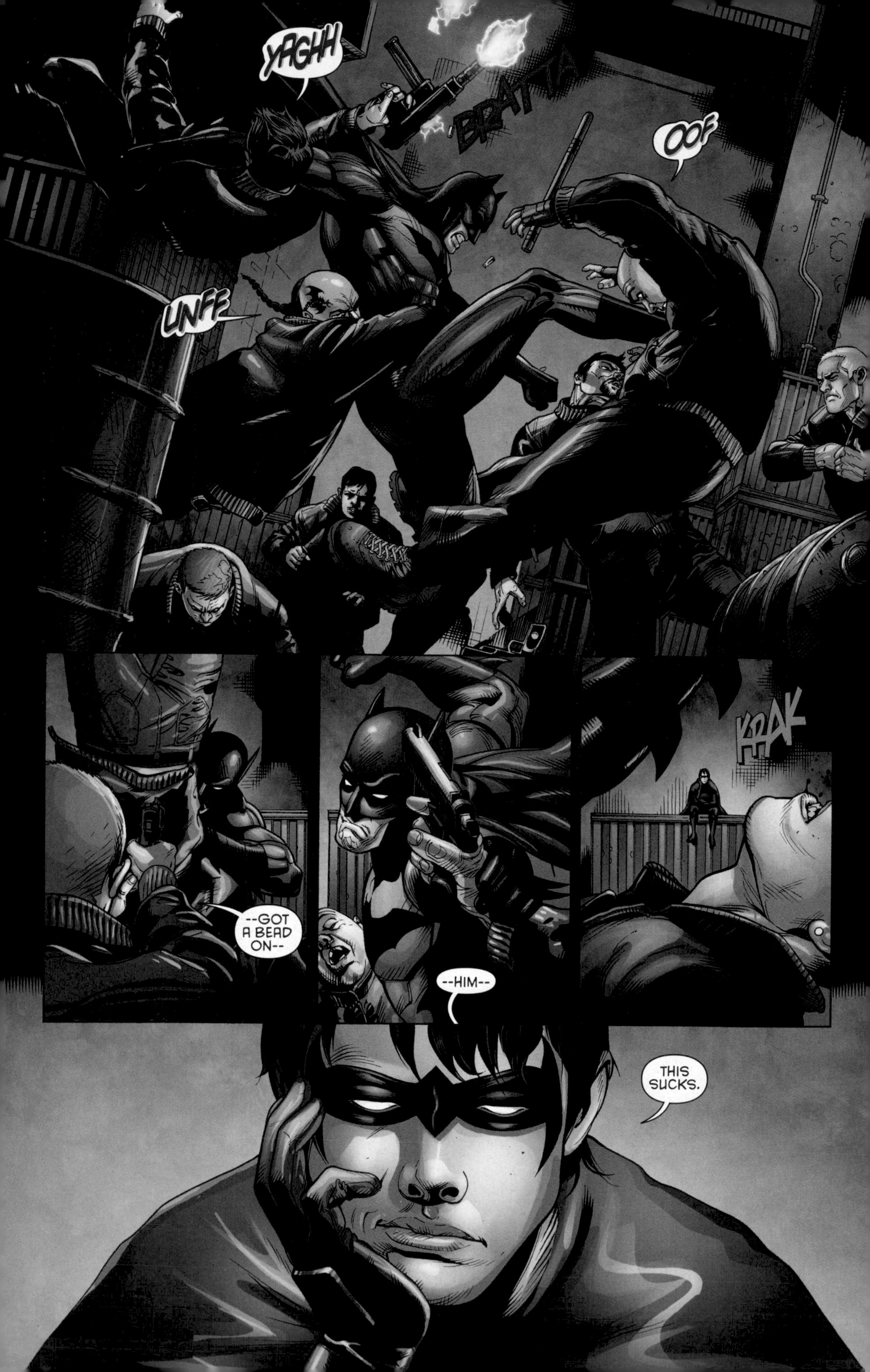
YAGHH
BRATTA
OOF
UNFF
KRAK
--GOT A BEAD ON--
--HIM--
THIS SUCKS.

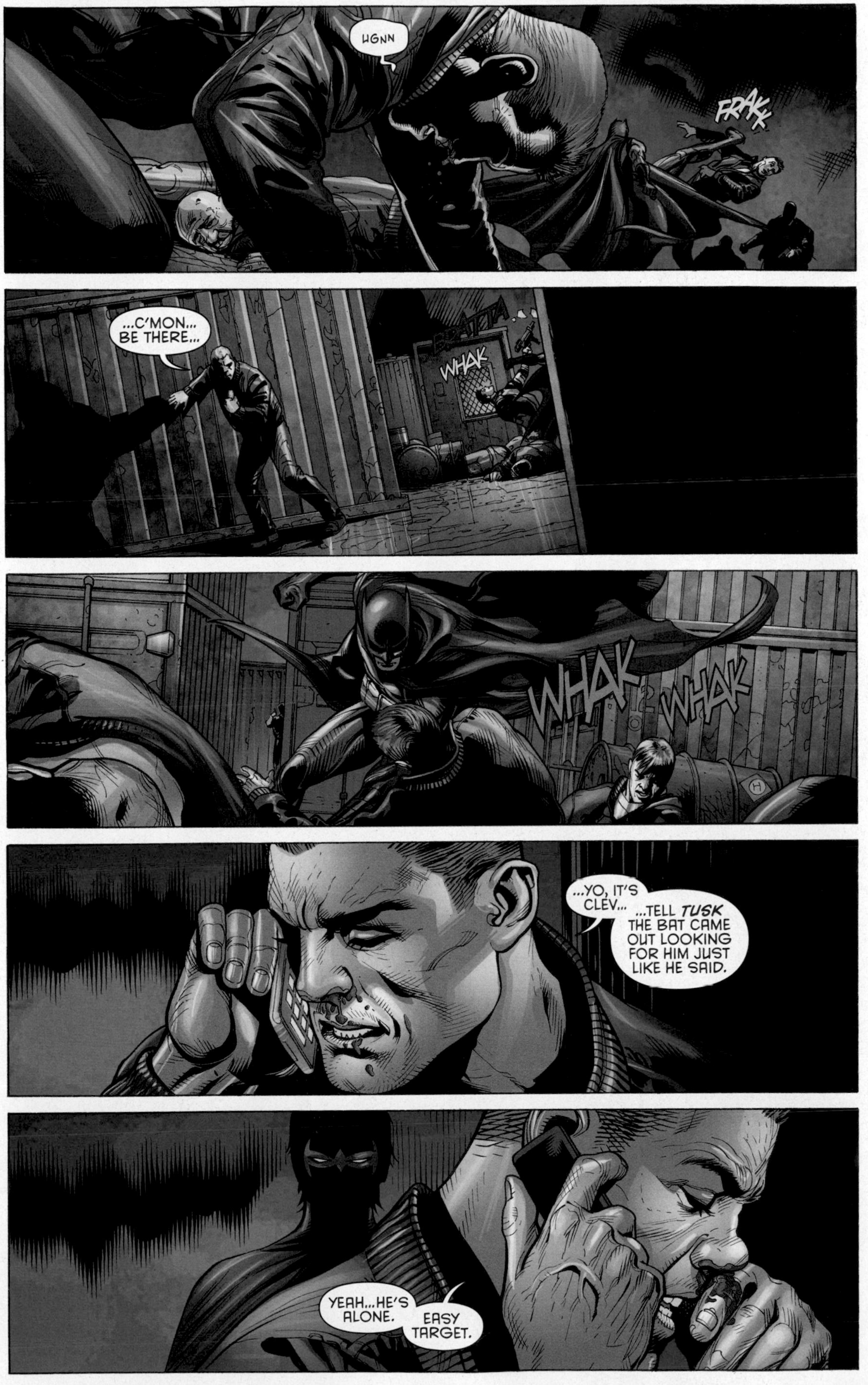
UGNN
FRAKK
...C'MON... BE THERE...
WHAK
WHAK
WHAK
...YO, IT'S CLEV...
...TELL TUSK THE BAT CAME OUT LOOKING FOR HIM JUST LIKE HE SAID.
YEAH...HE'S ALONE.
EASY TARGET.

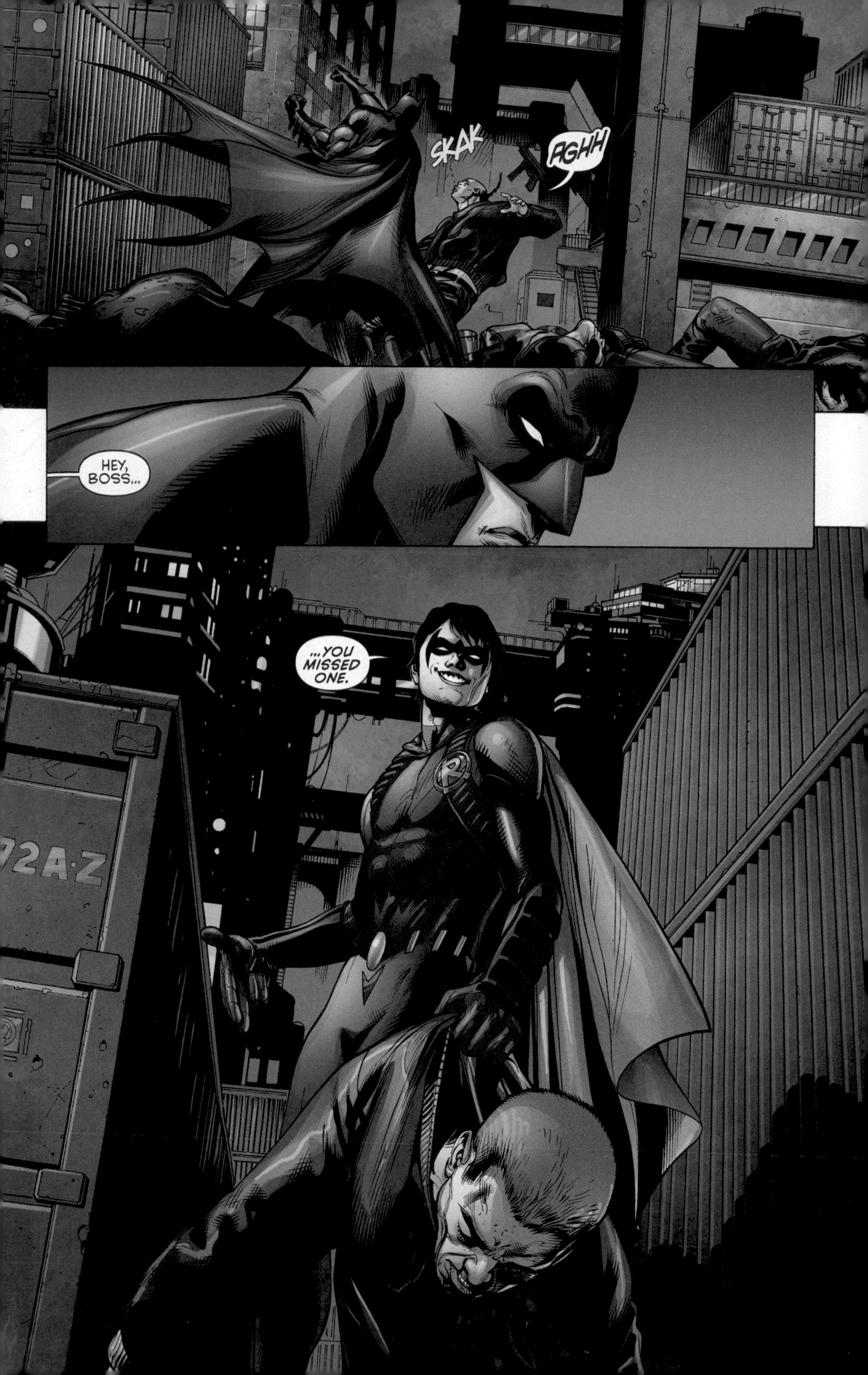
SKAK
AGHH
HEY, BOSS...
...YOU MISSED ONE.
72A-Z

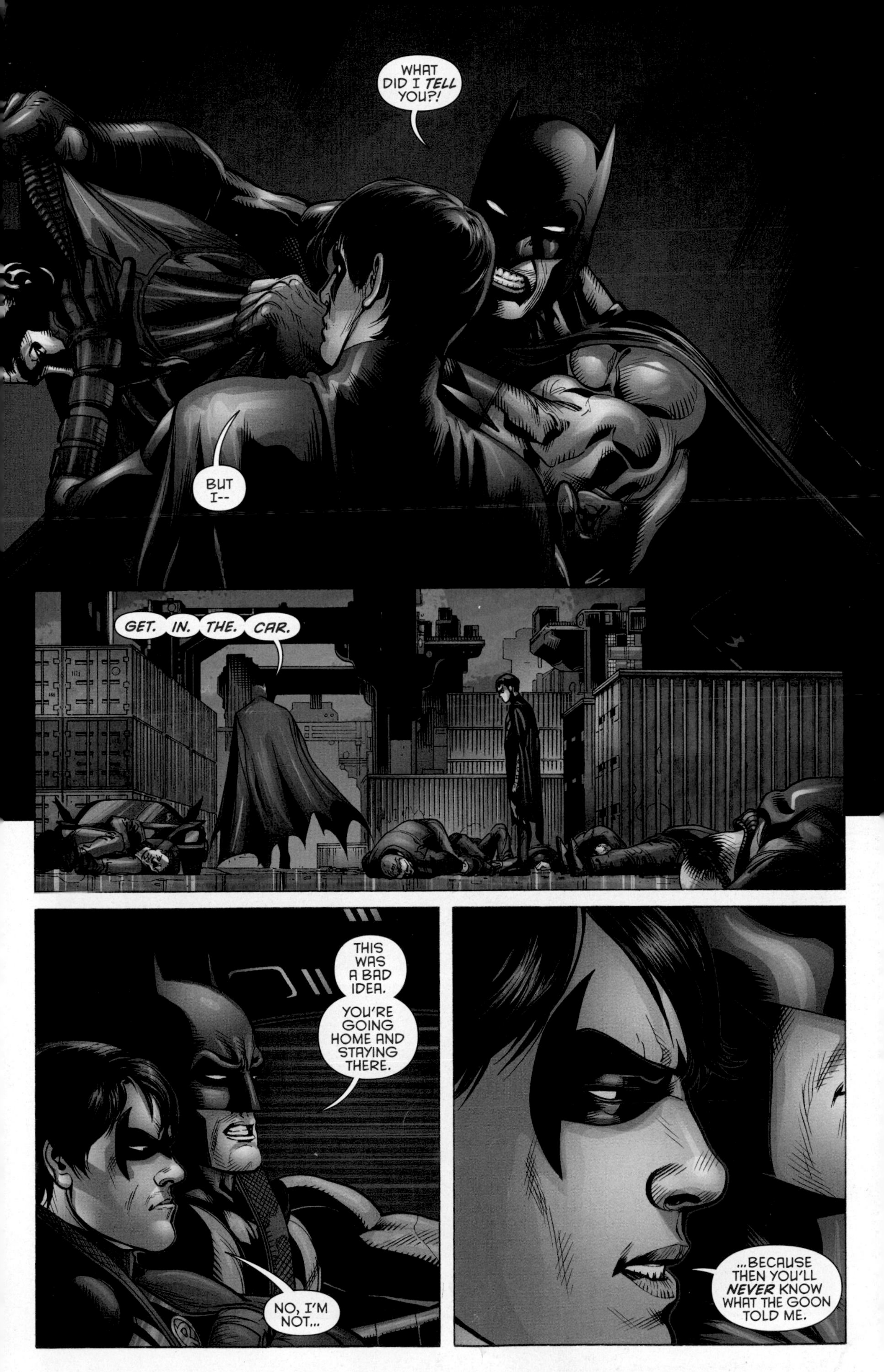
WHAT DID I TELL YOU?!
BUT I--
GET. IN. THE. CAR.
THIS WAS A BAD IDEA.
YOU'RE GOING HOME AND STAYING THERE.
NO, I'M NOT...
...BECAUSE THEN YOU'LL NEVER KNOW WHAT THE GOON TOLD ME.

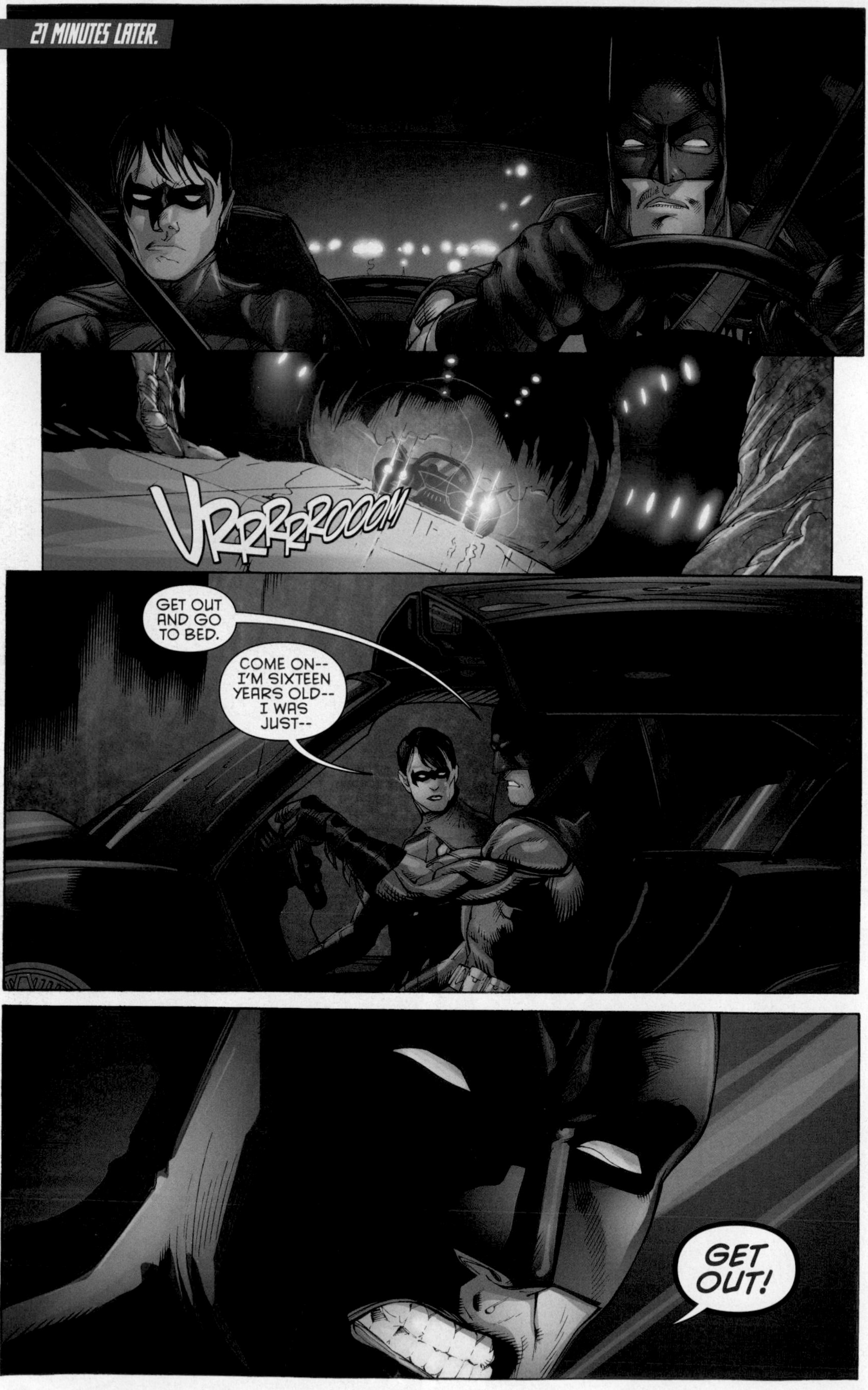
21 MINUTES LATER.
VRRRRROOOOM
GET OUT AND GO TO BED.
COME ON-- I'M SIXTEEN YEARS OLD-- I WAS JUST--
GET OUT!

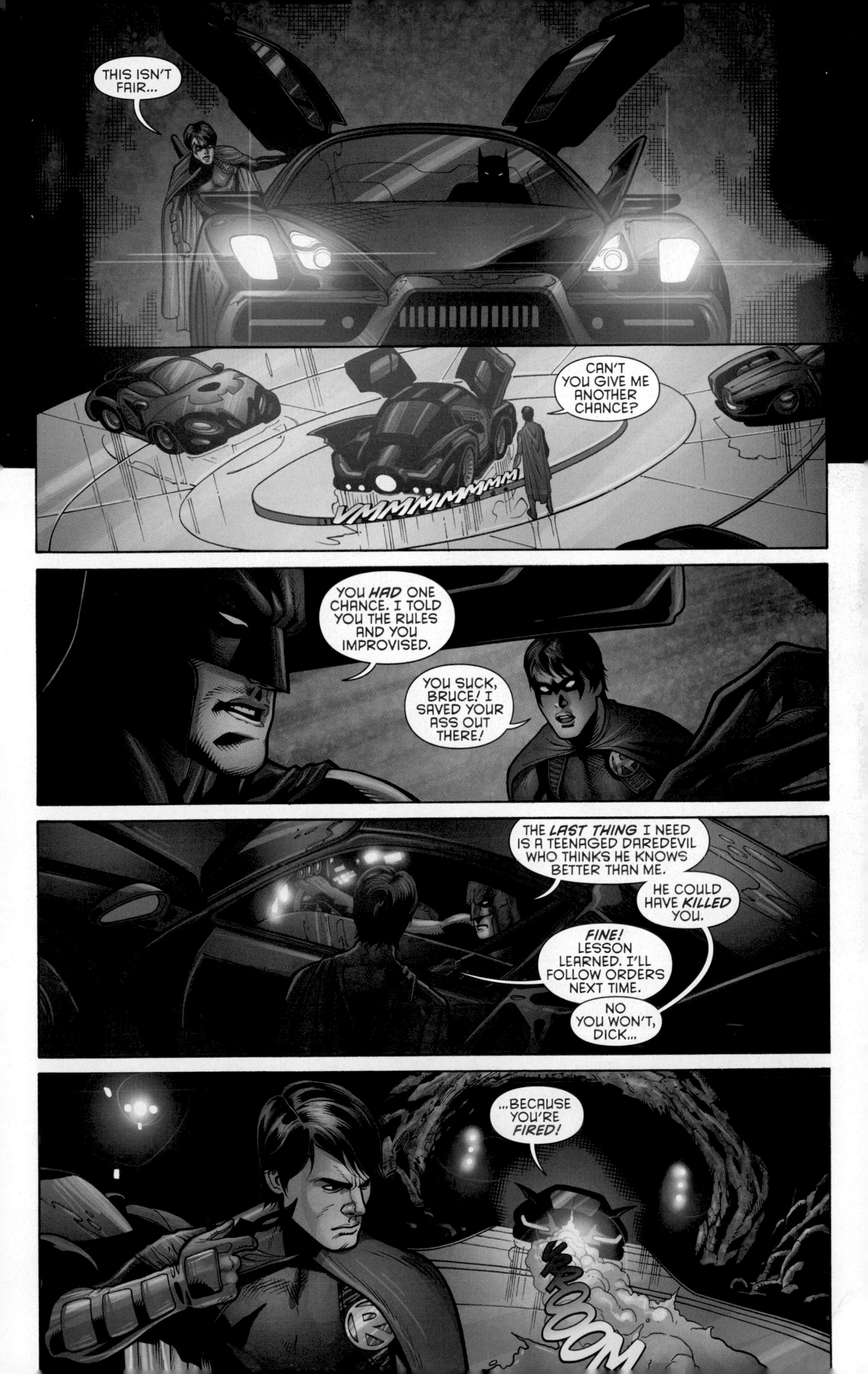
THIS ISN'T FAIR...
CAN'T YOU GIVE ME ANOTHER CHANCE?
VMMMMMMMMM
YOU *HAD* ONE CHANCE. I TOLD YOU THE RULES AND YOU IMPROVISED.
YOU SUCK, BRUCE! I SAVED YOUR ASS OUT THERE!
THE *LAST THING* I NEED IS A TEENAGED DAREDEVIL WHO THINKS HE KNOWS BETTER THAN ME.
HE COULD HAVE *KILLED* YOU.
FINE! LESSON LEARNED. I'LL FOLLOW ORDERS NEXT TIME.
NO YOU WON'T, DICK...
...BECAUSE YOU'RE *FIRED!*
VROOOOM

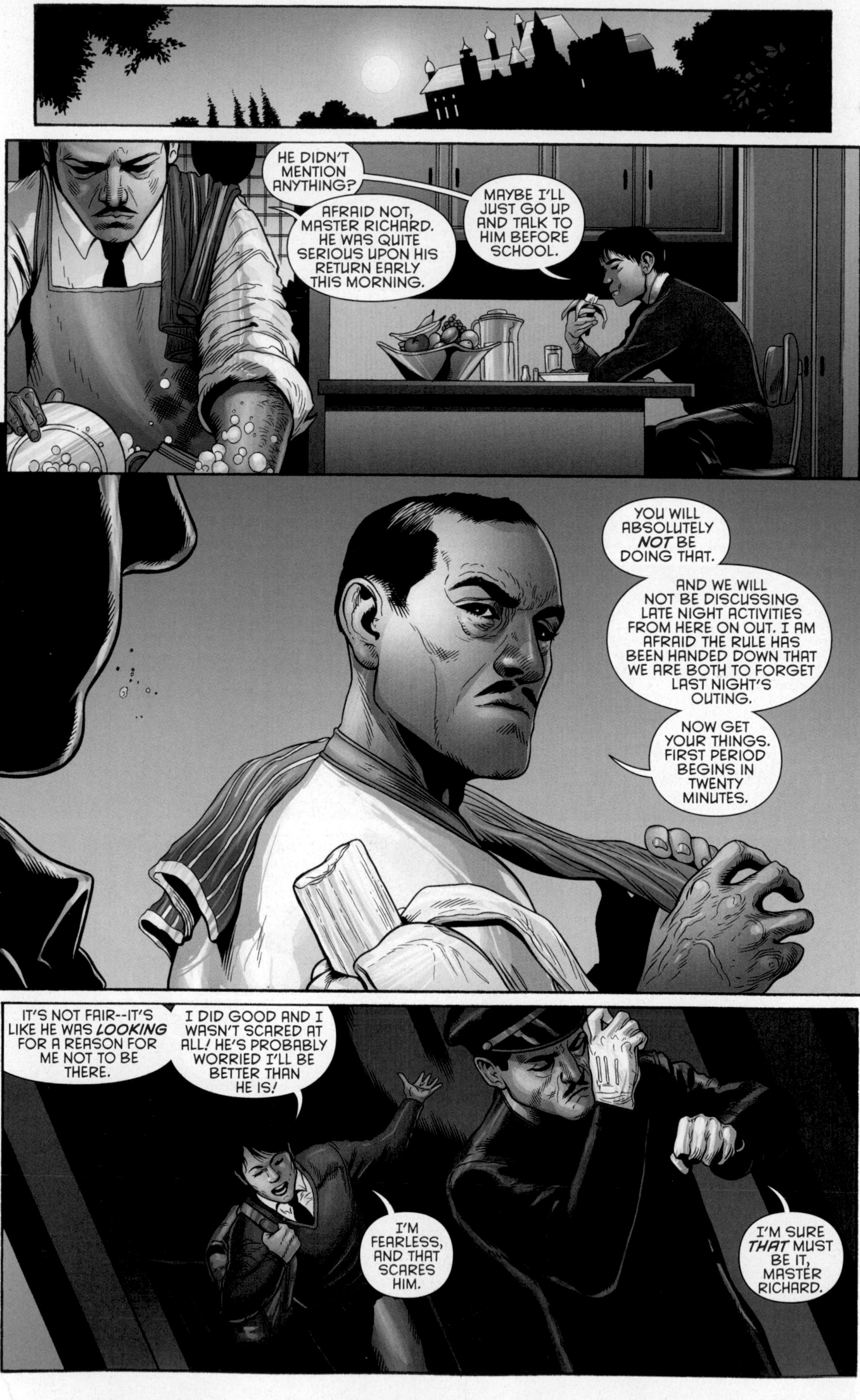
HE DIDN'T MENTION ANYTHING?
AFRAID NOT, MASTER RICHARD. HE WAS QUITE SERIOUS UPON HIS RETURN EARLY THIS MORNING.
MAYBE I'LL JUST GO UP AND TALK TO HIM BEFORE SCHOOL.
YOU WILL ABSOLUTELY *NOT* BE DOING THAT.
AND WE WILL NOT BE DISCUSSING LATE NIGHT ACTIVITIES FROM HERE ON OUT. I AM AFRAID THE RULE HAS BEEN HANDED DOWN THAT WE ARE BOTH TO FORGET LAST NIGHT'S OUTING.
NOW GET YOUR THINGS. FIRST PERIOD BEGINS IN TWENTY MINUTES.
IT'S NOT FAIR--IT'S LIKE HE WAS *LOOKING* FOR A REASON FOR ME NOT TO BE THERE.
I DID GOOD AND I WASN'T SCARED AT ALL! HE'S PROBABLY WORRIED I'LL BE BETTER THAN HE IS!
I'M FEARLESS, AND THAT SCARES HIM.
I'M SURE *THAT* MUST BE IT, MASTER RICHARD.

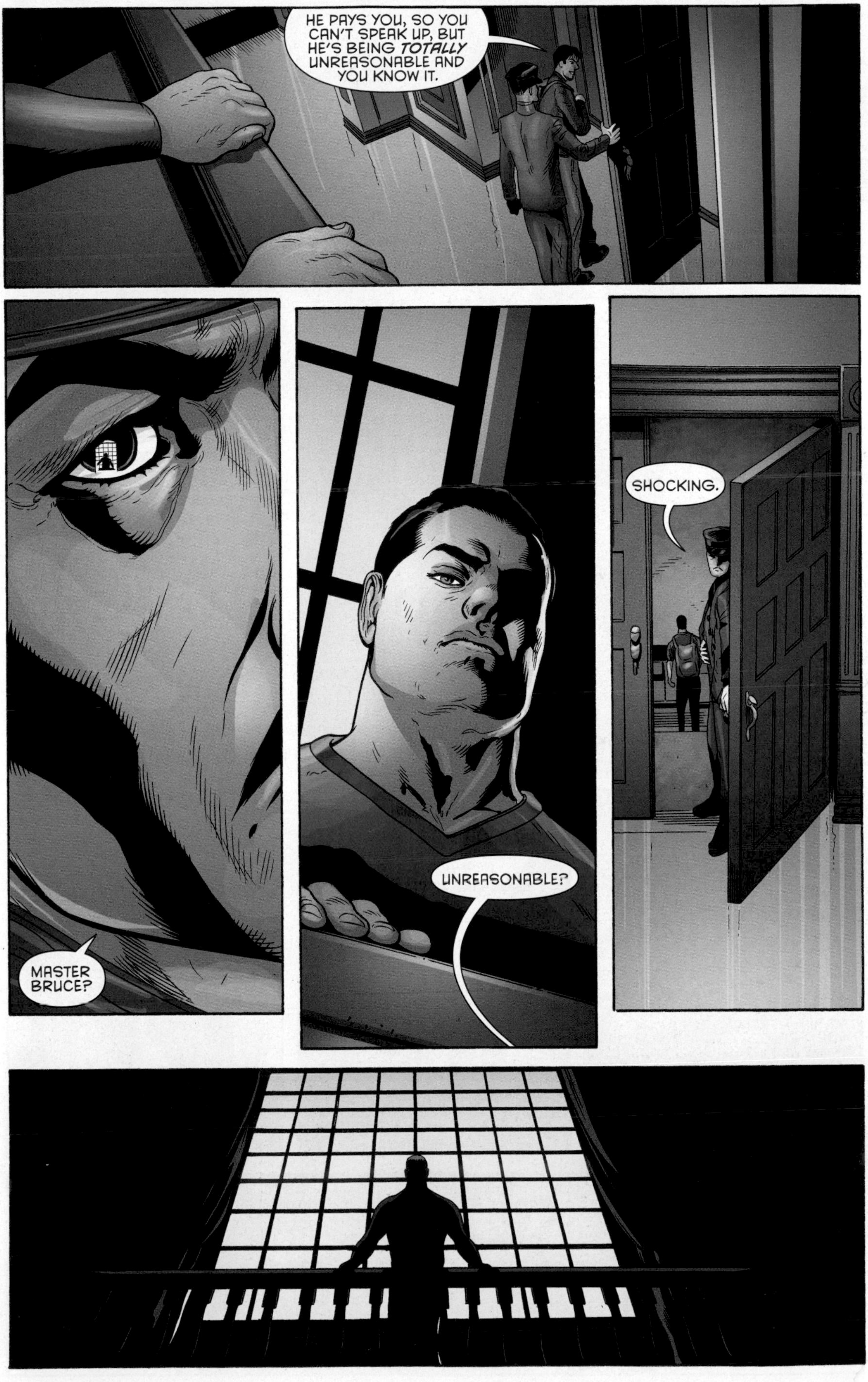
HE PAYS YOU, SO YOU CAN'T SPEAK UP, BUT HE'S BEING *TOTALLY* UNREASONABLE AND YOU KNOW IT.
MASTER BRUCE?
UNREASONABLE?
SHOCKING.

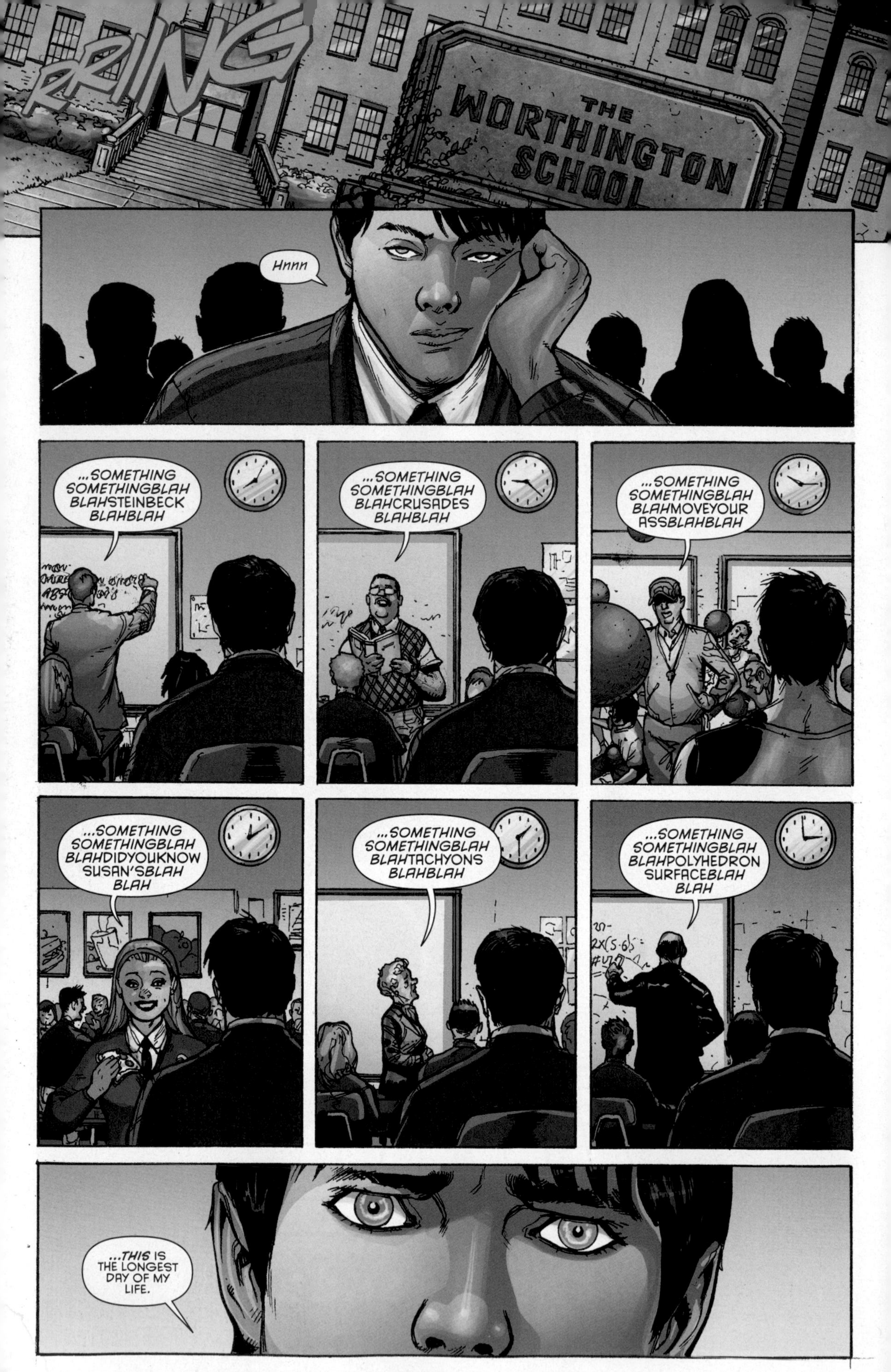
RRING
THE WORTHINGTON SCHOOL
Hnnn
...SOMETHING SOMETHINGBLAH BLAHSTEINBECK BLAHBLAH
...SOMETHING SOMETHINGBLAH BLAHCRUSADES BLAHBLAH
...SOMETHING SOMETHINGBLAH BLAHMOVEYOUR ASSBLAHBLAH
...SOMETHING SOMETHINGBLAH BLAHDIDYOUKNOW SUSAN'SBLAH BLAH
...SOMETHING SOMETHINGBLAH BLAHTACHYONS BLAHBLAH
...SOMETHING SOMETHINGBLAH BLAHPOLYHEDRON SURFACEBLAH BLAH
...THIS IS THE LONGEST DAY OF MY LIFE.

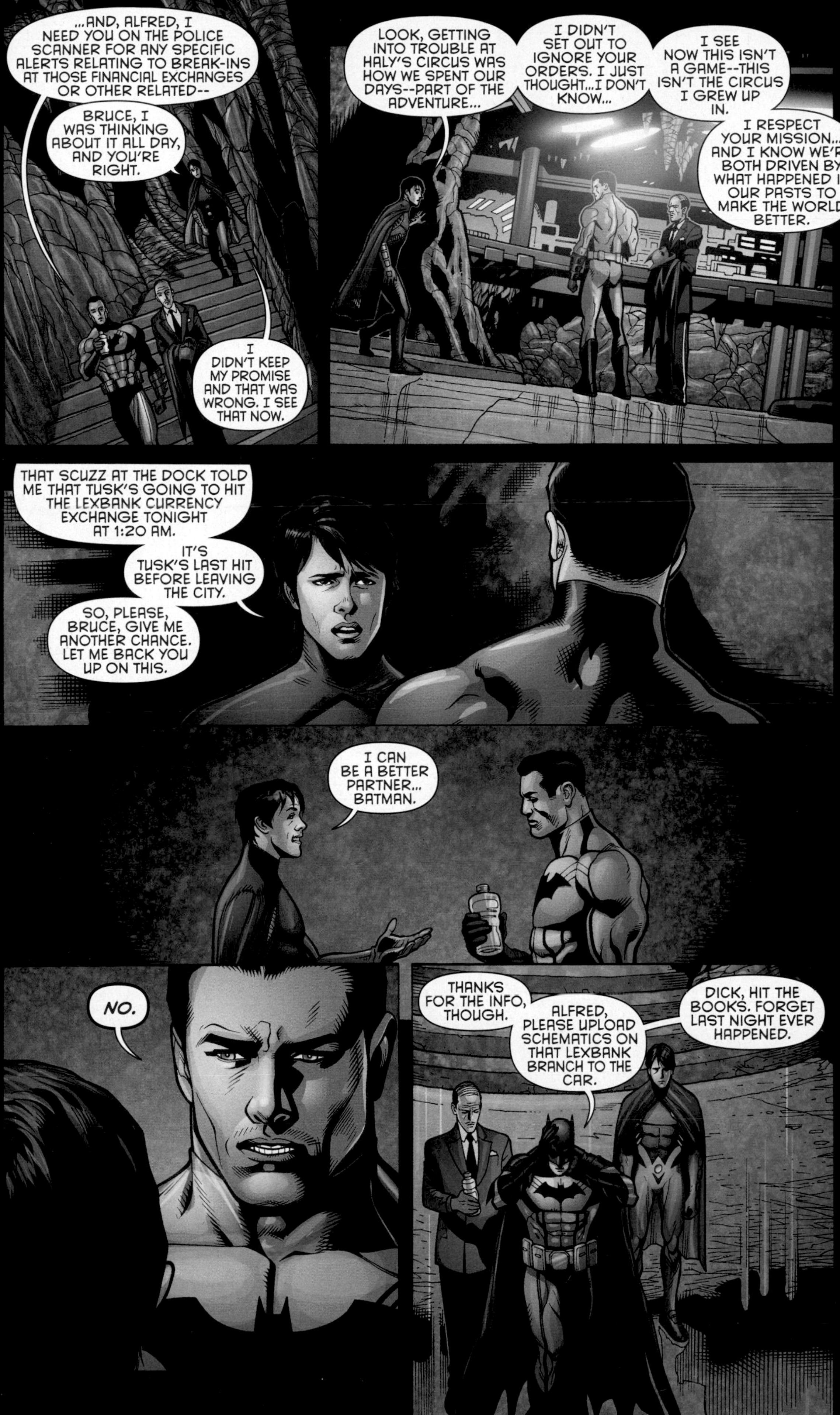
...AND, ALFRED, I NEED YOU ON THE POLICE SCANNER FOR ANY SPECIFIC ALERTS RELATING TO BREAK-INS AT THOSE FINANCIAL EXCHANGES OR OTHER RELATED--
BRUCE, I WAS THINKING ABOUT IT ALL DAY, AND YOU'RE RIGHT.
I DIDN'T KEEP MY PROMISE AND THAT WAS WRONG. I SEE THAT NOW.
LOOK, GETTING INTO TROUBLE AT HALY'S CIRCUS WAS HOW WE SPENT OUR DAYS--PART OF THE ADVENTURE...
I DIDN'T SET OUT TO IGNORE YOUR ORDERS. I JUST THOUGHT...I DON'T KNOW...
I SEE NOW THIS ISN'T A GAME--THIS ISN'T THE CIRCUS I GREW UP IN.
I RESPECT YOUR MISSION... AND I KNOW WE'RE BOTH DRIVEN BY WHAT HAPPENED IN OUR PASTS TO MAKE THE WORLD BETTER.
THAT SCUZZ AT THE DOCK TOLD ME THAT TUSK'S GOING TO HIT THE LEXBANK CURRENCY EXCHANGE TONIGHT AT 1:20 AM.
IT'S TUSK'S LAST HIT BEFORE LEAVING THE CITY.
SO, PLEASE, BRUCE, GIVE ME ANOTHER CHANCE. LET ME BACK YOU UP ON THIS.
I CAN BE A BETTER PARTNER... BATMAN.
NO.
THANKS FOR THE INFO, THOUGH.
ALFRED, PLEASE UPLOAD SCHEMATICS ON THAT LEXBANK BRANCH TO THE CAR.
DICK, HIT THE BOOKS. FORGET LAST NIGHT EVER HAPPENED.

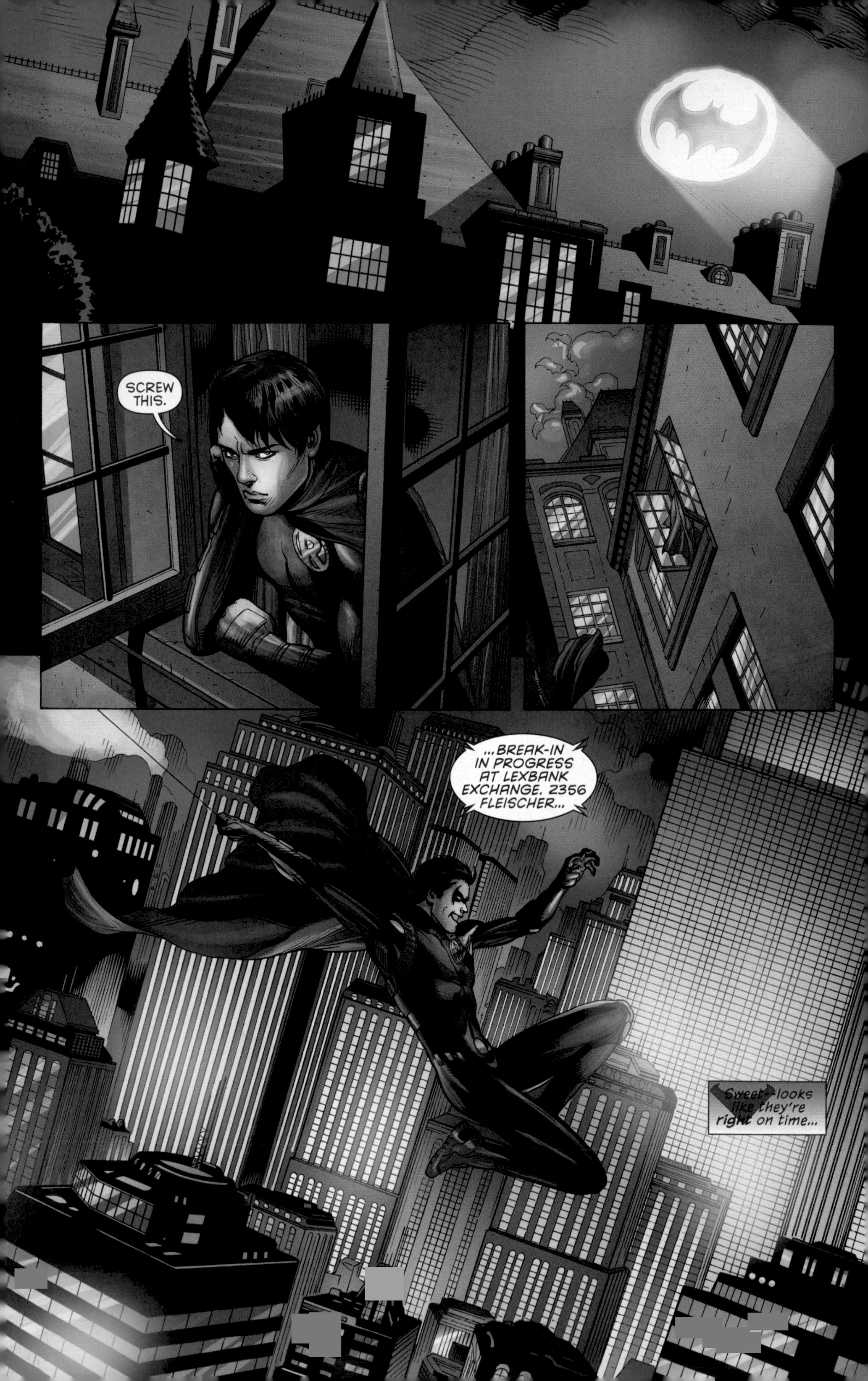
SCREW THIS.
...BREAK-IN IN PROGRESS AT LEXBANK EXCHANGE. 2356 FLEISCHER...
Sweet--looks like they're right on time...

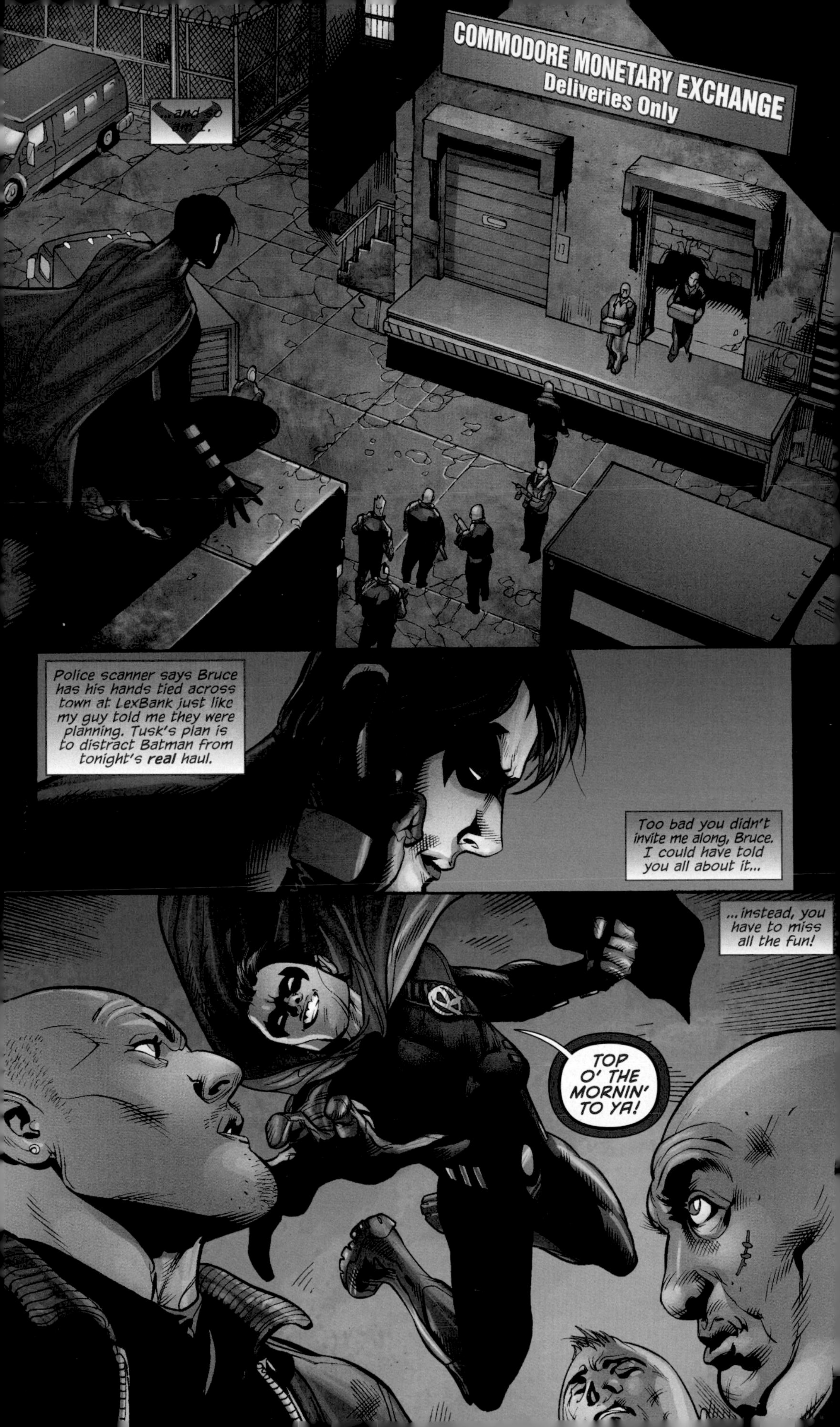
COMMODORE MONETARY EXCHANGE
Deliveries Only
Police scanner says Bruce has his hands tied across town at LexBank just like my guy told me they were planning. Tusk's plan is to distract Batman from tonight's **real** haul.
Too bad you didn't invite me along, Bruce. I could have told you all about it...
...instead, you have to miss all the fun!
TOP O' THE MORNIN' TO YA!

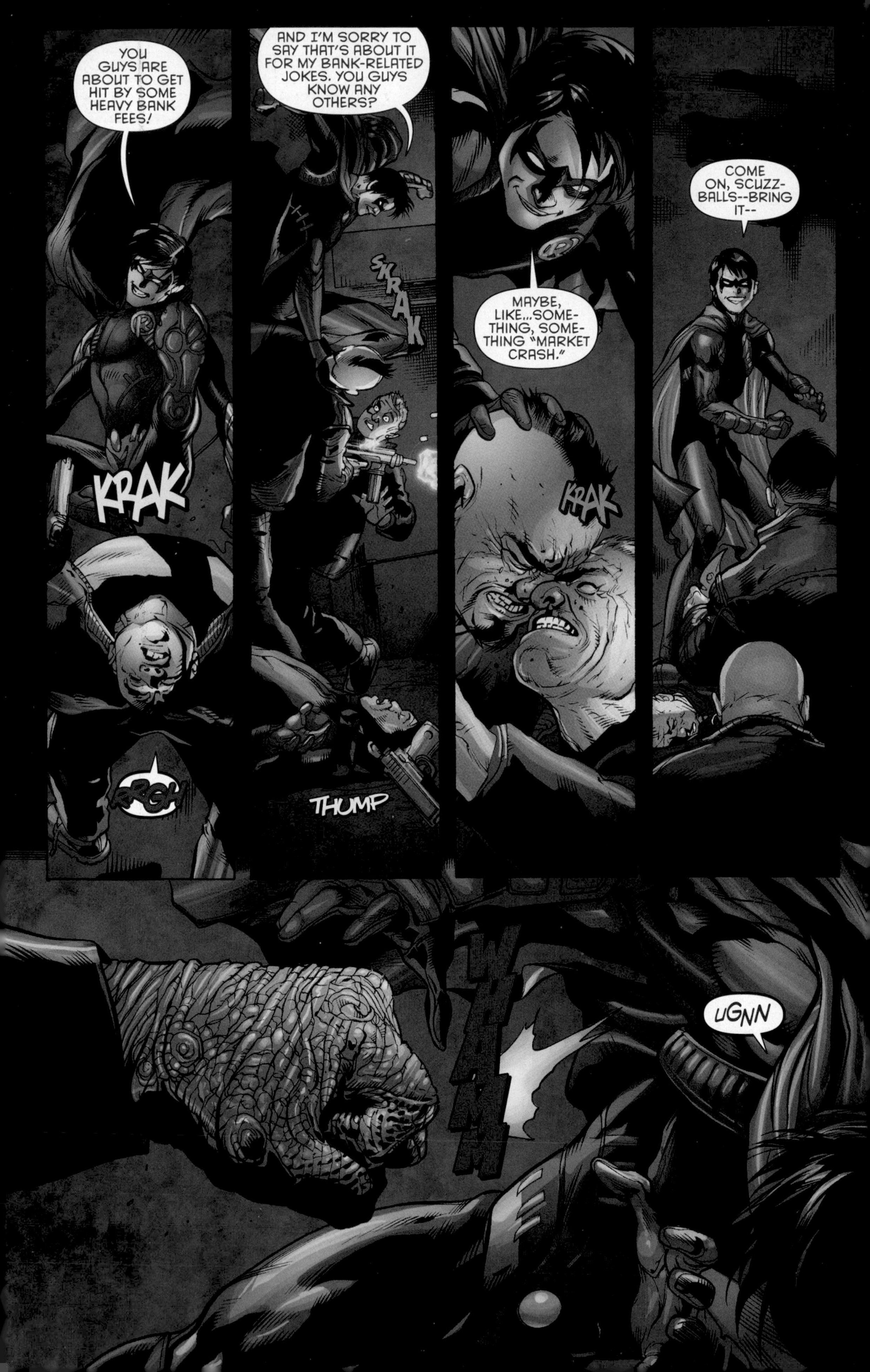
YOU GUYS ARE ABOUT TO GET HIT BY SOME HEAVY BANK FEES!
KRAK
RRGH
AND I'M SORRY TO SAY THAT'S ABOUT IT FOR MY BANK-RELATED JOKES. YOU GUYS KNOW ANY OTHERS?
SKRAK
THUMP
MAYBE, LIKE...SOME-THING, SOME-THING "MARKET CRASH."
KRAK
COME ON, SCUZZ-BALLS--BRING IT--
WHAM
UGNN

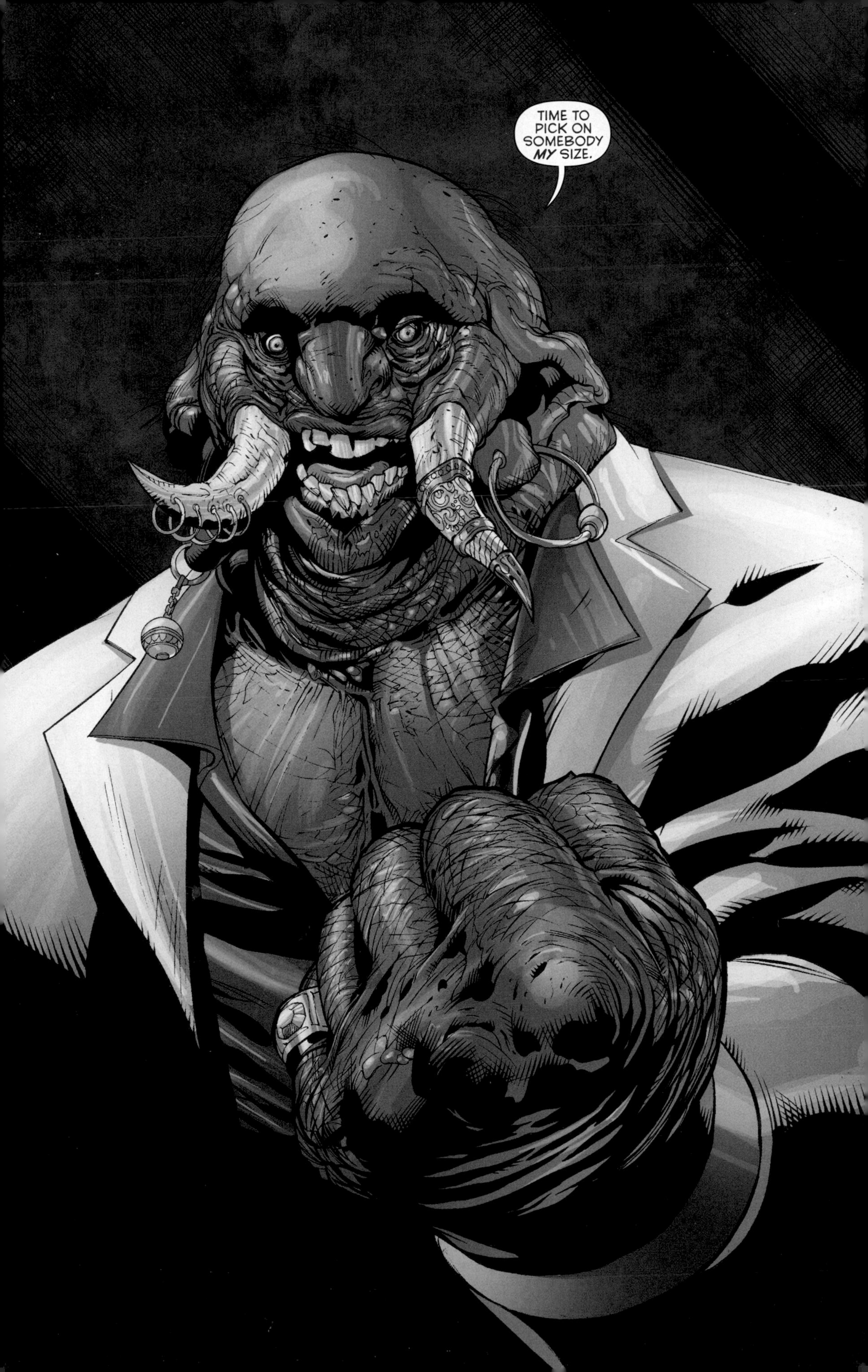
TIME TO PICK ON SOMEBODY *MY* SIZE.

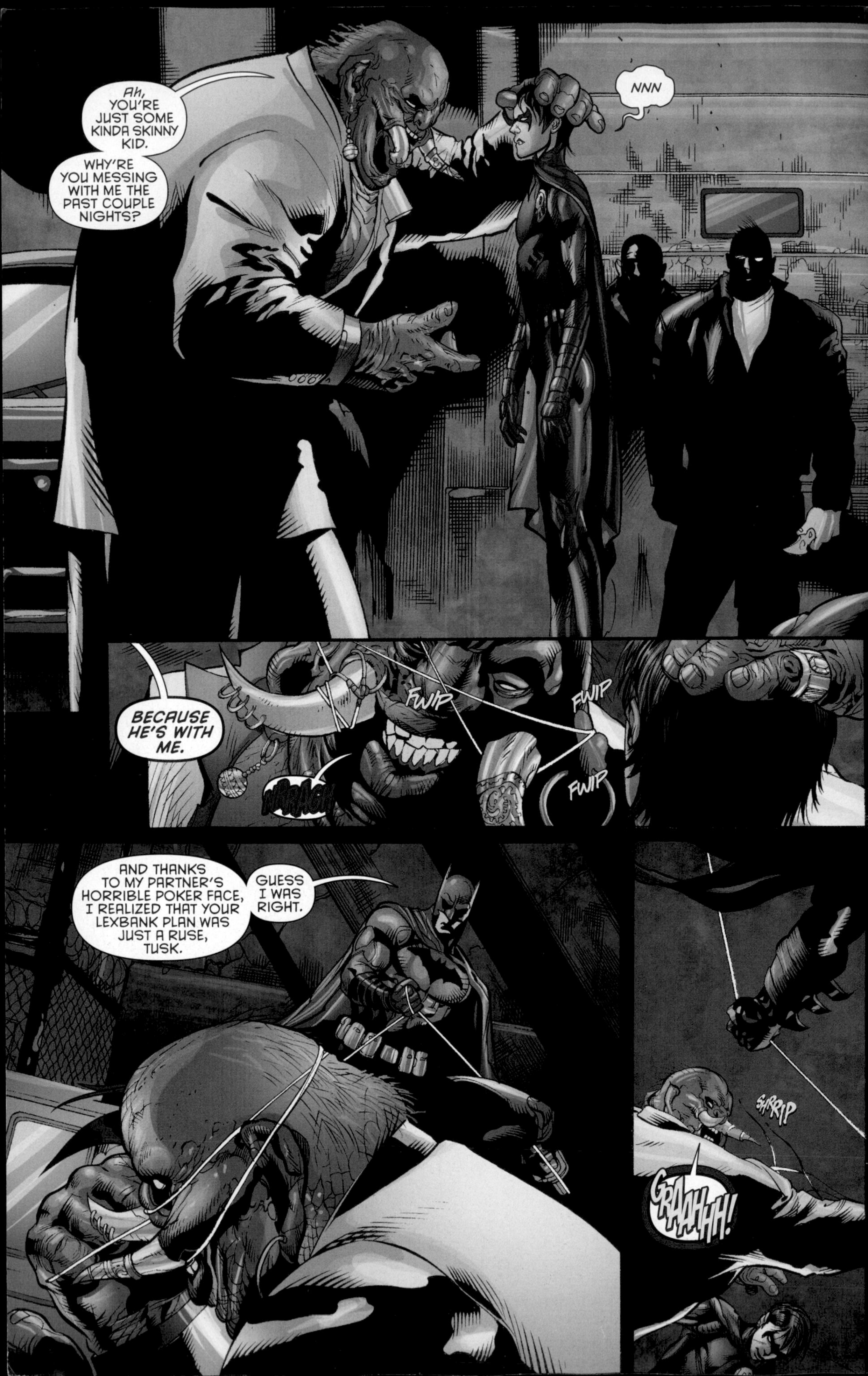

Ah, YOU'RE JUST SOME KINDA SKINNY KID.
WHY'RE YOU MESSING WITH ME THE PAST COUPLE NIGHTS?
NNN
BECAUSE HE'S WITH ME.
FWIP
FWIP
FWIP
AND THANKS TO MY PARTNER'S HORRIBLE POKER FACE, I REALIZED THAT YOUR LEXBANK PLAN WAS JUST A RUSE, TUSK.
GUESS I WAS RIGHT.
SHRRIP
GRAAHHH!

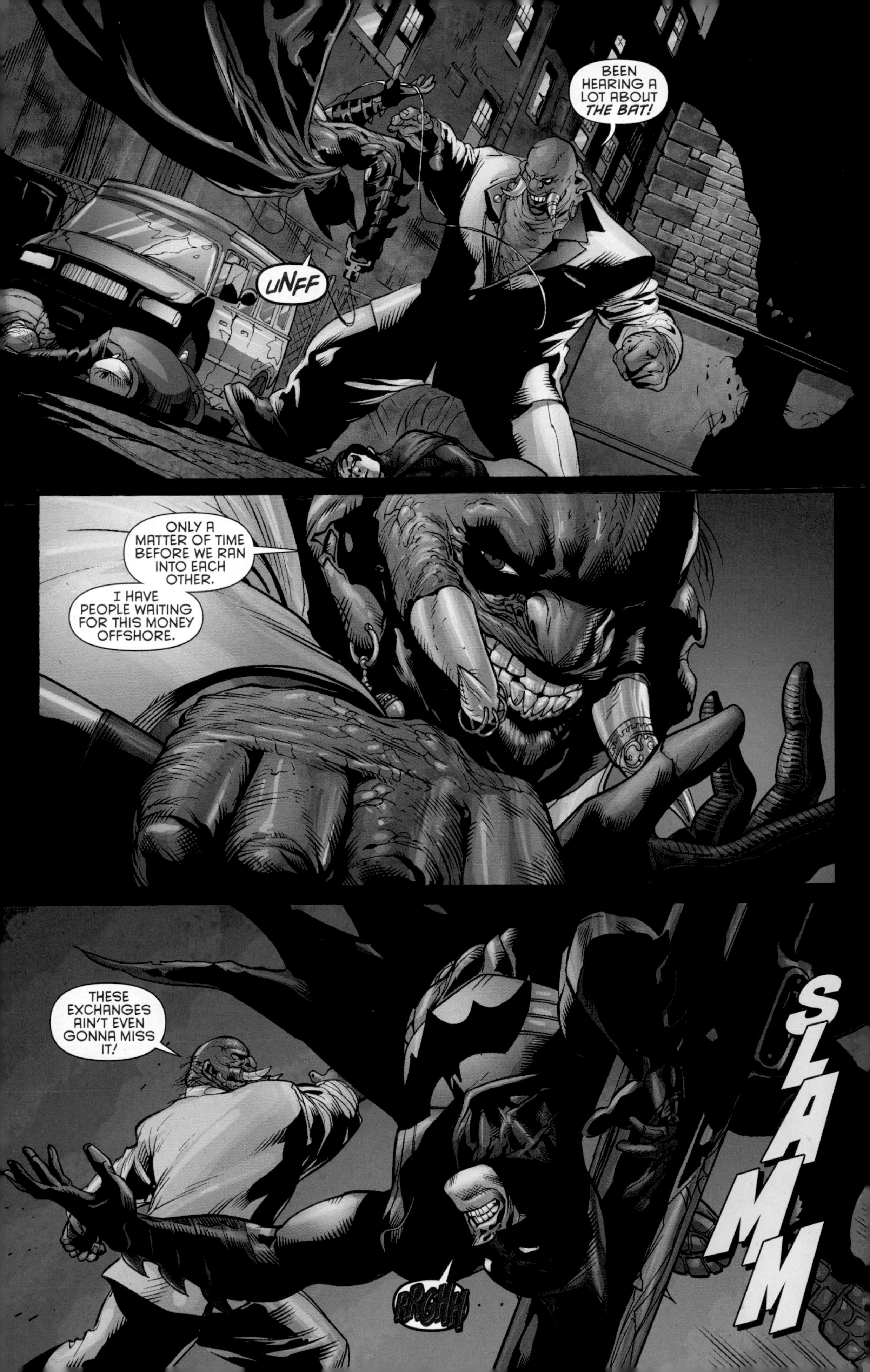
BEEN HEARING A LOT ABOUT THE BAT!
UNFF
ONLY A MATTER OF TIME BEFORE WE RAN INTO EACH OTHER.
I HAVE PEOPLE WAITING FOR THIS MONEY OFFSHORE.
THESE EXCHANGES AIN'T EVEN GONNA MISS IT!
SLAMM
RRGHH

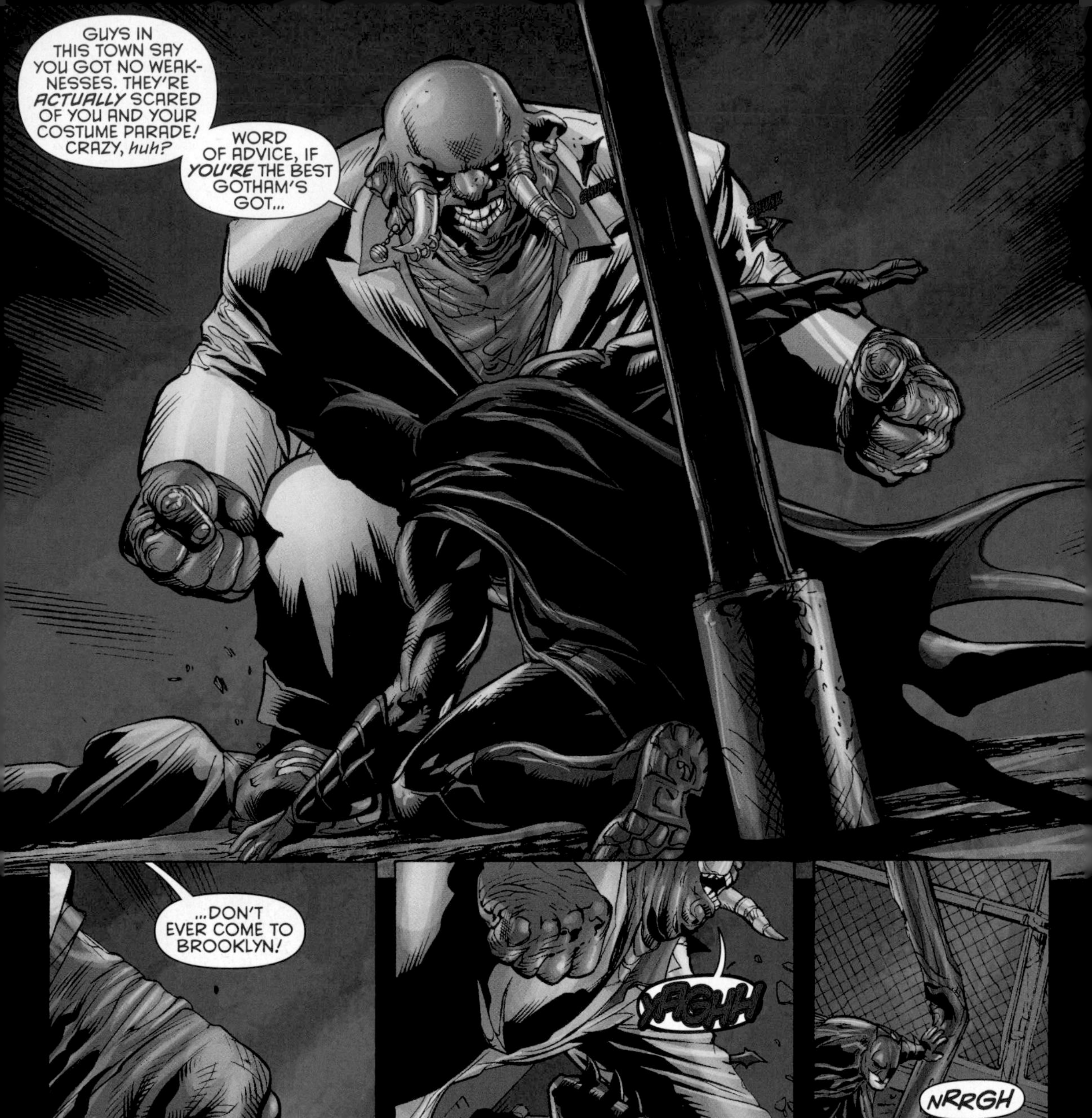
GUYS IN THIS TOWN SAY YOU GOT NO WEAK-NESSES. THEY'RE ACTUALLY SCARED OF YOU AND YOUR COSTUME PARADE! CRAZY, huh?
WORD OF ADVICE, IF YOU'RE THE BEST GOTHAM'S GOT...
...DON'T EVER COME TO BROOKLYN!
YAGHH
SKRAK
KOOOMM
NRRGH
SHOOT THE KID!

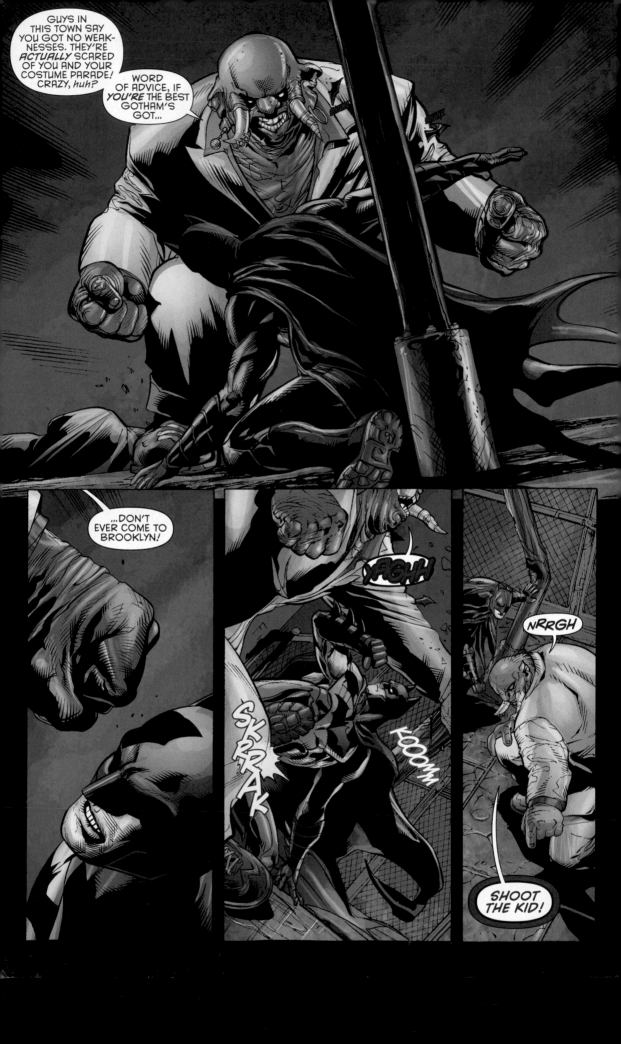

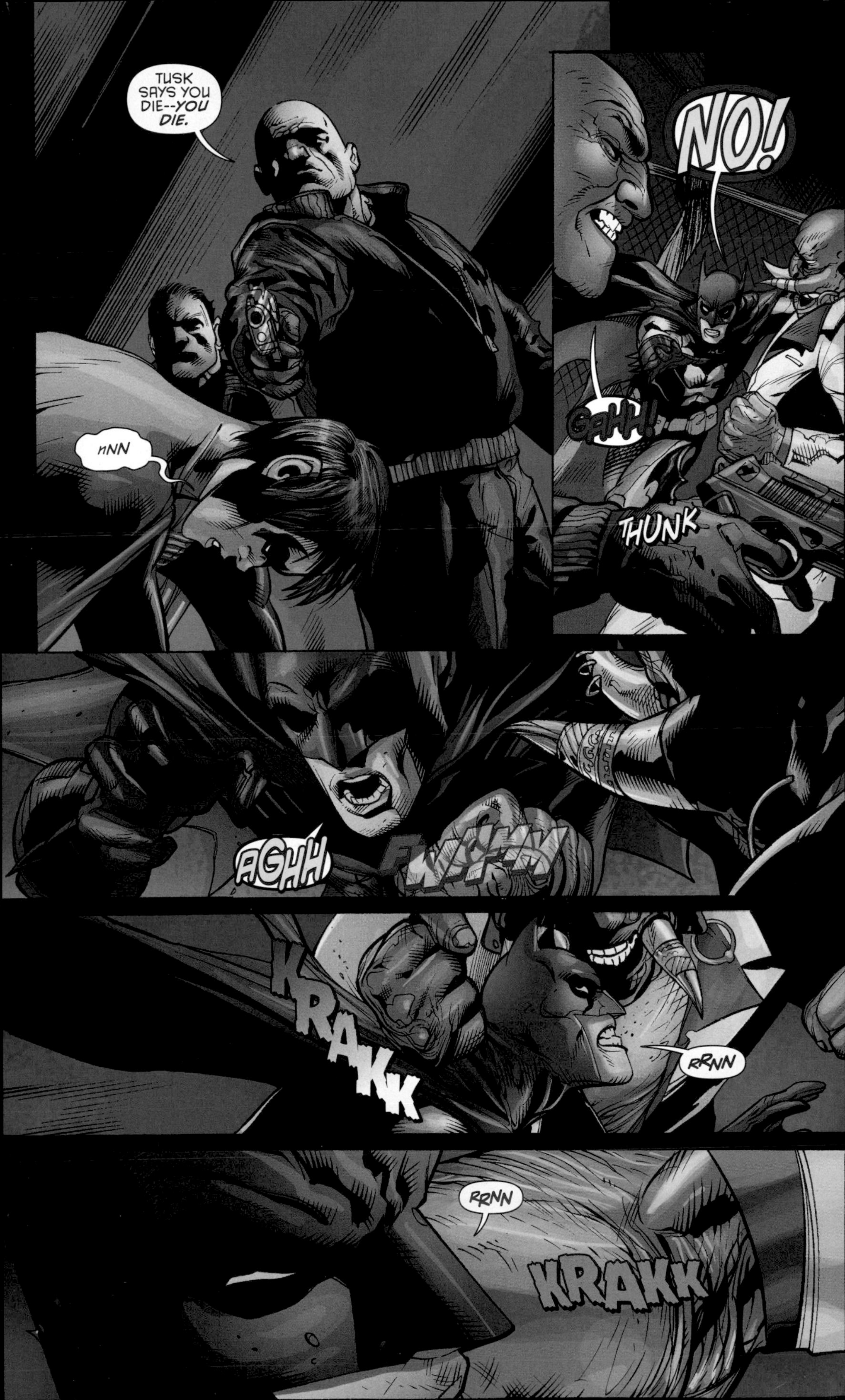
TUSK SAYS YOU DIE--YOU DIE.
NO!
MNN
GAHH!
THUNK
AGHH
FWHMM
KRAKK
RRNN
RRNN
KRAKK

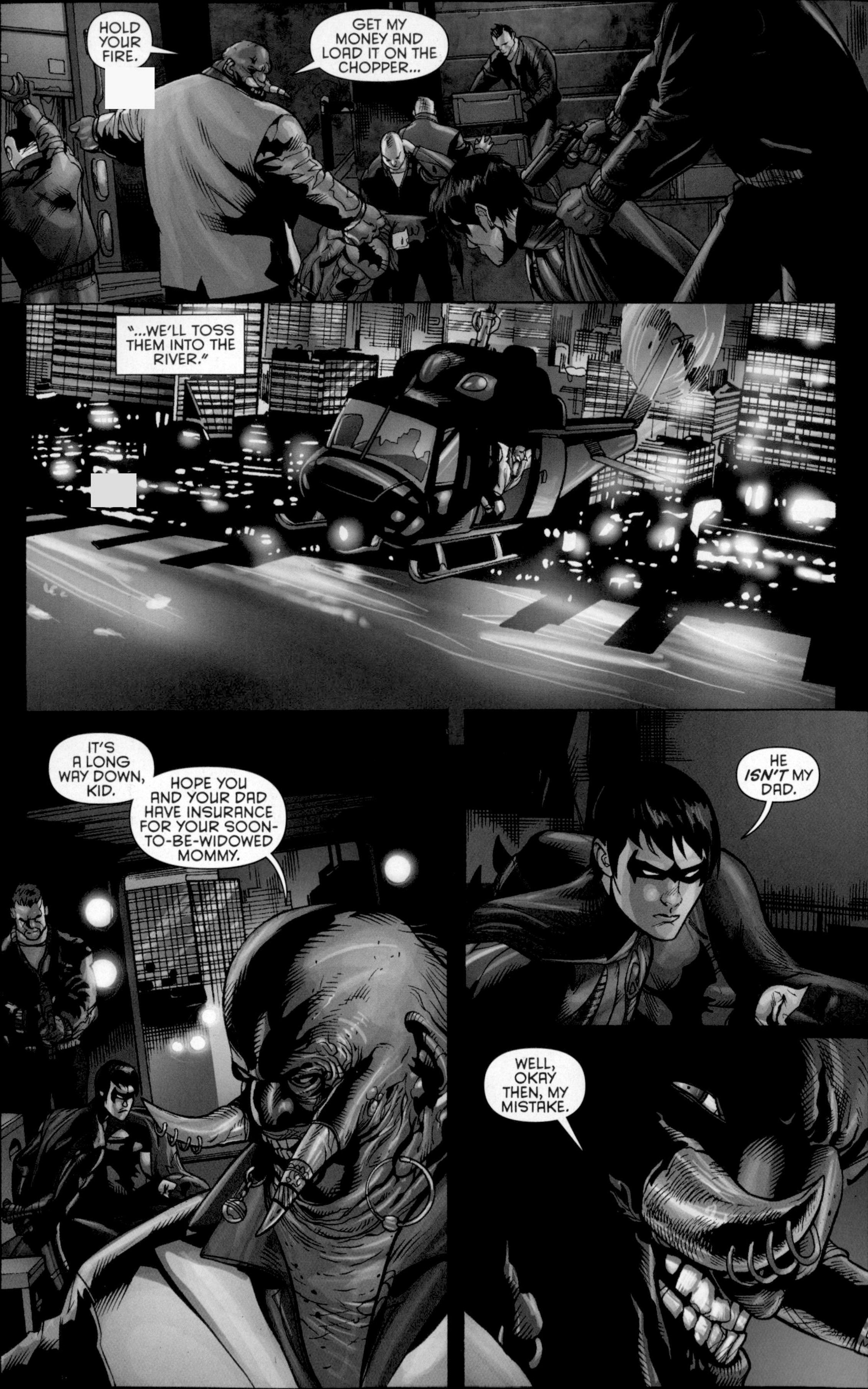
HOLD YOUR FIRE.
GET MY MONEY AND LOAD IT ON THE CHOPPER...
"...WE'LL TOSS THEM INTO THE RIVER."
IT'S A LONG WAY DOWN, KID.
HOPE YOU AND YOUR DAD HAVE INSURANCE FOR YOUR SOON-TO-BE-WIDOWED MOMMY.
HE *ISN'T* MY DAD.
WELL, OKAY THEN, MY MISTAKE.

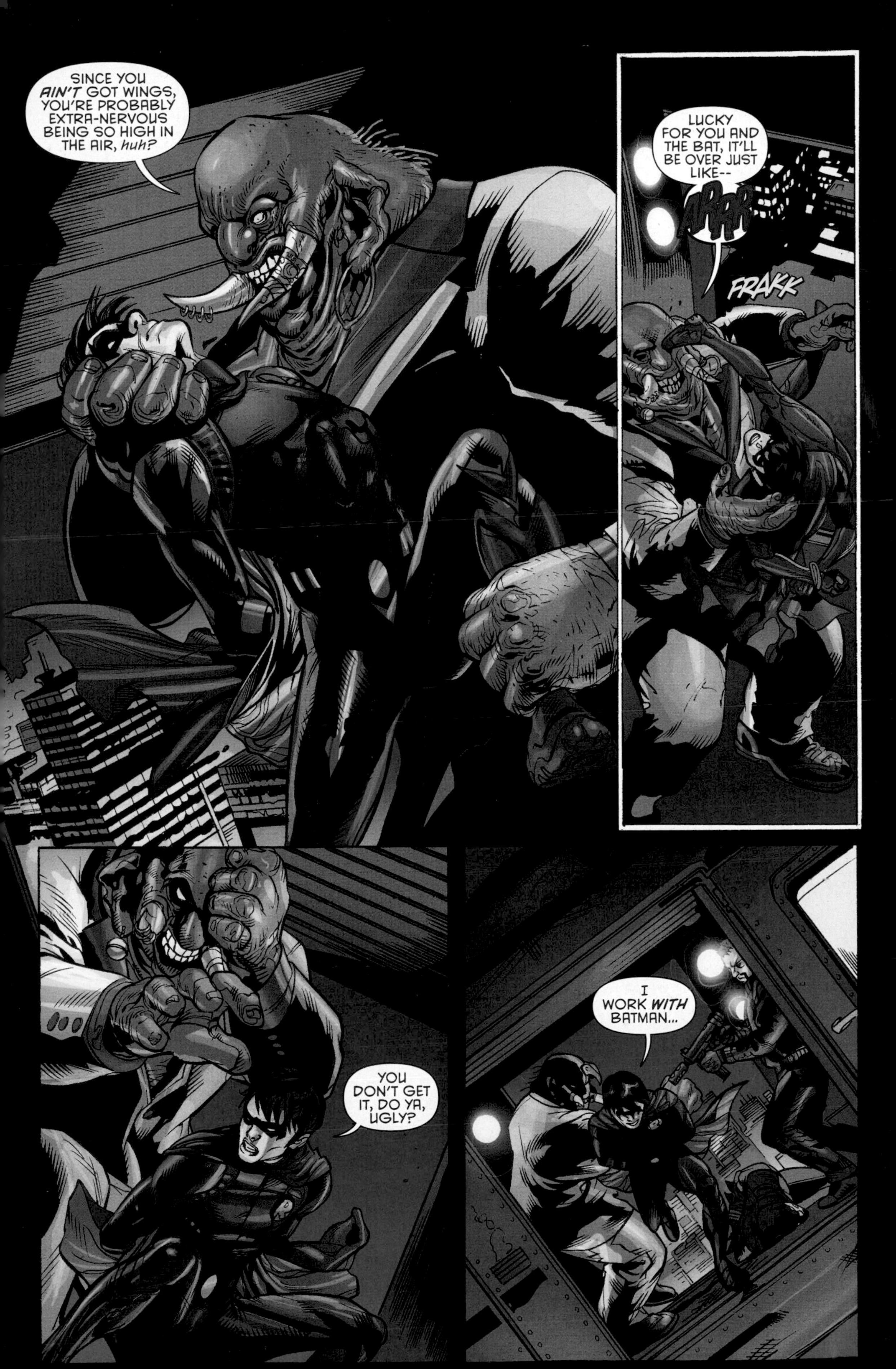
SINCE YOU *AIN'T* GOT WINGS, YOU'RE PROBABLY EXTRA-NERVOUS BEING SO HIGH IN THE AIR, *huh?*
LUCKY FOR YOU AND THE BAT, IT'LL BE OVER JUST LIKE--
ARRR
FRAKK
YOU DON'T GET IT, DO YA, UGLY?
I WORK *WITH* BATMAN...

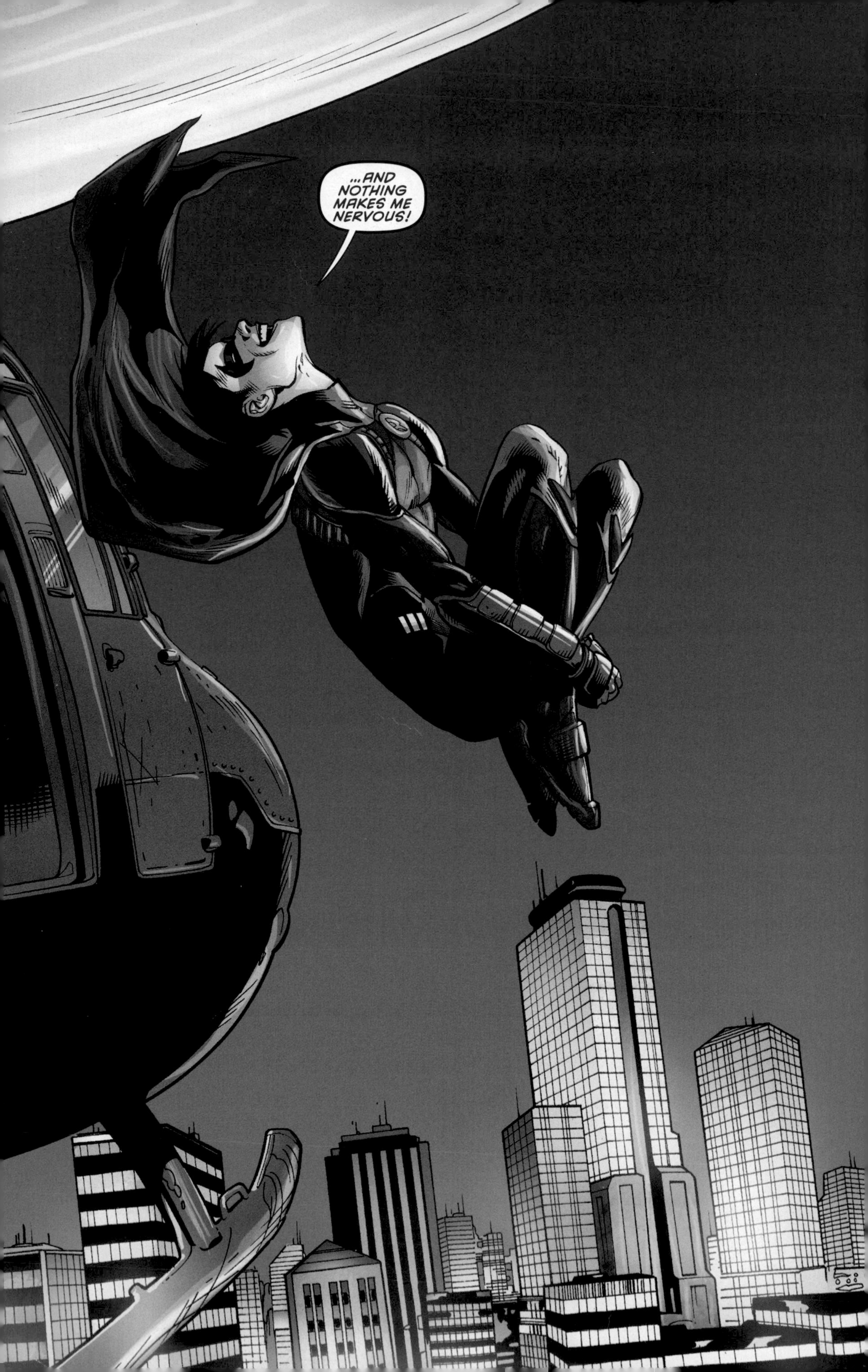
...AND NOTHING MAKES ME NERVOUS!

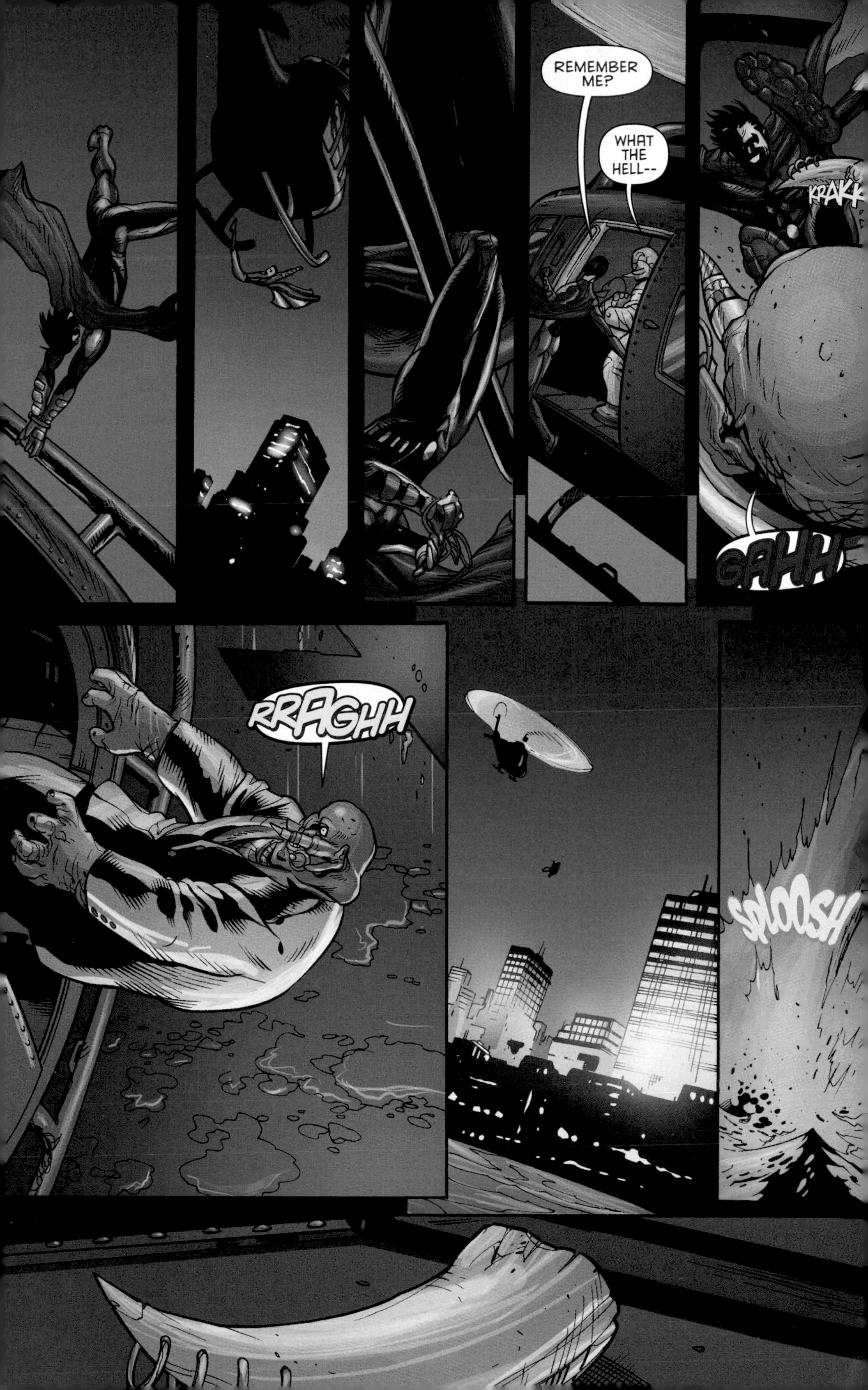
REMEMBER ME?
WHAT THE HELL--
KRAKK
GAHH
RRAGHH
SPLOOSH

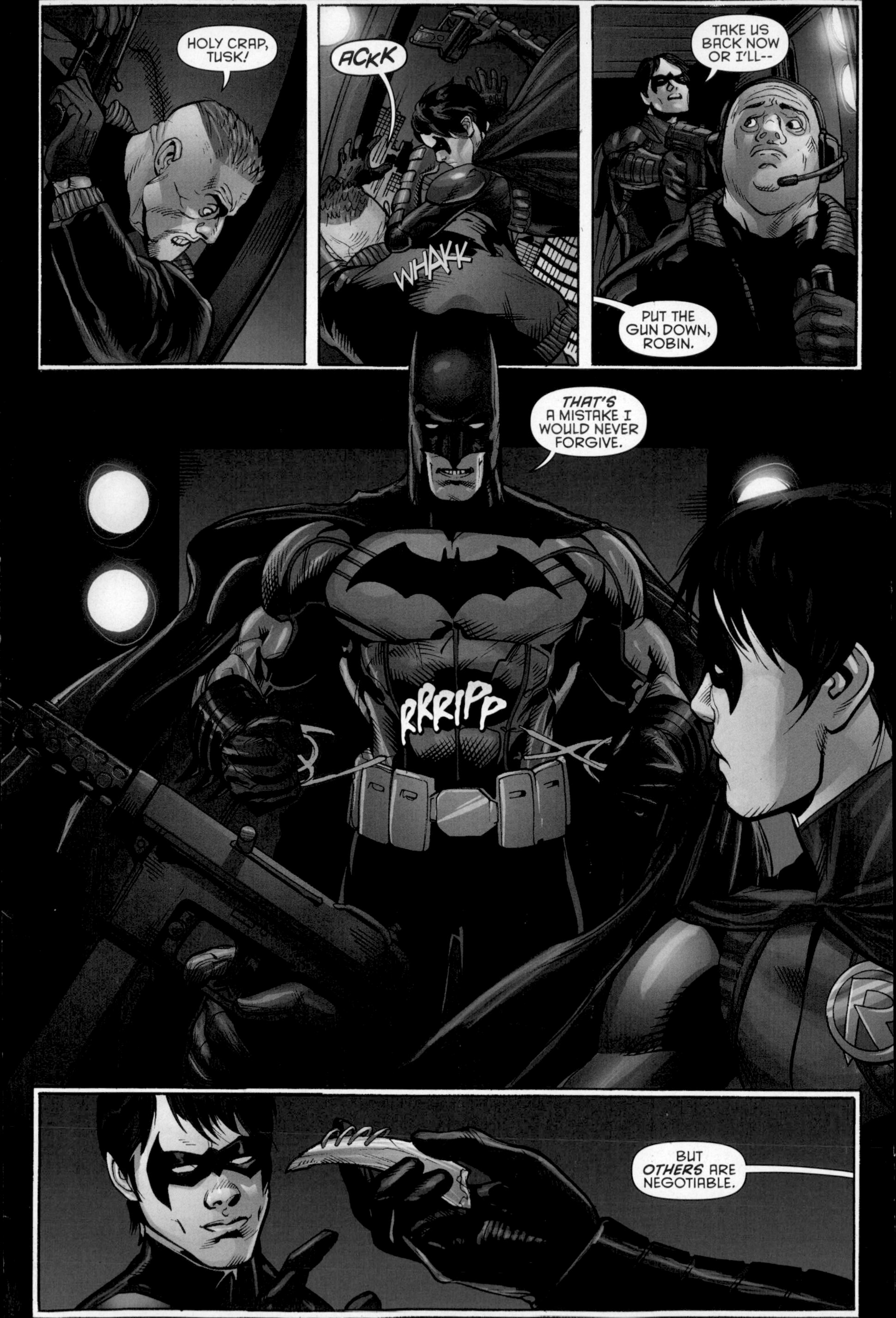
HOLY CRAP, TUSK!
ACKK
WHAKK
TAKE US BACK NOW OR I'LL--
PUT THE GUN DOWN, ROBIN.
THAT'S A MISTAKE I WOULD NEVER FORGIVE.
RRRIPP
BUT OTHERS ARE NEGOTIABLE.

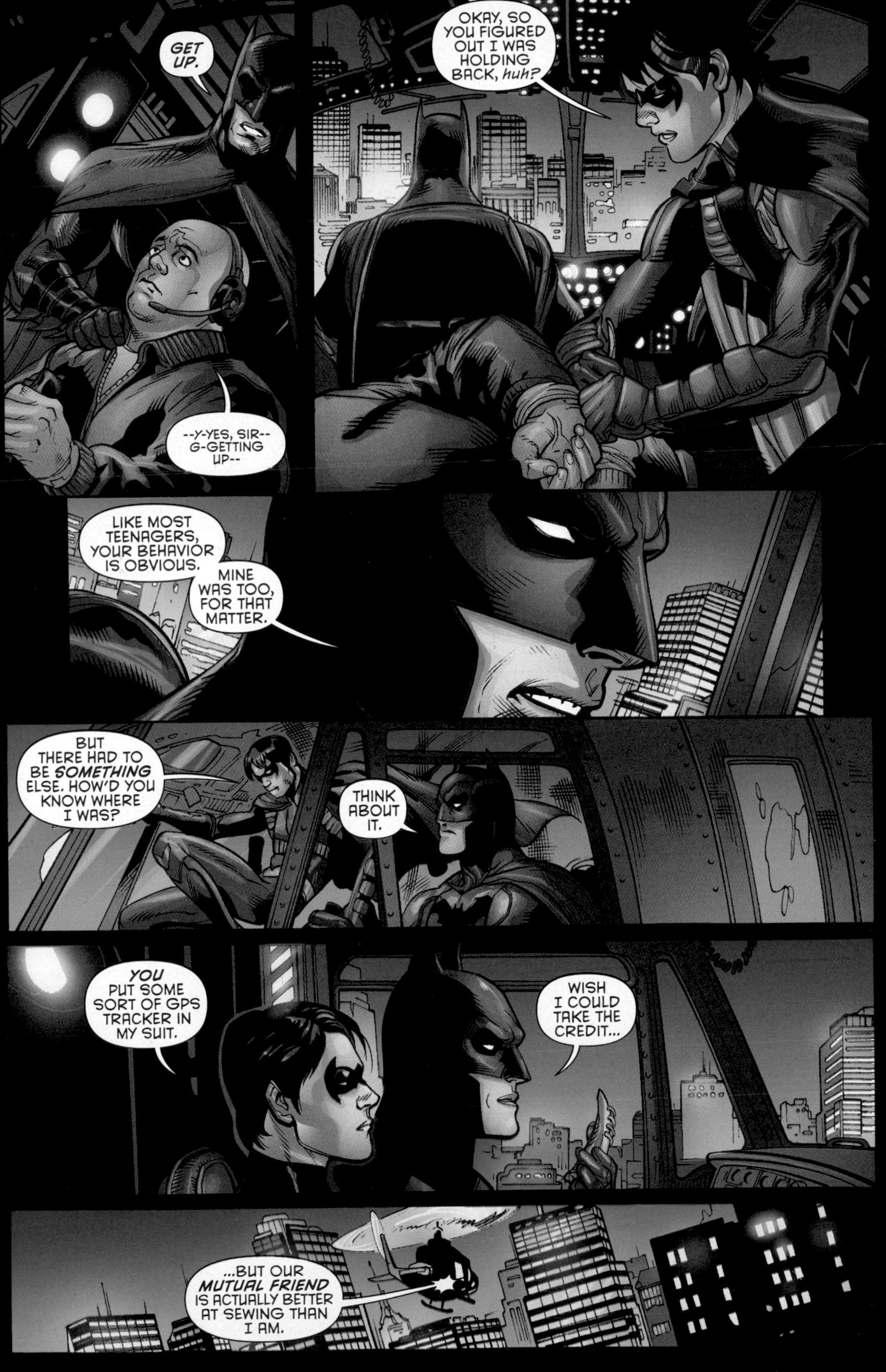
GET UP.
--Y-YES, SIR-- G-GETTING UP--
OKAY, SO YOU FIGURED OUT I WAS HOLDING BACK, huh?
LIKE MOST TEENAGERS, YOUR BEHAVIOR IS OBVIOUS.
MINE WAS TOO, FOR THAT MATTER.
BUT THERE HAD TO BE SOMETHING ELSE. HOW'D YOU KNOW WHERE I WAS?
THINK ABOUT IT.
YOU PUT SOME SORT OF GPS TRACKER IN MY SUIT.
WISH I COULD TAKE THE CREDIT...
...BUT OUR MUTUAL FRIEND IS ACTUALLY BETTER AT SEWING THAN I AM.

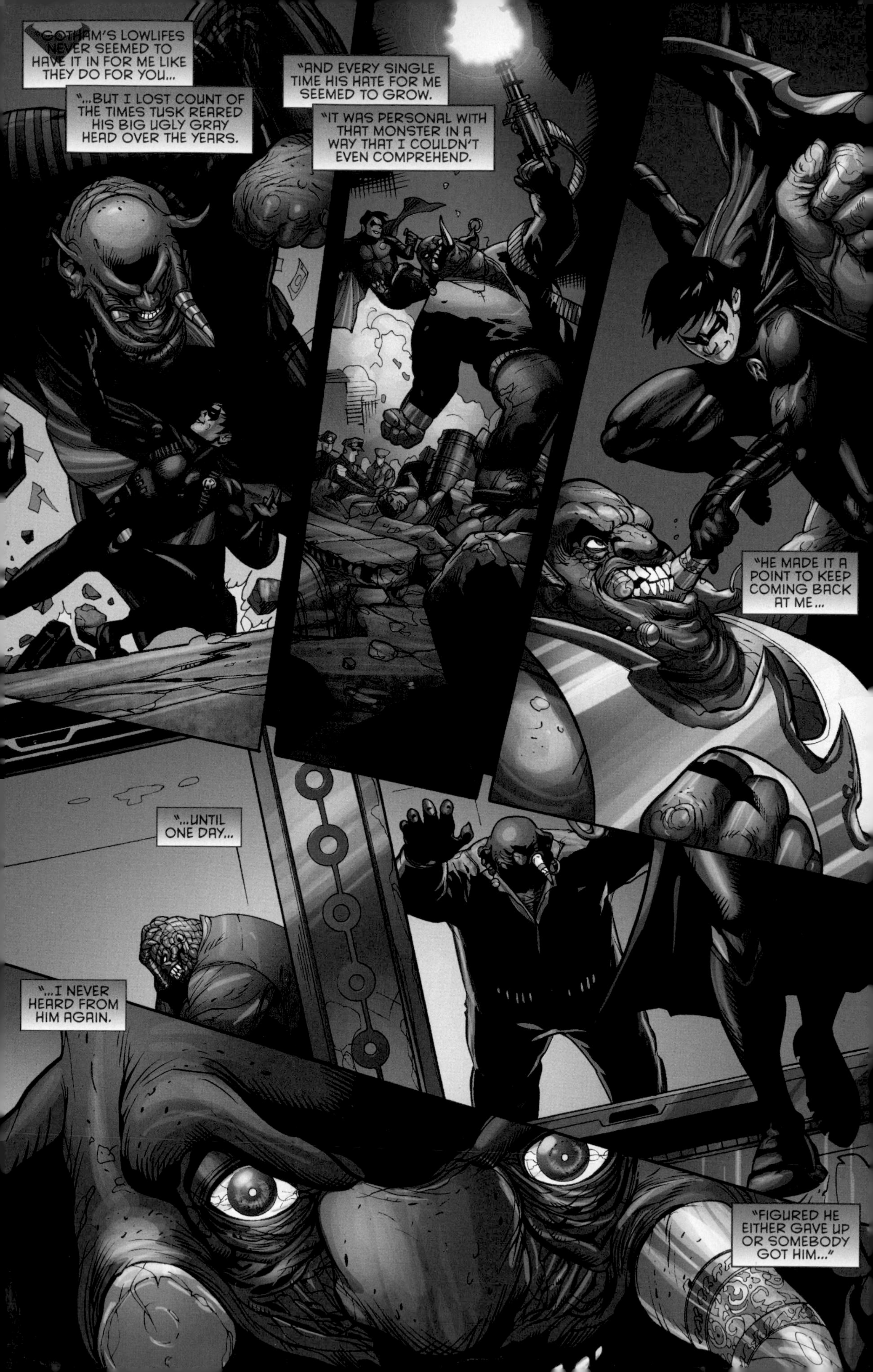
"GOTHAM'S LOWLIFES NEVER SEEMED TO HAVE IT IN FOR ME LIKE THEY DO FOR YOU...
"...BUT I LOST COUNT OF THE TIMES TUSK REARED HIS BIG UGLY GRAY HEAD OVER THE YEARS.
"AND EVERY SINGLE TIME HIS HATE FOR ME SEEMED TO GROW.
"IT WAS PERSONAL WITH THAT MONSTER IN A WAY THAT I COULDN'T EVEN COMPREHEND.
"HE MADE IT A POINT TO KEEP COMING BACK AT ME...
"...UNTIL ONE DAY...
"...I NEVER HEARD FROM HIM AGAIN.
"FIGURED HE EITHER GAVE UP OR SOMEBODY GOT HIM..."

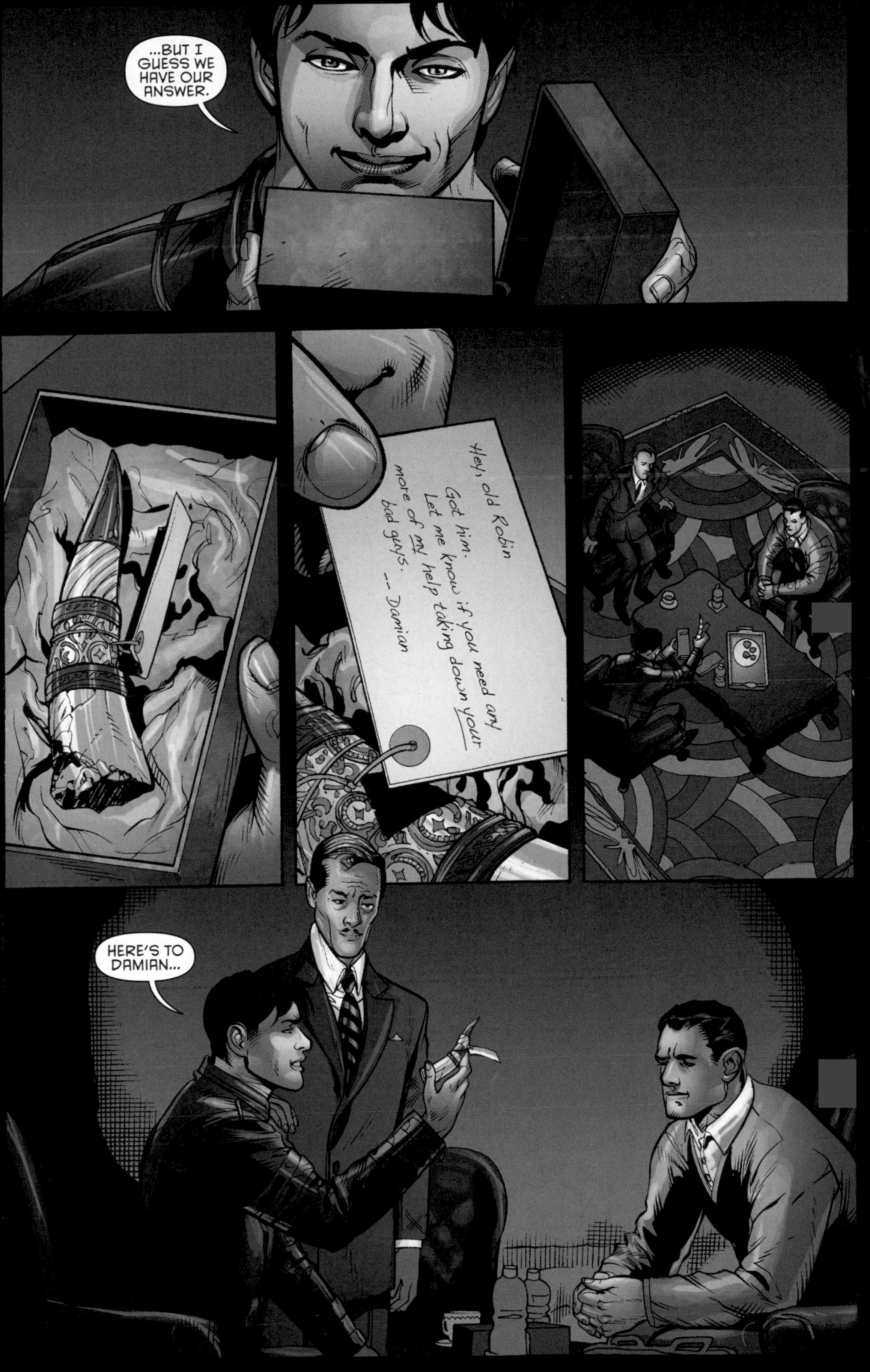
...BUT I GUESS WE HAVE OUR ANSWER.
Hey, old Robin
Got him.
Let me know if you need any more of my help taking down your bad guys.
-- Damian
HERE'S TO DAMIAN...

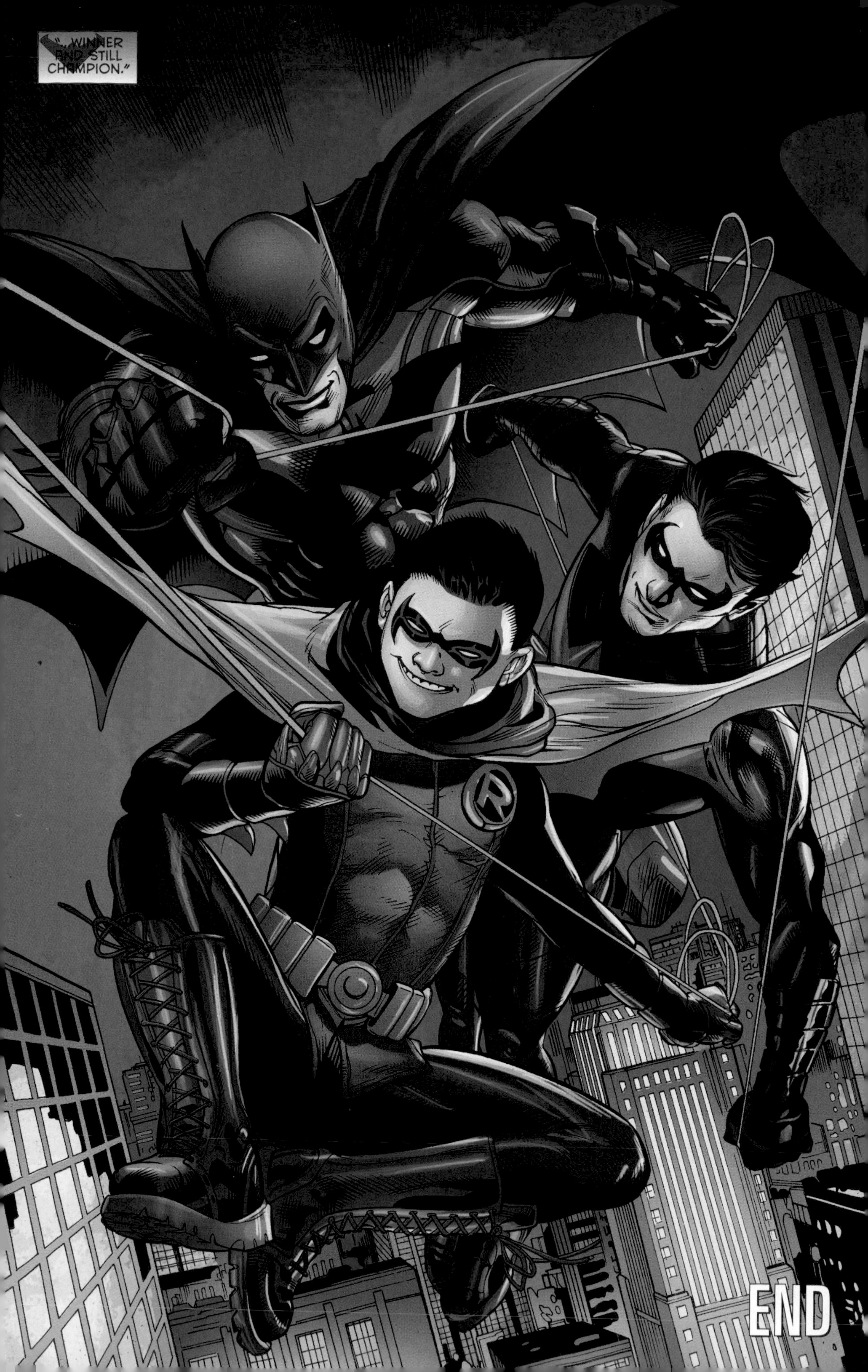
"...WINNER AND STILL CHAMPION."
END

Issue #25 Variant Cover by Brian Bolland

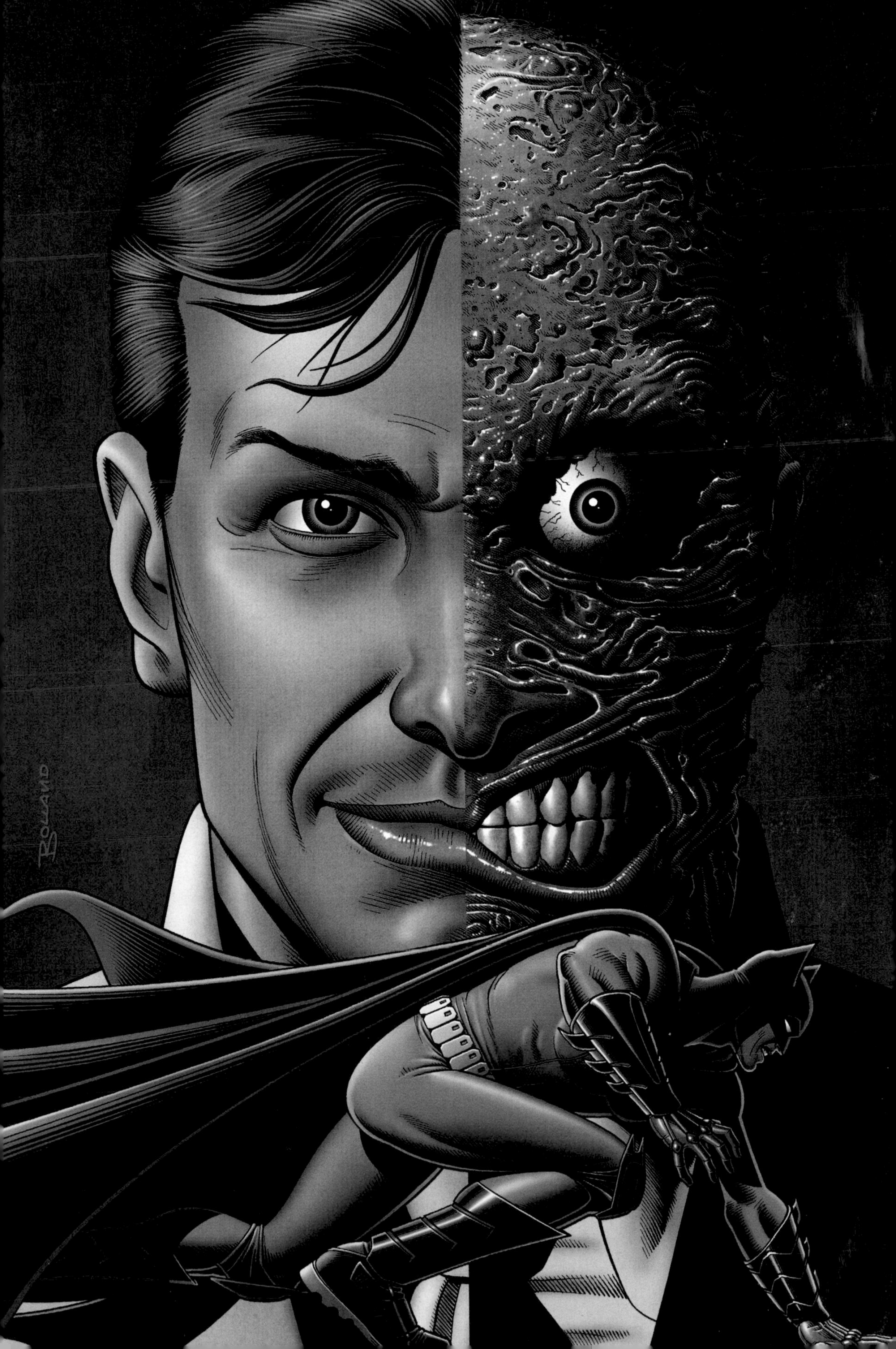
BOLLAND

Issue #27 Scribblenauts Variant Cover by Jon Katz, after Frank Quitely

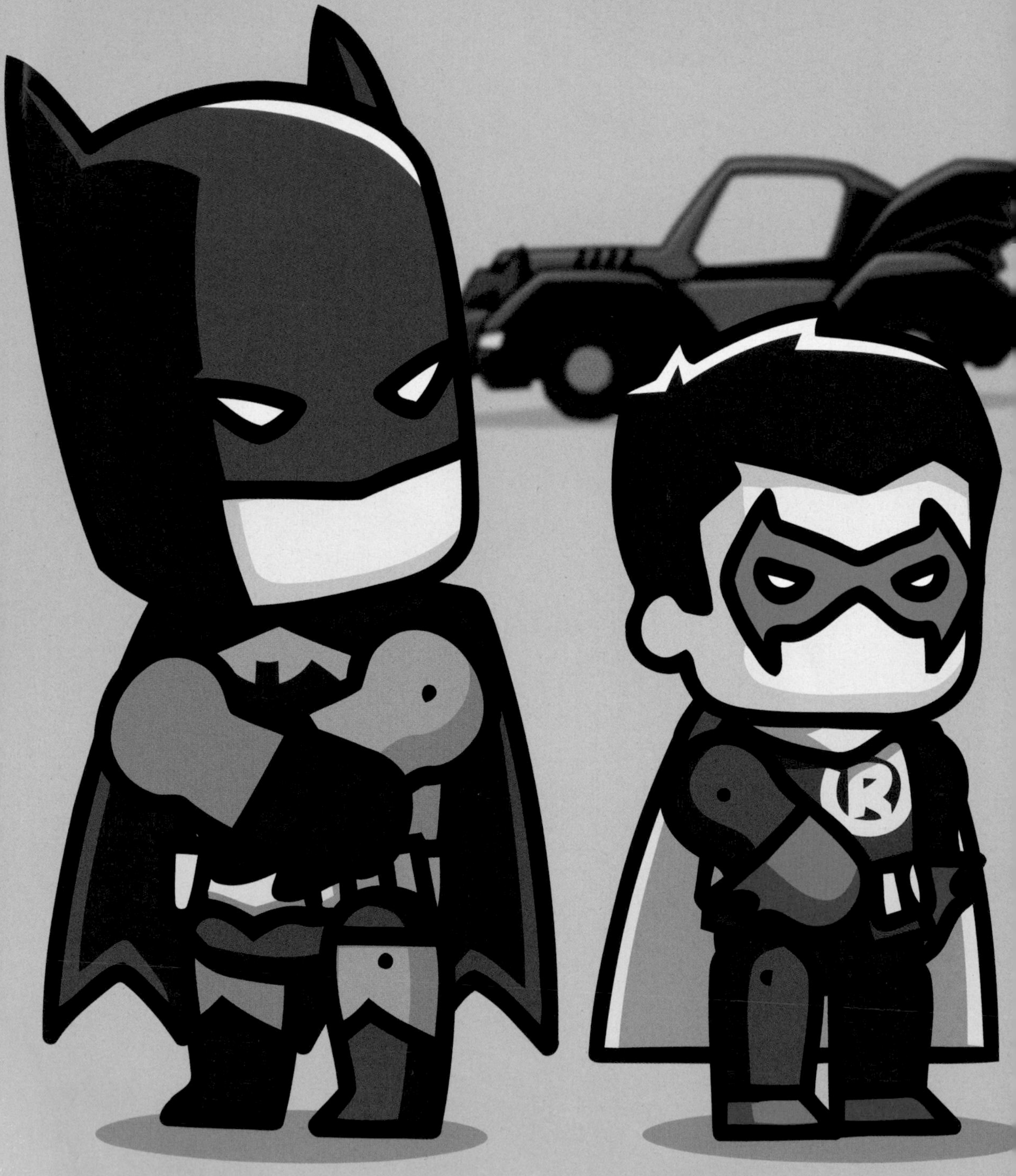

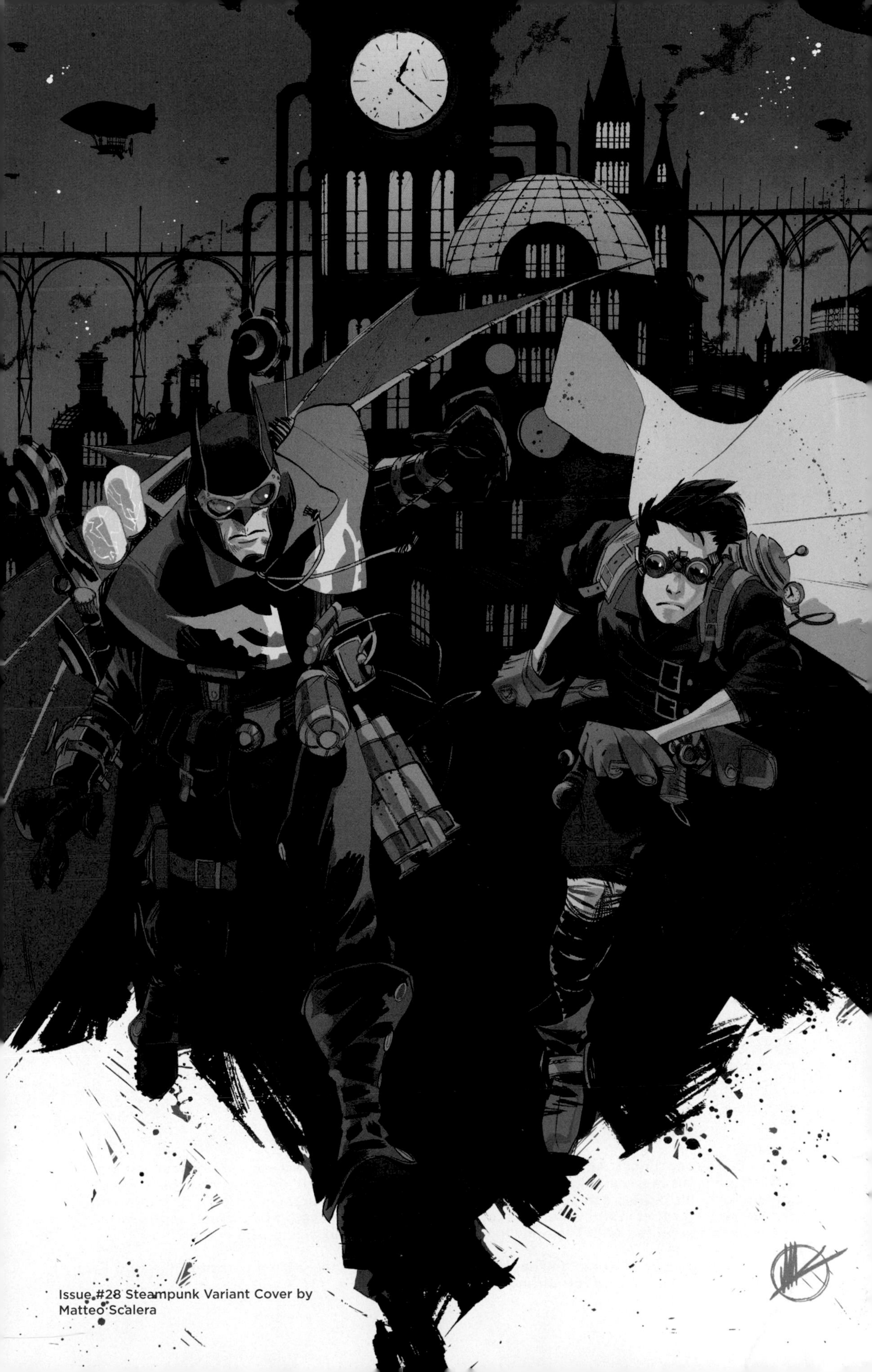

Issue #28 Steampunk Variant Cover by
Matteo Scalera

PAGE 1
panel 1
Horizontal panels across the page, Gleason, or a grid of six equal-sized panels. Or just do whatever ya want as ya usually do! Night, of course. Angle close on BATMAN driving, hands gripped tightly on the steering wheel as he's turning hard left. ERIN is in the seat next to him, bracing hard with her handcuffed hands against the dashboard. You can go with a plastic hand-tie if ya want. Also put in the red tear running down her face.

ERIN: Keeping me cuffed isn't a great motivator!

BATMAN: Earn my trust and stop playing games, McKillen --

ELEC (off): ...what you're watching tonight, Gotham, is an untraceable live feed from a secure location...

panel 2
Angle on the PENGUIN sipping a martini as he's intently watching a flat-screen TV in his office at the Iceberg of Two-Face tied to the chair.

ELEC: ...as we perform the first of many needed operations...

TWO-FACE: NNFFF (he can't speak due to muffler across mouth)

panel 3
Angle from behind Batman and Erin's heads so we can see that a HOLOGRAM of TWO-FACE is on the windshield from the live feed transmission right between them. It should be a close-up of Two-Face, with a thin muffler of some kind over his mouth to prevent him from talking. We can't see where he's at just yet, but it's the SOUNDSTAGE COURTHOUSE SET RIGHT OUT OF A LAW AND ORDER EPISODE we spoke about. Remember, soundstages don't have windows. We'll see shortly that Dent's tied to a chair on the witness stand beside the judge's bench. Batman's making a hard right.

ERIN: I'm not playing at anything -- turn right!

BATMAN: You're burning minutes damn it -- got us making random turns -- you just want those goons to take Harvey out for you!

BATMAN: Tell me where they're holding him!

ELEC: ...to remove the psychotic blight spreading across our great city.

panel 4
Angle on MANBAT from behind, arms/wings crossed over him, hanging upside down on the ledge of a building looking through an open window at Two-Face on the flatscreen TV that a family is watching in their living room, unaware that Manbat hangs outside.

ELEC: For obvious reasons we can't reveal our identities to you...

panel 5
Angle on Batman, pissed, as he's now turning the steering wheel for another hard right as he screams directly into Erin's face as she points her handcuffed hands towards the window. Keep the hologram of Two Face on the windshield.

BATMAN: I said where?!?

ERIN: The courthouse -- Dent's being held at the old courthouse!

ELEC: ...but we'd like to think of ourselves as benefactors...

panel 6
We're in a sewer tunnel. Angle on KILLER CROC watching Two-Face on a 15-inch laptop literally sitting in his lap, several of his UNDERGROUND FOLLOWERS are crowded around him, looking over his big-ass scaly broad shoulders, focused on the screen. Croc's legs dangle off the walkway, his feet in the water. We can see the laptop is powered by a cord tapped into a city power box on the wall. The only light source is the laptop giving us a creepy feel.

ELEC: ...with a vested interest in keeping this city safe and secure from parasites like Two-Face who enjoy watching blood run through its streets.

PAGE 2

panel 1
Close on Batman's eyes, studying the Holo of Two-Face off-panel as he drives.

BATMAN: Computer -- zoom in on holo screen -- quadrant two -- highest res.

ELEC: If there are any kids watching this program...

panel 2
We're now actually at the soundstage revealing visually where Two-Face is being held for the first time as I described earlier. We see he's tied to a chair on the stand with heavy belts beside the judge's bench and don't forget the thin muffler in his mouth. Behind him we can make out one of those iconic and carved circular city seals that are usually on the wall behind a judge. The phrase: LIBERTY AND JUSTICE FOR ALL is along the bottom curve of the seal. Two-Face is filled with rage, struggling to no avail. Standing beside Two-Face is MOB GUY 1 holding a flamethrower (make it streamlined, not clunky like those WW2 era flamethrowers). This Mob Guy is dressed all in black with a mask keeping his identity hidden, sorta like a Black Ops guy except without all the stuff as he plays to a newscamera being held by MOB GUY 2 also dressed in black with a mask. A point of info, Pat: what we don't see yet is the fact that a bunch of the MOB BOSSES are sitting around a large table and watching this go down like some kinda backroom fight so don't go wide until I give ya the high-sign. Their GOONS stand behind them also watching, and we'll have some with fire extinguishers at the ready.

MOB 1: ...we suggest sending them into another room...

panel 3
Angle from behind Batman on the WINDSHIELD HOLO of Two-Face where we can see the bottom of the circular city seal behind Dent's shoulder. The phrase: LIBERTY AND JUSTICE FOR ALL can be seen, but focus in on the word JUSTICE because that's what Bats is zeroing in on even as he turns the wheel hard.

BATMAN: The 'U' in Justice -- on the courtroom's actual seal it's a Roman 'V' --

ELEC: ...because it's only fitting that someone who turned their back on justice...

panel 4
Back at soundstage. Mob Guy sprays the flamethrower around Two-Face but not on him. They want it to be a slow burn. Dent strains at his bindings, raging, unable to talk/scream.

MOB 1:   ...burns at its altar.

TWO FACE: NRRGH

panel 5
Angle on Batman and Erin as Batman suddenly turns the wheel violently, the canopy of the batmobile opening. Batman has a look of disgust on his face. All the words he used on Erin back at the manor fell on deaf ears. She stares at him, another bloody tear running down her cheek.

ERIN: What are you doing -- we're almost there?!?

BATMAN: No we're not, thanks to you.

BATMAN: They're not downtown -- they're across town at the condemned old Gotham Studios!

BATMAN: Had a chance to do the right thing, but you just couldn't do it!

SFX: SKREEEE

PAGE 3
panel 1
Angle on Erin literally being EJECTED super-fast from the car with the passenger seat still under her as Batman looks on in disgust. Remember, her hands are still bound.

BATMAN: Here's where you get off, McKillen!

ERIN: YAAGHH

SFX: FOOOM

panel 2
Angle from behind Batman, hunched, hands gripped tight on the wheel, as we see the WINDSHIELD HOLO of Two-Face struggling in his chair as the stand and the judge's bench is burning all around him. By the way, the overhead canopy's still open.

ELEC: So, for all you twisted deviants watching from the shadows...

TWO-FACE: GHHRR

panel 3
Erin in the passenger seat, small chute trailing behind it, lands on a police car roof parked in front of an electronics shop where 2 COPS, who were a second earlier watching TWO-FACE on the various flatscreen TVs in the window, have turned only their heads towards Erin's unexpected entrance. I'm seeing Erin in the foreground trying to tear the plastic binding around her hands away with her teeth and the Cops and TVs in the background.

ELEC: ...this is your future...

SFX: THUNKK

panel 4
Angle on Erin still on the roof of the car, hands still bound, the harness safety belts of the seat still tight around her. She's got a wicked smile on her face as the Cops are drawing their guns.

ERIN: I want my phone call.

panel 5
Profile angle on Batman as he's ejected himself super-fast from the Batmobile, fisted hands extended out front like Superman as the driver's seat falls away behind him. Firing out of his gauntlets (we established those tranq packs on the tops of his hands last issue) are several small explosives which'll be used to blow out the wall he's heading for.

ELEC: ...unless you leave Gotham!

PAGES 4 and 5
panel 1
Double-page spread. Three visual tiers across, one thin black panel across bottom.
Biggest panel across both pages as Batman smashes through the exploding wall with both fists extended as he's coming right at us like a bat outta hell.

SFX: SKOOOM

panel 2
Okay, this is our establishing shot of the soundstage layout and it's a courtroom set with a clear indication it's fake; wall flats, leftover appleboxes, a stray light stand or two — you know the look we're going for. On the far left side of the page, Two-Face is on the stand, the flames all around him, and as mentioned earlier, the MOB BOSSES, on the far right side of the page, sitting around a large table and watching this go down like some kinda backroom fight with their respective GOONS behind them, are all now turning their attention to BATMAN as he comes smashing through the wall somewhere between Two-Face and the Mob Guys. Batman has already fired his wirepoon towards Two-Face. Make sure MOB GUY 2 with the newscamera is still filming and Mob Guy 1 with the flamethrower is spinning around to aim it at Batman.

MOB BOSS 1: Batman!

MOB BOSS 2: Cook 'em both!

panel 3
Two-Face, surrounded by flames, looks up from his chair at Batman in mid-air dropping towards him, the stream of fire from the flamethrower off-panel engulfing Batman, who's got his cape up like Dracula as he throws a batarang cutting Two-Face's mouth strap.

TWO-FACE: Didn't know I have a dark angel on my shoulder too?

panel 4
White letters of title/credits against thin black panel running across bottom of both pages.

panel 1
Batman, now standing beside Two-Face in the raging flames, quickly slices the other bindings with one swipe of his gauntlets as he throws 3 rangs with the other hand from between his fingers like we've shown before in the series. Remember, Two-Face was shot in the shoulder.

BATMAN: Saving you is getting to be a bad habit, Harvey.

TWO-FACE: Nagging guilt for letting Erin get away from you the night she paid Gilda and I a visit's still eating at you, hmm?

panel 2
Angle on Mob Guy 2 WITH THE CAMERA getting hit by a rang in the mouth along with MOB GUY 1 with the FLAMETHROWER getting hit in the shoulder and neck that causes him to fall to the ground, the flame shooting from the nozzle coming to a stop. And make sure the CAMERA is falling from Mob 2 Guy's hands.

MOB 2: GAKK

MOB 1: YAGHH

SFX: shunk shunk shunk (from embedded rangs)

panel 3
Angle through the sideways camera lens lying on the floor as we see GOONS, guns out, firing, slowly advancing towards the burning judicial platform and stand that Batman and Two Face are crouching behind, the bullets chewing into the wood.

SFX: BRATTABRATTABLAMBLAM

panel 4
Let's cut away to the Penguin in his office enjoying the action-packed program. He's clapping like a kid at the circus, a wicked smile on his face.

PENGUIN: Rollicking good show!

panel 5
Angle on Batman and Two-Face crouching behind the judge's wooden bench that's getting chewed up by bullets as Batman smashes several flame retardant marble capsules that snuff out the flames around them with one hand while he FLIPS TWO-FACE'S COIN to Dent who holds up his good hand to catch it as he clutches his bloody shoulder with his other hand. Have there be an after-image of the coin flipping in the air to indicate it going from Batman to Dent's hand. Dent should look a little weak from the loss of blood but he's still filled with bile and rage.

BATMAN: Dropped this in the tunnel.

SFX: pling (flipped coin)

TWO-FACE: Don't expect me to say thanks.

SFX: pafpafpafpaf (marble capsules)

SFX: SWHOOOSH (putting out flame)

SFX: BRATTABRATTA

SFX: pokpokpokpokpok

PAGE 7
panel 1
Angle on the Goons as they keep firing at the judicial bench, wood chips flying, the metal state SHIELD that hangs on the wall behind the judge's seat is FALLING off towards the back of the bench where Bats and Dent are, though not visible at this moment.

SFX: BRATTABRATTA

panel 2
Closer on Batman and Two-Face as Bats positions the large shield that's fallen in front of them with one hand as he grabs Two-Face's wrist holding the coin before he can pocket it. Batman's filled with anger, frustration and desperation, trying to reach his old friend.

BATMAN: We were once on a mission together, damn it -- you, me, and Gordon --

TWO-FACE: Yeah, crusaders all -- a holy trinity of law and order -- except you let McKillen destroy my life!

BATMAN: How could you let yourself fall so far?! Why couldn't you steel yourself -- channel the pain -- turn it into something good?!?

TWO-FACE: Like you did, Bruce.

panel 3
Close on Batman and Two-Face, bullets still flying, taken aback but not in some big melodramatic way. Bats, jaw tight, stares at Two-Face.

SILENT

panel 4
Bats is still holding Two-Face's wrist with the coin closed in his fist. Two-Face isn't sympathetic here. He's matter-of-fact about this revelation. He jams his finger into his ruined face with his other hand. Bullets are still chewing up the scenery for rest of scene.

TWO-FACE: You pushed me into the D.A. job and I got to watch that Irish witch snuff out Gilda's light like she was nothing more than a goddamn floor lamp?!?

TWO-FACE: If you only knew the battles I've fought in my head to keep you alive these last few years.

TWO-FACE: Justice was served. I earned this for my sins.

TWO-FACE: I am this.

panel 5
Even closer on Batman and Two-Face as Two-Face yanks his hand away from Bat's grip.

BATMAN: Harvey Dent's still in there — I know it — I believe it.

TWO-FACE: He's gone, Bruce. Long gone.

panel 1
Angle on Batman, a mix of anger and determination, as he's grabbed Two-Face with both hands by the collar as bullets rip the air and wood all around them, as he tries to shake some sense into his old friend. Two-Face is defiantly pocketing his coin in his shirt. Think of that great final scene in Vietnam in the Deerhunter when DeNiro grabs Walken by the collar as Walken ignores him and wants to get to the Russian Roulette table.

BATMAN: No he's not!

BATMAN: Whenever you're about to flip, look at the third side of your coin, Harvey.

TWO-FACE: Only two sides to my coin.

BATMAN: Third side's the edge, the spot the two sides come together, where heads meets tails --

panel 2
Angle on Batman and Two-Face as they rush forward from behind the judicial bench, Bats holding the Gotham shield like Captain America in front of them, but more in front of Two-Face since Bats knows his armor can absorb some of the hit which it's indeed doing. The shield's taking the brunt of the bullets meant for Two-Face. Also, make sure the words we saw earlier, LIBERTY AND JUSTICE FOR ALL, are visible as is the words GOTHAM CITY.

BATMAN: — that's the best side because it bonds opposites together --

BATMAN: — and you've got to find a way to embrace it!

panel 3
Angle on Batman plowing hard into the armed Goons with the shield as Two Face falls away from Batman to-wards the floor.

panel 4
Angle close on Two-Face, pressing his foot into the back of the head of the struggling and wounded Mob Guy 1's head as he pulls the FLAMETHROWER from his back as he's still lying on the floor with the batarangs in him.

MOB GUY 1: UGNNN

panel 1
Angle on Two-Face, looking like some kinda demonic maniac, is shooting the Flamethrower, an arc of flame IGNITING BATMAN and THE GOONS and the inside of the soundstage as the Mob Bosses all run for the exits with their clothes also catching..

TWO-FACE: Scorched earth time!

panel 2
Close only on Batman, enveloped in flames, as he slams his fist into a LARGE RED BUTTON THAT READS RE-TRACTABLE ROOF even as he grabs a grenade mushroom like you drew last issue with the Russian in the tunnel from the barrel of a fallen gun. It's only the grenade bulb with short projectile stick attached, not the gun.

SFX: PAKK (roof button being pushed)

panel 3
Angle close on a demonic Two-Face continuing to spray the flamethrower. Don't show anybody burning here though. If we see the roof of the soundstage, feel free to have it being pulled back.

TWO-FACE: You're all gonna burn until you've got no face!

panel 4
Angle on Batman as he's fired his wirepoon to the ceiling, already rising fast, as he shoves the grenade bulb stick into his forearm gauntlet he fired the tranqs from last issue. Have the flames from the soundstage below licking at his feet a bit. The roof of the soundstage is on its way to being pulled back by ancient gears.

SFX: klak (insertion of grenade into his gauntlet)

panel 5
Angle from behind Batman as his wirepoon pulls him closer to the ceiling as he FIRES the grenade from his wrist gauntlet out of a section of the retracting roof.

SFX: POOM

panel 6
Thin horizontal across bottom as we're outside now and see the grenade blasting through the window, leaving a smoky trail as it IMPACTS against a massive dilapidated WB Studios-type water-tower (without the WB logo of course) situated right above the soundstage. Put a GC Studios worn and battered logo instead.

SFX: BABOOM

PAGE 10
panel 1
Biggest on page, as the WATER COMES RUSHING THROUGH THE NOW OPEN SOUNDSTAGE ROOF. The roof doesn't need to be fully retracted, but just enough for the water to pour in and not cave in the roof itself and kill anybody below.

SFX: FRRRAOOOSSSH

panel 2
Angle on Batman suspended in the air holding on for dear life to the wirepoon wire as a HUGE RUSH OF WATER RUSHES OVER HIM.

SFX: FRRRROOSHHH

panel 3
Angle on the Goons and Mob Guys being hit with the wave of water, immediately snuffing out their burning clothes and bodies. In other words, Batman's saved the bad guys.

SFX: FLLOOOOOSSH

panel 4
Angle close from behind Two-Face, flamethrower in hand, as he simply watches a wall of water literally coming right at him. It's important that the front of his face/body is visibly reflected back at him in the wall of water.

SFX: FWWARRSSSH

PAGE 11
panel 1
FLASHBACK. TRANSITIONAL CUT. Angle close from behind DENT, drink in hand, as he stands in front of a KNIGHT'S shining suit of armor and stares at his reflection on it. Bruce and Dent are about 21/22. During rest of scene feel free to toss ALFRED in the background with a drink tray along with other servers moving around the crowded room. Bruce was already keeping up the 'persona' back then, maintaining a big personality and a big lifestyle. Keep the crowd young.

BRUCE (off): Keep staring at yourself any longer, Harvey, and you'll crack it.

panel 2
Angle on Dent as he turns to face Bruce, a pretty BRUNETTE on his arm, but Dent's focus is on the girl. He's been hit by cupid. This is GILDA, the future, Mrs. Dent.

DENT: Nice bash as usual, Prince Bruce. Invitation didn't mention an occasion.

BRUCE: Figured I'd have a college graduation party that I could live vicariously through my friends and old classmates.

DENT: Almost as lavish as your pre-school graduation party which you at least got a diploma from.

BRUCE: Almost.

panel 3
Angle on Dent still maintaining his gaze on the girl beside Bruce.

DENT: And still monopolizing all the girls as usual.

BRUCE: I escorted this incredibly smart and beautiful woman over to meet you, dummy.

panel 4
Angle on Bruce, Gilda and Harvey as he makes introductions. Dent takes Gilda's hand.

BRUCE: Gilda Gold, Harvey Dent. Harvey Dent, Gilda Gold.

DENT: Um, hello.

GILDA: Pleasure.

panel 1
Angle on Bruce, acting slightly rakish, as he starts walking off from Dent and Gilda, we can see ERIN in the deep background arguing with someone who's spilled a drink on her, while SHAN-NON is taking her arm and trying to lead her away and diffuse the fight.

BRUCE: Now excuse me, seems like the McKillen twins are causing a ruckus with Erin leading the way as usual.

DENT: I think her bark's worse than her bite.

BRUCE: I hope not.

panel 2
Angle on Gilda and Dent. Focused only on each other. The party bleeds around the edges.

GILDA: So, Mister Dent, what do you want to be when you grow up?

DENT: A defense attorney. I start Gotham Law in September. What about you, Miss Gold?

GILDA: Marketing. My father's a partner in an advertising agency.

DENT: Maybe you could help market me at some point, raise my q level.

panel 3
Angle closer on Gilda and Dent as Dent leans closer to whisper in her ear.

GILDA: Maybe.

GILDA: And what made you want to embark on a law career?

DENT: I believe everyone deserves a fair trial...

DENT: ...and honestly, I always loved TV shows about lawyers -- they looked cool as hell and could talk their way out of just about anything.

panel 4
Angle on Dent and Gilda. These two people are already in love with each other.

DENT: If you don't have any boyfriends or husbands that'd object, how about dinner and a movie tomorrow night?

GILDA: You move fast, Mister Dent.

DENT: LIfe moves fast, Miss Gold.

PAGE 13
panel 1
BACK TO PRESENT. GORDON, gun drawn, edges along back wall slowly as he tilts his head upwards hearing an explosion off-panel (water tower being breached by Bats).

GORDON: I want units positioned — what the hell —

panel 2
Two-Face is suddenly washed out a back door slamming hard into an unsuspecting Gordon in a wall of water. Gordon's glasses are knocked off as he loses grip on his pistol as they're both hit by the mini-tidal wave, also establish a radio clipped on his belt.

TWO-FACE/GORDON: UNFFF

panel 3
Gordon, soaking wet, belly down in the mud, searching for his glasses only a foot away from his hand while he reaches into his pants leg for the .38 snub in his ankle holster.

GORDON: GNNN

TWO-FACE (off): No worries, James —

panel 4
Angle on Two Face, dripping wet, holding his own bleeding shoulder, FIRING Gordon's other gun just as Gordon pulls the .38 snub free from his ankle holster, his arm arcing around to-wards Dent just as the BULLET TEARS through Gordon's shoulder.

TWO-FACE: — I found your other gun.

SFX: BLAMM

panel 5
Angle on Two Face as he kneels down in the mud beside Gordon, tossing away the .38. Gor-don, wet, now leans up against some junction box clutching his bloody shoulder.

ELEC: Commissioner — we just had a damn tsunami pour out of the building — what's your 20?!? (from Gordon's radio)

GORDON: ...you were the best of us, Dent...you know that, don't you...?

TWO-FACE: No, James, you were — you're the only good man left — that's why I'm giving you a choice: take me in or let me go.

GORDON: You know that's no choice at all, Dent.

PAGE 14
panel 1
Angle close on Two Face and Gordon as Dent flips his coin in the air.

TWO-FACE: Then I guess I have to make my own.

GORDON: Guess you do.

TWO-FACE: Heads I surrender, tails you die.

SFX: pling

panel 2
Angle close on Two-Face as he misses the coin — it falls past his hand.

SILENT

panel 3
Angle close on the COIN AS IT LANDS IN THE MUD RIGHT ON ITS EDGE beside Two-Face's shoe, neither heads or tails.

SFX: sklitch

panel 4
Angle on Two-Face at a loss. He stares at the coin emotionless, waiting for it to fall but it doesn't. His moral compass has malfunctioned.

SILENT

panel 5
Angle close on Two-Face's hand as he plucks the Coin from the mud.

SFX: plik

panel 6
Two-Face suddenly places the barrel of Gordon's gun against Gordon's forehead and screams. Gordon simply stares back at him, giving him nothing, not a drop of emotion.

TWO FACE: YAARGGHH

panel 7
Angle on Two-Face as he's pulled the gun away from Gordon's forehead as they stare back at each other, no emotion whatsoever.

SILENT

PAGE 15
panel 1
Two-Face suddenly places the barrel of Gordon's gun back against Gordon's forehead and screams again. Again, Gordon stares back at him, giving him not a drop of emotion.

TWO-FACE: YAARGGHH

panel 2
Two-Face pulls the gun away again from Gordon's forehead as they stare back at each other again, no emotion whatsoever.

SILENT

panel 3
Two-Face suddenly places the gun barrel back against Gordon's forehead and screams again. Again, Gordon stares back at him, giving him nothing, not a drop of emotion except this time a BATARANG knocks Two-Face's hand away just as the gun fires.

TWO FACE: YAARGGHH

panel 4
Angle on Two-Face at full run as he swings a pipe into the helmet of a MOTORCYCLE COP arriving on the scene knocking him from his seat. Stage this so the Cop doesn't see Two-Face because he's passing a column of some kind or whatever you feel works.

COP: UGNN

panel 5
Angle on Gordon in the midground, back to us, firing his .38 at Two-Face driving off on motor-cycle in deep background as Batman's boots land in foreground mud of the panel.

SFX: BLAMBLAMBLAM (Gordon's gun)

panel 6
Batman's at Gordon's side, pushing his hands down hard against the BLOODY WOUND.

GORDON: — damn it — what are you doing? — get after him!

BATMAN: Artery tear -- bleeding bad, Jim — got to apply pressure — I'm not leaving.

panel 7
Thin horizontal from behind Batman holding Gordon's radio with one hand and the other over Gordon's wound as Two Face fades into distance in the background.

BATMAN: Medics — south side of building — Gordon down!

PAGE 16
panel 1
Angle close only on Erin's eye, the side that got burned. We can just make out the start of a bloody tear about to run down her face.

ERIN: A change is going to come...

panel 2
Pull out a little more so we're now seeing her whole face, as the bloody tear runs down the thin furrow on her cheek.

ERIN: ...when the old men with old views are pushed aside...

panel 3
Angle close on Erin as she dabs the blood from her cheek with a white handkerchief.

ERIN: ...and the much needed transfusion of new blood...

panel 4
Day. Angle on Erin outside in a prison yard, a high-security fence behind her as we now see she is holding court in front of SEVERAL WOMEN of different ethnic backgrounds, all of them wearing orange jumpsuits.

ERIN: ...with a distinct and powerful perspective takes their place.

panel 5
Angle close on Erin only, chest high, a determined look on her face.

ERIN: An old friend once told me a story about a young Indian girl who keeps having night-mares about twin wolves from the same family tearing each other to pieces.

ERIN: This little girl goes to her grandmother to make sense of these nightmares and she tells her there are two forces inside each of us, always fighting for power, one symbolizing light, and the other darkness.

panel 6
Angle even closer on Erin, a slight smile on her face, as she holds out her bloody handkerchief.

ERIN: And we're all sitting here because we know which one we want to feed, don't we?

We're back where we started from, Pat, the circle is now complete. We're in Dent's basement apartment from issue 24. Timeline wise, I see this happening shortly after he leaves Gordon lying shot on the ground.

panel 1
Angle close on Dent's CLOTHES we last saw him in scattered about the floor. Obviously they're torn, bloody, and singed with some burns.

SILENT

panel 2
Angle close looking directly down on Dent's feet beside the drain in the shower. Blood and dirt is running into the drain.

SILENT

panel 3
Angle close on Dent, the warm water from the shower-head running over his face. We should see his full face by the way, both sides, his good eye closed, his bad eye open. This is Dent's act of baptism.

SILENT

panel 4
Angle on Dent now out of the shower, he stands shirtless in front of a mirror almost done shaving only the good side of his face so there shouldn't be much shaving cream left on his skin. We should see that he's got a taped patch over the bullet wound in his shoulder and there should be some blood already spotting the new patch. Have some indication of the FLY buzzing around.

SILENT

panel 5
Angle on the FLY now resting on the TIP OF ONE OF THE SIX BULLETS bedside his 357. revolver lying on the same table from issue 24.

SILENT

PAGE 18

panel 1
Angle from behind Dent now at the closet with a button-down shirt on and a tie loose around his open collar as he's now combing his hair straight back so it looks like it did when he was younger. We can see several of the same exact suits you had him wearing in the opening of issue 24 visibly hanging in the closet.

SILENT

panel 2
Angle close on Dent's face, his eyes looking down at something.

panel 3
Angle from Dent's POV, close on the BAD SIDE OF THE COIN resting in the palm of his now clean hand.

panel 4
Biggest on page. Angle close on Dent's hands as he holds the coin upright on edge with one finger and has two fingers on his other hand poised to flick the coin and set it spinning on the same table as Gilda's picture. Make sure this is the GOOD SIDE of the coin we see.

SILENT

panel 5
Same angle as previous panel, only now the COIN IS SPINNING, just a blur.

panel 6
Angle on Dent as he now lifts the one bullet and .357 from the table. We can see the FLY flit away.

panel 7
Angle close on Dent's hand placing only the one bullet into the gun's cylinder.